OPERATIONS MANAGEMENT STUDENT LECTURE GUIDE

Seventh Edition

Jay Heizer
Jesse H. Jones Professor of Business Administration
Texas Lutheran University

Barry Render
Charles Harwood Professor of Operations Management
Crummer Graduate School of Business
Rollins College

PEARSON
Prentice Hall

Upper Saddle River, New Jersey 07458

Executive Editor: Tom Tucker
Editor-in-Chief: P.J. Boardman
Assistant Editor: Erika Rusnak
Editorial Assistant: Dawn Stapleton
Senior Media Project Manager: Nancy Welcher
Executive Marketing Manager: Debbie Clare
Marketing Assistant: Amanda Fisher
Managing Editor (Production): Cynthia Regan
Permissions Supervisor: Suzanne Grappi
Production Manager: Arnold Vila
Design Manager: Maria Lange
Designer: Blair Brown
Interior/Cover Design: Blair Brown
Cover Photo: Courtesy of Hard Rock Cafe International, Inc.
Photo Researcher: Mary Ann Price
Image Permission Coordinator: Carolyn Gauntt
Manager, Print Production: Christy Mahon
Composition/Illustration (Interior): UG / GGS Information Services, Inc.
Full-Service Project Management: UG / GGS Information Services, Inc.
Printer/Binder: R.R. Donnelley & Sons Company

Credits and acknowledgments borrowed from other sources and reproduced, with permission, in this textbook appear on appropriate page within text.

Microsoft Excel, Solver, and Windows are registered trademarks of Microsoft Corporation in the U.S.A. and other countries. Screen shots and icons reprinted with permission from the Microsoft Corporation. This book is not sponsored or endorsed by or affiliated with Microsoft Corporation.

Pearson Education LTD.
Pearson Education Australia PTY, Limited
Pearson Education Singapore, Pte. Ltd
Pearson Education North Asia Ltd
Pearson Education, Canada, Ltd
Pearson Educación de Mexico, S.A. de C.V.
Pearson Education—Japan
Pearson Education Malaysia, Pte. Ltd

PEARSON
Prentice
Hall

10 9 8 7 6 5 4 3 2 1
ISBN 0-13-142273-1

Brief Contents

Letter to the Student

Operations Management can be one of the most exciting courses in your college program. As a student of operations management, we hope you will find *Operations Management, Seventh Edition, Flexible Version* an ideal way to learn the subject. We have created this new and innovative learning system to help you in your study of the field. This unique combination of *text*, *Student Lecture Guide,* and *Student CD-ROM,* with extensive Web site support, costs significantly less than a traditional textbook. Moreover, the *Student Lecture Guide* (the part you should bring to each class) is smaller and lighter than the standard text—easing weight in your backpack! The idea is for the text to be a reference and the *Student Lecture Guide* to bridge the gap between the text and the lecture.

The first page of each chapter in the *Student Lecture Guide* begins with a chapter outline, a brief introduction, and a series of questions that address the major ideas and concepts of the chapter. If you answer these questions before attending class, you will have an important head start.

Each chapter contains headings for the major topics and critical teaching points, figures, charts, and tables relevant to that topic—but most importantly, each chapter has lots of extra space for you to take notes. We think you can take better notes and get more from the lecture when you can focus on note taking rather than redrawing outlines, figures, charts, and tables. Practice Problems are also included, as is room for the solutions and necessary notes. The *Student Lecture Guide* also contains all the homework problems in case your instructor wants to assign any of this material in class.

The full support and resources of the Student CD-ROM and the extensive Web site (www.prenhall.com/heizer) are also available to make the learning process complete. For instance, the Web site includes a study guide that contains quizzes for each chapter. These quizzes are automatically graded and can be forwarded to the instructor if you so desire.

We hope that this new approach to learning helps you enjoy your operations management journey.

Jay Heizer
Texas Lutheran University
1000 W. Court St.
Seguin, Texas 78155
Phone: (830) 372-6056
Fax: (830) 372-6065
Email: jheizer@tlu.edu

Barry Render
Graduate School of Business
Rollins College
Winter Park, Florida 32789
Phone: (407) 646-2657
Fax: (407) 646-1550
Email: Barry.Render@rollins.edu

Chapter 1

Operations and Productivity

Chapter Outline

WHAT IS OPERATIONS MANAGEMENT?

ORGANIZING TO PRODUCE GOODS
AND SERVICES

WHY STUDY OM?

WHAT OPERATIONS MANAGERS DO

THE HERITAGE OF OPERATIONS
MANAGEMENT

OPERATIONS IN THE SERVICE SECTOR

EXCITING NEW TRENDS IN OPERATIONS
MANAGEMENT

THE PRODUCTIVITY CHALLENGE

THE CHALLENGE OF SOCIAL RESPONSIBILITY

Production is the creation of goods and services. Operations Management is the set of activities that creates value by using labor, capital, and management to transform inputs (raw materials) into desired outputs (goods and services). The operations manager's job is to ensure that this transformation takes place efficiently. This text identifies 10 decisions that are critical to effective and efficient operations management.

BEFORE COMING TO CLASS, READ CHAPTER 1 IN YOUR TEXT AND ANSWER THESE QUESTIONS.

1. What is the distinction between production and productivity? ____
_____
_____

2. Identify and define the 10 critical decisions of operations management. _____
_____
_____
_____

3. What are the critical variables in productivity? _____
_____
_____

4. Identify some career opportunities in operations management. ____
_____
_____

5. What are the distinctions between goods and services? _____
_____
_____

6. Who are three twentieth-century pioneers in operations management? _____
_____

WHAT IS OPERATIONS MANAGEMENT?

Production

ORGANIZING TO PRODUCE GOODS AND SERVICES

Three Functions All Organizations Perform

1. _____

2. _____

3. _____

WHY STUDY OM?

WHAT OPERATIONS MANAGERS DO

Ten Decision Areas of OM

1. Design of Goods and Services (Chapter 5)
2. Managing Quality (Chapter 6 and Supplement 6)
3. Process and Capacity Design (Chapter 7 and Supplement 7)
4. Location (Chapter 8)
5. Layout Design (Chapter 9)
6. Human Resources and Job Design (Chapter 10 and Supplement 10)
7. Supply Chain Management (Chapter 11 and Supplement 11)
8. Inventory, MRP, and JIT (Chapters 12, 14, and 16)
9. Scheduling (Chapters 13 and 15)
10. Maintenance (Chapter 17)

HERITAGE OF OPERATIONS MANAGEMENT

Whitney
Taylor
Ford/Sorensen
Gilbreth
Shewhart
Deming

OPERATIONS IN THE SERVICE SECTOR

TABLE 1.3 ■ Differences between Goods and Services

ATTRIBUTES OF GOODS (TANGIBLE PRODUCT)	ATTRIBUTES OF SERVICES (INTANGIBLE PRODUCT)
Product can be resold.	Reselling a service is unusual.
Product can be inventoried.	Many services cannot be inventoried.
Some aspects of quality are measurable.	Many aspects of quality are difficult to measure.
Selling is distinct from production.	Selling is often a part of the service.
Product is transportable.	Provider, not product, is often transportable.
Site of facility is important for cost.	Site of facility is important for customer contact.
Often easy to automate.	Service is often difficult to automate.
Revenue is generated primarily from the tangible product.	Revenue is generated primarily from the intangible services.

EXCITING NEW TRENDS IN OPERATIONS MANAGEMENT

1. Global focus
2. JIT shipments
3. Partnering with suppliers, ERP, e-commerce
4. Rapid product development
5. Mass customization
6. Empowerment, lean production
7. Green manufacturing, recycling

THE PRODUCTIVITY CHALLENGE

$$\text{Productivity} = \frac{\text{Units produced}}{\text{Input used}} \qquad (1\text{-}1)$$

PRACTICE PROBLEM 1.1 ■ Productivity

Mance Fraily, the production manager at Ralts Mills, can currently expect his operation to produce 1,000 square yards of fabric for each ton of raw cotton. Each ton of raw cotton requires 5 labor-hours to process. He believes that he can buy a better quality raw cotton, which will enable him to produce 1,200 square yards per ton of raw cotton with the same labor-hours.

What will be the impact on productivity (measured in square yards per labor-hour) if he purchases the higher quality raw cotton?

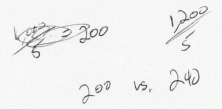

PRACTICE PROBLEM 1.2 ■ Productivity

C. A. Ratchet, the local auto mechanic, finds that it usually takes him 2 hours to diagnose and fix a typical problem. What is his daily productivity (assume an 8-hour day)?

Mr. Ratchet believes he can purchase a small computer trouble shooting device, which will allow him to find and fix a problem in the incredible (at least to his customers!) time of 1 hour. He will, however, have to spend an extra hour each morning adjusting the computerized diagnostic device. What will be the impact on productivity if he purchases the device?

Multifactor Productivity

$$\text{Productivity} = \frac{\text{Output}}{\text{Labor} + \text{Material} + \text{Energy} + \text{Capital} + \text{Miscellaneous}} \qquad (1\text{-}2)$$

PRACTICE PROBLEM 1.3 ■ Multifactor Productivity

Joanna French is currently working a total of 12 hours per day to produce 240 dolls. She thinks that by changing the paint used for the facial features and fingernails that she can increase her rate to 360 dolls per day. Total material cost for each doll is approximately $3.50; she has to invest $20 in the necessary supplies (expendables) per day; energy costs are assumed to be only $4 per day; and she thinks she should be making $10 per hour for her time. Viewing this from a total (multifactor) productivity perspective, what is her productivity at present and with the new paint?

PRACTICE PROBLEM 1.4 ■ Multifactor Productivity

How would total (multifactor) productivity change if using the new paint raised Ms. French's material costs by $0.50 per doll?

PRACTICE PROBLEM 1.5 ■ Multifactor Productivity

If she uses the new paint, by what amount could Ms. French's material cost increase without reducing total (multifactor) productivity?

Additional Practice Problem Space

Productivity Variables

1. Labor
2. Capital
3. Management

THE CHALLENGE OF SOCIAL RESPONSIBILITY

DISCUSSION QUESTIONS

1. Why should one study operations management?
2. Who are some of the people who have contributed to the theory and techniques of operations management?
3. Briefly describe the contributions of the individuals identified in the preceding question.
4. Figure 1.1 in your text outlines the operations, finance/accounting, and marketing functions of three organizations. Prepare a chart similar to Figure 1.1 outlining the same functions for one of the following:
   (a) a newspaper
   (b) a drugstore
   (c) a college library
   (d) a summer camp
   (e) a small costume jewelry factory
5. Answer question 4 for some other organization, perhaps an organization where you have worked.
6. What are the three basic functions of a firm?

7. Name the 10 decision areas of operations management.
8. Name four areas that are significant to improving labor productivity.
9. The U.S., and indeed much of the world, has been described as a "knowledge society." How does this affect productivity measurement and the comparison of productivity between the U.S. and other countries?
10. What are the measurement problems that occur when attempting to measure productivity?
11. Mass customization and rapid product development were identified as current trends in modern manufacturing operations. What is the relationship, if any, between these trends? Can you cite any examples?
12. What are the five reasons why productivity is difficult to improve in the service sector?
13. Describe some of the actions taken by Taco Bell to increase productivity that have resulted in Taco Bell's ability to serve "twice the volume with half the labor."

CRITICAL THINKING EXERCISE

Productivity in the U.S. averaged 2.5% for almost 100 years preceding 1973, when it dropped to about half of that and where it remained for about 25 years. In recent years, productivity increases have returned to the 2.5% range. To what do you attribute the 25-year drop in productivity?

PROBLEMS

- **1.1** John Lucy makes wooden boxes in which to ship motorcycles. John and his three employees invest 40 hours per day making the 120 boxes.
   a) What is their productivity? *3$ boxes/hour*
   b) John and his employees have discussed redesigning the process to improve efficiency. If they can increase the rate to 125 per day, what would be their new productivity? *3.5 boxes/hour*
   c) What would be their *increase* in productivity?

- **1.2** Riverside Metal Works produces cast bronze valves on a 10-person assembly line. On a recent day, 160 valves were produced during an 8-hour shift. Calculate the labor productivity of the line.

- **1.3** Browse the *Wall Street Journal*, the money section of a daily paper, or read business news online. Obtain articles about goods versus services, about productivity, about production technology. Be prepared to share your articles in a class discussion.

- **1.4** As a library or Internet assignment, find the U.S. productivity rate (increase) last year for the (a) national economy, (b) manufacturing sector, and (c) service sector.

- **1.5** Lori produces "Final Exam Care Packages" for resale by the sorority. She is currently working a total of 5 hours per day to produce 100 care packages.
   a) What is Lori's productivity?
   b) Lori thinks that by redesigning the package she can increase her total productivity to 133 care packages per day. What would be her new productivity?
   c) What will be the increase in productivity if Lori makes the change?

- **1.6** Eric Johnson makes billiard balls in his New England plant. With recent increases in his costs, he has a new-found interest in efficiency. Eric is interested in determining the productivity of his organization. He would like to know if his organization is maintaining the manufacturing average of 3% increase in productivity. He has the following data representing a month from last year and an equivalent month this year:

	LAST YEAR	NOW
Units Produced	1,000	1,000
Labor (hours)	300	275
Resin (pounds)	50	45
Capital invested ($)	10,000	11,000
Energy (BTU)	3,000	2,850

Show the productivity change for each category and then determine the improvement for labor-hours, the typical standard for comparison.

1.7 Eric Johnson (using data from Problem 1.6) determines his costs to be as follows:
- labor $10 per hour;
- resin $5 per pound;
- capital 1% per month of investment;
- energy $.50 per BTU.

Show the productivity change, for one month last year versus one month this year, on a multifactor basis with dollars as the common denominator.

1.8 Kleen Karpet cleaned 65 rugs in October, consuming the following resources:

Labor:	520 hours at $13 per hour
Solvent:	100 gallons at $5 per gallon
Machine rental:	20 days at $50 per day

a) What is the labor productivity?
b) What is the multifactor productivity?

1.9 David Upton is president of Upton Manufacturing, a producer of Go-Kart tires. Upton makes 1,000 tires per day with the following resources:

Labor:	400 hours @ $12.50 per hour
Raw material:	20,000 pounds per day @ $1 per pound
Energy:	$5,000 per day
Capital:	$10,000 per day

a) What is the labor productivity for these tires at Upton Manufacturing?
b) What is the multifactor productivity for these tires at Upton Manufacturing?
c) What is the percent change in multifactor productivity if Upton can reduce the energy bill by $1,000 without cutting production or changing any other inputs?

1.10 Sawyer's, a local bakery, is worried about increased costs—particularly energy. Last year's records can provide a fairly good estimate of the parameters for this year. Judy Sawyer, the owner, does not believe things have changed much, but she did invest an additional $3,000 for modifications to the bakery's ovens to make them more energy-efficient. The modifications were supposed to make the ovens at least 15% more efficient. Sawyer has asked you to check the energy savings of the new ovens and also to look over other measures of the bakery's productivity to see if the modifications were beneficial. You have the following data to work with:

	LAST YEAR	NOW
Production (dozen)	1,500	1,500
Labor (hours)	350	325
Capital investment ($)	15,000	18,000
Energy (BTU)	3,000	2,750

1.11 Cunningham Performance Auto, Inc., modifies 375 autos per year. The manager, Peter Cunningham, is interested in obtaining a measure of overall performance. He has asked you to provide him with a multifactor measure of last year's performance as a benchmark for future comparison. You have assembled the following data. Resource inputs were: labor, 10,000 hours; 500 suspension and engine modification kits; and energy, 100,000 Kilowatt-hours. Average labor cost last year was $20 per hour, kits cost $1,000 each, and energy costs were $3 per Kilowatt-hour. What do you tell Mr. Cunningham?

1.12 Lake Charles Seafood makes 500 wooden packing boxes for fresh seafood per day, working in two 10-hour shifts. Due to higher demand, plant managers have decided to operate three 8-hour shifts instead. The plant is now able to produce 650 boxes per day. Calculate the company's productivity before the change in work rules and after the change. What is the percentage increase in productivity?

1.13 Charles Lackey operates a bakery in Idaho Falls, Idaho. Because of its excellent product and excellent location, demand has increased by 25% in the last year. On far too many occasions, customers have not been able to purchase the bread of their choice. Because of the size of the store, no new ovens can be added. At a staff meeting, one employee suggested ways to load the ovens differently so that more loaves of bread can be cooked at one time. This new process will require that the ovens be loaded by hand and take additional workers. This is the only thing to be changed. The pay will be $8 per hour for employees. If the bakery made 1,500 loaves this tim~

last year with a labor productivity of 2.344 loaves per labor-hour, how many workers will Lackey need to add? (*Hint:* Each worker works 160 hours per month.)

1.14   Refer to Problem 1.13. Charles Lackey can also improve the yield by purchasing an improved blender. The new blender will mean an increase in his investment. This added investment has a cost of $100 per month, but he will achieve the same output as the change in labor (an increase to 1,875). What is the better decision?
a)   Show the productivity change with an increase in labor (from 640 to 800 hours).
b)   Show the productivity change with an increase in investment ($100 per month more).

1.15   Refer to Problems 1.13 and 1.14. If Charles Lackey's utility costs remain constant at $500 per month, labor at $8 per hour, and cost of ingredients at $0.35 per pound, but Charles does not purchase the blender suggested in Problem 1.14, what will the productivity of the bakery be? What will be the percentage of increase or decrease?

INTERNET HOMEWORK PROBLEMS

See our Internet home page, www.prenhall.com/heizer, for these additional homework problems: 1.16 and 1.17.

CASE STUDY

National Air Express

National Air is a competitive air-express firm with offices around the country. Frank Smith, the Chattanooga, Tennessee, station manager, is preparing his quarterly budget report, which will be presented at the Southeast regional meeting next week. He is very concerned about adding capital expense to the operation when business has not increased appreciably. This has been the worst first quarter he can remember: snowstorms, earthquakes, and bitter cold. He has asked Martha Lewis, field services supervisor, to help him review the available data and offer possible solutions.

Service Methods

National Air offers door-to-door overnight air-express delivery within the U.S. Smith and Lewis manage a fleet of 24 trucks to handle freight in the Chattanooga area. Routes are assigned by area, usually delineated by zip code boundaries, major streets, or key geographical features, such as the Tennessee River. Pickups are generally handled between 3:00 P.M. and 6:00 P.M., Monday through Friday. Driver routes are a combination of regularly scheduled daily stops and pickups that the customer calls in as needed. These call-in pickups are dispatched by radio to the driver. Commitments are made in advance, with regular pickup stops concerning the time the package will be ready. However, most call-in customers want as late a pickup as possible, just before closing (usually at 5:00 P.M.).

When the driver arrives at each pickup location, he or she provides supplies as necessary (an envelope or box if requested) and must receive a completed air waybill for each package. Because the industry is extremely competitive, a professional, courteous driver is essential to retaining customers. Therefore, Smith has always been concerned about drivers not rushing a customer to complete his or her package and paperwork.

Budget Considerations

Smith and Lewis have found that they have been unable to meet their customers' requests for a scheduled pickup on many occasions in the past quarter. While, on average, drivers are not handling any more business, they are unable on some days to arrive at each location on time. Smith does not think he can justify increasing costs by $1,200 per week for additional trucks and drivers while productivity (measured in shipments per truck/day) has remained flat. The company has established itself as the low-cost operator in the industry but has at the same time committed itself to offering quality service and value for its customers.

Discussion Questions

1. Is the productivity measure of shipments per day per truck still useful? Are there alternatives that might be effective?
2. What, if anything, can be done to reduce the daily variability in pickup call-ins? Can the driver be expected to be at several locations at once at 5:00 P.M.?
3. How should we measure package pickup performance? Are standards useful in an environment that is affected by the weather, traffic, and other random variables? Are other companies having similar problems?

Source: Adapted from a case by Phil Pugliese under the supervision of Professor Marilyn M. Helms, University of Tennessee at Chattanooga. Reprinted by permission.

CASE STUDY

Zychol Chemicals Corporation

Bob Richards, the production manager of Zychol Chemicals, in Houston, Texas, is preparing his quarterly report which is to include a productivity analysis for his department. One of the inputs is production data prepared by Sharon Walford, his operations analyst. The report, which she gave him this morning, showed the following:

	2002	2003
Production (units)	4,500	6,000
Raw Material Used (barrels of petroleum by-products)	700	900
Labor Hours	22,000	28,000
Capital Cost Applied to the Department ($)	$375,000	$620,000

Bob knew that his labor cost per hour had increased from an average of $13 per hour to an average of $14 per hour, primarily due to a move by management to become more competitive with a new company that had just opened a plant in the area. He also knew that his average cost per barrel of raw material had increased from $320 to $360. He had concern about the accounting procedures that increased his capital cost from $375,000 to $620,000, but earlier discussions with his boss suggested that there was nothing that could be done about that allocation.

Bob wondered if his productivity had increased at all. He called Sharon into the office and conveyed the above information to her and asked her to proceed with preparing this part of the report.

Discussion Questions

1. Prepare the productivity part of the report for Mr. Richards. He probably expects some analysis of productivity inputs for all factors, as well as a multifactor analysis for both years with the change in productivity (up or down) and the amount noted.
2. The producer price index had increased from 120 to 125, and this fact seemed to indicate to Mr. Richards that his costs were too high. What do you tell him are the implications of this change in the producer price index?
3. Management's expectation for departments such as Mr. Richards's is an annual productivity increase of 5%. Did he reach this goal?

Source: Professor Hank Maddux III, Sam Houston State University.

VIDEO CASE STUDY

Hard Rock Cafe: Operations Management in Services

In its 30 years of existence, Hard Rock has grown from a modest London pub to a global power managing 110 cafes, three hotels, casinos, live music venues, a rock museum, and a huge annual Rockfest concert. This puts Hard Rock firmly in the service industry—a sector that employs over 75% of the people in the U.S. Hard Rock moved its world headquarters to Orlando, Florida, in 1988 and has expanded to more than 40 locations throughout the U.S., serving over 100,000 meals each day. Hard Rock chefs are modifying the menu from classic American—burgers and chicken wings—to include higher-end items such as stuffed veal chops and lobster tails. Just as taste in music changes over time, so does Hard Rock Cafe, with new menus, layouts, memorabilia, services, and strategies.

At Orlando's Universal Studios, a traditional tourist destination, Hard Rock Cafe serves over 3,500 meals each day. The cafe employs about 400 people. Most are employed in the restaurant, but some work in the retail shop. Retail is now a standard and increasingly prominent feature in Hard Rock Cafes (since close to 48% of revenue comes from this source). Cafe employees include kitchen and wait staff, hostesses, and bartenders. Hard Rock employees are not only competent in their job skills; they are also passionate about music and have engaging personalities. Cafe staff is scheduled down to 15-minute intervals to meet seasonal and daily demand changes in the tourist environment of Orlando. Surveys are done on a regular basis to evaluate quality of food and service at the cafe. Scores are done on a 1 to 7 scale, and if the score is not a 7, the food or service is a failure.

Hard Rock is adding a new emphasis on live music and is redesigning its restaurants to accommodate the changing tastes. Since Eric Clapton hung his guitar on the wall to mark his favorite bar stool, Hard Rock has become the world's leading collector and exhibitor of rock 'n' roll memorabilia, with changing exhibits at its cafes throughout the world. The collection includes 1,000's of pieces, valued at $40 million. In keeping with the times, Hard Rock also maintains a Web site, www.hardrock.com, which receives over 100,000 hits per week, and a weekly cable television program on VH-1. Hard Rock's brand recognition, at 92%, is one of the highest in the world.

Discussion Questions*

1. From your knowledge of restaurants, from the video, from the *Global Company Profile* that opens this chapter, and from the case itself, identify how each of the 10 decisions of operations management is applied at Hard Rock Cafe.
2. How would you determine the productivity of the kitchen staff and wait staff at Hard Rock?
3. How are the 10 decisions of OM different when applied to the operations manager of a service operation such as Hard Rock versus an automobile company such as Ford Motor Company?

*You may wish to play this video case on your CD-ROM before addressing these questions.

Source: Professors Barry Render (Rollins College), Jay Heizer (Texas Lutheran University) and Beverly Amer (Northern Arizona University)

Chapter **2**

Operations Strategy in a Global Environment

Chapter Outline

A GLOBAL VIEW OF OM

DEVELOPING MISSIONS AND STRATEGIES

ACHIEVING COMPETITIVE ADVANTAGE THROUGH OPERATIONS

TEN STRATEGIC OM DECISIONS

ISSUES IN OPERATIONS STRATEGY

STRATEGY DEVELOPMENT AND IMPLEMENTATION

GLOBAL OPERATIONS STRATEGY OPTIONS

Today's operations manager must have a global view of operations strategy. The rapid growth of world trade means that many organizations are compelled to extend their firms into an unforgiving global environment. Well-designed missions and strategies must obtain a competitive advantage while providing an economic purpose that satisfies customers.

The idea is to create customer value in an efficient and sustainable way. Managers create value via some combination of three strategies. The three strategies are *differentiation*, *low cost*, and *response*.

BEFORE COMING TO CLASS, READ CHAPTER 2 IN YOUR TEXT AND ANSWER THESE QUESTIONS.

1. What is a mission?

2. What is a strategy?

3. Identify three conceptual strategies of operations management.

4. What are four global approaches to operations?

5. What are the 10 critical decisions of operations management?

6. What is SWOT analysis?

A GLOBAL VIEW OF OM

1. Cost Reduction
2. Supply Chain Improvement
3. Better Goods/Services
4. Learning
5. Global Talent

DEVELOPING MISSIONS AND STRATEGIES

Mission

Strategy

ACHIEVING COMPETITIVE ADVANTAGE THROUGH OPERATIONS

Competing on Differentiation

Competing on Cost

Competing on Response

TEN STRATEGIC OM DECISIONS

1. Design of Goods and Services
2. Managing Quality
3. Process and Capacity Design
4. Location
5. Layout Design
6. Human Resources and Job Design
7. Supply Chain Management
8. Inventory, MRP, and JIT
9. Scheduling
10. Maintenance

ISSUES IN OPERATIONS STRATEGY

STRATEGY DEVELOPMENT AND IMPLEMENTATION

SWOT Analysis

Strengths
Weaknesses
Opportunities
Threats

Critical Success Factors (CSF)

PRACTICE PROBLEM 2.1 ■ OM Strategy

Identify how changes in the external environment may affect the OM strategy for a company. For example, what impact are the following factors likely to have on OM strategy?

a. The occurrence of a major storm or hurricane.

b. Terrorist attacks of September 11, 2001.

c. The much discussed decrease in the quality of American primary and secondary school systems.

d. Trade legislation such as WTO and NAFTA and changes in tariffs and quotas.

e. The rapid rate at which the cost of health insurance is increasing.

f. The Internet.

PRACTICE PROBLEM 2.2 ■ OM Strategy

Identify how the changes in the internal environment affect the OM strategy for a company. For example, what impact are the following factors likely to have on OM strategy?

a. The increased use of local and wide area networks (LANs and WANs).

b. An increased emphasis on service.

c. The increased role of women in the workplace.

d. The seemingly increasing rate at which both internal and external environments change.

GLOBAL OPERATIONS STRATEGY OPTIONS

International Strategy

Multi-Domestic Strategy

Global Strategy

Transnational Strategy

DISCUSSION QUESTIONS

1. Based on the descriptions and analyses in your text, would Boeing be better described as a global firm or a transnational firm? Discuss.
2. List six reasons to internationalize operations.
3. Coca-Cola is called a global product. Does this mean that Coca-Cola is formulated in the same way throughout the world? Discuss.
4. Define *mission*.
5. Define *strategy*.
6. Describe how an organization's *mission* and *strategy* have different purposes.
7. Identify the mission and strategy of your automobile repair garage. What are the manifestations of the 10 OM decisions at the garage? That is, how is each of the 10 decisions accomplished?
8. As a library or Internet assignment, identify the mission of a firm and the strategy that supports that mission.
9. How does an OM strategy change during a product's life cycle?
10. There are three primary ways to achieve competitive advantage. Provide an example, not included in the text, of each. Support your choices.
11. Describe PIMS's five characteristics of high-return-on-investment (ROI) firms.
12. Given the discussion of Southwest Airlines in the text, define an *operations* strategy for that firm.
13. How must an operations strategy integrate with marketing and accounting?

 CRITICAL THINKING EXERCISE

As a manufacturer of athletic shoes whose image, indeed performance, is widely regarded as socially responsible, you find your costs increasing. Traditionally, your athletic shoes have been made in Indonesia and South Korea. Although the ease of doing business in those countries has been improving, wage rates have also been increasing. The labor-cost differential between your present suppliers and a contractor who will get the shoes made in China now exceeds $1 per pair. Your sales next year are projected to be 10 million pairs, and your analysis suggests that this cost differential is not offset by any other tangible costs; you face only the political risk and potential damage to your commitment to social responsibility. Thus, this $1 per pair savings should improve your bottom line. There is no doubt that the Chinese government remains repressive and is a long way from a democracy. What do you do and on what basis do you make your decision?

PROBLEMS

· 2.1 Your text provides three primary ways—strategic approaches—for achieving competitive advantage. Provide an example of each not provided in your text. Support your choices. (*Hint:* Note the examples provided in your text.)

: 2.2 Within the food service industry (restaurants that serve meals to customers, but not just fast food), find examples of firms that have sustained competitive advantage by competing on the basis of (1) cost leadership, (2) response, and (3) differentiation. Cite one example in each category; provide a sentence or two in support of each choice. Do not use fast-food chains for all categories. (*Hint:* A "99¢ menu" is very easily copied and is not a good source of sustained advantage.)

: 2.3 Browse through the *Wall Street Journal*, the financial section of a daily paper, or read business news online. Seek articles about manufacturing issues that don't work everywhere—workers aren't allowed to do this, workers can't be trained to do that, this technology is not allowed, this material cannot be handled by workers, and so forth. Be prepared to share your articles in class discussion.

: 2.4

Match the Product with the Proper Parent Company and Country

PRODUCT	PARENT COMPANY	COUNTRY
Arrow Shirts	**a.** Volkswagen	**1.** France
Braun Household Appliances	**b.** Bidermann International	**2.** Great Britain
Lotus Autos	**c.** Bridgestone	**3.** Germany
Firestone Tires	**d.** Campbell Soup	**4.** Japan
Godiva Chocolate	**e.** Credit Lyonnais	**5.** U.S.
Häagen-Daz Ice Cream	**f.** Ford Motor Company	**6.** Switzerland
Jaguar Autos	**g.** Gillette	**7.** Malaysia
MGM Movies	**h.** Grand Metropolitan	
Lamborghini Autos	**i.** Michelin	
Goodrich Tires	**j.** Nestlé	
Alpo Petfoods	**k.** Proton	

:   **2.5**   Identify how changes in the internal environmental affect the OM strategy for a company. For instance, discuss what impact the following internal factors might have on OM strategy:

a)   Maturing of a product.

b)   Technology innovation in the manufacturing process.

c)   Changes in product design that move disk drives from $3\frac{1}{2}$-inch floppy drives to CD-ROM drives.

:   **2.6**   Identify how changes in the external environment affect the OM strategy for a company. For instance, discuss what impact the following external factors might have on OM strategy:

a)   Major increases in oil prices.

b)   Water- and air-quality legislation.

c)   Fewer young prospective employees entering the labor market.

d)   Inflation versus stable prices.

e)   Legislation moving health insurance from a benefit to taxable income.

:   **2.7**   Develop a ranking for corruption in the following countries: Mexico, Turkey, Denmark, the U.S., Taiwan, Brazil, and another country of your choice. (*Hint:* See sources such as *Transparency International, Asia Pacific Management News,* and *The Economist.*)

:   **2.8**   Develop a ranking for competitiveness and/or business environment for Britain, Singapore, the U.S., Hong Kong, and Italy. (*Hint:* See the *Global Competitive Report, World Economic Forum,* Geneva, and *The Economist.*)

CASE STUDY

Minit-Lube, Inc.

A substantial and continuing market exists for automobile tune-up and lubrication shops. This demand came about because of the change in consumer buying patterns as self-service gas stations proliferated. Consumers now pump their own gas, which makes a second stop necessary for oil and lubrication. Consequently, Minit-Lube, Mobil-Lube, Jiffy-Lube, and others developed a strategy to accommodate this opportunity.

Minit-Lube stations perform oil changes, lubrication, and interior cleaning in a spotless environment. The buildings are clean, painted white, and often surrounded by neatly trimmed landscaping. To facilitate fast service, cars can be driven through three abreast. At Minit-Lube, the customer is greeted by service representatives who are graduates of the Minit-Lube school in Salt Lake City. The Minit-Lube school is not unlike McDonald's Hamburger University near Chicago or Holiday Inn's training school in Memphis. The greeter takes the order, which typically includes fluid checks (oil, water, brake fluid, transmission fluid, differential grease) and the necessary lubrication, as well as filter changes for air and oil. Service personnel

in neat uniforms then move into action. The standard three-person team has one person checking fluid levels under the hood, another assigned interior vacuuming and window cleaning, and the third in the garage pit, removing the oil filter, draining the oil, checking the differential and transmission, and lubricating as necessary. Precise task assignments and good training are designed to put the car in and out of the bay in 10 minutes. The idea is to charge no more, and hopefully less, than gas stations, automotive repair chains, and auto dealers, while providing better service.

Discussion Questions

1. What constitutes the mission of Minit-Lube?

2. How does the Minit-Lube operations strategy provide competitive advantage? (*Hint:* Evaluate how Minit-Lube's traditional competitors perform the 10 decisions of operations management vs. how Minit-Lube performs them.)

3. Is it likely that Minit-Lube has increased productivity over its more traditional competitors? Why? How would we measure productivity in this industry?

VIDEO CASE STUDY

Strategy at Regal Marine

Regal Marine, one of the U.S.'s 10 largest power-boat manufacturers, achieves its mission—providing luxury performance boats to customers worldwide—using the strategy of differentiation. It differentiates its products through constant innovation, unique features, and high quality. Increasing sales at the Orlando, Florida, family-owned firm suggest that the strategy is working.

As a quality boat manufacturer, Regal Marine starts with continuous innovation, as reflected in computer-aided design (CAD), high-quality molds, and close tolerances that are controlled through both defect charts and rigorous visual inspection. In-house quality is not enough, however. Because a product is only as good as the parts put into it, Regal has established close ties with a large number of its suppliers to ensure both flexibility and perfect parts. With the help of these suppliers, Regal can profitably produce a product line of 22 boats, ranging from the $14,000 three-passenger Rush to the $500,000 42-foot Commodore Yacht.

"We build boats," says VP Tim Kuck, "but we're really in the 'fun' business. Our competition includes not only 300 other boat, canoe, and yacht manufacturers in our $17 billion industry, but home theaters, the Internet, and all kinds of alternative family entertainment." Fortunately for Regal, with the strong economy and the repeal of the boat luxury tax on its side, it has been paying down debt and increasing market share.

Regal has also joined with scores of other independent boat makers in the American Boat Builders Association. Through economies of scale in procurement, Regal is able to navigate against billion-dollar competitor Brunswick (makers of the Sea Ray and Bayliner brands). The *Global Company Profile* featuring Regal

Marine (which opens Chapter 5 in your text) provides further background on Regal and its strategy.

Discussion Questions*

1. State Regal Marine's mission in your own words.
2. Identify the strengths, weaknesses, opportunities, and threats that are relevant to the strategy of Regal Marine.
3. How would you define Regal's strategy?
4. How would each of the 10 operations management decisions apply to operations decision making at Regal Marine?

*You may wish to play this video case on your CD-ROM before addressing these questions.

VIDEO CASE STUDY

Hard Rock Cafe's Global Strategy

Hard Rock is bringing the concept of the "experience economy" to its cafe operation. The strategy is to incorporate a unique "experience" into its operations. This innovation is somewhat akin to mass customization in manufacturing. At Hard Rock, the experience concept is to provide not only a custom meal from the menu, but a dining event that includes a unique visual and sound experience not duplicated anywhere in the world. This strategy is succeeding. Other theme restaurants have come and gone while Hard Rock continues to grow. As Professor C. Markides of the London Business School says, "The trick is not to play the game better than the competition, but to develop and play an altogether different game."* At Hard Rock, the different game is the experience game.

From the opening of its first cafe in London in 1971, during the British rock music explosion, Hard Rock has been serving food and rock music with equal enthusiasm. Hard Rock Cafe has 40 U.S. locations, about a dozen in Europe, and the remainder scattered throughout the world, from Bangkok and Beijing to Beirut. New construction, leases, and investment in remodeling are long term, so a global strategy means special consideration of political risk, currency risk, and social norms in a context of a brand fit. While Hard Rock is one of the most recognized brands in the world, this does not mean its cafe is a natural everywhere. Special consideration must be given to the supply chain for the restaurant and its accompanying retail store. About 48% of a typical cafe's sales are from merchandise.

The Hard Rock Cafe business model is well defined, but because of various risk factors and differences in business practices and employment law, Hard Rock elects to franchise about half of its cafes. Social norms and preferences often suggest some tweaking of

menus for local taste. For instance, Europeans, particularly the British, still have some fear of mad cow disease; therefore, Hard Rock is focusing less on hamburgers and beef and more on fish and lobster in its British cafes.

Because 70% of Hard Rock's guests are tourists, recent years have found it expanding to "destination" cities. While this has been a winning strategy for decades, allowing the firm to grow from 1 London cafe to 110 facilities in 41 countries, it has made Hard Rock susceptible to economic fluctuations that hit the tourist business hardest. So Hard Rock is signing a long-term lease for a new location in Nottingham, England, to join recently opened cafes in Manchester and Birmingham—cities that are not standard tourist destinations. At the same time, menus are being upgraded. Hopefully, repeat business from locals in these cities will smooth demand and make Hard Rock less dependent on tourists.

Discussion Questions†

1. Identify the strategy changes that have taken place at Hard Rock Cafe since its founding in 1971.
2. As Hard Rock Cafe has changed its strategy, how has its responses to some of the 10 decisions of OM changed?
3. Where does Hard Rock fit in the four international operations strategies outlined in Figure 2.9 in your text? Explain your answer.

Source: Professors Barry Render (Rollins College), Jay Heizer (Texas Lutheran University), and Beverly Amer (Northern Arizona University).

*Constantinos Markides, "Strategic Innovation," *MIT Sloan Management Review* 38, no. 3 (spring 1997): 9.

†You may wish to play this video case on your CD-ROM before addressing these questions.

Project Management

Chapter Outline

Many projects that organizations undertake are large and complex. And almost every manager worries about how to manage such projects effectively. It is a difficult problem and the stakes are high. Expensive cost overruns and unnecessary delays can occur due to poor project planning.

The first step in planning and scheduling a project is to develop the work breakdown structure. The time, cost, resource requirements, predecessors, and person(s) responsible are identified for each activity. When this has been done, a schedule for the project can be developed using such techniques as *Program Evaluation and Review Technique* (PERT) and the *Critical Path Method* (CPM).

BEFORE COMING TO CLASS, READ CHAPTER 3 IN YOUR TEXT AND ANSWER THESE QUESTIONS.

1. Give an example of a situation in which project management is needed. _____

_____

2. What are the three phases involved in managing a large project? ____

_____

_____

3. What is the critical path and why is it important? _____

_____

_____

4. What are some of the questions that can be answered with PERT or CPM? _____

_____

_____

5. What does *slack* mean and how can it be computed? _____

_____

6. What would you do to "crash" a project? _____

_____

THE IMPORTANCE OF PROJECT MANAGEMENT

Three Phases in the Management of Projects

1. Planning
2. Scheduling
3. Controlling

PROJECT PLANNING

FIGURE 3.1 ■ Project Planning, Scheduling, and Controlling

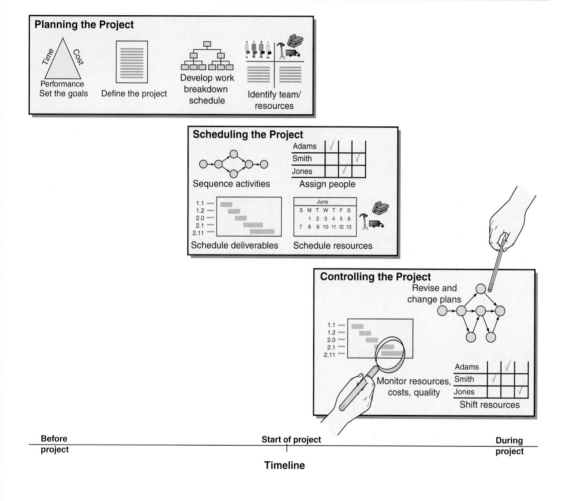

Work Breakdown Structure (WBS)

Level

1. Project
2.   Major tasks
3.   Subtasks
4.   Activities ("work package")

PROJECT SCHEDULING

Gantt Charts

FIGURE 3.4 ■ Gantt Chart of Service Activities for a Delta Jet during a 60-Minute Layover

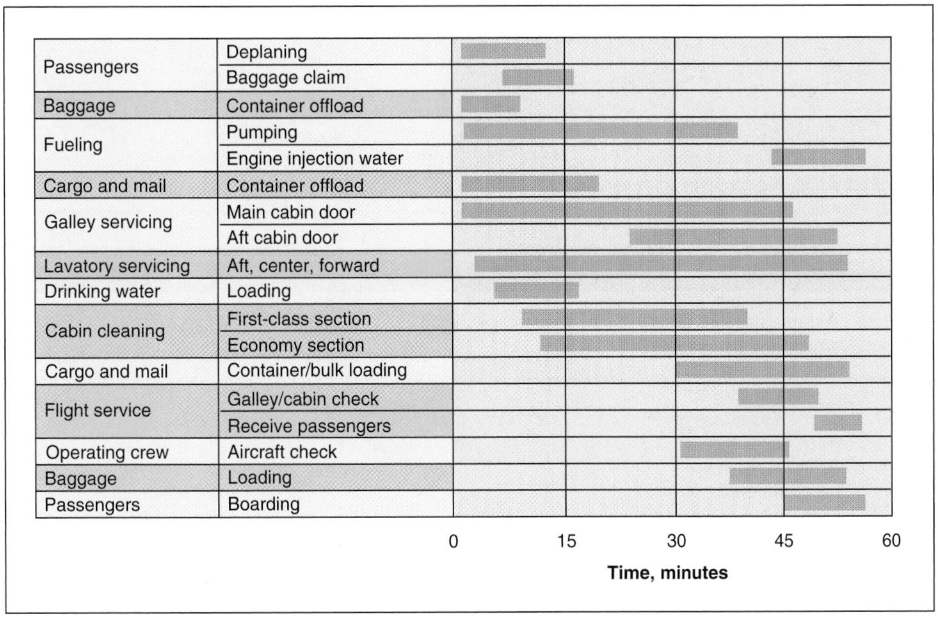

Passengers	Deplaning					
	Baggage claim					
Baggage	Container offload					
Fueling	Pumping					
	Engine injection water					
Cargo and mail	Container offload					
Galley servicing	Main cabin door					
	Aft cabin door					
Lavatory servicing	Aft, center, forward					
Drinking water	Loading					
Cabin cleaning	First-class section					
	Economy section					
Cargo and mail	Container/bulk loading					
Flight service	Galley/cabin check					
	Receive passengers					
Operating crew	Aircraft check					
Baggage	Loading					
Passengers	Boarding					

0   15   30   45   60

Time, minutes

PROJECT CONTROLLING

PROJECT MANAGEMENT TECHNIQUES: PERT AND CPM

Six Basic Steps in PERT and CPM

1. Define the project and prepare the WBS.
2. Develop the relationship among the activities.
3. Draw the network.
4. Assign time/cost estimates to activities.
5. Compute the critical path.
6. Use the network to plan, schedule, monitor, and control.

PERT and CPM Can Answer Several Questions

Network Diagrams and Approaches

Activity on Node (AON)

Activity on Arrow (AOA)

Dummy Activity

FIGURE 3.5 ■ A Comparison of AON and AOA Network Conventions

	Activity on Node (AON)	Activity Meaning	Activity on Arrow (AOA)
(a)	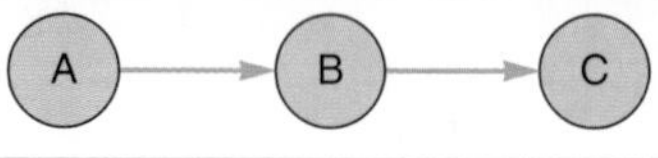	A comes before B, which comes before C.	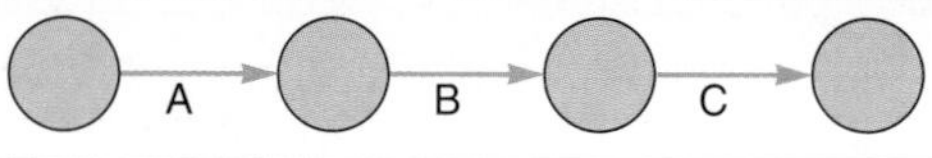
(b)	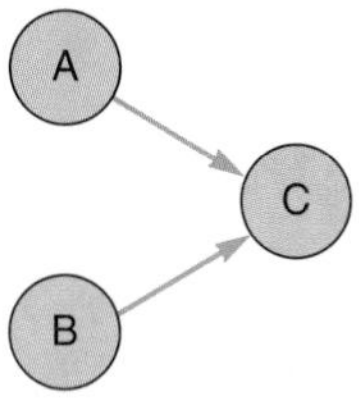	A and B must both be completed before C can start.	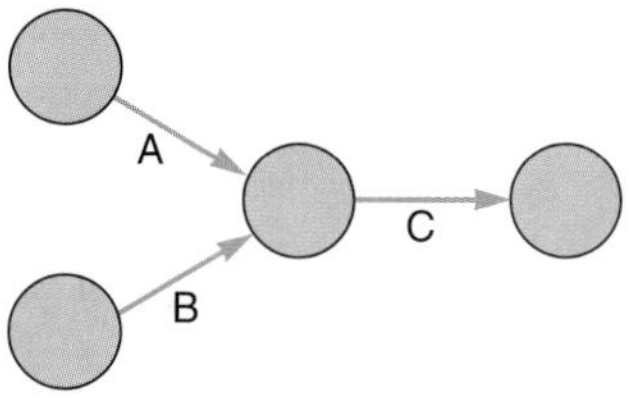
(c)	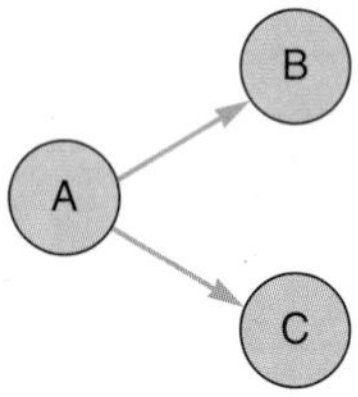	B and C cannot begin until A is completed.	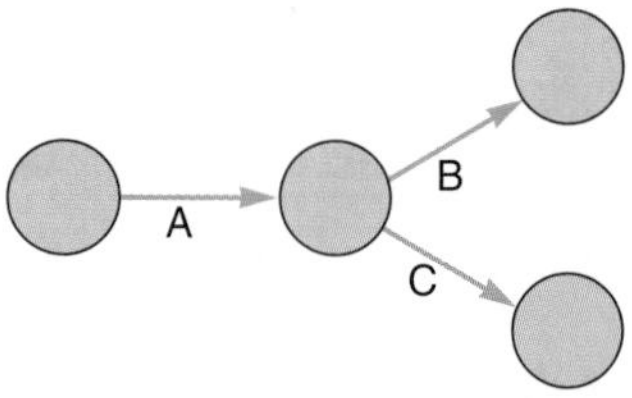
(d)	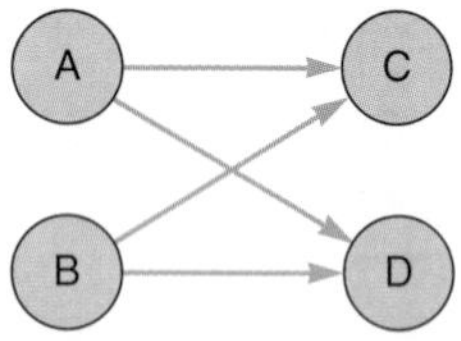	C and D cannot begin until A and B have both been completed.	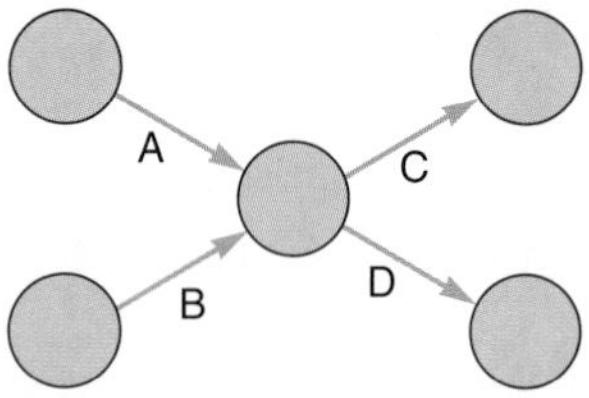
(e)	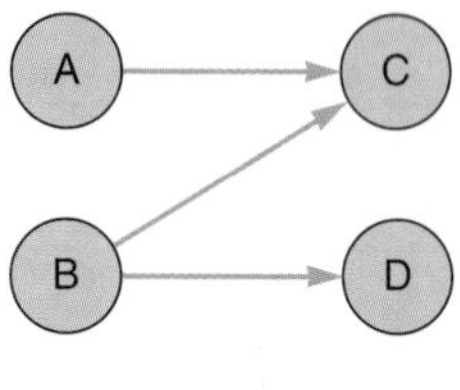	C cannot begin until both A and B are completed; D cannot begin until B is completed. A dummy activity is introduced in AOA.	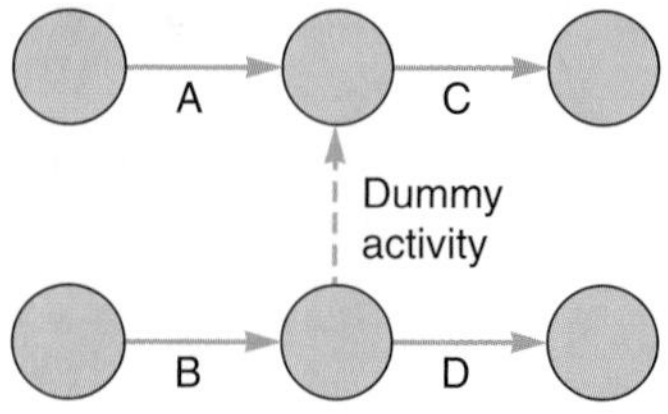
(f)	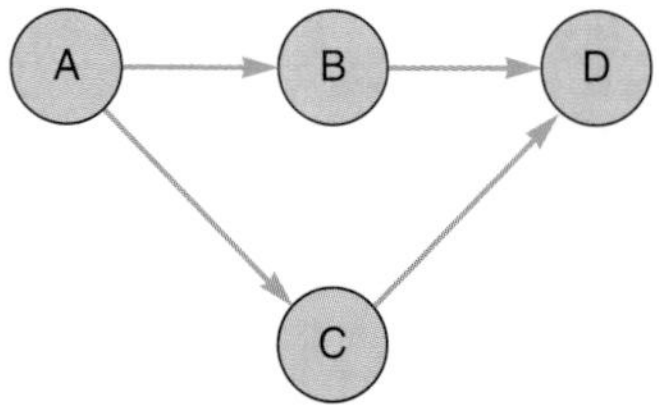	B and C cannot begin until A is completed. D cannot begin until both B and C are completed. A dummy activity is again introduced in AOA.	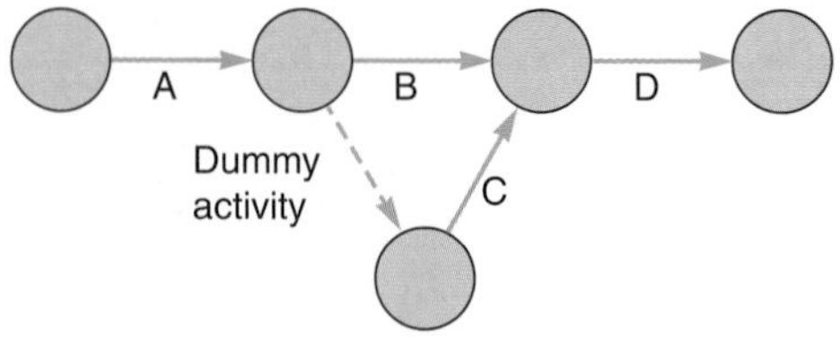

PRACTICE PROBLEM 3.1 ■ Drawing an AON Network

The following represent activities in a major construction project. Draw the network to represent this project.

ACTIVITY	IMMEDIATE PREDECESSOR
A	—
B	—
C	A
D	B
E	B
F	C, E
G	D
H	F, G

DETERMINING THE PROJECT SCHEDULE

Critical Path Analysis

Earliest Start (ES)

Earliest Finish (EF)

Latest Start (LS)

Latest Finish (LF)

Forward Pass

Backward Pass

FIGURE 3.10 ■ Notation Used in Nodes for
Forward and Backward Pass

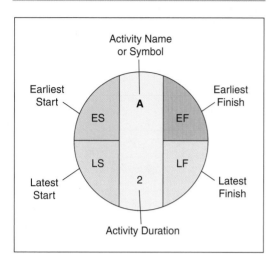

Slack Time

$$\text{Slack} = \text{LS} - \text{ES} \qquad \text{or} \qquad \text{Slack} = \text{LF} - \text{EF} \tag{3-5}$$

VARIABILITY IN ACTIVITY TIMES

Three Time Estimates in PERT

Optimistic Time (a)
Pessimistic Time (b)
Most Likely Time (m)

FIGURE 3.14 ■ Beta Probability Distribution with Three Time Estimates

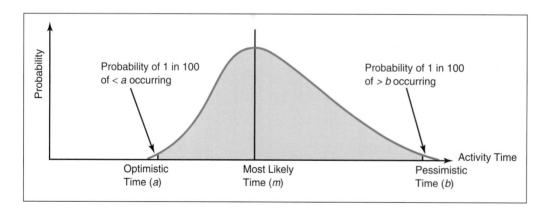

Expected time
$$t = (a + 4m + b)/6 \tag{3-6}$$
Variance of activity completion time $= [(b - a)/6]^2 \tag{3-7}$

PRACTICE PROBLEM 3.2 ■ Critical Path

Given the following time chart and network diagram, find the critical path.

ACTIVITY	a	m	b	t	VARIANCE
A	2	3	4	3	1/9
B	1	2	3	2	1/9
C	4	5	12	6	16/9
D	1	3	5	3	4/9
E	1	2	3	2	1/9

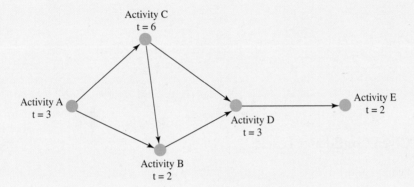

Additional Practice Problem Space

Probability of Project Completion

$$\text{Project variance } (\sigma_p^2) = \Sigma \text{ variance on critical path}$$

$$\text{Project standard deviation } (\sigma_p) = \sqrt{\text{Project variance}}$$

(3-8)

PRACTICE PROBLEM 3.3 ■ Variance

What is the variance in completion time for the critical path found in Practice Problem 3.2?

Project Completion Time for Given Confidence Levels

$$Z = (\text{due date} - \text{expected date of completion})/\sigma_p$$

(3-9)

PRACTICE PROBLEM 3.4 ■ Probabilities of Project Completion

A project has an expected completion time of 40 weeks and a standard deviation of 5 weeks. It is assumed that the project completion time is normally distributed.

   a. What is the probability of finishing the project in 50 weeks or less?

   b. What is the probability of finishing the project in 38 weeks or less?

   c. The due date for the project is set so that there is a 90% chance that the project will be finished by this date. What is the date?

Additional Practice Problem Space

COST-TIME TRADE-OFFS AND PROJECT CRASHING

Normal (or Standard) Time

Normal Cost

Crash Time

Crash Cost

$$\text{Crash cost per period} = \frac{(\text{Crash cost} - \text{Normal cost})}{(\text{Normal time} - \text{Crash time})} \tag{3-11}$$

Four Steps in Crashing a Project

1. _____

2. _____

3. _____

4. _____

PRACTICE PROBLEM 3.5 ■ Crashing

Development of a new deluxe version of a particular software product is being considered. The activities necessary for the completion of this project are listed in the following table along with their costs and completion times in weeks.

ACTIVITY	NORMAL TIME	CRASH TIME	NORMAL COST	CRASH COST	IMMEDIATE PREDECESSOR
A	4	3	2,000	2,600	—
B	2	1	2,200	2,800	A
C	3	3	500	500	A
D	8	4	2,300	2,600	A
E	6	3	900	1,200	B, D
F	3	2	3,000	4,200	C, E
G	4	2	1,400	2,000	F

a. What is the project expected completion date?

b. What is the total cost required for completing this project in normal time?

c. If you wish to reduce the time required to complete this project by 1 week, which activity should be crashed, and how much will this increase the total cost?

Additional Practice Problem Space

A CRITIQUE OF PERT AND CPM

Advantages

Disadvantages

USING MICROSOFT PROJECT TO MANAGE PROJECTS

PROGRAM 3.5 ■ Project Network in MS Project for Milwaukee General Hospital

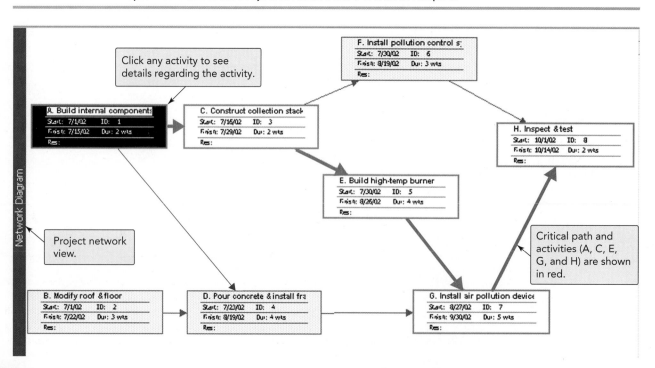

DISCUSSION QUESTIONS

1. Give an example of a situation where project management is needed.
2. Explain the purpose of project organization.
3. What are the three phases involved in the management of a large project?
4. What are some of the questions that can be answered with PERT and CPM?
5. Define *work breakdown structure*. How is it used?
6. What is the use of Gantt charts in project management?
7. What is the difference between an activity-on-arrow (AOA) network and an activity-on-node (AON) network? Which is primarily used in this chapter?
8. What is the significance of the critical path?
9. What would a project manager have to do to crash an activity?
10. Describe how expected activity times and variances can be computed in a PERT network.
11. Define *early start*, *early finish*, *late finish*, and *late start* times.
12. Students are sometimes confused by the concept of critical path, and want to believe that it is the *shortest* path through a network. Convincingly explain why this is not so.
13. What are dummy activities? Why are they used in activity-on-arrow (AOA) project networks?
14. What are the three time estimates used with PERT?
15. Would a project manager ever consider crashing a noncritical activity in a project network? Explain convincingly.
16. How is the variance of the total project computed in PERT?
17. Describe the meaning of slack, and discuss how it can be determined.
18. How can we determine the probability that a project will be completed by a certain date? What assumptions are made in this computation?
19. Name some of the widely used project management software programs.

CRITICAL THINKING EXERCISE

Construction of a new professional league basketball, football, or baseball stadium is a multiyear project which is so complex that the critical path method is almost a necessity. For example, when the Colorado Rockies, a National League baseball team, first began to select a Denver site, it took 4 years until the field was ready for play. Here are 18 actual activities involved *in random order*. Try to sequence them by correctly matching each activity with one of the dates listed.

ACTUAL DATES	MATCH ACTIVITIES IN THIS COLUMN WITH DATES ON THE LEFT
March 13, 1991	Contractor selected
December 31, 1991	Schematic design of ballpark starts
February 13, 1992	Construction starts
April 1, 1992	Architect presents exterior elevations of ballpark to the public
April 21, 1992	Sports lighting turned on at night
October 8, 1992	Field ready for opening day
October 16, 1992	Mass excavation commences
November 30, 1992	Agreement on final terms of lease
February 2, 1993	Caissons and foundation start
February 15, 1993	Scoreboard installed
July 14, 1993	Sod transplanted to playing field
September 24, 1993	Lower downtown site selected
October 6, 1993	First steel raised
March 11, 1994	Final seating capacity set
September 19, 1994	First bricks placed
October 25, 1994	Largest portion of land purchased
February 27, 1995	Final lease negotiations start
March 31, 1995	Last parcel of land purchased

ACTIVE MODEL EXERCISE

Milwaukee General Hospital. This Active Model allows you to evaluate changes in important elements on the hospital network we saw in this chapter, using your CD-ROM. See Active Model 3.1.

This Graph contains a Gantt Chart for the single time estimate hospital project. The critical activities appear in red in both the data table and the Gantt chart. Noncritical activities appear in green in the Gantt chart and the right side of these noncritical activities displays the amount of slack they have. You can use the scrollbars to change the

ACTIVE MODEL 3.1 ■

Project Management

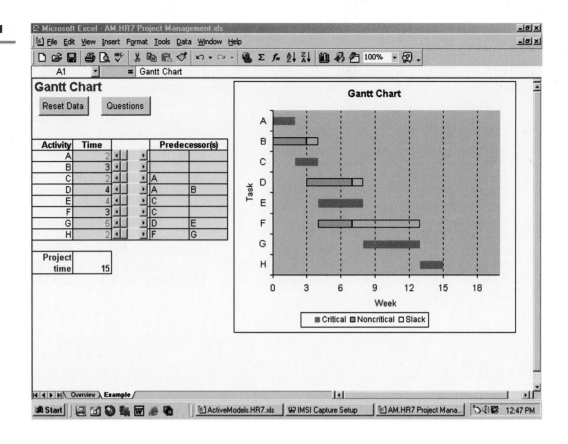

times of the individual activities. For critical activities, when you change the times the project times will change. For noncritical activities, if you increase the time then eventually they will become critical.

Questions

1. Both A and H are critical activities. Describe the difference between what happens on the graph when you increase A vs. increasing H.
2. Activity F is not critical. By how many weeks can you increase activity F until it becomes critical.
3. Activity B is not critical. By how many weeks can you increase activity B until it becomes critical. What happens when B becomes critical?
4. What happens when you increase B by 1 more week after it becomes critical?
5. Suppose that building codes change and as a result activity B would have to be completed before activity C could be started. How would this affect the project?

 # PROBLEMS*

· **3.1**   The work breakdown structure for building a house (levels 1 and 2) is shown below:

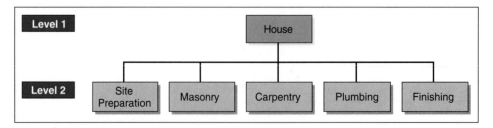

a) Add two level 3 activities to each of the level 2 activities to provide more detail to the WBS.
b) Select one of your level 3 activities and add two level 4 activities below it.

*Note: **P** means the problem may be solved with POM for Windows; ✕ means the problem may be solved with Excel OM; and **P✕** means the problem may be solved with POM for Windows and/or Excel OM.

3.2 Jerry Jacobs has decided to run for a seat as Congressman from the House of Representative district 34 in Florida. He views his 8-month campaign for office as a major project, and wishes to create a work breakdown structure (WBS) to help control the detailed scheduling. So far, he has developed the following pieces of the WBS:

LEVEL	LEVEL ID No.	ACTIVITY
1	1.0	Develop political campaign
2	1.1	Fund-raising plan
3	1.11	_____
3	1.12	_____
3	1.13	_____
2	1.2	Develop a position on major issues
3	1.21	_____
3	1.22	_____
3	1.23	_____
2	1.3	Staffing for campaign
3	1.31	_____
3	1.32	_____
3	1.33	_____
3	1.34	_____
2	1.4	Paperwork compliance for candidacy
3	1.41	_____
3	1.42	_____
2	1.5	Ethical plan/issues
3	1.51	_____

Help Mr. Jacobs by providing details where the blank lines appear. Are there any other major (level 2) activities to create? If so, add an ID no. 1.6 and insert them.

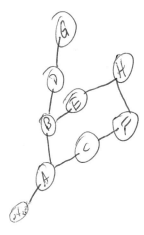

Px . 3.3 Draw the activity-on-node (AON) project network associated with the following activities for Girish Shambu's consulting company project. How long should it take Girish and his team to complete this project? What are the critical path activities?

ACTIVITY	IMMEDIATE PREDECESSOR(S)	TIME (DAYS)	ACTIVITY	IMMEDIATE PREDECESSOR(S)	TIME (DAYS)
A	—	3	E	B	4
B	A	4	F	C	4
C	A	6	G	D	6
D	B	6	H	E, F	8

Px . 3.4 Given the activities whose sequence is described by the following table, draw the appropriate activity-on-arrow (AOA) network diagram. Which activities are on the critical path? What is the length of the critical path?

ACTIVITY	IMMEDIATE PREDECESSOR(S)	TIME (DAYS)	ACTIVITY	IMMEDIATE PREDECESSOR(S)	TIME (DAYS)
A	—	5	F	C	5
B	A	2	G	E, F	2
C	A	4	H	D	3
D	B	5	I	G, H	5
E	B	5			

Px . 3.5 Using AOA, diagram the network described below for Sarah McComb's construction project. Calculate its critical path. How long is the minimum duration of this network?

ACTIVITY	NODES	TIME (WEEKS)	ACTIVITY	NODES	TIME (WEEKS)
J	1–2	10	N	3–4	2
K	1–3	8	O	4–5	7
L	2–4	6	P	3–5	5
M	2–3	3			

Px : 3.6 Shirley Hopkins is developing a program in leadership training for middle-level managers. Shirley has listed a number of activities that must be completed before a training program of this nature could be conducted. The activities, immediate predecessors, and times appear in the table on the top of the next page.

ACTIVITY	IMMEDIATE PREDECESSOR(S)	TIME (DAYS)	ACTIVITY	IMMEDIATE PREDECESSOR(S)	TIME (DAYS)
A	—	2	E	A, D	3
B	—	5	F	C	6
C	—	1	G	E, F	8
D	B	10			

a) Develop an AON network for this problem.
b) What is the critical path?
c) What is the total project completion time?
d) What is the slack time for each individual activity?

3.7 Task time estimates for a production line setup project at Robert Klassen's Ontario factory are as follows.

ACTIVITY	TIME (IN HOURS)	IMMEDIATE PREDECESSORS
A	6.0	—
B	7.2	—
C	5.0	A
D	6.0	B, C
E	4.5	B, C
F	7.7	D
G	4.0	E, F

a) Draw the project network using AON.
b) Identify the critical path.
c) What is the expected project length?
d) Draw a Gantt chart for the project.

3.8 A large playground for the new town square in Celebration, Florida, is in the planning stages. Here are the six activities to be completed:

ACTIVITY	HOURS NEEDED	IMMEDIATE PREDECESSOR(S)
Planning (A)	20	—
Buying supplies (B)	60	Planning (A)
Digging/grading (C)	100	Planning (A)
Sawing lumber (D)	30	Buying supplies (B)
Placing lumber (E)	20	Digging/grading (C) and Sawing (D)
Assembly/painting (F)	10	Placing lumber (E)

a) Develop an activity-on-arrow (AOA) network for this project.
b) What is the project completion time?

3.9 Refer to Problem 3.8. Develop an activity-on-node (AON) network for the project.

3.10 The activities needed to build an experimental chemical contaminant tracking machine at Billy Thornton Corp. are listed in the following table. Construct an AON network for these activities.

ACTIVITY	IMMEDIATE PREDECESSOR(S)	ACTIVITY	IMMEDIATE PREDECESSOR(S)
A	—	E	B
B	—	F	B
C	A	G	C, E
D	A	H	D, F

3.11 Billy Thornton (see Problem 3.10) was able to determine the activity times for constructing his chemical contaminant tracking machine. Thornton would like to determine ES, EF, LS, LF, and slack for each activity. The total project completion time and the critical path should also be determined. Here are the activity times:

ACTIVITY	TIME (WEEKS)	ACTIVITY	TIME (WEEKS)
A	6	E	4
B	7	F	6
C	3	G	10
D	2	H	7

P$_{\times}$. 3.12 The activities described by the following table are given for the Duplaga Corporation:

ACTIVITY	IMMEDIATE PREDECESSOR(S)	TIME
A	—	9
B	A	7
C	A	3
D	B	6
E	B	9
F	C	4
G	E, F	6
H	D	5
I	G, H	3

a) Draw the appropriate AON PERT diagram for Ed Duplaga's management team.
b) Find the critical path.
c) What is the project completion time?

P$_{\times}$. 3.13 A small renovation of a Hard Rock Cafe gift shop has six activities (in hours). For the following estimates of a, m and b, calculate the expected time and the standard deviation for each activity.

ACTIVITY	a	m	b
A	11	15	19
B	27	31	41
C	18	18	18
D	8	13	19
E	17	18	20
F	16	19	22

P$_{\times}$. 3.14 Latta Carpet and Trim installs carpeting in commercial offices. Carol Latta has been very concerned with the amount of time it took to complete several recent jobs. Some of her workers are very unreliable. A list of activities and their optimistic completion time, the most likely completion time, and the pessimistic completion time (all in days) for a new contract are given in the table below.

Determine the expected completion time and variance for each activity.

ACTIVITY	TIME (DAYS) a	m	b	IMMEDIATE PREDECESSOR(S)
A	3	6	8	—
B	2	4	4	—
C	1	2	3	—
D	6	7	8	C
E	2	4	6	B, D
F	6	10	14	A, E
G	1	2	4	A, E
H	3	6	9	F
I	10	11	12	G
J	14	16	20	C
K	2	8	10	H, I

P$_{\times}$: 3.15 Carol Latta would like to determine the total project completion time and the critical path for installing carpeting in a large new office building. See Problem 3.14 for details. In addition, determine ES, EF, LS, LF, and slack for each activity.

: 3.16 What is the probability that Latta Carpet and Trim will finish the project described in Problems 3.14 and 3.15 in 40 days or less?

P$_{\times}$: 3.17 Bill Fennema, president of Fennema Construction, has developed the tasks, durations, and predecessor relationships in the table on the top of the next page for building new motels. Draw the AON network and answer the questions that follow the table.

ACTIVITY	IMMEDIATE PREDECESSOR(S)	TIME ESTIMATES (IN WEEKS)		
		OPTIMISTIC	MOST LIKELY	PESSIMISTIC
A	—	4	8	10
B	A	2	8	24
C	A	8	12	16
D	A	4	6	10
E	B	1	2	3
F	E, C	6	8	20
G	E, C	2	3	4
H	F	2	2	2
I	F	6	6	6
J	D, G, H	4	6	12
K	I, J	2	2	3

a)   What is the expected time for activity C?
b)   What is the variance for activity C?
c)   Based on the calculation of estimated times, what is the critical path?
d)   What is the estimated time of the critical path?
e)   What is the activity variance along the critical path?
f)   What is the probability of completion of the project before week 36?

P : 3.18   What is the minimum cost of crashing the following project by 4 days?

ACTIVITY	NORMAL TIME (DAYS)	CRASH TIME (DAYS)	NORMAL COST	CRASH COST	IMMEDIATE PREDECESSOR(S)
A	6	5	$ 900	$1,000	—
B	8	6	300	400	—
C	4	3	500	600	—
D	5	3	900	1,200	A
E	8	5	1,000	1,600	C

P : 3.19   Three activities are candidates for crashing on a project network for a large computer installation (all are, of course, critical). Activity details are in the table below.

ACTIVITY	PREDECESSOR	NORMAL TIME	NORMAL COST	CRASH TIME	CRASH COST
A	—	7 days	$6,000	6 days	$6,600
B	A	4 days	1,200	2 days	3,000
C	B	11 days	4,000	9 days	6,000

a)   What action would you take to reduce the critical path by one day?
b)   Assuming no other paths become critical, what action would you take to reduce the critical path one additional day?
c)   What is the total cost of the two-day reduction?

P : 3.20   Development of a new deluxe version of a particular software product is being considered by Ravi Behara's software house. The activities necessary for the completion of this project are listed in the following table:

ACTIVITY	NORMAL TIME (WEEKS)	CRASH TIME (WEEKS)	NORMAL COST	CRASH COST	IMMEDIATE PREDECESSOR(S)
A	4	3	$2,000	$2,600	—
B	2	1	2,200	2,800	—
C	3	3	500	500	—
D	8	4	2,300	2,600	A
E	6	3	900	1,200	B
F	3	2	3,000	4,200	C
G	4	2	1,400	2,000	D, E

a)   What is the project completion date?
b)   What is the total cost required for completing this project on normal time?
c)   If you wish to reduce the time required to complete this project by 1 week, which activity should be crashed, and how much will this increase the total cost?
d)   What is the maximum time that can be crashed? How much would costs increase?

P : 3.21   The estimated times and immediate predecessors for the activities in a project at Caesar Douglas's retinal scanning company are given in the table on the top of the next page. Assume that the activity times are independent.

ACTIVITY	IMMEDIATE PREDECESSOR	TIME (WEEKS) *a*	*m*	*b*
A	—	9	10	11
B	—	4	10	16
C	A	9	10	11
D	B	5	8	11

a) Calculate the expected time and variance for each activity.

b) What is the expected completion time of the critical path? What is the expected completion time of the other path in the network?

c) What is the variance of the critical path? What is the variance of the other path in the network?

d) If the time to complete path A–C is normally distributed, what is the probability that this path will be finished in 22 weeks or less?

e) If the time to complete path B–D is normally distributed, what is the probability that this path will be finished in 22 weeks or less?

f) Explain why the probability that the *critical path* will be finished in 22 weeks or less is not necessarily the probability that the *project* will be finished in 22 weeks or less.

3.22 Ton Stam Manufacturing produces custom-built pollution-control devices for medium-size steel mills. The most recent project undertaken by Stam requires 14 different activities.

a) Stam's managers would like to determine the total project completion time (in days) and those activities that lie along the critical path. The appropriate data are shown in the following table.

b) What is the probability of being done in 53 days?

ACTIVITY	IMMEDIATE PREDECESSOR(S)	OPTIMISTIC TIME	MOST LIKELY TIME	PESSIMISTIC TIME
A	—	4	6	7
B	—	1	2	3
C	A	6	6	6
D	A	5	8	11
E	B, C	1	9	18
F	D	2	3	6
G	D	1	7	8
H	E, F	4	4	6
I	G, H	1	6	8
J	I	2	5	7
K	I	8	9	11
L	J	2	4	6
M	K	1	2	3
N	L, M	6	8	10

3.23 Dream Team Productions is in the final design phases of its new film, *Killer Worms*, to be released next summer. Market Wise, the firm hired to coordinate the release of *Killer Worms* toys, identified 16 activities to be completed before the release of the film.

a) How many weeks in advance of the film release should Market Wise start its marketing campaign? What are the critical paths? The tasks (in time units of weeks) are as follows:

ACTIVITY	IMMEDIATE PREDECESSORS	OPTIMISTIC TIME	MOST LIKELY TIME	PESSIMISTIC TIME
A	—	1	2	4
B	—	3	3.5	4
C	—	10	12	13
D	—	4	5	7
E	—	2	4	5
F	A	6	7	8
G	B	2	4	5.5
H	C	5	7.7	9
I	C	9.9	10	12
J	C	2	4	5
K	D	2	4	6
L	E	2	4	6
M	F, G, H	5	6	6.5
N	J, K, L	1	1.1	2
O	I, M	5	7	8
P	N	5	7	9

b) If activities I and J were not necessary, what impact would this have on the critical path and the number of weeks needed to complete the marketing campaign?

3.24 Using PERT, Harold Schramm was able to determine that the expected project completion time for the construction of a pleasure yacht is 21 months and the project variance is 4.
a) What is the probability that the project will be completed in 17 months?
b) What is the probability that the project will be completed in 20 months?
c) What is the probability that the project will be completed in 23 months?
d) What is the probability that the project will be completed in 25 months?

P : 3.25 Bolling Electronics manufactures DVD players for commercial use. W. Blaker Bolling, president of Bolling Electronics, is contemplating producing DVD players for home use. The activities necessary to build an experimental model and related data are given in the following table:

ACTIVITY	NORMAL TIME (WEEKS)	CRASH TIME (WEEKS)	NORMAL COST ($)	CRASH COST ($)	IMMEDIATE PREDECESSOR(S)
A	3	2	1,000	1,600	—
B	2	1	2,000	2,700	—
C	1	1	300	300	—
D	7	3	1,300	1,600	A
E	6	3	850	1,000	B
F	2	1	4,000	5,000	C
G	4	2	1,500	2,000	D, E

a) What is the project completion date?
b) Crash this project to 10 weeks at the least cost.
c) Crash this project to 7 weeks (which is the maximum it can be crashed) at the least cost.

P : 3.26 The Maser is a new custom-designed sports car. An analysis of the task of building the Maser reveals the following list of relevant activities, their immediate predecessors, and their duration.[1]

JOB LETTER	DESCRIPTION	IMMEDIATE PREDECESSOR(S)	NORMAL TIME (DAYS)
A	Start	—	0
B	Design	A	8
C	Order special accessories	B	0.1
D	Build frame	B	1
E	Build doors	B	1
F	Attach axles, wheels, gas tank	D	1
G	Build body shell	B	2
H	Build transmission and drivetrain	B	3
I	Fit doors to body shell	G, E	1
J	Build engine	B	4
K	Bench-test engine	J	2
L	Assemble chassis	F, H, K	1
M	Road-test chassis	L	0.5
N	Paint body	I	2
O	Install wiring	N	1
P	Install interior	N	1.5
Q	Accept delivery of special accessories	C	5
R	Mount body and accessories on chassis	M, O, P, Q	1
S	Road test car	R	0.5
T	Attach exterior trim	S	1
U	Finish	T	0

a) Draw a network diagram for the project.
b) Mark the critical path and state its length.
c) If the Maser had to be completed 2 days earlier, would it help to
  i) Buy preassembled transmissions and drivetrains?
  ii) Install robots to halve engine-building time?
  iii) Speed delivery of special accessories by 3 days?
d) How might resources be borrowed from activities on the noncritical path to speed activities on the critical path?

[1]*Source:* James A. D. Stoner and Charles Wankel, *Management*, 3rd ed. (Englewood Cliffs, NJ: Prentice Hall, 1986): 195.

3.27 A project in James He's South Carolina company has an expected completion time of 40 weeks and a standard deviation of 5 weeks. It is assumed that the project completion time is normally distributed.
a) What is the probability of finishing the project in 50 weeks or less?
b) What is the probability of finishing the project in 38 weeks or less?
c) The due date for the project is set so that there is a 90% chance that the project will be finished by this date. What is the due date?

INTERNET HOMEWORK PROBLEMS

See our Internet home page, at **www.prenhall.com/heizer**, for these additional homework problems: 3.28 through 3.34.

CASE STUDY

Southwestern University: (A)*

Southwestern University (SWU), a large state college in Stephenville, Texas, 30 miles southwest of the Dallas/Fort Worth metroplex, enrolls close to 20,000 students. In a typical town–gown relationship, the school is a dominant force in the small city, with more students during fall and spring than permanent residents.

A longtime football powerhouse, SWU is a member of the Big Eleven conference and is usually in the top 20 in college football rankings. To bolster its chances of reaching the elusive and long-desired number-one ranking, in 1997 SWU hired the legendary Bo Pitterno as its head coach.

One of Pitterno's demands on joining SWU had been a new stadium. With attendance increasing, SWU administrators began to face the issue head-on. After 6 months of study, much political arm wrestling, and some serious financial analysis, Dr. Joel Wisner, president of Southwestern University, had reached a decision to expand the capacity at its on-campus stadium.

Adding thousands of seats, including dozens of luxury skyboxes, would not please everyone. The influential Pitterno had argued the need for a first-class stadium, one with built-in dormitory rooms for his players and a palatial office appropriate for the coach of a future NCAA champion team. But the decision was made, and *everyone*, including the coach, would learn to live with it.

The job now was to get construction going immediately after the 2003 season ended. This would allow exactly 270 days until the 2004 season opening game. The contractor, Hill Construction (Bob Hill being an alumnus, of course), signed his contract. Bob Hill looked at

the tasks his engineers had outlined and looked President Wisner in the eye. "I guarantee the team will be able to take the field on schedule next year," he said with a sense of confidence. "I sure hope so," replied Wisner. "The contract penalty of $10,000 per day for running late is nothing compared to what Coach Pitterno will do to you if our opening game with Penn State is delayed or canceled." Hill, sweating slightly, did not need to respond. In football-crazy Texas, Hill Construction would be *mud* if the 270-day target were missed.

Back in his office, Hill again reviewed the data (see Table 3.6) and noted that optimistic time estimates can be used as crash times. He then gathered his foremen. "Folks, if we're not 75% sure we'll finish this stadium in less than 270 days, I want this project crashed! Give me the cost figures for a target date of 250 days—also for 240 days. I want to be *early*, not just on time!"

Discussion Questions

1. Develop a network drawing for Hill Construction and determine the critical path. How long is the project expected to take?
2. What is the probability of finishing in 270 days?
3. If it is necessary to crash to 250 or 240 days, how would Hill do so, and at what costs? As noted in the case, assume that optimistic time estimates can be used as crash times.

*This integrated study runs throughout the Student Lecture Guide. Other issues facing Southwestern's football expansion include: (B) Forecasting game attendance (Chapter 4); (C) Quality of facilities (Chapter 6); (D) Inventory planning of football programs (Chapter 12); (E) Scheduling of campus security officers/staff for game days (Chapter 13).

TABLE 3.6 ■ Southwestern University Project

			TIME ESTIMATES (DAYS)			
ACTIVITY	DESCRIPTION	PREDECESSOR(S)	OPTIMISTIC	MOST LIKELY	PESSIMISTIC	CRASH COST/DAY
A	Bonding, insurance, tax structuring	—	20	30	40	$1,500
B	Foundation, concrete footings for boxes	A	20	65	80	3,500
C	Upgrading skyboxes stadium seating	A	50	60	100	4,000
D	Upgrading walkways, stairwells, elevators	C	30	50	100	1,900
E	Interior wiring, lathes	B	25	30	35	9,500
F	Inspection approvals	E	0.1	0.1	0.1	0
G	Plumbing	D, E	25	30	35	2,500
H	Painting	G	10	20	30	2,000
I	Hardware/AC/metal workings	H	20	25	60	2,000
J	Tile/carpeting/windows	H	8	10	12	6,000
K	Inspection	J	0.1	0.1	0.1	0
L	Final detail work/cleanup	I, K	20	25	60	4,500

CASE STUDY

Bay Community Hospital

The staff of the Bay Community Hospital had committed itself to introduce a new diagnostic procedure in the clinic. This procedure required the acquisition, installation, and introduction of a new medical instrument. Dr. Ed Windsor was assigned the responsibility for assuring that the introduction be performed as quickly and smoothly as possible.

Dr. Windsor created a list of activities that would have to be completed before the new service could begin. Initially, three individual steps had to be taken: (1) write instructions and procedures, (2) select techniques to operate the equipment, and (3) procure the equipment. The instructions and selection of the operators had to be completed before training could commence. Dr. Windsor also believed it was necessary to choose the operators and evaluate their qualifications before formally announcing the new service to the local medical community. Upon arrival and installation of the equipment and completion of the operators' training, Edward Windsor wanted to spend a period checking out the procedures, operators, and equipment before declaring the project was successfully completed. The activities and times are listed in Table 3.7.

Jack Worth, a member of the Bay Community Hospital staff, reported that it would be possible to save time on the project by paying some premiums to complete certain activities faster than the normal schedule listed in Table 3.7. Specifically, if the equipment were shipped by express truck, one week could be saved. Air freight would save two weeks. However, a premium of $2,000 would be paid for the express truck shipment and $7,500 would be paid for air shipment. The operator training period could also be reduced by one week if the trainees worked overtime. However, this would cost the hospital an additional $6,000. The time required to complete the instructions could be reduced by one week with the additional expenditure of $4,000. However, $3,000 could be *saved* if this activity was allowed to take three weeks.

Discussion Questions

1. What is the shortest time period in which the project can be completed using the expected times listed in Table 3.7?
2. What is the shortest time in which the project can be completed?
3. What is the lowest cost schedule for this shortest time?

Source: Modified from W. Earl Sasser, Jr., R. Paul Olsen, and D. Daryl Wyckoff, *Management Service Operations*, pp. 97–98. Allyn and Bacon. Reprinted with permission.

TABLE 3.7 ■ Bay Community Hospital Activities Required to Introduce a New Diagnostic Procedure

ACTIVITY	DURATION (WEEKS)	IMMEDIATELY PRECEDING ACTIVITIES	IMMEDIATELY FOLLOWING ACTIVITIES
A. Write instructions	2	Start	C
B. Select operators	4	Start	C, D
C. Train operators	3	A, B	F
D. Announce new service	4	B	End
E. Purchase, ship, and receive equipment	8	Start	F
F. Test new operators on equipment	2	C, E	End

VIDEO CASE STUDY

Managing Hard Rock's Rockfest*

At the Hard Rock Cafe, like many organizations, project management is a key planning tool. With Hard Rock's constant growth in hotels and cafes, remodeling of existing cafes, scheduling for Hard Rock Live concert and event venues, and planning the annual Rockfest, managers rely on project management techniques and software to maintain schedule and budget performance.

"Without Microsoft Project," says Hard Rock Vice-President Chris Tomasso, "there is no way to keep so many people on the same page." Tomasso is in charge of the Rockfest event, which is attended by well over 100,000 enthusiastic fans. The challenge is pulling it off within a tight 9-month planning horizon. As the event approaches, Tomasso devotes greater energy to its activities. For the first 3 months, Tomasso updates his MS Project charts monthly. Then at the 6-month mark, he updates his progress weekly. At the 9-month mark, he checks and corrects his schedule twice a week.

Early in the project management process, Tomasso identifies 10 major tasks (called level 2 activities in a work breakdown structure, or WBS):[†] talent booking, ticketing, marketing/PR, online promotion, television, show production, travel, sponsorships, operations, and merchandising. Using a WBS, each of these is further divided into a series of subtasks. Table 3.8 identifies 26 of the major activities and subactivities, their immediate predecessors, and time estimates. Tomasso enters all of these into the MS Project software.[‡] Tomasso alters the MS Project document and the time line as the project progresses. "It's okay to change it as long as you keep on track," he states.

The day of the rock concert itself is not the end of the project planning. "It's nothing but surprises. A band not being able to get to the venue because of traffic jams is a surprise, but an 'anticipated' surprise. We had a helicopter on stand-by ready to fly the band in," says Tomasso.

On completion of Rockfest in July, Tomasso and his team have a 3-month reprieve before starting the project planning process again.

Discussion Questions[§]

1. Identify the critical path and its activities for Rockfest. How long does the project take?
2. Which activities have a slack time of 8 weeks or more?
3. Identify five major challenges a project manager faces in events such as this one.
4. Why is a work breakdown structure useful in a project such as this? Take the 26 activities and break them into what you think should be level 2, level 3, and level 4 tasks.

*Source: Professors Barry Render (Rollins College), Jay Heizer (Texas Lutheran University) and Beverly Amer (Northern Arizona University).

[†]The level one activity is the Rockfest concert itself.

[‡]There are actually 127 activities used by Tomasso—the list is abbreviated for this case study.

[§]You may wish to play this video case on your Student CD-ROM before addressing these questions.

TABLE 3.8 ■ Some of the Major Activities and Subactivities in the Rockfest Plan

ACTIVITY	DESCRIPTION	PREDECESSOR(S)	TIME (WEEKS)
A	Finalize site and building contracts	—	7
B	Select local promoter	A	3
C	Hire production manager	A	3
D	Design promotional Web site	B	5
E	Set TV deal	D	6
F	Hire director	E	4
G	Plan for TV camera placement	F	2
H	Target headline entertainers	B	4
I	Target support entertainers	H	4
J	Travel accommodations for talent	I	10
K	Set venue capacity	C	2
L	Ticketmaster contract	D, K	3
M	On-site ticketing	L	8
N	Sound and staging	C	6
O	Passes and stage credentials	G, R	7
P	Travel accommodations for staff	B	20
Q	Hire sponsor coordinator	B	4
R	Finalize sponsors	Q	4
S	Define/place signage for sponsors	R, X	3
T	Hire operations manager	A	4
U	Develop site plan	T	6
V	Hire security director	T	7
W	Set police/fire security plan	V	4
X	Power, plumbing, AC, toilet services	U	8
Y	Secure merchandise deals	B	6
Z	Online merchandise sales	Y	6

Chapter 4

Forecasting

Chapter Outline

Forecasts are an essential part of efficient service and manufacturing operations. Demand forecasts drive a firm's production, capacity, and scheduling decisions and affect the financial, marketing, and personnel planning functions.

Both qualitative and quantitative techniques are used to forecast demand. Qualitative approaches employ judgment, experience, intuition, and a host of other factors that are difficult to quantify. Quantitative forecasting uses historical data and causal, or associative, relations to project future demands.

BEFORE COMING TO CLASS, READ CHAPTER 4 IN YOUR TEXT AND ANSWER THESE QUESTIONS.

1. What is a qualitative forecasting model and when is it used? _____

_____

_____

2. What are the three forecasting time horizons? _____

_____

3. What is the difference between a weighted moving average and exponential smoothing? _____

_____

_____

4. What is time-series data? _____

_____

_____

5. What tools can be used to determine the accuracy of a given forecasting method? _____

_____

_____

6. What is a dependent variable? How does it differ from an independent variable? _____

_____

WHAT IS FORECASTING?

Forecasting Time Horizons
1. Short-range
2. Medium-range
3. Long-range

TYPES OF FORECASTS
1. Economic Forecasts
2. Technological Forecasts
3. Demand Forecasts

THE STRATEGIC IMPORTANCE OF FORECASTING

SEVEN STEPS IN THE FORECASTING SYSTEM
1. Determine the Use of the Forecast
2. Select the Items to be Forecasted
3. Determine the Time Horizon of the Forecast
4. Select the Forecasting Model(s)
5. Gather the Data Needed
6. Make the Forecast
7. Validate and Implement the Results

FORECASTING APPROACHES

Qualitative Methods

1. Jury of Executive Opinion

2. Delphi

3. Sales Force Composite

4. Consumer Market Survey

Quantitative Methods

1. Time-Series Models

2. Associative (Regression) Model

TIME-SERIES FORECASTING

Decomposition

1. Trend

2. Seasonality

3. Cycles

4. Random Variations

FIGURE 4.1 ■ Product Demand Charted over 4 Years with a Growth Trend and Seasonality Indicated

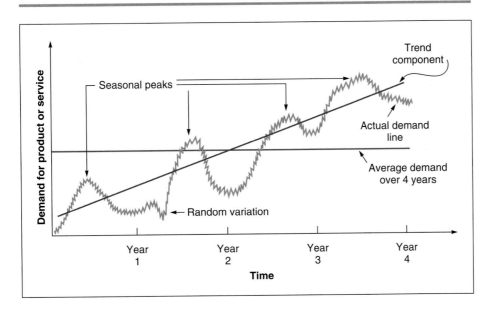

Naïve Approach

Moving Averages

$$\text{Moving average} = \frac{\Sigma \text{ demand in previous } n \text{ periods}}{n} \qquad (4\text{-}1)$$

PRACTICE PROBLEM 4.1 ■ Moving Averages

Auto sales at Carmen's Chevrolet are as follows. Develop a 3-week moving average.

WEEK	AUTO SALES
1	8
2	10
3	9
4	11
5	10
6	13
7	—

Additional Practice Problem Space

Weighted Moving Averages

$$\text{Weighted moving average} = \frac{\Sigma \ (\text{weight for period } n)(\text{demand in period } n)}{\Sigma \ \text{weights}} \qquad (4\text{-}2)$$

PRACTICE PROBLEM 4.2 ■ Practice Problem 4.1 with Weights

Carmen's decides to forecast auto sales by weighting the 3 weeks as follows:

Weights Applied	Period
3	Last week
2	Two weeks ago
1	Three weeks ago
6	Total

Additional Practice Problem Space

Exponential Smoothing

New forecast = last period's forecast
              + α (last period's actual demand – last period's forecast)   (4-3)

where α = smoothing constant between 0 and 1

PRACTICE PROBLEM 4.3 ■ Exponential Smoothing

A firm uses simple exponential smoothing with α = 0.1 to forecast demand. The forecast for the week of January 1 was 500 units whereas the actual demand turned out to be 450 units. Calculate the demand forecast for the week of January 8.

Additional Practice Problem Space

Measuring Forecast Error

1. Mean Absolute Deviation (MAD)

2. Mean Squared Error (MSE)

3. Mean Absolute Percent Error (MAPE)

$$\text{MAD} = \frac{\Sigma |\text{forecast errors}|}{n}$$ (4-5)

PRACTICE PROBLEM 4.4 ■ Using MAD to Evaluate Two Exponential Smoothing Models

Exponential smoothing is used to forecast automobile battery sales. Two values of α are examined: $\alpha = 0.8$ and $\alpha = 0.5$. Evaluate the accuracy of each smoothing constant. Which is preferable? (Assume the forecast for January was 22 batteries.) Actual sales are as follows:

Month	Actual Battery Sales	Forecast
January	20	22
February	21	
March	15	
April	14	
May	13	
June	16	

Additional Practice Problem Space

Exponential Smoothing with Trend Adjustment

Forecast including trend (FIT_t) = exponentially smoothed forecast (F_t)
         + exponentially smoothed trend (T_t) (4-8)

α = smoothing constant for average

β = smoothing constant for trend

Practice Problem Space

Trend Projections

Least Squares Method

$$\hat{y} = a + bx \tag{4-11}$$

Where: y is:

a is:

b is:

x is:

$$b = \frac{\sum xy - n\bar{x}\,\bar{y}}{\sum x^2 - n\bar{x}^2} \tag{4-12}$$

$$a = \bar{y} - b\bar{x} \tag{4-13}$$

FIGURE 4.4 ■ The Least Squares Method for Finding the Best-Fitting Straight Line, Where the Asterisks Are the Locations of the Seven Actual Observations or Data Points

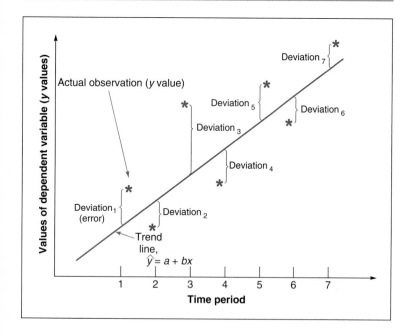

PRACTICE PROBLEM 4.5 ■ Trend Projection

Use the sales data given below to determine (a) the least squares trend line and (b) the predicted value for 2003 sales.

YEAR	SALES (UNITS)
1996	100
1997	110
1998	122
1999	130
2000	139
2001	152
2002	164

To minimize computations, transform the value of x (time) to simpler numbers. In this case, designate year 1996 as year 1, 1997 as year 2, and so on.

Additional Practice Problem Space

Seasonal Variations in Data

PRACTICE PROBLEM 4.6 ■ Quarterly Seasons

Over the past year, Meredith and Smunt Manufacturing had annual sales of 10,000 portable water pumps. The average quarterly sales for the past 5 years have averaged: spring 4,000; summer 3,000; fall 2,000; and winter 1,000. Compute the quarterly index.

PRACTICE PROBLEM 4.7 ■ Forecasting with Seasonal Data

Using the data in Practice Problem 4.6, Meredith and Smunt Manufacturing expects sales of pumps to grow by 10% next year. Compute next year's sales and the sales for each quarter.

Additional Practice Problem Space

ASSOCIATIVE FORECASTING METHODS: REGRESSION AND CORRELATION ANALYSIS

Associative Model

Dependent Variable (y)

Independent Variable (x)

$$\hat{y} = a + bx$$

Practice Problem Space

Standard Error of the Estimate

Correlation Coefficients (r)

$$r = \frac{n\sum xy - \sum x \sum y}{\sqrt{\left[n\sum x^2 - (\sum x)^2\right]\left[n\sum y^2 - (\sum y)^2\right]}} \tag{4-16}$$

FIGURE 4.10 ■ Four Values of the Correlation Coefficient

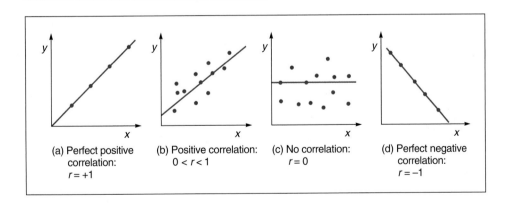

(a) Perfect positive correlation: $r = +1$

(b) Positive correlation: $0 < r < 1$

(c) No correlation: $r = 0$

(d) Perfect negative correlation: $r = -1$

Coefficient of Determination (r^2)

Multiple Regression Analysis

$$\hat{y} = a + b_1 x_1 + b_2 x_2 + \cdots + b_n x_n \tag{4-17}$$

MONITORING AND CONTROLLING FORECASTS

Tracking Signal

$$\text{Tracking signal} = \frac{\text{RSFE}}{\text{MAD}} = \frac{\Sigma \ (\text{actual demand in period } i - \text{forecast demand in period } i)}{\text{MAD}} \tag{4-18}$$

$$\text{where MAD} = \frac{\Sigma \left| \text{actual} - \text{forecast} \right|}{n}$$

FIGURE 4.11 ■ A Plot of Tracking Signals

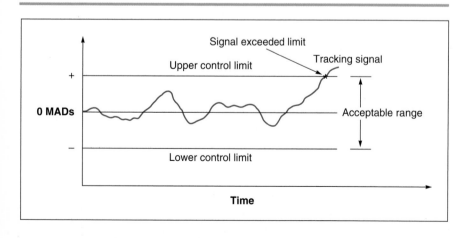

PRACTICE PROBLEM 4.8 ■ Tracking Signals and MAD

Given the following forecast demand and actual demand for 10-foot fishing boats, compute the tracking signal and MAD.

YEAR	FORECAST DEMAND	ACTUAL DEMAND
1	78	71
2	75	80
3	83	101
4	84	84
5	88	60
6	85	73

Additional Practice Problem Space

FORECASTING IN THE SERVICE SECTOR

TABLE 4.2 ■ Summary of Forecasting Formulas

Moving averages—forecasts based on an average of recent values

$$\text{Moving average} = \frac{\Sigma \text{ demand in previous } n \text{ periods}}{n} \qquad (4\text{-}1)$$

Weighted moving averages—a moving average with weights that vary

$$\text{Weighted moving average} = \frac{\Sigma \text{ (weight for period } n)(\text{demand in period } n)}{\Sigma \text{ weights}} \qquad (4\text{-}2)$$

Exponential smoothing—a moving average with weights following an exponential distribution

$$\text{New forecast} = \text{last period's forecast} + \alpha \text{ (last period's actual} \\ \text{demand} - \text{last period's forecast} \qquad (4\text{-}3)$$

$$F_t = F_{t-1} + \alpha(A_{t-1} - F_{t-1}) \qquad (4\text{-}4)$$

Mean absolute deviation—a measure of overall forecast error

$$\text{MAD} = \frac{\Sigma |\text{forecast errors}|}{n} \qquad (4\text{-}5)$$

Mean squared error—a second measure of forecast error

$$\text{MSE} = \frac{\Sigma \text{ (forecast errors)}^2}{n} \qquad (4\text{-}6)$$

Mean absolute percent error—a third measure of forecast error

$$\text{MAPE} = \frac{100 \displaystyle\sum_{i=1}^{n} |\text{actual}_i - \text{forecast}_i| / \text{actual}_i}{n} \qquad (4\text{-}7)$$

Exponential smoothing with trend adjustment—an exponential smoothing model that can accommodate trend

$$\text{Forecast including trend } (FIT_t) = \text{exponentially smoothed forecast } (F_t) \\ + \text{exponentially smoothed trend } (T_t) \qquad (4\text{-}8)$$

$$F_t = \alpha(A_{t-1}) + (1-\alpha)(F_{t-1} + T_{t-1}) \qquad (4\text{-}9)$$

$$T_t = \beta(F_t - F_{t-1}) + (1-\beta)T_{t-1} \qquad (4\text{-}10)$$

Trend projection and regression analysis—fitting a trend line to historical data or a regression line to an independent variable

$$\hat{y} = a + bx \qquad (4\text{-}11)$$

$$b = \frac{\Sigma xy - n\bar{x}\,\bar{y}}{\Sigma x^2 - n\bar{x}^2} \qquad (4\text{-}12)$$

$$a = \bar{y} - b\bar{x} \qquad (4\text{-}13)$$

Multiple regression analysis—a regression model with more than one independent (predicting) variable

$$\hat{y} = a + b_1 x_1 + b_2 x_2 + \cdots + b_n x_n \qquad (4\text{-}17)$$

Tracking signal—a measurement of how well the forecast is predicting actual values

$$\text{Tracking signal} = \frac{\text{RSFE}}{\text{MAD}} = \frac{\Sigma \text{ (actual demand in period } i - \text{forecast demand in period } i)}{\text{MAD}} \qquad (4\text{-}18)$$

DISCUSSION QUESTIONS

1. What is a qualitative forecasting model, and when is it appropriate?
2. Identify and briefly describe the two general forecasting approaches.
3. Identify the three forecasting time horizons. State an approximate duration for each.
4. Briefly describe the steps that are used to develop a forecasting system.
5. A skeptical manager asks what medium-range forecasts can be used for. Give the manager three possible uses/purposes.
6. Explain why such forecasting devices as moving averages, weighted moving averages, and exponential smoothing are not well suited for data series that have trends.
7. What is the basic difference between a weighted moving average and exponential smoothing?
8. What three methods are used to determine the accuracy of any given forecasting method? How would you determine whether time series regression or exponential smoothing is better in a specific application?
9. Briefly describe the Delphi technique. How would it be used by an employer you have worked for?
10. What is the primary difference between a time series model and a causal model?
11. Define time series.
12. What effect does the value of the smoothing constant have on the weight given to the recent values?
13. Explain the value of seasonal indexes in forecasting. How are seasonal patterns different from cyclical patterns?
14. Which forecasting technique can place the most emphasis on recent values? How does it do this?
15. In your own words, explain adaptive forecasting.
16. What is the purpose of a tracking signal?
17. Explain, in your own words, the meaning of the correlation coefficient. Discuss the meaning of a negative value of the correlation coefficient.
18. What is the difference between a dependent and an independent variable?
19. Give examples of industries that are affected by seasonality. Why would these businesses want to filter out seasonality?
20. Give examples of industries where demand forecasting is dependent on the demand for other products.
21. What happens to our ability to forecast as we forecast for periods farther into the future?

CRITICAL THINKING EXERCISE

In 2002, the board of regents responsible for all public higher education funding in a large midwestern state hired a consultant to develop a series of enrollment forecasting models, one for each college. These models used historical data and exponential smoothing to forecast the following year's enrollments. Based on the model, which included a smoothing constant (α) for each school, each college's budget was set by the board. The head of the board personally selected each smoothing constant, based on what she called her "gut reactions and political acumen."

What do you think the advantages and disadvantages of this system are? Answer from the perspective of (a) the board of regents and (b) the president of each college. How can this model be abused and what could be done to remove any biases? How can a *regression model* be used to produce results that favor one forecast over another?

ACTIVE MODEL EXERCISE

This Active Model, as well as the three others in Chapter 4 in your text, appears on your CD-ROM. It allows you to evaluate important elements of an exponential smoothing forecast.

ACTIVE MODEL 4.2 ■

Exponential Smoothing Using Data from Example 4 in Your Text

Note that error terms in Example 4 are rounded off, so MAD is slightly different here.

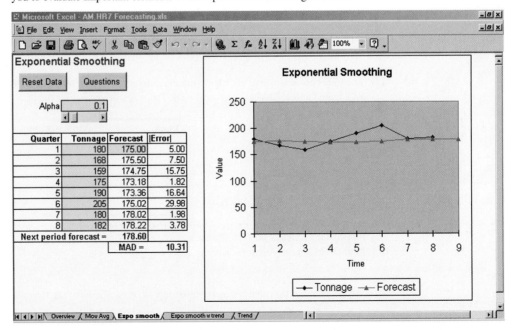

Quarter	Tonnage	Forecast	|Error|
1	180	175.00	5.00
2	168	175.50	7.50
3	159	174.75	15.75
4	175	173.18	1.82
5	190	173.36	16.64
6	205	175.02	29.98
7	180	178.02	1.98
8	182	178.22	3.78
Next period forecast =	178.60		
		MAD =	10.31

Questions

1. What happens to the graph when alpha equals zero?
2. What happens to the graph when alpha equals 1?
3. Generalize what happens to a forecast as alpha increases.
4. At what level of alpha is the mean absolute deviation (MAD) minimized?

PROBLEMS*

4.1   The following gives the number of pints of type A blood used at Woodlawn Hospital in the past 6 weeks.

WEEK OF	PINTS USED
August 31	360
September 7	389
September 14	410
September 21	381
September 28	368
October 5	374

a) Forecast the demand for the week of October 12 using a 3-week moving average.
b) Use a 3-week weighted moving average, with weights of .1, .3, and .6, using .6 for the most recent week. Forecast demand for the week of October 12.
c) Compute the forecast for the week of October 12 using exponential smoothing with a forecast for August 31 of 360 and $\alpha = .2$.

4.2

Year	1	2	3	4	5	6	7	8	9	10	11
Demand	7	9	5	9	13	8	12	13	9	11	7

a) Plot the above data on a graph. Do you observe any trend, cycles, or random variations?
b) Starting in year 4 and going to year 12, forecast demand using a 3-year moving average. Plot your forecast on the same graph as the original data.
c) Starting in year 4 and going to year 12, forecast demand using a 3-year moving average with weights of .1, .3, and .6, using .6 for the most recent year. Plot this forecast on the same graph.
d) As you look at the forecasts against the original data, which seems to give the better results?

4.3   Refer to Problem 4.2. Develop a forecast for years 2 through 12 using exponential smoothing with $\alpha = .4$ and a forecast for year 1 of 6. Plot your new forecast on a graph with the actual data and the naive forecast. Based on a visual inspection, which forecast is better?

4.4   A check-processing center uses exponential smoothing to forecast the number of incoming checks each month. The number of checks received in June was 40 million, while the forecast was 42 million. A smoothing constant of .2 is used.
a) What is the forecast for July?
b) If the center received 45 million checks in July, what would be the forecast for August?
c) Why might this be an inappropriate forecasting method for this situation?

4.5   The Carbondale Hospital is considering the purchase of a new ambulance. The decision will rest partly on the anticipated mileage to be driven next year. The miles driven during the past 5 years are as follows.

YEAR	MILEAGE
1	3,000
2	4,000
3	3,400
4	3,800
5	3,700

a) Forecast the mileage for next year using a 2-year moving average.
b) Find the MAD for your forecast in part (a).

*Note: **P** means the problem may be solved with POM for Windows; **X** means the problem may be solved with Excel OM; and **P𝗫** means the problem may be solved with POM for Windows and/or Excel OM.

c) Use a weighted 2-year moving average with weights of .4 and .6 to forecast next year's mileage. (The weight of .6 is for the most recent year.) What is the MAD of this forecast?

d) Compute the forecast for year 6 using exponential smoothing, an initial forecast for year 1 of 3,000 miles, and $\alpha = .5$.

P : 4.6   The monthly sales for Telco Batteries, Inc. were as follows:

MONTH	SALES
January	20
February	21
March	15
April	14
May	13
June	16
July	17
August	18
September	20
October	20
November	21
December	23

a) Plot the monthly sales data on a sheet of graph paper.

b) Forecast January sales using each of the following:
   1) Naive method.
   2) A 3-month moving average.
   3) A 6-month weighted average using .1, .1, .1, .2, .2, and .3, with the heaviest weights applied to the most recent months.
   4) Exponential smoothing using an $\alpha = .3$ and a September forecast of 18.
   5) A trend projection.

c) With the data given, which method would allow you to forecast next March's sales?

: 4.7   Doug Moodie is the president of Garden Products Limited. Over the last 5 years, he has asked both his vice president of marketing and his vice president of operations to provide sales forecasts. The actual sales and the forecasts are given below. Using MAD, which vice president is better at forecasting?

YEAR	SALES	VP/MARKETING	VP/OPERATIONS
1	167,325	170,000	160,000
2	175,362	170,000	165,000
3	172,536	180,000	170,000
4	156,732	180,000	175,000
5	176,325	165,000	165,000

P . 4.8   Daily high temperatures in the city of Houston for the last week have been as follows: 93, 94, 93, 95, 96, 88, 90 (yesterday).

a) Forecast the high temperature today, using a 3-day moving average.

b) Forecast the high temperature today, using a 2-day moving average.

c) Calculate the mean absolute deviation based on a 2-day moving average.

d) Compute the mean squared error for the 2-day moving average.

e) Calculate the mean absolute percent error for the 2-day moving average.

P : 4.9   H-P uses an X63 chip in some of its computers. The prices for the chip during the last 12 months have been:

MONTH	PRICE PER CHIP	MONTH	PRICE PER CHIP
January	$1.80	July	1.80
February	1.67	August	1.83
March	1.70	September	1.70
April	1.85	October	1.65
May	1.90	November	1.70
June	1.87	December	1.75

a) Use a 2-month moving average on all of the data and plot the averages and the prices.

b) Use a 3-month moving average and add the 3-month plot to the graph created in part (a).

c)   Which is better (using the mean absolute deviation): the 2-month average or the 3-month average?
d)   Compute the forecasts for each month using exponential smoothing, with an initial forecast for January of $1.80. Use $\alpha = .1$, then $\alpha = .3$, and finally $\alpha = .5$. Using MAD, which α is the best?

4.10   Data collected on the yearly registrations for a Six Sigma seminar at the Quality College are shown in the following table:

Year	1	2	3	4	5	6	7	8	9	10	11
Registrations (000)	4	6	4	5	10	8	7	9	12	14	15

a)   Develop a 3-year moving average to forecast registrations from year 4 to year 12.
b)   Estimate demand again for years 4 to 12 with a weighted moving average in which registrations in the most recent year are given a weight of 2 and registrations in the other 2 years are each given a weight of 1.
c)   Graph the original data and the two forecasts. Which of the two forecasting methods seems better?

4.11   Use exponential smoothing with a smoothing constant of 0.3 to forecast the registrations at the seminar given in Problem 4.10. To begin the procedure, assume that the forecast for year 1 was 5,000 people signing up.

4.12   In Problems 4.10 and 4.11, three different forecasts were developed for seminar registrations. These three forecasts are a 3-year moving average, a weighted moving average, and exponential smoothing. Using MAD as the criterion, which forecast method is best? Why?

4.13   As you can see in the following table, demand for heart transplant surgery at Washington General Hospital has increased steadily in the past few years:

Year	1	2	3	4	5	6
Heart Transplants	45	50	52	56	58	?

The director of medical services predicted 6 years ago that demand in year 1 would be 41 surgeries.
a)   Use exponential smoothing, first with a smoothing constant of .6 and then with one of .9, to develop forecasts for years 2 through 6.
b)   Use a 3-year moving average to forecast demand in years 4, 5, and 6.
c)   Use the trend-projection method to forecast demand in years 1 through 6.

4.14   Refer to Problem 4.13. With MAD as the criterion, which of the four forecasting methods is best?

4.15   Refer to Solved Problem 4.1 in your text. Use a 3-year moving average to forecast the sales of Volkswagen Beetles in Nevada through 2003.

4.16   Refer to Solved Problem 4.1. Using the trend projection method, develop a forecast for the sales of Volkswagen Beetles in Nevada through 2003.

4.17   Refer to Solved Problem 4.1. Using smoothing constants of .6 and .9, develop forecasts for the sales of VW Beetles. What effect did the smoothing constant have on the forecast? Use MAD to determine which of the three smoothing constants (.3, .6, or .9) gives the most accurate forecast.

4.18   Refer to Solved Problem 4.1 and Problems 4.15 and 4.16. Using MAD as the criterion, would you use exponential smoothing with a smoothing constant of .3 as shown in Solved Problem 4.1, a 3-year moving average, or trend to predict the sales of Volkswagen Beetles? Why?

P :   4.19   Income at the law firm of Smith and Wesson for the period February to July has been as follows:

Month	February	March	April	May	June	July
Income (in $ thousands)	70.0	68.5	64.8	71.7	71.3	72.8

Use trend-adjusted exponential smoothing to forecast the law firm's August income. Assume that the initial forecast for February is $65,000 and the initial trend adjustment is 0. The smoothing constants selected are $\alpha = .1$ and $\beta = .2$.

P :   4.20   Resolve Problem 4.19 with $\alpha = .1$ and $\beta = .8$. Using MSE, which smoothing constants provide a better forecast?

P ·   4.21   Refer back to the trend-adjusted exponential smoothing illustration in Example 7 in your text. Using $\alpha = .2$ and $\beta = .4$, we forecast sales for 9 months, showing the detailed calculations for months 2 and 3. In Solved Problem 4.2, we continued the process for month 4.
    In this problem, show your calculations for months 5 and 6 for F_t, T_t, and FIT_t.

P · 4.22 Refer to Problem 4.21. Complete the trend-adjusted exponential-smoothing forecast computations for periods 7, 8, and 9. Confirm that your numbers for F_t, T_t, and FIT_t match those in Table 4.1 in your text.

: 4.23 Sales of vegetable dehydrators at Bud Banis's discount department store in St. Louis over the past year are shown below. Management prepared a forecast using a combination of exponential smoothing and its collective judgment for the upcoming 4 months (March, April, May, and June of 2002).

MONTH	2001–2002 UNIT SALES	MANAGEMENT'S FORECAST
July	100	
August	93	
September	96	
October	110	
November	124	
December	119	
January	92	
February	83	
March	101	120
April	96	114
May	89	110
June	108	108

a) Compute MAD and MAPE for management's technique.
b) Do management's results outperform (have smaller MAD and MAPE than) a naïve forecast?
c) Which forecast do you recommend, based on lower forecast error?

P 4.24 The operations manager of a musical instrument distributor feels that demand for bass drums may be related to the number of television appearances by the popular rock group Green Shades during the previous month. The manager has collected the data shown in the following table:

Demand for Bass Drums	3	6	7	5	10	8
Green Shades TV Appearances	3	4	7	6	8	5

a) Graph these data to see whether a linear equation might describe the relationship between the group's television shows and bass drum sales.
b) Use the least squares regression method to derive a forecasting equation.
c) What is your estimate for bass drum sales if the Green Shades performed on TV nine times last month?

P 4.25 The following gives the number of accidents that have occurred on Florida State Highway 101 during the last 4 months.

MONTH	NUMBER OF ACCIDENTS
January	30
February	40
March	60
April	90

Forecast the number of accidents that will occur in May, using least squares regression to derive a trend equation.

· 4.26 In the past, Larry Youdelman's tire dealership sold an average of 1,000 radials each year. In the past 2 years, 200 and 250, respectively, were sold in fall, 350 and 300 in winter, 150 and 165 in spring, and 300 and 285 in summer. With a major expansion planned, Youdelman projects sales next year to increase to 1,200 radials. What will be the demand during each season?

: 4.27 Pasta Alfredo, a Des Moines restaurant, bases its manpower scheduling on the anticipated customer demand. Customer demand shows little trend, but shows substantial variability among the days of the week. The restaurant therefore wants to build a forecasting system that will enable it to adequately predict the number of customers for any given day in the near future. Alfredo has collected data for the past 4 weeks, as shown in the data that follows. Calculate the seasonal (daily) indexes for the restaurant.

Mon., 9/9	84	Mon., 9/16	82	Mon., 9/23	93	Mon., 9/30	80
Tue., 9/10	82	Tue., 9/17	71	Tue., 9/24	77	Tue., 10/1	67
Wed., 9/11	78	Wed., 9/18	89	Wed., 9/25	83	Wed., 10/2	98
Thu., 9/12	95	Thu., 9/19	94	Thu., 9/26	103	Thu., 10/3	96
Fri., 9/13	130	Fri., 9/20	144	Fri., 9/27	135	Fri., 10/4	125
Sat., 9/14	144	Sat., 9/21	135	Sat., 9/28	140	Sat., 10/5	136
Sun., 9/15	42	Sun., 9/22	48	Sun., 9/29	37	Sun., 10/6	40

4.28   Attendance at Orlando's newest Disneylike attraction, Vacation World, has been as follows:

QUARTER	GUESTS (IN THOUSANDS)	QUARTER	GUESTS (IN THOUSANDS)
Winter '01	73	Summer '02	124
Spring '01	104	Fall '02	52
Summer '01	168	Winter '03	89
Fall '01	74	Spring '03	146
Winter '02	65	Summer '03	205
Spring '02	82	Fall '03	98

Compute seasonal indices using all of the data.

4.29   Central States Elecric Company estimates its demand trend line (in millions of kilowatt hours) to be

$$D = 77 + 0.43Q$$

where Q refers to the sequential quarter number and $Q = 1$ for winter 1980. In addition, the multiplicative seasonal factors are as follows:

QUARTER	FACTOR (INDEX)
Winter	.8
Spring	1.1
Summer	1.4
Fall	.7

Forecast energy use for the four quarters of 2005, beginning with winter.

4.30   Brian Buckley has developed the following forecasting model:

$$\hat{y} = 36 + 4.3x$$

where $\hat{y}$ = demand for Aztec air conditioners and
x = the outside temperature (°F)

a)   Forecast demand for the Aztec when the temperature is 70°F.
b)   What is demand when the temperature is 80°F?
c)   What is demand when the temperature is 90°F?

4.31   The sales of Gemini lawn mowers for the last 3 years are given by season as follows:

YEAR	SEASON	SALES
1	Spring/Summer	26,825
	Fall/Winter	5,722
2	Spring/Summer	28,630
	Fall/Winter	7,633
3	Spring/Summer	30,255
	Fall/Winter	8,745

a)   Use linear regression to find the best fit line.
b)   What is wrong with this line?
c)   How should forecasts be made for year 4?

P$_x$ · **4.32**   The following data relate the sales figures of the bar in Marty and Polly Starr's small bed-and-breakfast inn in Marathon, Florida, to the number of guests registered that week:

WEEK	GUESTS	BAR SALES
1	16	$330
2	12	270
3	18	380
4	14	300

a)   Perform a linear regression that relates bar sales to guests (not to time).
b)   If the forecast is for 20 guests next week, what are the sales expected to be?

P$_x$ · **4.33**   The number of transistors (in millions) made at a plant in Japan during the past 5 years follows:

YEAR	TRANSISTORS
1	140
2	160
3	190
4	200
5	210

a)   Forecast the number of transistors to be made next year, using linear regression.
b)   Compute the mean squared error (MSE) when using linear regression.
c)   Compute the mean absolute percent error (MAPE).

· **4.34**   The number of auto accidents in a certain region is related to the regional number of registered automobiles in thousands (X_1), alcoholic beverage sales in $10,000s ($X_2$), and rainfall in inches (X_3). Furthermore, the regression formula has been calculated as

$$Y = a + b_1X_1 + b_2X_2 + b_3X_3$$

where Y = number of automobile accidents,

$$a = 7.5, b_1 = 3.5, b_2 = 4.5, \text{ and } b_3 = 2.5$$

Calculate the expected number of automobile accidents under conditions a, b, and c:

	X_1	X_2	X_3
(a)	2	3	0
(b)	3	5	1
(c)	4	7	2

P :   **4.35**   Barbara Downey, a Missouri real estate developer, has devised a regression model to help determine residential housing prices in Lake Charles, Louisiana. The model was developed using recent sales in a particular neighborhood. The price (Y) of the house is based on the size (square footage = X) of the house. The model is

$$Y = 13,473 + 37.65X$$

The coefficient of correlation for the model is 0.63.
a)   Use the model to predict the selling price of a house that is 1,860 square feet.
b)   An 1,860-square-foot house recently sold for $95,000. Explain why this is not what the model predicted.
c)   If you were going to use multiple regression to develop such a model, what other quantitative variables might be included?
d)   What is the value of the coefficient of determination in this problem?

P ·   **4.36**   Accountants at the firm Doke and Reed believed that several traveling executives were submitting unusually high travel vouchers when they returned from business trips. First, they took a sample of 200 vouchers submitted from the past year. Then they developed the following multiple-regression equation relating expected travel cost to number of days on the road (x_1) and distance traveled (x_2) in miles:

$$\hat{y} = \$90.00 + \$48.50x_1 + \$.40x_2$$

The coefficient of correlation computed was .68.

a)   If Bill Tomlinson returns from a 300-mile trip that took him out of town for 5 days, what is the expected amount he should claim as expenses?

b)   Tomlinson submitted a reimbursement request for $685. What should the accountant do?

c)   Should any other variables be included? Which ones? Why?

4.37   Sales of music stands at Johnny Ho's music store, in Columbus, Ohio, over the past 10 weeks are shown in the table below. Forecast demand, including week 10, using exponential smoothing with $\alpha = .5$ (initial forecast = 30). Compute the MAD. Compute the tracking signal.

WEEK	DEMAND	WEEK	DEMAND
1	13	6	29
2	21	7	36
3	28	8	22
4	37	9	25
5	25	10	28

4.38   City government has collected the following data on annual sales tax collections and new car registrations:

Annual Sales Tax Collections (in millions)	1.0	1.4	1.9	2.0	1.8	2.1	2.3
New Car Registrations (in thousands)	10	12	15	16	14	17	20

Determine the following:

a)   The least squares regression equation.

b)   Using the results of part (a), find the estimated sales tax collections if new car registrations total 22,000.

c)   The coefficients of correlation and determination.

4.39   Dr. Susan Sweeney, a Providence psychologist, specializes in treating patients who are agoraphobic (afraid to leave their homes). The following table indicates how many patients Dr. Sweeney has seen each year for the past 10 years. It also indicates what the robbery rate was in Providence during the same year.

Year	1	2	3	4	5	6	7	8	9	10
Number of Patients	36	33	40	41	40	55	60	54	58	61
Robbery Rate per 1,000 Population	58.3	61.1	73.4	75.7	81.1	89.0	101.1	94.8	103.3	116.2

Using trend analysis, predict the number of patients Dr. Sweeney will see in years 11 and 12. How well does the model fit the data?

4.40   Using the data in Problem 4.39, apply linear regression to study the relationship between the robbery rate and Dr. Sweeney's patient load. If the robbery rate increases to 131.2 in year 11, how many phobic patients will Dr. Sweeney treat? If the robbery rate drops to 90.6, what is the patient projection?

4.41   Bus and subway ridership for the summer months in London, England, is believed to be tied heavily to the number of tourists visiting the city. During the past 12 years, the following data have been obtained:

YEAR (SUMMER MONTHS)	NUMBER OF TOURISTS (IN MILLIONS)	RIDERSHIP (IN MILLIONS)	YEAR (SUMMER MONTHS)	NUMBER OF TOURISTS (IN MILLIONS)	RIDERSHIP (IN MILLIONS)
1	7	1.5	7	16	2.4
2	2	1.0	8	12	2.0
3	6	1.3	9	14	2.7
4	4	1.5	10	20	4.4
5	14	2.5	11	15	3.4
6	15	2.7	12	7	1.7

a)   Plot these data and decide if a linear model is reasonable.

b)   Develop a regression relationship.

c)   What is expected ridership if 10 million tourists visit London in a year?

d)   Explain the predicted ridership if there are no tourists at all.

e)   What is the standard error of the estimate?

f)   What is the model's correlation coefficient and coefficient of determination?

4.42 Des Moines Power and Light has been collecting data on demand for electric power in its western subregion for only the past 2 years. Those data are shown in the following table:

MONTH	DEMAND IN MEGAWATTS		MONTH	DEMAND IN MEGAWATTS	
	LAST YEAR	THIS YEAR		LAST YEAR	THIS YEAR
Jan.	5	17	July	23	44
Feb.	6	14	Aug.	26	41
Mar.	10	20	Sept.	21	33
Apr.	13	23	Oct.	15	23
May	18	30	Nov.	12	26
June	15	38	Dec.	14	17

In order to plan for expansion and to arrange to borrow power from neighboring utilities during peak periods, the utility needs to be able to forecast demand for each month next year. However, the standard forecasting models discussed in this chapter will not fit the data observed for the 2 years.

a) What are the weaknesses of the standard forecasting techniques as applied to this set of data?

b) Because known models are not really appropriate here, propose your own approach to forecasting. Although there is no perfect solution to tackling data such as these (in other words, there are no 100% right or wrong answers), justify your model.

c) Forecast demand for each month next year using the model you propose.

4.43 Emergency calls to the 911 system of Gainesville, Florida, for the past 24 weeks are shown in the following table:

Week	1	2	3	4	5	6	7	8	9	10	11	12
Calls	50	35	25	40	45	35	20	30	35	20	15	40

Week	13	14	15	16	17	18	19	20	21	22	23	24
Calls	55	35	25	55	55	40	35	60	75	50	40	65

a) Compute the exponentially smoothed forecast of calls for each week. Assume an initial forecast of 50 calls in the first week, and use $\alpha = .2$. What is the forecast for week 25?

b) Reforecast each period using $\alpha = .6$.

c) Actual calls during week 25 were 85. Which smoothing constant provides a superior forecast? Explain and justify the measure of error that you used.

4.44 Using the 911 call data in Problem 4.43, forecast calls for weeks 2 through 25 with a trend-adjusted exponential smoothing model. Assume an initial forecast for 50 calls for week 1 and an initial trend of zero. Use smoothing constants of $\alpha = .3$ and $\beta = .2$. Is this model better than that of Problem 4.43? What adjustment might be useful for further improvement? (Again, assume actual calls in week 25 were 85.)

4.45 The East Dubuque school district is trying to forecast its needs for kindergarten teachers for the next 5 years. The district has data on births and kindergarten enrollments for the past 10 years. *The enrollments lag the births by 5 years.* Forecast kindergarten enrollments for the next 2 years, given the following data from the past 10 years:

YEAR	BIRTHS	ENROLLMENTS	YEAR	BIRTHS	ENROLLMENTS
1	131	161	6	130	148
2	192	127	7	128	188
3	158	134	8	124	155
4	93	141	9	97	110
5	107	112	10	147	124

4.46 Thirteen students entered the OM program at Rollins College 2 years ago. The following table indicates what each student scored on the high school SAT math exam and their grade-point averages (GPAs) after students were in the Rollins program for 2 years.

a) Is there a meaningful relationship between SAT math scores and grades?

b) If a student scores a 350, what do you think his or her GPA will be?

c) What about a student who scores 800?

Student	A	B	C	D	E	F	G	H	I	J	K	L	M
SAT Score	421	377	585	690	608	390	415	481	729	501	613	709	366
GPA	2.90	2.93	3.00	3.45	3.66	2.88	2.15	2.53	3.22	1.99	2.75	3.90	1.60

P :   **4.47**   The manufacturer of a new type of virtual reality software game is trying to determine how Internet advertising expenditures affect its sales. Given the data below, use least squares regression to develop a relationship between advertising and the sales of software. What are expected sales when advertising is $65,000?

MONTH	1	2	3	4	5	6	7	8	9	10
Unit Sales (in thousands)	21	24	27	32	29	37	43	43	54	66
Advertising (in $ thousands)	14	17	25	25	35	35	45	50	60	60

P :   **4.48**   Sundar Balakrishnan, the general manager of Precision Engineering Corporation (PEC), thinks that his firm's engineering services contracted to highway construction firms are directly related to the volume of highway construction business contracted with companies in his geographic area. He wonders if this is really so, and if it is, can this information help him plan his operations better by forecasting the quantity of his engineering services required by construction firms in each quarter of the year? The table below presents the sales of his services and total amounts of contracts for highway construction over the last 8 quarters:

QUARTER	1	2	3	4	5	6	7	8
Sales of PEC Services (in $ thousands)	8	10	15	9	12	13	12	16
Contracts Released (in $ thousands)	153	172	197	178	185	199	205	226

a)   Using this data, develop a regression equation for predicting the level of demand of Precision's services.
b)   Determine the coefficient of correlation and the standard error of the estimate.

P :   **4.49**   Salinas Savings and Loan is proud of its long tradition in Topeka, Kansas. Begun by Teresita Salinas 13 years after World War II, the S&L has bucked the trend of financial and liquidity problems that has plagued the industry since 1985. Deposits have increased slowly but surely over the years, despite recessions in 1960, 1983, 1988, 1991, and 2001. Ms. Salinas believes it is necessary to have a long-range strategic plan for her firm, including a 1-year forecast and preferably even a 5-year forecast of deposits. She examines the past deposit data and also peruses Kansas's Gross State Product (GSP), over the same 44 years. (GSP is analogous to Gross National Product, GNP, but on the state level.) The resulting data are in the following table:

YEAR	DEPOSITS[a]	GSP[b]	YEAR	DEPOSITS[a]	GSP[b]	YEAR	DEPOSITS[a]	GSP[b]
1959	.25	.4	1974	2.3	1.6	1989	24.1	3.9
1960	.24	.4	1975	2.8	1.5	1990	25.6	3.8
1961	.24	.5	1976	2.8	1.6	1991	30.3	3.8
1962	.26	.7	1977	2.7	1.7	1992	36.0	3.7
1963	.25	.9	1978	3.9	1.9	1993	31.1	4.1
1964	.30	1.0	1979	4.9	1.9	1994	31.7	4.1
1965	.31	1.4	1980	5.3	2.3	1995	38.5	4.0
1966	.32	1.7	1981	6.2	2.5	1996	47.9	4.5
1967	.24	1.3	1982	4.1	2.8	1997	49.1	4.6
1968	.26	1.2	1983	4.5	2.9	1998	55.8	4.5
1969	.25	1.1	1984	6.1	3.4	1999	70.1	4.6
1970	.33	.9	1985	7.7	3.8	2000	70.9	4.6
1971	.50	1.2	1986	10.1	4.1	2001	79.1	4.7
1972	.95	1.2	1987	15.2	4.0	2002	94.0	5.0
1973	1.70	1.2	1988	18.1	4.0			

[a]In $ millions.
[b]In $ billions.

a)   Using exponential smoothing, with $\alpha = .6$, then trend analysis, and finally linear regression, discuss which forecasting model fits best for Salinas's strategic plan. Justify the selection of one model over another.
b)   Carefully examine the data. Can you make a case for excluding a portion of the information? Why? Would that change your choice of model?

INTERNET HOMEWORK PROBLEMS

See our Internet home page at www.prenhall.com/heizer for these additional homework problems: 4.50 through 4.62.

CASE STUDY

Southwestern University: (B)*

Southwestern University (SWU), a large state college in Stephenville, Texas, enrolls close to 20,000 students. The school is a dominant force in the small city, with more students during fall and spring than permanent residents.

Always a football powerhouse, SWU is usually in the top 20 in college football rankings. Since hiring the legendary Bo Pitterno as its head coach in 1997 (in hopes of reaching the elusive number 1 ranking), attendance at the five Saturday home games each year increased. Prior to Pitterno's arrival, attendance generally averaged 25,000 to 29,000 per game. Season ticket sales bumped up by 10,000 just with the announcement of the new coach's arrival. Stephenville and SWU were ready to move to the big time!

The immediate issue facing SWU, however, was not NCAA ranking. It was capacity. The existing SWU stadium, built in 1953, has seating for 54,000 fans. The following table indicates attendance at each game for the past 6 years.

One of Pitterno's demands upon joining SWU had been a stadium expansion, or possibly even a new stadium. With attendance increasing, SWU administrators began to face the issue head-on. Pitterno had wanted dormitories solely for his athletes in the stadium as an additional feature of any expansion.

SWU's president, Dr. Joel Wisner, decided it was time for his vice president of development to forecast when the existing stadium would "max out." The expansion was, in his mind, a given. But Wisner needed to know how long he could wait. He also sought a revenue projection, assuming an average ticket price of $20 in 2004 and a 5% increase each year in future prices.

Discussion Questions

1. Develop a forecasting model, justifying its selection over other techniques, and project attendance through 2005.
2. What revenues are to be expected in 2004 and 2005?
3. Discuss the school's options.

*This integrated case study runs throughout the Student Lecture Guide. Other issues facing Southwestern's football stadium include: (A) managing the stadium project (Chapter 3); (C) quality of facilities (Chapter 6); (D) inventory planning of football programs (Chapter 12); and (E) scheduling of campus security officers/staff for game days (Chapter 13).

Southwestern University Football Game Attendance, 1998–2003

	1998		**1999**		**2000**	
GAME	**ATTENDEES**	**OPPONENT**	**ATTENDEES**	**OPPONENT**	**ATTENDEES**	**OPPONENT**
1	34,200	Baylor	36,100	Oklahoma	35,900	TCU
2[a]	39,800	Texas	40,200	Nebraska	46,500	Texas Tech
3	38,200	LSU	39,100	UCLA	43,100	Alaska
4[b]	26,900	Arkansas	25,300	Nevada	27,900	Arizona
5	35,100	USC	36,200	Ohio State	39,200	Rice

	2001		**2002**		**2003**	
GAME	**ATTENDEES**	**OPPONENT**	**ATTENDEES**	**OPPONENT**	**ATTENDEES**	**OPPONENT**
1	41,900	Arkansas	42,500	Indiana	46,900	LSU
2[a]	46,100	Missouri	48,200	North Texas	50,100	Texas
3	43,900	Florida	44,200	Texas A&M	45,900	Prairie View A&M
4[b]	30,100	Miami	33,900	Southern	36,300	Montana
5	40,500	Duke	47,800	Oklahoma	49,900	Arizona State

[a]Homecoming games.

[b]During the 4th week of each season, Stephenville hosted a hugely popular southwestern crafts festival. This event brought tens of thousands of tourists to the town, especially on weekends, and had an obvious negative impact on game attendance.

CASE STUDY

Analog Cell Phone, Inc.

Paul Jordan has just been hired as a management analyst at Analog Cell Phone, Inc. Analog Cell manufactures a broad line of phones for the consumer market. Paul's boss, John Smithers, chief operations officer, has asked Paul to stop by his office this morning. After a brief exchange of pleasantries over a cup of coffee, he says he has a special assignment for Paul: "We've always just made an educated guess
(continued)

about how many phones we need to make each month. Usually we just look at how many we sold last month and plan to produce about the same number. This sometimes works fine. But most months we either have too many phones in inventory or we are out of stock. Neither situation is good."

Handing Paul the table shown here, Smithers continues, "Here are our actual orders entered for the past 36 months. There are 144 phones per case. I was hoping that since you graduated recently from the University of Alaska, you might have studied some techniques that would help us plan better. It's been a while since I was in college—I think I forgot most of the details I learned then. I'd like you to analyze these data and give me an idea of what our business will look like over the next 6 to 12 months. Do you think you can handle this?"

"Of course," Paul replies, sounding more confident than he really is. "How much time do I have?"

"I need your report on the Monday before Thanksgiving—that would be November 20th. I plan to take it home with me and read it during the holiday. Since I'm sure you will not be around during the holiday, be sure that you explain things carefully so that I can understand your recommendation without having to ask you any more questions. Since you are new to the company, you should know that I like to see all the details and complete justification for recommendations from my staff."

With that, Paul was dismissed. Arriving back at his office, he began his analysis.

Orders Received by Month

MONTH	CASES 2000	CASES 2001	CASES 2002
January	480	575	608
February	436	527	597
March	482	540	612
April	448	502	603
May	458	508	628
June	489	573	605
July	498	508	627
August	430	498	578
September	444	485	585
October	496	526	581
November	487	552	632
December	525	587	656

Discussion Question

1. Prepare Paul Jordan's report to John Smithers. Provide a summary of the cell phone industry outlook (using print or Internet resources) as part of Paul's response.

Source: Professor Victor E. Sower, Sam Houston State University.

VIDEO CASE STUDY

Forecasting at Hard Rock Cafe

With the growth of Hard Rock Cafe—from one pub in London in 1971 to more than 110 restaurants in over 40 countries today—came a corporatewide demand for better forecasting. Hard Rock uses long-range forecasting in setting a capacity plan and intermediate-term forecasting for locking in contracts for leather goods (used in jackets) and for such food items as beef, chicken, and pork. Its short-term sales forecasts are conducted each month, by cafe, and then aggregated for a headquarters view.

The heart of the sales forecasting system is the point-of-sale system (POS), which, in effect, captures transaction data on nearly every person who walks through a cafe's door. The sale of each entrée represents one customer; the entrée sales data are transmitted daily to the Orlando corporate headquarters' database. There, the financial team, headed by Todd Lindsey, begins the forecast process. Lindsey forecasts monthly guest counts, retail sales, banquet sales, and concert sales (if applicable) at each cafe. The general managers of individual cafes tap into the same database to prepare a daily forecast for their sites. A cafe manager pulls up prior years' sales for that day, adding information from the local Chamber of Commerce or Tourist Board on upcoming events such as a major convention, sporting event, or concert in the city where the cafe is located. The daily forecast is further broken into hourly sales, which drives employee scheduling. An hourly forecast of $5,500 in sales translates into 19 workstations, which are further broken down into a specific number of wait staff, hosts, bartenders, and kitchen staff. Computerized scheduling software plugs in people based on their availability. Variances between forecast and actual sales are then examined to see why errors occurred.

Hard Rock doesn't limit its use of forecasting tools to sales. To evaluate managers and set bonuses, a 3-year weighted moving average is applied to cafe sales. If cafe general managers exceed their targets, a bonus is computed. Todd Lindsey, at corporate headquarters, applies weights of 40% to the most recent year's sales, 40% to the year before, and 20% to sales 2 years ago in reaching his moving average.

An even more sophisticated application of statistics is found in Hard Rock's menu planning. Using multiple regression, managers can compute the impact on demand of other menu items if the price of one item is changed. For example, if the price of a cheeseburger increases from $6.99 to $7.99, Hard Rock can predict the effect this will have on sales of chicken sandwiches, pork sandwiches, and salads. Managers do the same analysis on menu placement, with the center section driving higher sales volumes. When an item such as a hamburger is moved off the center to one of the side flaps, the corresponding effect on related items, say french fries, is determined.

Discussion Questions*

1. Describe three different forecasting applications at Hard Rock. Name three other areas in which you think Hard Rock could use forecasting models.
2. What is the role of the POS system in forecasting at Hard Rock?
3. Justify the use of the weighting system used for evaluating managers for annual bonuses.
4. Name several variables besides those mentioned in the case that could be used as good predictors of daily sales in each cafe.

*You may wish to review this video case on your CD before answering these questions.

Source: Professors Barry Render (Rollins College), Jay Heizer (Texas Lutheran University) and Bev Amer (Northern Arizona University).

Design of Goods and Services

Chapter Outline

Selection and design of goods and services are fundamental to an organization's strategy and have major implications throughout the operations function. The objective of product decisions is to develop and implement a product strategy that meets the demands of the marketplace with a competitive advantage. The product strategy often determines the focus of the competitive advantage—a focus that may be via differentiation, low cost, rapid response, or a combination of these.

BEFORE COMING TO CLASS, READ CHAPTER 5 IN YOUR TEXT AND ANSWER THESE QUESTIONS.

1. What is the objective of a firm's product strategy? _____

_____

_____

2. Identify the four stages of a product's life cycle. _____

_____

_____

3. Why are product design and selection so important?_____

_____

_____

4. What are the four ways firms organize for product development? __

_____

_____

5. Identify how firms define a product. _____

_____

_____

6. What documents are used to facilitate production of products?_____

_____

_____

GOODS AND SERVICES SELECTION

Product Life Cycles

Product-by-Value Analysis

GENERATING NEW PRODUCTS

Opportunities, Considerations, and Issues

Importance of New Products

PRODUCT DEVELOPMENT

FIGURE 5.3 ■ Product Development Stages

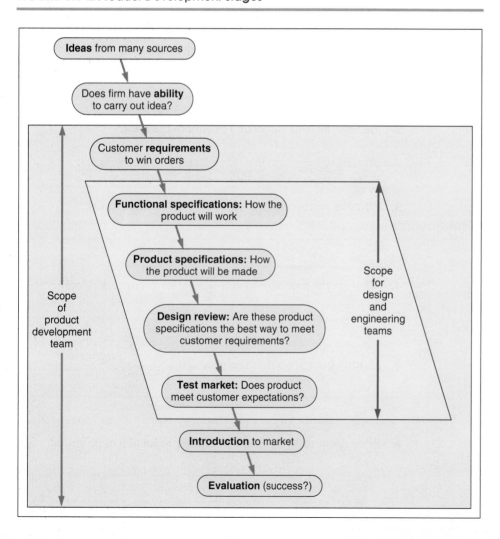

Quality Function Deployment

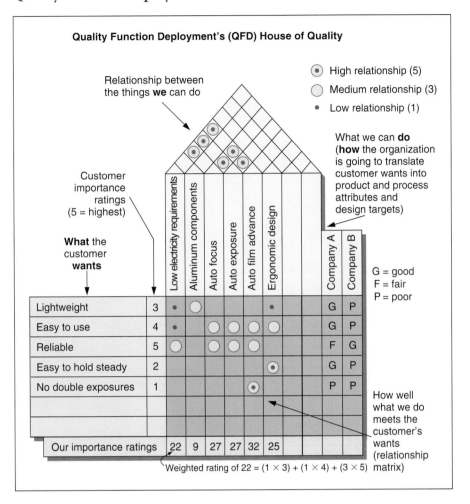

Quality Function Deployment's (QFD) House of Quality

PRACTICE PROBLEM 5.1 ■ QFD

You wish to compete in the superpremium ice cream market. The task is to determine the *wants* of the super premium market and the attributes/*hows* to be met by their firm. Use the house of quality concept.

Market research has revealed that customers feel four factors are significant when making a buying decision. A "rich" taste is most important, followed by smooth texture, distinct flavor, and a sweet taste. From a production standpoint, important factors are the sugar content, the amount of butterfat, low air content, and natural flavors.

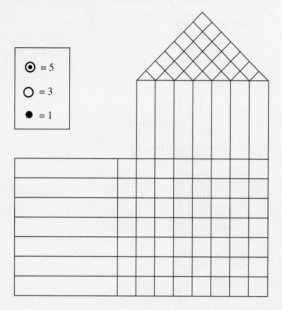

ISSUES FOR PRODUCT DESIGN

Robust Design

Modular Design

Computer-Aided Design (CAD)

Computer-Aided Manufacturing (CAM)

Virtual Reality Technology

Value Analysis

Environmentally Friendly Designs

TIME-BASED COMPETITION

FIGURE 5.6 ■ Product Development Continuum

Product Development Continuum

External Development Strategies

Alliances

Joint Ventures

Purchase Technology or Expertise
by Acquiring the Developer

Internal Development Strategies

Migrations of Existing Products

Enhancements to Existing Products

New Internally Developed Products

Internal ←	Cost of Product Development	→ Shared
Lengthy ←	Speed of Product Development	→ Rapid and/or Existing
High ←	Risk of Product Development	→ Shared

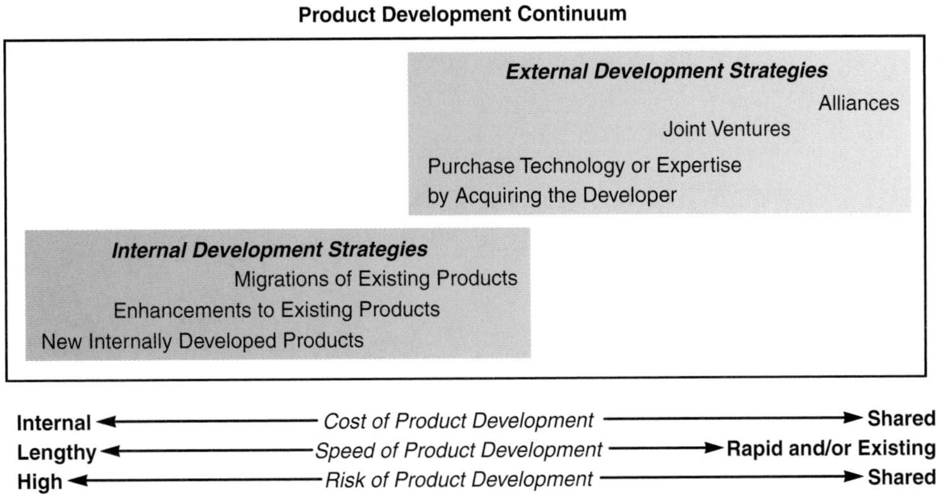

DEFINING THE PRODUCT

Written Specifications

Engineering Drawings

Bills-of-Material

FIGURE 5.9 ■ Bills of Material Take Different Forms in a Manufacturing Plant (a) and a Restaurant (b), but in Both Cases, the Product Must Be Defined

(a)	**Bill of Material for a Panel Weldment**		(b)	**Hard Rock Cafe's Hickory BBQ Bacon Cheeseburger**	

NUMBER	DESCRIPTION	QTY	DESCRIPTION	QTY
A 60-71	PANEL WELDM'T	1	Bun	1
			Hamburger patty	8 oz.
A 60-7	LOWER ROLLER ASSM.	1	Cheddar cheese	2 slices
R 60-17	ROLLER	1	Bacon	2 strips
R 60-428	PIN	1	BBQ onions	1/2 cup
P 60-2	LOCKNUT	1	Hickory BBQ sauce	1 oz.
			Burger set	
A 60-72	GUIDE ASSM. REAR	1	Lettuce	1 leaf
R 60-57-1	SUPPORT ANGLE	1	Tomato	1 slice
A 60-4	ROLLER ASSEM.	1	Red onion	4 rings
02-50-1150	BOLT	1	Pickle	1 slice
			French fries	5 oz.
A 60-73	GUIDE ASSM. FRONT	1	Seasoned salt	1 tsp.
A 60-74	SUPPORT WELDM'T	1	11-inch plate	1
R 60-99	WEAR PLATE	1	HRC flag	1
02-50-1150	BOLT	1		

PRACTICE PROBLEM 5.2 ■ BOM

Prepare a bill-of-material for a ham and cheese sandwich.

DOCUMENTS FOR PRODUCTION

Assembly Drawing

Assembly Chart

Route Sheet

Work Order

Engineering Change Notices (ECNs)

FIGURE 5.11 ■ Assembly Drawing and Assembly Chart

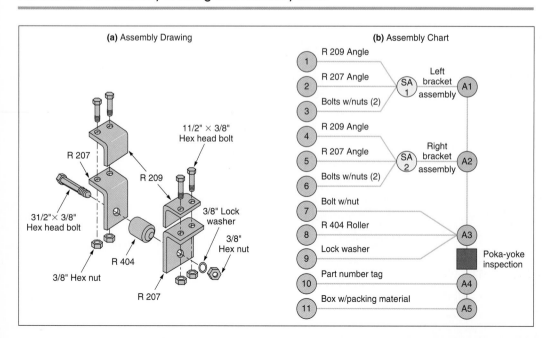

PRACTICE PROBLEM 5.3 ■ Assembly Chart

Prepare an assembly chart for a ham and cheese sandwich.

SERVICE DESIGN

APPLICATION OF DECISION TREES TO PRODUCT DESIGN

PRACTICE PROBLEM 5.4 ■ Decision Tree

Michael's Engineering, Inc., manufactures components for the ever-changing notebook computer business. Michael is considering moving from a small custom design facility to an operation capable of much more rapid design of components. This means that Michael must consider upgrading his CAD equipment. Option 1 is to purchase two new desktop CAD systems at $100,000 each. Option 2 is to purchase an integrated system and the related server at $500,000. Michael's sales manager has estimated that if the market for notebook computers continues to expand, sales over the life of the system will be $1,000,000. He places the odds of this happening at 40%. He thinks the likelihood of the market having already peaked to be 60% and the sales to be only $700,000. What do you suggest Michael do and what is the EMV of this decision?

Additional Practice Problem Space

TRANSITION TO PRODUCTION

DISCUSSION QUESTIONS

1. Why is it necessary to document a product explicitly?
2. What techniques do we use to define a product?
3. In what ways is product strategy linked to product decisions?
4. Once a product is defined, what documents are used to assist production personnel in its manufacture?
5. What is time-based competition?
6. Describe the differences between joint ventures and alliances.
7. Describe four organizational approaches to product development. Which of these is generally thought to be best?
8. Explain what is meant by robust design.
9. What are three specific ways in which computer-aided design (CAD) benefits the design engineer?
10. What information is contained in a bill of materials?
11. What information is contained in an engineering drawing?
12. What information is contained in an assembly chart? In a process sheet?
13. Explain what is meant in service design by the "moment-of-truth."
14. Explain how the house of quality translates customer desires into product/service attributes.
15. What are the advantages of computer-aided design?
16. What strategic advantages does computer-aided design provide?

 CRITICAL THINKING EXERCISE

The design of successful new products, as suggested in this chapter, is a complex task. The task is performed in a variety of ways that include functional hand offs from one department to another, integrated organizations, project managers, and teams. What are the advantages and disadvantages of each? Moreover, as environmental issues become increasingly significant, how might these issues be integrated into the new-product design process?

ACTIVE MODEL EXERCISE

This Active Model appears on your Student CD-ROM. It allows you to evaluate important elements in a decision tree such as that in Example 3 in your text. A sequential decision tree is one of the models in Operations Management that contains probabilities. Generally, probabilities are estimates (forecasts), and there is much uncertainty associated with these probabilities. We use this Active Model to explore the sensitivity of the initial decision (hiring more engineers or purchase CAD) to the probabilities. In addition, we explore the sensitivity of the decision to the estimated (forecasted) payoffs in each sequence of decisions and probabilistic events.

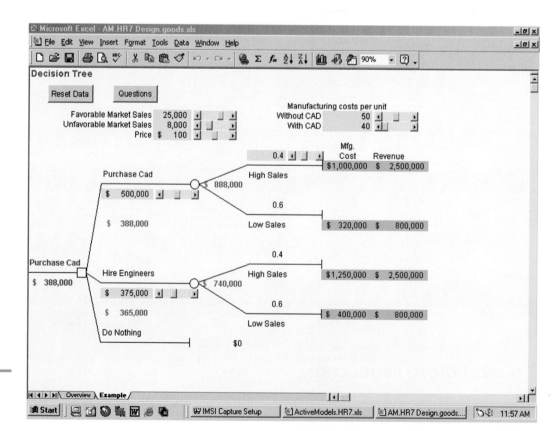

ACTIVE MODEL 5.1 ■

Decision Tree Analysis
Using Data from
Example 3 in Your Text

Questions

1. For what range of probabilities of high sales should we purchase the CAD system?
2. "Favorable market sales" has been defined as 25,000 units. Suppose this is optimistic. At what value would we change our decision and hire engineers?
3. "Unfavorable market sales" has been defined as 8,000 units. Suppose this is optimistic. At what value would we change our decision and hire engineers?
4. How does the price affect our decision?
5. How sensitive is the decision to the manufacturing costs without CAD?
6. How sensitive is the decision to the manufacturing costs with CAD?

PROBLEMS

5.1 Construct a house of quality matrix for a wristwatch. Be sure to indicate specific customer wants that you think the general public desires. Then complete the matrix to show how an operations manager might identify specific attributes that can be measured and controlled to meet those customer desires.

5.2 Using the house of quality, pick a real product (a good or service) and analyze how an existing organization satisfies customer requirements.

5.3 Using a houses of quality sequence, as described in Figure 5.4 in the text, determine how you might deploy resources to achieve the desired quality. (*Hint:* Choose a product/service that you understand.)

5.4 Conduct an interview with a prospective purchaser of a new bicycle and translate the customer's *wants* into the specific *hows* of the firm.

5.5 Prepare a bill of material for a pair of eyeglasses in a case.

5.6 Draw an assembly chart for a ballpoint pen.

5.7 Draw an assembly chart for a pair of eyeglasses.

5.8 Prepare an assembly chart for a table lamp.

5.9 Visit a local sandwich shop, like Subway, Blimpie, Quizno's, and so forth. Construct a bill of material for one of their trademark sandwiches. Perhaps the store clerk or manager will provide you with details on the quantity or weight of various ingredients. Otherwise, estimate quantities.

5.10 Given the contribution made on each of the three products in the following table and their position in the life cycle, identify a reasonable operations strategy for each.

PRODUCT	PRODUCT CONTRIBUTION (% OF SELLING PRICE)	COMPANY CONTRIBUTION (%: TOTAL ANNUAL CONTRIBUTION DIVIDED BY TOTAL ANNUAL SALES)	POSITION IN LIFE CYCLE
Notebook computer	30	40	Growth
Palm-held computer	30	50	Introduction
Hand calculator	50	10	Decline

5.11 The product design group of Flores Electric Supplies, Inc., has determined that it needs to design a new series of switches. It must decide on one of three design strategies. The market forecast is for 200,000 units. The better and more sophisticated the design strategy and the more time spent on value engineering, the less will be the variable cost. The chief of engineering design, Dr. W. L. Berry, has decided that the following costs are a good estimate of the initial and variable costs connected with each of the three strategies:

a) Low-tech: a low-technology, low-cost process consisting of hiring several new junior engineers. This option has a cost of $45,000 and variable cost probabilities of .3 for $.55 each, .4 for $.50, and .3 for $.45.

b) Subcontract: a medium-cost approach using a good outside design staff. This approach would have an initial cost of $65,000 and variable cost probabilities of .7 of $.45, .2 of $.40, and .1 of $.35.

c) High-tech: a high-technology approach using the very best of the inside staff and the latest computer-aided design technology. This approach has a fixed cost of $75,000 and variable cost probabilities of .9 of $.40 and .1 of $.35. What is the best decision based on an expected monetary value (EMV) criterion? (*Note:* We want the lowest EMV as we are dealing with costs in this problem.)

5.12   Clarkson Products, Inc., of Clarkson, New York, has the option of (a) proceeding immediately with production of a new top-of-the-line stereo TV that has just completed prototype testing or (b) having the value analysis team complete a study. If Ed Lusk, VP for operations, proceeds with the existing prototype (option a), the firm can expect sales to be 100,000 units at $550 each, with a probability of .6 and a .4 probability of 75,000 at $550. If, however, he uses the value analysis team (option b), the firm expects sales of 75,000 units at $750, with a probability of .7 and a .3 probability of 70,000 units at $750. Cost of the value analysis is $100,000. Which option has the highest expected monetary value (EMV)?

5.13   Residents of Mill River have fond memories of ice skating at a local park. An artist has captured the experience in a drawing and is hoping to reproduce it and sell framed copies to current and former residents. He thinks that if the market is good he could sell 400 copies of the elegant version at $125 each. If the market is not good, he would only sell 300 at $90 each. He could make a deluxe version of the same drawing instead. He feels that if the market were good he could sell 500 copies of the deluxe version at $100 each. If the market is not good, he would only sell 400 copies at $70 each. In either case, production costs would be approximately $35,000. He could also choose to do nothing at this time. If he believes there is a 50% probability of a good market, what should he do? Why?

5.14   Ritz Products' materials manager, Bruce Elwell, must determine whether to make or buy a new semiconductor for the wrist TV that the firm is about to produce. One million units are expected to be produced over the life cycle. If the product is made, start-up and production costs of the *make* decision total $1 million with a probability of .4 that the product will be satisfactory and a .6 probability that it will not. If the product is not satisfactory, the firm will have to reevaluate the decision. If the decision is reevaluated, the choice will be whether to spend another $1 million to redesign the semiconductor or to purchase. Likelihood of success the second time that the make decision is made is .9. If the second *make* decision also fails, the firm must purchase. Regardless of when the purchase takes place, Elwell's best judgment of cost is that Ritz will pay $.50 for each purchased semiconductor plus $1 million in vendor development cost.

a)   Assuming that Ritz must have the semiconductor (stopping or doing without is not a viable option), what is the best decision?

b)   What criteria did you use to make this decision?

c)   What is the worst that can happen to Ritz as a result of this particular decision? What is the best that can happen?

5.15   Page Engineering designs and constructs the air conditioning and heating (HVAC) systems for hospitals and clinics. Currently the company's staff is overloaded with design work. There is a major design project due in 8 weeks. The penalty for completing the design late is $14,000 per week since any delay will cause the facility to open later than anticipated, costing the client significant revenue. If the company uses its inside engineers to complete the design, it will have to pay them overtime for all work. Page has estimated that it will cost $12,000 per week (wages and overhead) to have company engineers complete the design. Page is also considering having an outside engineering firm do the design. A bid of $92,000 has been received for the completed design. Yet another option for completing the design is to conduct a joint design by having a third engineering company complete all electro-mechanical components of the design at a cost of $56,000. Page would then complete the rest of the design and control systems at an estimated cost of $30,000.

Page has estimated the following probabilities of completing the project within various time frames when using each of the three options. Those estimates are shown in the following table:

	PROBABILITY OF COMPLETING THE DESIGN			
OPTION	ON TIME	ONE WEEK LATE	TWO WEEKS LATE	THREE WEEKS LATE
Internal Engineers	.4	.5	.1	—
External Engineers	.2	.4	.3	.1
Joint Design	.1	.3	.4	.2

What is the best decision based on an expected monetary value criterion? (*Note:* You want the lowest EMV because we are dealing with costs in this problem.)

5.16   Use the data in Solved Problem 5.1 to examine what happens to the decision if Sarah King can increase yields from 59,000 to 64,000 by applying an expensive phosphorus to the screen at an added cost of $250,000. Prepare the modified decision tree. What are the payoffs, and which branch has the greatest EMV?

5.17   As a library or Internet project, find a series of group technology codes.

INTERNET HOMEWORK PROBLEMS

See our Internet home page at **www.prenhall.com/heizer** for these additional homework problems: 5.18 through 5.24.

CASE STUDY

De Mar's Product Strategy

De Mar, a plumbing, heating, and air-conditioning company located in Fresno, California, has a simple but powerful product strategy: *Solve the customer's problem no matter what, solve the problem when the customer needs it solved, and make sure the customer feels good when you leave.* De Mar offers guaranteed, same-day service for customers requiring it. The company provides 24-hour-a-day, 7-day-a-week service at no extra charge for customers whose air-conditioning dies on a hot summer Sunday or whose toilet overflows at 2:30 in the morning. As assistant service coordinator Janie Walter puts it: "We will be there to fix your A/C on the fourth of July, and it's not a penny extra. When our competitors won't get out of bed, we'll be there!"

De Mar guarantees the price of a job to the penny before the work begins. Whereas most competitors guarantee their work for 30 days, De Mar guarantees all parts and labor for one year. The company assesses no travel charge because "it's not fair to charge customers for driving out." Owner Larry Harmon says: "We are in an industry that doesn't have the best reputation. If we start making money our main goal, we are in trouble. So I stress customer satisfaction; money is the by-product."

De Mar uses selective hiring, ongoing training and education, performance measures and compensation that incorporate customer satisfaction, strong teamwork, peer pressure, empowerment, and aggressive promotion to implement its strategy. Says credit manager Anne Semrick: "The person who wants a nine-to-five job needs to go somewhere else."

De Mar is a premium pricer. Yet customers respond because De Mar delivers value—that is, benefits for costs. In 8 years, annual sales increased from about $200,000 to more than $3.3 million.

Discussion Questions

1. What is De Mar's product? Identify the tangible parts of this product and its service components.
2. How should other areas of De Mar (marketing, finance, personnel) support its product strategy?
3. Even though De Mar's product is primarily a service product, how should each of the 10 OM decisions in the text be managed to ensure that the product is successful?

Source: Reprinted with the permission of The Free Press, from *On Great Service: A Framework for Action* by Leonard L. Berry. Copyright © 1995 by Leonard L. Berry.

VIDEO CASE STUDY

Product Design at Regal Marine

With hundreds of competitors in the boat business, Regal Marine must work to differentiate itself from the flock. As we saw in the *Global Company Profile* that opened Chapter 5 in your text, Regal continuously introduces innovative, high-quality new boats. Its differentiation strategy is reflected in a product line consisting of 22 models.

To maintain this stream of innovation, and with so many boats at varying stages of their life cycles, Regal constantly seeks design input from customers, dealers, and consultants. Design ideas rapidly find themselves in the styling studio, where they are placed onto CAD machines in order to speed the development process. Existing boat designs are always evolving as the company tries to stay stylish and competitive. Moreover, with life cycles as short as 3 years, a steady stream of new products is required. A few years ago, the new product was the three-passenger $11,000 Rush, a small but powerful boat capable of pulling a water-skier. This was followed with a 20-foot inboard–outboard performance boat with so many innovations that it won prize after prize in the industry. Another new boat is a redesigned 42-foot Commodore that sleeps six in luxury staterooms. With all these models and innovations, Regal designers and production personnel are under pressure to respond quickly.

By getting key suppliers on board early and urging them to participate at the design stage, Regal improves both innovations and qual-

ity while speeding product development. Regal finds that the sooner it brings suppliers on board, the faster it can bring new boats to the market. After a development stage that constitutes concept and styling, CAD designs yield product specifications. The first stage in actual production is the creation of the "plug," a foam-based carving used to make the molds for fiberglass hulls and decks. Specifications from the CAD system drive the carving process. Once the plug is carved, the permanent molds for each new hull and deck design are formed. Molds take about 4 to 8 weeks to make and are all handmade. Similar molds are made for many of the other features in Regal boats—from galley and stateroom components to lavatories and steps. Finished molds can be joined and used to make thousands of boats.

Discussion Questions*

1. How does the concept of product life cycle apply to Regal Marine products?
2. What strategy does Regal use to stay competitive?
3. What kind of engineering savings is Regal achieving by using CAD technology rather than traditional drafting techniques?
4. What are the likely benefits of the CAD design technology?

*You may wish to view this video case on your CD-ROM before addressing these questions.

Managing Quality

Chapter Outline

Regardless of the organization's strategy, defining and managing quality is crucial. Quality, or lack of quality, impacts the entire organization from supplier to customer and from product design to maintenance. Successful quality management begins with an organizational environment that fosters quality, followed by an understanding of the principles of quality, and then engaging employees in the necessary activities to implement quality. When these things are done well, the product typically obtains a competitive advantage and wins customers.

BEFORE COMING TO CLASS, READ CHAPTER 6 IN YOUR TEXT AND ANSWER THESE QUESTIONS.

1. How do firms define quality? _____

_____

_____

2. Why is quality important? _____

_____

_____

3. What is meant by TQM? _____

_____

_____

4. What are quality robust products? _____

_____

_____

5. What are ISO standards and why are they important? _____

_____

_____

6. What are seven tools of TQM? _____

_____

_____

QUALITY AND STRATEGY

DEFINING QUALITY

Quality is the totality of features and characteristics of a product or service that bears on the ability to satisfy stated or implied needs.

Three Other Perspectives to Defining Quality

1. User based:

2. Manufacturing based:

3. Product based:

INTERNATIONAL QUALITY STANDARDS

The Two Major International Standards for Quality

1. ISO 9000

2. ISO 14000

TOTAL QUALITY MANAGEMENT (TQM)

The Six Ingredients of Total Quality Management

1. Continuous improvement

2. Employee empowerment

3. Benchmarking

4. Just-in-time

5. Taguchi concepts

6. TQM tools

Taguchi Concepts

Quality loss function

$$L = D^2C$$

where
L = loss to society
D^2 = square of the distance from the target value
C = cost of the deviation at the specification limit

FIGURE 6.4 ■ Quality Loss Function (a) and Distribution of Specifications for Products Produced (b)

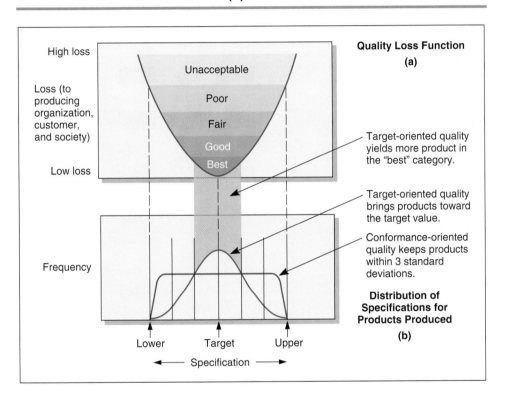

The Other Two Taguchi Concepts

1. Target-oriented quality

2. Quality robust products

FIGURE 6.5 ■ Seven Tools of TQM

Tools for Generating Ideas

(a) *Check Sheet:* An organized method of recording data.

Defect	Hour							
	1	2	3	4	5	6	7	8
A	///	/		/	/	/	///	/
B	//	/	/	/			//	///
C	/	//					//	////

(b) *Scatter Diagram:* A graph of the value of one variable vs. another variable.

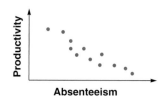

(c) *Cause and Effect Diagram:* A tool that identifies process elements (causes) that might effect an outcome.

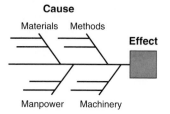

Tools to Organize the Data

(d) *Pareto Charts:* A graph to identify and plot problems or defects in descending order of frequency.

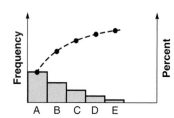

(e) *Flow Charts (Process Diagrams):* A chart that describes the steps in a process.

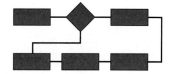

Tools for Identifying Problems

(f) *Histogram:* A distribution showing the frequency of occurrences of a variable.

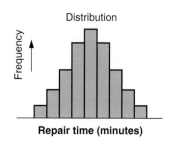

(g) *Statistical Process Control Chart:* A chart with time on the horizontal axis to plot values of a statistic.

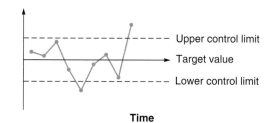

PRACTICE PROBLEM 6.1 ■ Pareto Chart

The accounts receivable department has documented the following defects over a 30-day period:

CATEGORY	FREQUENCY
Invoice amount does not agree with the check amount	108
Invoice not on record (not found)	24
No formal invoice issued	18
Check (payment) not received on time	30
Check not signed	8
Invoice number and invoice referenced do not agree	12

Draw the Pareto chart. What conclusions can you draw about defects in the accounts receivable department?

Additional Practice Problem Space

PRACTICE PROBLEM 6.2 ■ Flowchart

Prepare a flowchart for purchasing a Big Mac at the drive-through window at McDonald's.

PRACTICE PROBLEM 6.3 ■ Fishbone Chart

Draw a fishbone chart detailing reasons why a part might not be machined correctly.

PRACTICE PROBLEM 6.4 ■ Process Chart

Develop a process chart for changing an automobile tire.

THE ROLE OF INSPECTION

When and Where to Inspect

Source Inspection

Poka-Yoke

Attribute Inspection

Variable Inspection

TQM IN SERVICES

Determinants of Quality

Reliability

Responsiveness

Competence

Access

Courtesy

Communication

Credibility

Security

Understanding/Knowing the Customer

Tangibles

DISCUSSION QUESTIONS

1. Explain how higher quality can lead to lower costs.
2. As an Internet exercise, determine the Baldrige Award Criteria. See the Web site **www.quality.nist.gov**.
3. Which 3 of Deming's 14 points do you feel are most critical to the success of a TQM program? Why?
4. List the six concepts that are necessary for an effective TQM program. How are these related to Deming's 14 points?
5. Name three of the important people associated with the quality concepts of this chapter. In each case, write a short sentence about each one summarizing their primary contribution to the field of quality management.
6. What are seven tools of TQM?
7. How does fear in the workplace (and in the classroom) inhibit learning?
8. How can a university control the quality of its output (that is, its graduates)?

9. Philip Crosby suggested quality is free. Why?
10. List the three concepts central to Taguchi's approach?
11. What is the purpose of using a Pareto chart for a given problem?
12. What are the four broad categories of "causes" to help initially structure an Ishikawa diagram or cause-and-effect diagram?
13. Of the several points where inspection may be necessary, which apply especially well to manufacturing?
14. What roles do operations managers play in addressing the major aspects of service quality?
15. Explain, in your own words, what is meant by *source inspection*.
16. What are 10 determinants of service quality?
17. Name several products that do not require high quality.
18. What does the formula $L = D^2C$ mean?

CRITICAL THINKING EXERCISE

In this chapter, we have suggested that building quality into a process and its people is difficult. Inspections are also difficult. To indicate just how difficult inspections are, count the number of *E*s (both capital *E*, and small *e*) in the *OM in Action* box, "Richey International's Spies," on page 169 in your text (include the title, but not the footnote). How many did you find? If each student does this individually, you are very likely to find a distribution rather than a single number!

ACTIVE MODEL EXERCISE

This Active Model appears on your CD-ROM. It allows you to evaluate important elements in the Pareto Chart.

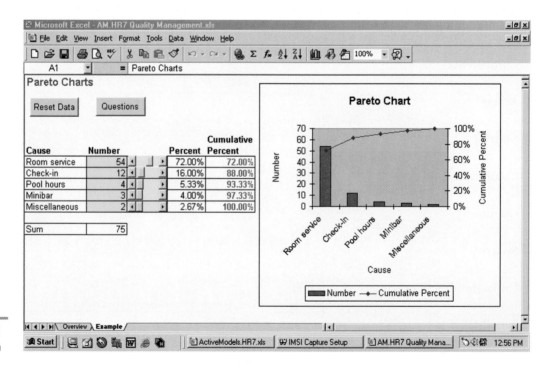

ACTIVE MODEL 6.1 ■

Pareto Analysis of Hotel Data from Example 1 in Your Text

Questions

1. What percentage of overall defects do the room service complaints account for?
2. If we could reduce the room service complaints in half how does this affect the chart?

PROBLEMS

6.1   Develop a Pareto analysis of the following causes of delay in Lument Technology's production process. What do you conclude?

REASON FOR DELAY	FREQUENCY
Awaiting engineering decision	11
No schematic available	10
Test equipment down	22
Delay in inspection	15
Inadequate parts	40
Lack of personnel available	3

6.2   Develop a scatter diagram for two variables of interest (say pages in the newspaper by day of the week; see example in Figure 6.5b on page 6-4).

6.3   Develop a Pareto analysis of the following causes of poor grades on an exam:

REASON FOR POOR GRADE	FREQUENCY
Insufficient time to complete	15
Late arrival to exam	7
Difficulty understanding material	25
Insufficient preparation time	2
Studied wrong material	2
Distractions in exam room	9
Calculator batteries died during exam	1
Forgot exam was scheduled	3
Felt ill during exam	4

6.4   Develop a histogram of the time it took for you or your friends to receive six recent orders at a fast-food restaurant.

6.5   Visit a fast-food drive-through window operation during off-peak service hours. Record each time a vehicle arrives at the order window or the end of the line. Also record the number of people in the vehicle. Then record the time that the vehicle begins to drive away from the serving window and compute the throughput time (time between arrival and departure) of each vehicle. (Include 30 vehicles or more in the study.)

      Using these data, construct a scatter diagram of the two variables: number of vehicle occupants and throughput time. Use occupants as the X variable. Does there appear to be a relationship between the two variables?

6.6   Develop a flow chart (as in Figure 6.5[e] on page 6-4; and Example 2 in your text) showing all the steps involved in planning a party.

6.7   Consider the types of poor driving habits that might occur at a traffic light. Make a list of the 10 you consider most likely to happen. Add the category of "other" to that list.

a)   Compose a check sheet (like that in Figure 6.5[a] on page 6-4) to collect the frequency of occurrence of these habits. Using your check sheet, visit a busy traffic light intersection at four different times of the day, with two of these times being during high-traffic periods (rush hour, lunch hour). For 15 to 20 minutes each visit, observe the frequency with which the habits you listed occurred.

b)   Construct a Pareto chart showing the relative frequency of occurrence of each habit.

6.8   Draw a fish-bone chart detailing reasons why a bolt might not be correctly matched to a nut on an assembly line.

6.9   Consider the everyday task of getting to work on time or arriving at your first class on time in the morning. Draw a fish-bone chart showing reasons why you might arrive late in the morning.

6.10   Construct a cause-and-effect diagram to reflect "Student dissatisfied with university registration process." Use the "four Ms" or create your own organizing scheme. Include at least 12 causes.

6.11   Draw a fish-bone chart depicting the reasons that might give rise to an incorrect fee statement at the time you go to pay for your registration at school.

6.12   Mary Beth Marrs, the manager of an apartment complex, feels overwhelmed by the number of complaints she is receiving. Below is the check sheet she has kept for the last 12 weeks. Develop a Pareto chart using this information. What recommendations would you make?

WEEK	GROUNDS	PARKING/ DRIVES	POOL	TENANT ISSUES	ELECTRICAL/ PLUMBING
1	✓✓✓	✓	✓	✓✓✓	
2	✓	✓✓✓	✓✓	✓✓	✓
3	✓✓✓	✓✓✓	✓✓	✓	
4	✓	✓✓✓✓	✓	✓	✓✓
5	✓✓	✓✓✓	✓✓✓✓	✓✓	
6	✓	✓✓✓✓	✓✓		
7		✓✓✓	✓✓	✓✓	
8	✓	✓✓✓✓✓	✓✓	✓✓✓	✓
9	✓	✓✓	✓		
10	✓	✓✓✓✓	✓✓	✓✓	
11		✓✓✓	✓✓	✓	
12	✓✓	✓✓✓	✓✓✓	✓	

6.13 Use Pareto analysis to investigate the following data collected on a printed-circuit-board assembly line.
a) Prepare a graph of the data.
b) What conclusions do you reach?

DEFECT	NUMBER OF DEFECT OCCURRENCES
Components not adhering	143
Excess adhesive	71
Misplaced transistors	601
Defective board dimension	146
Mounting holes improperly positioned	12
Circuitry problems on final test	90
Wrong component	212

6.14 An auto repair shop has recorded the following complaints. Use them to prepare a cause-and-effect diagram based on the "four Ms" (that is, label the diagram, and place each complaint on the proper branch of the diagram).
a) I was overcharged—your labor rates are too high.
b) The mechanic left grease on the driver's seat.
c) I wish you took appointments for service and repairs.
d) You weren't finished with my car when you promised.
e) The replacement part has failed.
f) The replacement part is not as good as the factory original.
g) You didn't tighten the drain plug properly—it's leaking.
h) My problem is minor and easy to fix—why can't you take care of it right now, and let some of the longer repairs wait?
i) Your estimate of repair costs was *way* off.
j) I brought my car in for a simple oil change, but you did that and a complete tune-up as well.
k) Your mechanic is just changing parts—he doesn't have a clue what's wrong with my car.
l) I don't think your diagnostic computer is working right.
m) You charged me for work that wasn't done.

6.15 Develop a flow chart for one of the following:
a) Filling up with gasoline at a self-serve station.
b) Determining your account balance and making a withdrawal at an ATM.
c) Getting a cone of yogurt or ice cream from an ice cream store.

6.16 Southwest Wood Treating has been getting many complaints from its major customer, Home Station, about the quality of its shipments of pressure-treated products. Rick Summers, the plant manager, is alarmed that a customer is providing him with the only information the company has on shipment quality. He decided to collect information on defective shipments through a form he asked his drivers to complete on arrival at customers' stores. The forms for the first 284 shipments have been turned in. They show the following over the last 8 weeks:

			REASON FOR DEFECTIVE SHIPMENT			
WEEK	NO. OF SHIPMENTS	NO. OF SHIPMENTS WITH DEFECTS	INCORRECT BILL OF LADING *1*	INCORRECT TRUCKLOAD *2*	DAMAGED PRODUCT *3*	TRUCKS LATE *4*
1	23	5	2	2	1	
2	31	8	1	4	1	2
3	28	6	2	3	1	
4	37	11	4	4	1	2
5	35	10	3	4	2	1
6	40	14	5	6	3	
7	41	12	3	5	3	1
8	44	15	4	7	2	2

Even though Rick increased his capacity by adding more workers to his normal contingent of 30, he knew that for many weeks he exceeded his regular output of 30 shipments per week. A review of his turnover over the last 8 weeks shows the following:

WEEK	NO. OF NEW HIRES	NO. OF TERMINATIONS	TOTAL NO. OF WORKERS
1	1	0	30
2	2	1	31
3	3	2	32
4	2	0	34
5	2	2	34
6	2	4	32
7	4	1	35
8	3	2	36

a) Develop a scatter diagram using total number of shipments and number of defective shipments. Does there appear to be any relationship?

b) Develop a scatter diagram using the variable "turnover" (number of new hires plus number of terminations) and the number of defective shipments. Does the diagram depict a relationship between the two variables?

c) Develop a Pareto chart for the type of defects that have occurred.

d) Draw a fish-bone chart showing the possible causes of the defective shipments.

INTERNET HOMEWORK PROBLEMS

See our Internet home page at **www.prenhall.com/heizer** for these additional homework problems: 6.17 through 6.20.

CASE STUDY

Southwestern University: (C)*

The popularity of Southwestern University's football program under its new coach, Bo Pitterno, has surged in each of the 5 years since his arrival at the Stephenville, Texas, college. (See Southwestern University: (A) in Chapter 3 and (B) in Chapter 4.) With a football stadium close to maxing out at 54,000 seats and a vocal coach pushing for a new stadium, SWU president Joel Wisner faced some difficult decisions. After a phenomenal upset victory over its archrival, the University of Texas, at the homecoming game in the fall, Dr. Wisner was not as happy as one would think. Instead of ecstatic alumni, students, and faculty, all Wisner heard were complaints. "The lines at the concession stands were too long"; "Parking was harder to find and farther away than in the old days" (that is, before

the team won regularly); "Seats weren't comfortable"; "Traffic was backed up halfway to Dallas"; and on and on. "A college president just can't win," muttered Wisner to himself.

At his staff meeting the following Monday, Wisner turned to his VP of administration, Leslie Gardner. "I wish you would take care of these football complaints, Leslie," he said. "See what the *real* problems are and let me know how you've resolved them." Gardner wasn't surprised at the request. "I've already got a handle on it, Joel," she replied. "We've been randomly surveying 50 fans per game for the past year to see what's on their minds. It's all part of my campuswide TQM effort. Let me tally things up and I'll get back to you in a week."

When she returned to her office, Gardner pulled out the file her assistant had compiled (see Table 6.5). "There's a lot of information here," she thought. *(continued)*

TABLE 6.5

Fan Satisfaction
Survey Results
(N = 250)

		OVERALL GRADE				
		A	B	C	D	E
GAME DAY	A. Parking	90	105	45	5	5
	B. Traffic	50	85	48	52	15
	C. Seating	45	30	115	35	25
	D. Entertainment	160	35	26	10	19
	E. Printed Program	66	34	98	22	30
TICKETS	A. Pricing	105	104	16	15	10
	B. Season Ticket Plans	75	80	54	41	0
CONCESSIONS	A. Prices	16	116	58	58	2
	B. Selection of Foods	155	60	24	11	0
	C. Speed of Service	35	45	46	48	76

RESPONDENTS

Alumnus 113
Student 83
Faculty/Staff 16
None of the above 38

OPEN-ENDED COMMENTS ON SURVEY CARDS:

Parking a mess	Lines are awful	Coach is terrific
Add a sky box	Seats are uncomfortable	More water fountains
Get better cheerleaders	I will pay more for better view	Better seats
Double the parking attendants	Get a new stadium	Seats not comfy
Everything is okay	Student dress code needed	Bigger parking lot
Too crowded	I want cushioned seats	I'm too old for bench seats
Seats too narrow	Not enough police	No coffee served at game
Great food	Students too rowdy	My company will buy a sky box—build it!
Joe P. for President!	Parking terrible	Programs overpriced
I smelled drugs being smoked	Toilets weren't clean	Want softer seats
Stadium is ancient	Not enough handicap spots in lot	Beat those Longhorns!
Seats are like rocks	Well done, SWU	I'll pay for a sky box
Not enough cops for traffic	Put in bigger seats	Band was terrific
Game starts too late	Friendly ushers	Love Pitterno
Hire more traffic cops	Need better seats	Everything is great
Need new band	Expand parking lots	Build new stadium
Great!	Hate the bleacher seats	Move games to Dallas
More hot dog stands	Hot dogs cold	No complaints
Seats are all metal	$3 for a coffee? No way!	Dirty bathroom
Need sky boxes	Get some sky boxes	Seats too small
Seats stink	Love the new uniforms	
Go SWU!	Took an hour to park	

Discussion Questions

1. Using at least two different quality tools, analyze the data and present your conclusions.
2. How could the survey have been more useful?
3. What is the next step?

*This integrated case study runs throughout the Student Lecture Guide. Other issues facing Southwestern's football stadium include: (A) Managing the renovation project (Chapter 3); (B) Forecasting game attendance (Chapter 4); (D) Inventory planning of football programs (Chapter 12); and (E) Scheduling of campus security officers/staff for game days (Chapter 13).

VIDEO CASE STUDY

Quality at the Ritz-Carlton Hotel Company

Ritz-Carlton. The name alone evokes images of luxury and quality. As the first hotel company to win the Malcolm Baldrige National Quality Award, the Ritz treats quality as if it is the heartbeat of the company. This means a daily commitment to meeting customer expectations and making sure that each hotel is free of any deficiency.

In the hotel industry, quality can be hard to quantify. Guests do not purchase a product when they stay at the Ritz: They buy an experience. Thus, creating the right combination of elements to make the experience stand out is the challenge and goal of every employee, from maintenance to management.

Before applying for the Baldrige Award, company management undertook a rigorous self-examination of its operations in an attempt to measure and quantify quality. Nineteen processes were studied, including room service delivery, guest reservation and registration, message delivery, and breakfast service. This period of self-study included statistical measurement of process work flows and cycle times for areas ranging from room service delivery times and reservations to valet parking and housekeeping efficiency. The results were used to develop performance benchmarks against which future activity could be measured.

With specific, quantifiable targets in place, Ritz-Carlton managers and employees now focus on continuous improvement. The goal is 100% customer satisfaction: If a guest's experience does not meet expectations, the Ritz-Carlton risks losing that guest to competition.

One way the company has put more meaning behind its quality efforts is to organize its employees into "self-directed" work teams. Employee teams determine work scheduling, what work needs to be done, and what to do about quality problems in their own areas. In order that they can see the relationship of their specific area to the overall goals, employees are also given the opportunity to take additional training in hotel operations. Ritz-Carlton believes that a more educated and informed employee is in a better position to make decisions in the best interest of the organization.

Discussion Questions*

1. In what ways could the Ritz-Carlton monitor its success in achieving quality?
2. Many companies say that their goal is to provide quality products or services. What actions might you expect from a company that intends quality to be more than a slogan or buzzword?
3. Why might it cost the Ritz-Carlton less to "do things right" the first time?
4. How could control charts, Pareto diagrams, and cause-and-effect diagrams be used to identify quality problems at a hotel?
5. What are some nonfinancial measures of customer satisfaction that might be used by the Ritz-Carlton?

*You may wish to view this video case on your CD-ROM before addressing these questions.

Source: Adapted from C. T. Horngren, G. Foster, and S. M. Dator, *Cost Accounting*, 11th ed. (Upper Saddle River, NJ: Prentice Hall, 2003).

Statistical Process Control

Supplement Outline

Statistical process control (SPC) is a major tool of quality control. We use SPC to measure performance of a process. Control charts for SPC help operations managers distinguish between natural and assignable variations. A process is said to be operating in statistical control when the only source of variation is common (natural) causes. The $\bar{x}$-chart and the R-chart are used for variable sampling, and the p-chart and the c-chart for attribute sampling. The C_{pk} index is a way to express process capability. Operating characteristic (OC) curves facilitate acceptance sampling and provide the manager with tools to evaluate the quality of a production run or shipment.

BEFORE COMING TO CLASS, READ SUPPLEMENT 6 IN YOUR TEXT AND ANSWER THESE QUESTIONS.

1. Why do firms use $\bar{x}$- and R-charts? _____

_____

_____

2. What might be a reason for a process to be "out of control"? _____

_____

_____

3. When are p- or c-charts used? _____

_____

_____

4. What are the two types of variation? _____

_____

_____

5. Explain what C_p and C_{pk} mean. _____

_____

_____

6. What is an operating characteristic (OC) curve? _____

_____

_____

STATISTICAL PROCESS CONTROL (SPC)

Natural Variations

Assignable Variations

Samples

Control Charts

FIGURE S6.2 ■ Process Control: Three Types of Process Outputs

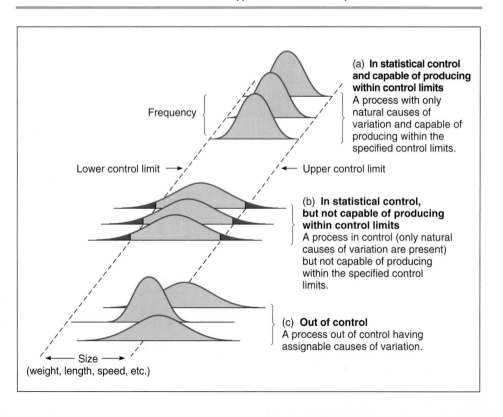

Central Limit Theorem

$$\bar{\bar{x}} = \mu \qquad \text{Population mean} \qquad \text{(S6-1)}$$

$$\sigma_{\bar{x}} = \frac{\sigma}{\sqrt{n}} \qquad \text{Standard deviation of the sampling distribution} \qquad \text{(S6-2)}$$

FIGURE S6.3 ■ The Relationship between Population and Sampling Distributions

Regardless of the population distribution (e.g., normal, beta, uniform), each with its own mean (μ) and standard deviation (σ), the distribution of sample means is normal.

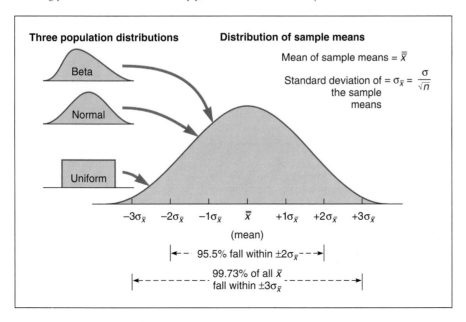

Creating $\bar{x}$ Charts

If we know the standard deviation of the process population, σ

Upper control limit (UCL) = $\bar{\bar{x}} + z\sigma_{\bar{x}}$ $\qquad\qquad\qquad\qquad\qquad\qquad$ (S6-3)

Lower control limit (LCL) = $\bar{\bar{x}} - z\sigma_{\bar{x}}$ $\qquad\qquad\qquad\qquad\qquad\qquad$ (S6-4)

where $\quad\bar{\bar{x}}$ = mean of the sample means or a target value set for the process

$\quad\quad z$ = number of normal standard deviations (2 for 95.45% confidence, 3 for 99.73%)

$\quad\quad \sigma_{\bar{x}}$ = standard deviation of the sample means = $\sigma/\sqrt{n}$

$\quad\quad \sigma$ = population (process) standard deviation

$\quad\quad n$ = sample size

PRACTICE PROBLEM S6.1 ■ Setting $\bar{x}$ Control Limits

Twenty-five engine mounts are sampled each day and found to have an average width of 2 inches, with a standard deviation of 0.1 inches. What are the control limits that include 99.73% of the sample means ($Z = 3$)?

Additional Practice Problem Space

Using the range to set control limits

$$\text{UCL}_{\bar{x}} = \bar{\bar{x}} + A_2 \bar{R}$$

(S6-5)

and

$$\text{LCL}_{\bar{x}} = \bar{\bar{x}} - A_2 \bar{R}$$

(S6-6)

where $\bar{R}$ = average range of the samples
A_2 = value found in Table S6.1
$\bar{\bar{x}}$ = mean of the sample means

TABLE S6.1 ■ Factors for Computing Control Chart Limits (3 sigma)

SAMPLE SIZE, n	MEAN FACTOR, A_2	UPPER RANGE, D_4	LOWER RANGE, D_3
2	1.880	3.268	0
3	1.023	2.574	0
4	.729	2.282	0
5	.577	2.115	0
6	.483	2.004	0
7	.419	1.924	0.076
8	.373	1.864	0.136
9	.337	1.816	0.184
10	.308	1.777	0.223
12	.266	1.716	0.284

PRACTICE PROBLEM S6.2 ■ $\bar{x}$-Chart with Ranges and Use of Table S6.1

Several samples of size $n = 8$ have been taken from today's production of fence posts. The average post was 3 yards in length, and the average sample range was 0.015 yard. Find the 99.73% upper and lower control limits.

Additional Practice Problem Space

Creating *R*-Charts

$$\text{UCL}_R = D_4 \overline{R} \qquad\qquad\qquad \text{(S6-7)}$$

$$\text{LCL}_R = D_3 \overline{R} \qquad\qquad\qquad \text{(S6-8)}$$

where UCL_R = upper control chart limit for the range
LCL_R = lower control chart limit for the range
D_4 and D_3 = values from Table S6.1

PRACTICE PROBLEM S6.3 ■ Range Chart

The average range of a process is 10 pounds. The sample size is 10. Use Table S6.1 to develop upper and lower control limits on the *range*.

Additional Practice Problem Space

Steps to Follow When Using Control Charts

1. Collect 20 to 25 samples of n = 4 or 5 each from a stable process and compute the mean and range of each.
2. Compute the overall means, set control limits, and compute the UCL and LCL.
3. Graph the sample means and ranges and see if they fall outside the limits.
4. Investigate points and patterns out of control.
5. Collect additional samples and revalidate limits if necessary.

Control Charts for Attributes

Attributes

p-Charts

$$\text{UCL}_p = \bar{p} + z\sigma_{\hat{p}} \qquad\qquad\qquad \text{(S6-9)}$$

$$\text{LCL}_p = \bar{p} - z\sigma_{\hat{p}} \qquad\qquad\qquad \text{(S6-10)}$$

where $\bar{p}$ = mean fraction defective in the sample
z = number of standard deviations ($z = 2$ for 95.45% limits; $z = 3$
for 99.73% limits)
$\sigma_{\hat{p}}$ = standard deviation of the sampling distribution

$\sigma_{\hat{p}}$ is estimated by the formula:

$$\sigma_{\hat{p}} = \sqrt{\frac{\bar{p}(1-\bar{p})}{n}} \qquad\qquad\qquad \text{(S6-11)}$$

where n = size of *each* sample.

PRACTICE PROBLEM S6.4 ■ p-Chart Limits

Based on samples of 20 IRS auditors, each handling 100 files, we find that the total number of mistakes in handling files is 220. Find the 95.45% upper and lower control limits.

Additional Practice Problem Space

c-Charts

$$\text{control limits} = \bar{c} \pm 3\sqrt{\bar{c}} \qquad\qquad (S6\text{-}12)$$

PRACTICE PROBLEM S6.5 ■ c-Chart Limits

There have been complaints that the sports page of the *Dubuque Register* has lots of typos. The past 6 days have been examined carefully and the number of typos per page is recorded below. Is the process in control using $Z = 2$?

DAY	NUMBER OF TYPOS
Monday	2
Tuesday	1
Wednesday	5
Thursday	3
Friday	4
Saturday	0

Additional Practice Problem Space

FIGURE S6.7 ■ Patterns to Look for on Control Charts

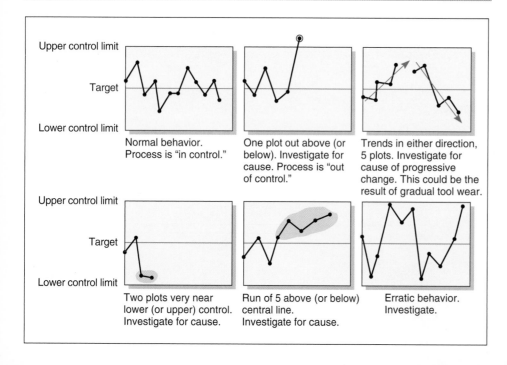

Normal behavior. Process is "in control."

One plot out above (or below). Investigate for cause. Process is "out of control."

Trends in either direction, 5 plots. Investigate for cause of progressive change. This could be the result of gradual tool wear.

Two plots very near lower (or upper) control. Investigate for cause.

Run of 5 above (or below) central line. Investigate for cause.

Erratic behavior. Investigate.

PROCESS CAPABILITY

Process Capability Ratio (C_p)

$$C_p = \frac{\text{Upper Specification} - \text{Lower Specification}}{6\sigma} \qquad \text{(S6-13)}$$

Process Capability Index (C_{pk})

$$C_{pk} = \text{minimum of} \left[\frac{\text{Upper Specification Limit} - \overline{X}}{3\sigma}, \frac{\overline{X} - \text{Lower Specification Limit}}{3\sigma} \right] \qquad \text{(S6-14)}$$

where $\overline{X}$ = process mean
σ = standard deviation of the process population

Additional Practice Problem Space

FIGURE S6.8 ■ Meanings of C_{pk} Measures

A C_{pk} index of 1.0 indicates that the process variation is centered within the upper and lower control limits. As the C_{pk} index goes above 1, the process becomes increasingly target-oriented with fewer defects. If the C_{pk} is less than 1.0, the process will not produce within the specified tolerance.

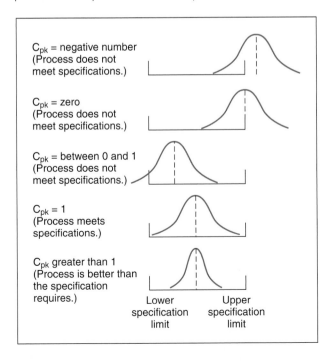

ACCEPTANCE SAMPLING

Operating Characteristic (OC) Curve

Producer's Risk

Consumer's Risk

Acceptable Quality Level (AQL)

Lot Tolerance Percent Defective (LTPD)

FIGURE S6.9 ■ An Operating Characteristic (OC) Curve Showing Producer's and Consumer's Risks

A good lot for this particular acceptance plan has less than or equal to 2% defectives. A bad lot has 7% or more defectives.

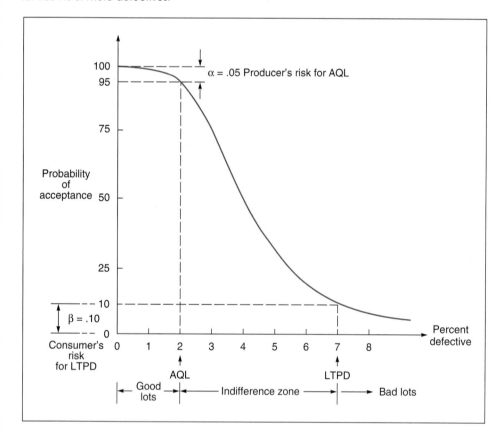

Average Outgoing Quality (AOQ)

$$AOQ = \frac{(P_d)(P_a)(N - n)}{N}$$

(S6-15)

where P_d = true percent defective of the lot

P_a = probability of accepting the lot

N = number of items in the lot

n = number of items in the sample

DISCUSSION QUESTIONS

1. List Shewhart's two types of variation. What are they also called?
2. Define "in statistical control."
3. Explain briefly what an $\bar{x}$-chart and an R-chart do.
4. What might cause a process to be out of control?
5. List five steps in developing and using $\bar{x}$-charts and R-charts.
6. List some possible causes of assignable variation.
7. Explain how a person using 2-sigma control charts will more easily find samples "out of bounds" than 3-sigma control charts. What are some possible consequences of this fact?
8. When is the desired mean, μ, used in establishing the centerline of a control chart instead of $\bar{\bar{x}}$?
9. Can a production process be labeled as "out of control" because it is too good? Explain.
10. In a control chart, what would be the effect on the control limits if the sample size varied from one sample to the next?
11. Define C_{pk} and explain what a C_{pk} of 1.0 means. What is C_p?
12. What does a run of 5 points above or below the centerline in a control chart imply?
13. What are the acceptable quality level (AQL) and the lot tolerance percent defective (LTPD)? How are they used?
14. What is a run test and when is it used?
15. Discuss the managerial issues regarding the use of control charts.
16. What is an OC curve?
17. What is the purpose of acceptance sampling?
18. What two risks are present when acceptance sampling is used?
19. Is a *capable* process a *perfect* process? That is, does a capable process generate only output that meets specifications? Explain.

ACTIVE MODEL EXERCISE

This Active Model appears on your CD. It allows you to evaluate important elements in the *p*-charts.

ACTIVE MODEL S6.1 ■

P-chart for the Arco Insurance Co. in Example S4 in Your Text

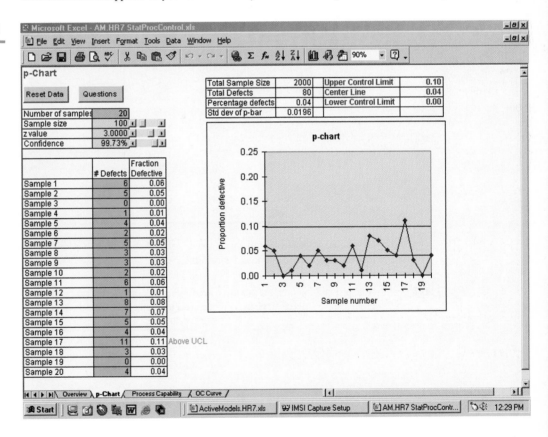

Questions

1. Has the process been in control?
2. Suppose we use a 95 percent *p*-chart. What are the upper and lower control limits? Has the process gotten more out of control?
3. Suppose that the sample size used was actually 120 instead of the 100 that it was supposed to be. How does this affect the chart?
4. What happens to the chart as we reduce the *z*-value?
5. What happens to the chart as we reduce the percentage?

PROBLEMS*

✗ . S6.1   Boxes of Organic Flakes are produced to contain 14 ounces, with a standard deviation of .1 ounce. Set up the 3-sigma $\bar{x}$-chart for a sample size of 36 boxes.

P✗ . S6.2   The overall average on a process you are attempting to monitor is 50 units. The process standard deviation is 1.72. Determine the upper and lower control limits for a mean chart, if you choose to use a sample size of 5. Set $z = 3$.

P✗ . S6.3   Thirty-five samples of size 7 each were taken from a fertilizer-bag-filling machine. The results were: Overall mean = 57.75 lb.; Average range = 1.78 lb.
   a) Determine the upper and lower control limits of the $\bar{x}$-chart.
   b) Determine the upper and lower control limits of the R-chart.

P✗ . S6.4   Food Storage Technologies produces refrigeration units for food producers and retail food establishments. The overall average temperature that these units maintain is 46° Fahrenheit. The average range is 2° Fahrenheit. Samples of 6 are taken to monitor the production process. Determine the upper and lower control limits for both a mean chart and a range chart for these refrigeration units.

P✗ . S6.5   Len Liter is attempting to monitor a filling process that has an overall average of 705 cc. The average range is 6 cc. If you use a sample size of 10, what are the upper and lower control limits for the mean and range?

P✗ : S6.6   Sampling 4 pieces of precision-cut wire (to be used in computer assembly) every hour for the past 24 hours has produced the following results:

HOUR	$\bar{x}$	R	HOUR	$\bar{x}$	R
1	3.25"	.71"	13	3.11"	.85"
2	3.10	1.18	14	2.83	1.31
3	3.22	1.43	15	3.12	1.06
4	3.39	1.26	16	2.84	.50
5	3.07	1.17	17	2.86	1.43
6	2.86	.32	18	2.74	1.29
7	3.05	.53	19	3.41	1.61
8	2.65	1.13	20	2.89	1.09
9	3.02	.71	21	2.65	1.08
10	2.85	1.33	22	3.28	.46
11	2.83	1.17	23	2.94	1.58
12	2.97	.40	24	2.64	.97

Develop appropriate control charts and determine whether there is any cause for concern in the cutting process. Plot the information and look for patterns.

P✗ : S6.7   Auto pistons (155 mm) are produced in a forging process, and the diameter is a critical factor that must be controlled. From sample sizes of 10 pistons produced each day, the mean and the range of this diameter have been as follows:

DAY	MEAN	RANGE
1	156.9	4.2
2	153.2	4.6
3	153.6	4.1
4	155.5	5.0
5	156.6	4.5

Construct the 3-sigma $\bar{x}$-chart and the 3-sigma R-chart for this dimension.

P✗ : S6.8   Small boxes of NutraFlakes cereal are labeled "net weight 10 ounces." Each hour, random samples of size $n = 4$ boxes are weighed to check process control. Five hours of observations yielded the following data:

Note: **P** means the problem may be solved with POM for Windows; **✗** means the problem may be solved with Excel OM; and **P✗** means the problem may be solved with POM for Windows and/or Excel OM.

		WEIGHTS		
TIME	BOX 1	BOX 2	BOX 3	BOX 4
9 A.M.	9.8	10.4	9.9	10.3
10 A.M.	10.1	10.2	9.9	9.8
11 A.M.	9.9	10.5	10.3	10.1
Noon	9.7	9.8	10.3	10.2
1 P.M.	9.7	10.1	9.9	9.9

a) Using these data, construct limits for $\bar{x}$- and R-charts (use Table S6.1 on page S6-5).
b) Is the process in control?
c) What other steps should the quality control department follow at this point?

: **S6.9** Whole Grains LLC uses statistical process control to ensure that its health-conscious, low-fat, multigrain sandwich loaves have the proper weight of 6 oz. Based on a previously stable and in-control process, the control limits of the $\bar{x}$- and R-charts are: $UCL_{\bar{x}} = 6.56$, $LCL_{\bar{x}} = 5.84$, $UCL_R = 1.141$, $LCL_R = 0$. Over the past few days, they have taken five random samples of four loaves each and have found the following:

		NET WEIGHT		
SAMPLE	LOAF #1	LOAF #2	LOAF #3	LOAF #4
1	6.3	6.0	5.9	5.9
2	6.0	6.0	6.3	5.9
3	6.3	4.8	5.6	5.2
4	6.2	6.0	6.2	5.9
5	6.5	6.6	6.5	6.9

Is the process still in control?

: **S6.10** A process that is considered to be in control measures an ingredient in ounces. Below are the last 10 samples (each of size $n = 5$) taken.

				SAMPLES					
1	2	3	4	5	6	7	8	9	10
10	9	13	10	12	10	10	13	8	10
9	9	9	10	10	10	11	10	8	12
10	11	10	11	9	8	10	8	12	9
9	11	10	10	11	12	8	10	12	8
12	10	9	10	10	9	9	8	9	12

a) What is the process standard deviation? What is $\sigma_{\bar{x}}$?
b) If $z = 3$, what are the control limits for the mean chart?
c) What are the control limits for the range chart?
d) Is the process in control?

P⨯ : S6.11 Twelve samples, each containing five parts, were taken from a process that produces steel rods which should measure 10 inches in length. The length of each rod in the samples was determined. The results were tabulated and sample means and ranges were computed. The results were:

SAMPLE	SAMPLE MEAN (IN.)	RANGE (IN.)
1	10.002	0.011
2	10.002	0.014
3	9.991	0.007
4	10.006	0.022
5	9.997	0.013
6	9.999	0.012
7	10.001	0.008
8	10.005	0.013
9	9.995	0.004
10	10.001	0.011
11	10.001	0.014
12	10.006	0.009

Determine the upper and lower control limits and the overall means for $\bar{x}$-charts and R-charts. Draw the chart and plot the values of the sample means and ranges. Do the data indicate a process that is in control? Why or why not?

P $\bar{x}$: **S6.12**   For the last 2 months, Pat LaPoint has been concerned about the number 5 machine at the West Factory. In order to make sure that the machine is operating correctly, samples are taken, and the average and range for each sample is computed. Each sample consists of 10 items produced from the machine. Recently 12 samples were taken and the sample range and average computed for each. The sample range and sample average were 1.1 and 46 for the first sample, 1.31 and 45 for the second, .91 and 46 for the third, and 1.1 and 47 for the fourth. After the fourth sample, the sample averages increased. For the fifth sample, the range was 1.21 and the average was 48; for number 6, it was .82 and 47; for number 7, it was .86 and 50; and for the eighth sample, it was 1.11 and 49. After the eighth sample, the sample average continued to increase, never getting below 50. For sample number 9, the range and average were 1.12 and 51; for number 10, they were .99 and 52; for number 11, they were .86 and 50; and for number 12, they were 1.2 and 52.

During installation, the supplier set an average of 47 for the process with an average range of 1.0. It was LaPoint's feeling that something was definitely wrong with machine number 5. Do you agree? (*Hint:* Use manufacturer's specifications to set the control limits. Run charts may be helpful.)

P $\bar{x}$. **S6.13**   The defect rate for data entry of insurance claims has historically been about 1.5%. What are the upper and lower control chart limits if you wish to use a sample size of 100 and 3-sigma limits?

P : **S6.14**   You are attempting to develop a quality monitoring system for some parts purchased from Warton & Kotha Manufacturing Co. These parts are either good or defective. You have decided to take a sample of 100 units. Develop a table of the appropriate upper and lower control chart limits for various values of the fraction defective in the sample taken. The values for p in this table should range from 0.02 to 0.10 in increments of 0.02. Develop the upper and lower control limits for a 99.73% confidence level.

n = 100		
P	UCL	LCL
0.02		
0.04		
0.06		
0.08		
0.10		

P $\bar{x}$: **S6.15**   The results of inspection of DNA samples taken over the past 10 days are given below. Sample size is 100.

DAY	DEFECTIVE
1	7
2	6
3	6
4	9
5	5
6	6
7	0
8	8
9	9
10	1

a)   Construct a 3-sigma p-chart using this information.
b)   If the number of defectives on the next three days are 12, 5, and 13, is the process in control?

P $\bar{x}$. **S6.16**   In the past, the defect rate for your product has been 1.5%. What are the upper and lower control chart limits if you wish to use a sample size of 500 and $z = 3$?

P $\bar{x}$. **S6.17**   Refer to Problem S6.16. If the defect rate was 3.5% instead of 1.5%, what would be the control limits ($z = 3$)?

P $\bar{x}$: **S6.18**   Refer to the Problems S6.16 and S6.17. Management would like to reduce the sample size to 100 units. If the past defect rate has been 3.5%, what would happen to the control limits ($z = 3$)? Should this action be taken? Explain your answer.

P $\bar{x}$: **S6.19**   Detroit Central Hospital is trying to improve its image by providing a positive experience for its patients and their relatives. Part of the "image" program involves providing tasty, inviting patient meals that are also healthy. A questionnaire accompanies each meal served, asking the patient, among other things, whether he or she is satisfied or unsatisfied with the meal. A 100-patient sample of the survey results over the past 7 days yielded the following data:

DAY	NO. OF UNSATISFIED PATIENTS	SAMPLE SIZE
1	24	100
2	22	100
3	8	100
4	15	100
5	10	100
6	26	100
7	17	100

Construct a *p*-chart that plots the percentage of patients unsatisfied with their meals. Set the control limits to include 99.73% of the random variation in meal satisfaction. Comment on your results.

S6.20 Chicago Supply Company manufactures paper clips and other office products. Although inexpensive, paper clips have provided the firm with a high margin of profitability. Samples of 200 are taken. Below are the results of the last 10 samples. Establish upper and lower control limits for the control chart and graph the data. Is the process in control?

Sample	1	2	3	4	5	6	7	8	9	10
Defectives	5	7	4	4	6	3	5	6	2	8

S6.21 Peter Ittig's department store, Ittig Brothers, is Amherst's largest independent clothier. The store receives an average of six returns per day. Using $z = 3$, would nine returns in a day warrant action?

S6.22 A random sample of 100 Modern Art dining room tables that came off the firm's assembly line is examined. Careful inspection reveals a total of 2,000 blemishes. What are the 99.73% upper and lower control limits for the number of blemishes? If one table had 42 blemishes, should any special action be taken?

S6.23 The school board is trying to evaluate a new math program introduced to second-graders in five elementary schools across the county this year. A sample of the student scores on standardized math tests in each elementary school yielded the following data:

SCHOOL	NO. OF TEST ERRORS
A	52
B	27
C	35
D	44
E	55

Construct a *c*-chart for test errors, and set the control limits to contain 99.73% of the random variation in test scores. What does the chart tell you? Has the new math program been effective?

S6.24 Telephone inquiries of 100 IRS "customers" are monitored daily at random. Incidents of incorrect information or other nonconformities (such as impoliteness to customers) are recorded. The data for last week are:

DAY	NO. OF NONCONFORMITIES
1	5
2	10
3	23
4	20
5	15

Construct a 3-standard deviation *c*-chart of nonconformities. What does the control chart tell you about the IRS telephone operators?

S6.25 The accounts receivable department at Rick Wing Manufacturing has been having difficulty getting customers to pay the full amount of their bills. Many customers complain that the bills are not correct and do not reflect the materials that arrived at their receiving docks. The department has decided to implement SPC in its billing process. In order to set up control charts, 10 samples of 50 bills each were taken over a month's time and the items on the bills checked against the bill of lading sent by the company's shipping department to determine the number of bills that were not correct. The results are shown in the table on the top of the next page.

SAMPLE NO.	NO. OF INCORRECT BILLS	SAMPLE NO.	NO. OF INCORRECT BILLS
1	6	6	5
2	5	7	3
3	11	8	4
4	4	9	7
5	0	10	2

a) Determine the value of p-bar, the mean fraction defective. Then determine the control limits for the p-chart using a 99.73% confidence level (3 standard deviations). Is this process in control? If not, which samples(s) were out of control?

b) How might you use the quality tools discussed in Chapter 6 to determine the source of the billing defects and where you might start your improvement efforts to eliminate the causes?

S6.26   The difference between the upper specification and the lower specification for a process is 0.6″. The standard deviation is 0.1″. What is the process capability ratio, C_p? Interpret this number.

S6.27   Meena Chavan Corp.'s computer chip production process yields DRAM chips with an average life of 1,800 hours and a $\sigma = 100$ hours. The tolerance upper and lower specification limits are 2,400 hours and 1,600 hours, respectively. Is this process capable of producing DRAM chips to specification?

S6.28   Blackburn, Inc., an equipment manufacturer in Nashville, has submitted a sample cutoff valve to improve your manufacturing process. Your process engineering department has conducted experiments and found that the valve has a mean (μ) of 8.00 and a standard deviation (σ) of .04. Your desired performance is $\mu = 8.0$ and $\sigma = .045$. What is the C_{pk} of the Blackburn valve?

S6.29   The specifications for a plastic liner for concrete highway projects calls for a thickness of 3.0 mm ±.1mm. The standard deviation of the process is estimated to be 0.02 mm. What are the upper and lower specification limits for this product? The process is known to operate at a mean thickness of 3.0 mm. What is the C_{pk} for this process? About what percentage of all units of this liner will meet specifications?

S6.30   The manager of a food processing plant desires a quality specification with a mean of 16 ounces, an upper specification limit of 16.5, and a lower specification limit of 15.5. The process has a standard deviation of 1 ounce. Determine the C_{pk} of the process.

S6.31   A process filling small bottles with baby formula has a target of 3 ounces ±0.150 ounces. Two-hundred bottles from the process were sampled. The results showed the average amount of formula placed in the bottles was 3.042 ounces. The standard deviation of the amounts was 0.034 ounces. Determine the value of C_{pk}. Roughly what proportion of bottles meets the specifications?

S6.32   In an acceptance sampling plan developed for lots containing 1,000 units, the sample size is 80 and c is 3. The percent defective of the incoming lots is 3%, and the probability of acceptance, which was obtained from an OC curve, is .79. What is the average outgoing quality?

S6.33   An acceptance sampling plan has lots of 500 units, a sample size of 60, and c is 2. The incoming lots have a percent defective of 4%, and the probability of acceptance, based on an OC curve, is .57. What is the AOQ?

S6.34   West Battery Corp. has recently been receiving complaints from retailers that its 9-volt batteries are not lasting as long as other name brands. James West, head of the TQM program at West's Austin plant, believes there is no problem because his batteries have had an average life of 50 hours, about 10% longer than competitors' models. To raise the lifetime above this level would require a new level of technology not available to West. Nevertheless, he is concerned enough to set up hourly assembly line checks. He decides to take size-5 samples of 9-volt batteries for each of the next 25 hours to create the standards for control chart limits (see the following table):

West Battery Data—Battery Lifetimes (in hours)

HOUR	SAMPLE 1	2	3	4	5	$\overline{X}$	R
1	51	50	49	50	50	50.0	2
2	45	47	70	46	36	48.8	34
3	50	35	48	39	47	43.8	15
4	55	70	50	30	51	51.2	40
5	49	38	64	36	47	46.8	28
6	59	62	40	54	64	55.8	24

(continued)

West Battery Data—Battery Lifetimes (in hours) (continued)

HOUR	SAMPLE					$\overline{X}$	R
	1	2	3	4	5		
7	36	33	49	48	56	44.4	23
8	50	67	53	43	40	50.6	27
9	44	52	46	47	44	46.6	8
10	70	45	50	47	41	50.6	29
11	57	54	62	45	36	50.8	26
12	56	54	47	42	62	52.2	20
13	40	70	58	45	44	51.4	30
14	52	58	40	52	46	49.6	18
15	57	42	52	58	59	53.6	17
16	62	49	42	33	55	48.2	29
17	40	39	49	59	48	47.0	20
18	64	50	42	57	50	52.6	22
19	58	53	52	48	50	52.2	10
20	60	50	41	41	50	48.4	19
21	52	47	48	58	40	49.0	18
22	55	40	56	49	45	49.0	16
23	47	48	50	50	48	48.6	3
24	50	50	49	51	51	50.2	2
25	51	50	51	51	62	53.0	12

With these limits in place, West now takes 5 more hours of data, which are shown in the following table:

HOUR	SAMPLE				
	1	2	3	4	5
26	48	52	39	57	61
27	45	53	48	46	66
28	63	49	50	45	53
29	57	70	45	52	61
30	45	38	46	54	52

a)   Is the manufacturing process in control?
b)   Comment on the lifetimes observed.

INTERNET HOMEWORK PROBLEMS

See our Internet home page at **www.prenhall.com/heizer** for these additional homework problems: S6.35 through S6.51.

CASE STUDY

Bayfield Mud Company

In November 2002, John Wells, a customer service representative of Bayfield Mud Company, was summoned to the Houston warehouse of Wet-Land Drilling, Inc., to inspect three boxcars of mud-treating agents that Bayfield had shipped to the Houston firm. (Bayfield's corporate offices and its largest plant are located in Orange, Texas, which is just west of the Louisiana–Texas border.) Wet-Land had filed a complaint that the 50-pound bags of treating agents just received from Bayfield were short-weight by approximately 5%.

The short-weight bags were initially detected by one of Wet-Land's receiving clerks, who noticed that the railroad scale tickets indicated that net weights were significantly less on all three boxcars than those of identical shipments received on October 25, 2002. Bayfield's traffic department was called to determine if lighter-weight pallets were used on the shipments. (This might explain the lighter net weights.) Bayfield indicated, however, that no changes had been made in loading or palletizing procedures. Thus, Wet-Land engineers randomly checked 50 bags and discovered that the average net weight was 47.51 pounds. They noted from past shipments that the process yielded bag net weights averaging exactly 50.0 pounds, with an acceptable standard deviation of 1.2 pounds. Consequently, they concluded that the sample indicated a significant short-weight. (The reader may wish to verify this conclusion.) Bayfield was then contacted, and Wells was sent to investigate the complaint. Upon arrival, Wells verified the complaint and issued a 5% credit to Wet-Land.

Wet-Land management, however, was not completely satisfied with the issuance of credit. The charts followed by their mud engineers on the drilling platforms were based on 50-pound bags of treating

Time	Average Weight (Pounds)	Range Smallest	Range Largest		Time	Average Weight (Pounds)	Range Smallest	Range Largest
6:00 A.M.	49.6	48.7	50.7		6:00	46.8	41.0	51.2
7:00	50.2	49.1	51.2		7:00	50.0	46.2	51.7
8:00	50.6	49.6	51.4		8:00	47.4	44.0	48.7
9:00	50.8	50.2	51.8		9:00	47.0	44.2	48.9
10:00	49.9	49.2	52.3		10:00	47.2	46.6	50.2
11:00	50.3	48.6	51.7		11:00	48.6	47.0	50.0
12 Noon	48.6	46.2	50.4		12 Midnight	49.8	48.2	50.4
1:00 P.M.	49.0	46.4	50.0		1:00 A.M.	49.6	48.4	51.7
2:00	49.0	46.0	50.6		2:00	50.0	49.0	52.2
3:00	49.8	48.2	50.8		3:00	50.0	49.2	50.0
4:00	50.3	49.2	52.7		4:00	47.2	46.3	50.5
5:00	51.4	50.0	55.3		5:00	47.0	44.1	49.7
6:00	51.6	49.2	54.7		6:00	48.4	45.0	49.0
7:00	51.8	50.0	55.6		7:00	48.8	44.8	49.7
8:00	51.0	48.6	53.2		8:00	49.6	48.0	51.8
9:00	50.5	49.4	52.4		9:00	50.0	48.1	52.7
10:00	49.2	46.1	50.7		10:00	51.0	48.1	55.2
11:00	49.0	46.3	50.8		11:00	50.4	49.5	54.1
12 Midnight	48.4	45.4	50.2		12 Noon	50.0	48.7	50.9
1:00 A.M.	47.6	44.3	49.7		1:00 P.M.	48.9	47.6	51.2
2:00	47.4	44.1	49.6		2:00	49.8	48.4	51.0
3:00	48.2	45.2	49.0		3:00	49.8	48.8	50.8
4:00	48.0	45.5	49.1		4:00	50.0	49.1	50.6
5:00	48.4	47.1	49.6		5:00	47.8	45.2	51.2
6:00	48.6	47.4	52.0		6:00	46.4	44.0	49.7
7:00	50.0	49.2	52.2		7:00	46.4	44.4	50.0
8:00	49.8	49.0	52.4		8:00	47.2	46.6	48.9
9:00	50.3	49.4	51.7		9:00	48.4	47.2	49.5
10:00	50.2	49.6	51.8		10:00	49.2	48.1	50.7
11:00	50.0	49.0	52.3		11:00	48.4	47.0	50.8
12 Noon	50.0	48.8	52.4		12 Midnight	47.2	46.4	49.2
1:00 P.M.	50.1	49.4	53.6		1:00 A.M.	47.4	46.8	49.0
2:00	49.7	48.6	51.0		2:00	48.8	47.2	51.4
3:00	48.4	47.2	51.7		3:00	49.6	49.0	50.6
4:00	47.2	45.3	50.9		4:00	51.0	50.5	51.5
5:00	46.8	44.1	49.0		5:00	50.5	50.0	51.9

agents. Lighter-weight bags might result in poor chemical control during the drilling operation and thus adversely affect drilling efficiency. (Mud-treating agents are used to control the pH and other chemical properties of the cone during drilling operation.) This defect could cause severe economic consequences because of the extremely high cost of oil and natural gas well-drilling operations. Consequently, special-use instructions had to accompany the delivery of these shipments to the drilling platforms. Moreover, the short-weight shipments had to be isolated in Wet-Land's warehouse, causing extra handling and poor space utilization. Thus, Wells was informed that Wet-Land might seek a new supplier of mud-treating agents if, in the future, it received bags that deviated significantly from 50 pounds.

The quality control department at Bayfield suspected that the lightweight bags may have resulted from "growing pains" at the Orange plant. Because of the earlier energy crisis, oil and natural gas exploration activity had greatly increased. In turn, this increased activity created increased demand for products produced by related industries, including drilling muds. Consequently, Bayfield had to expand from a one-shift (6:00 A.M. to 2:00 P.M.) to a two-shift (2:00 P.M. to 10:00 P.M.) operation in mid-2000, and finally to a three-shift operation (24 hours per day) in the fall of 2002.

The additional night-shift bagging crew was staffed entirely by new employees. The most experienced foremen were temporarily assigned to supervise the night-shift employees. Most emphasis was placed on increasing the output of bags to meet ever increasing demand. It was suspected that only occasional reminders were made to double-check the bag weight-feeder. (A double-check is performed by systematically weighing a bag on a scale to determine if the proper weight is being loaded by the weight-feeder. If there is significant deviation from 50 pounds, corrective adjustments are made to the weight-release mechanism.)

To verify this expectation, the quality control staff randomly sampled the bag output and prepared the chart above. Six bags were sampled and weighed each hour.

Discussion Questions

1. What is your analysis of the bag-weight problem?
2. What procedures would you recommend to maintain proper quality control?

Source: Professor Jerry Kinard, Western Carolina University.

CASE STUDY

Alabama Airlines' On-Time Schedule

Alabama Airlines opened its doors in December 2001 as a commuter service with its headquarters and only hub located in Birmingham. A product of airline deregulation, Alabama Air joined the growing number of short-haul, point-to-point airlines, including Lone Star, Comair, Atlantic Southeast and Skywest.

Alabama Air was started and managed by two former pilots, David Douglas (who had been with now-defunct Midway Airlines) and Michael Hanna (formerly with Continental). It acquired a fleet of 12 used prop-jet planes and the airport gates vacated by Delta Airlines in 2001 when it curtailed flights due to the terrorist attacks of 9-11.

One of Alabama Air's top competitive priorities is on-time arrivals. The airline defines "on-time" to mean any arrival that is within 20 minutes of the scheduled time.

Mike Hanna decided to personally monitor Alabama Air's performance. Each week for the past 30 weeks, Hanna checked a random sample of 100 flight arrivals for on-time performance. The table that follows contains the number of flights that did not meet Alabama Air's definition of on-time:

SAMPLE (WEEK)	LATE FLIGHTS	SAMPLE (WEEK)	LATE FLIGHTS
1	2	16	2
2	4	17	3
3	10	18	7
4	4	19	3
5	1	20	2
6	1	21	3
7	13	22	7
8	9	23	4
9	11	24	3
10	0	25	2
11	3	26	2
12	4	27	0
13	2	28	1
14	2	29	3
15	8	30	4

Discussion Questions

1. Using a 95% confidence level, plot the overall percentage of late flights (p) and the upper and lower control limits on a control chart.
2. Assume that the airline industry's upper and lower control limits for flights that are not on-time are .1000 and .0400, respectively. Draw them on your control chart.
3. Plot the percentage of late flights in each sample. Do all samples fall within Alabama Airlines' control limits? When one falls outside the control limits, what should be done?
4. What can Mike Hanna report about the quality of service?

Chapter 7

Process Strategy

A process strategy is an organization's approach to transforming resources into goods and services. The objective of a process strategy is to find a way to produce goods and services that meet customer requirements and product specifications within cost and other managerial constraints. This is typically done in one of four ways: (1) process focus, (2) repetitive focus, (3) product focus, and (4) mass customization. In this chapter we examine these four processes and the issues connected with their design.

BEFORE COMING TO CLASS, READ CHAPTER 7 IN YOUR TEXT AND ANSWER THESE QUESTIONS.

1. What are the differences between the four process strategies? _____

_____

_____

2. What are the differences between flow diagrams and time-function mapping? _____

_____

_____

3. What is service blueprinting? _____

_____

_____

4. What is computer-integrated manufacturing (CIM)? _____

_____

_____

5. What is a flexible manufacturing system (FMS)? _____

_____

_____

6. What operations changes are occurring in service processes? _____

_____

FOUR PROCESS STRATEGIES

Process Focus

Repetitive Focus

Product Focus

Mass Customization Focus

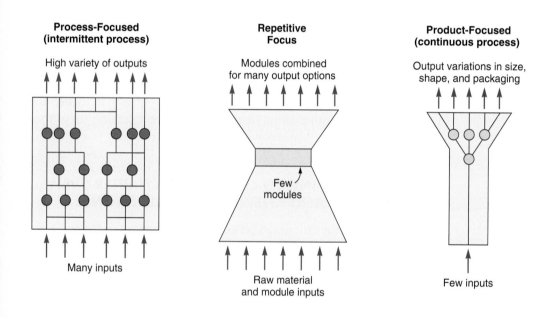

FIGURE 7.1 ■ Process Selected Must Fit with Volume and Variety

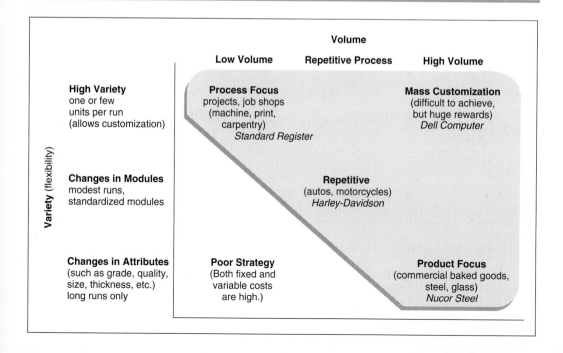

Crossover Charts

PRACTICE PROBLEM 7.1 ■ Crossover Chart Calculations

Taggert Custom Machine Shop has a contract for 130,000 units of a new product. James Taggert, the owner, has calculated the cost for three process alternatives. Which process should he choose for this new contract?

	GENERAL PURPOSE EQUIPMENT (GPE)	FLEXIBLE MANUFACTURING (FMS)	DEDICATED AUTOMATION (DA)
Fixed Costs	$150,000	$350,000	$950,000
Variable Costs	$10	$8	$6

PRACTICE PROBLEM 7.2 ■ Crossover Chart Graph

Solve Practice Problem 7.1 graphically.

PRACTICE PROBLEM 7.3 ■ Crossover Points

Using either your analytical solution found in Practice Problem 7.1 or the graphical solution found in Practice Problem 7.2, identify the volume ranges where each process should be used.

PRACTICE PROBLEM 7.4 ■ Crossover Analysis

If Taggert Custom Machine is able to convince the customer to renew the contract for another 1 or 2 years, what implications does this have for James Taggert's decision?

Additional Practice Problem Space

PROCESS ANALYSIS AND DESIGN

Flow Diagrams

Time-Function Mapping

Process Charts

Service Blueprinting

SERVICE PROCESS DESIGN

FIGURE 7.10 ■ Operation Changes within the Service Process Matrix

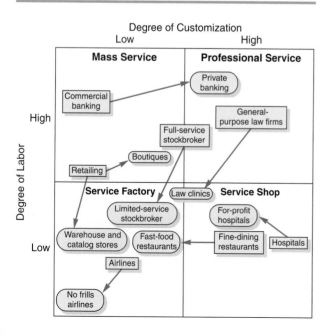

SELECTION OF EQUIPMENT AND TECHNOLOGY

PRODUCTION TECHNOLOGY

1. Computer Numeric Control (CNC)

2. Automatic Identification System (AIS)

3. Process Control

4. Vision Systems

5. Robots

6. Automated Storage and Retrieval System (ASRS)

7. Automated Guided Vehicle (AGV)

8. Flexible Manufacturing System (FMS)

9. Computer Integrated Manufacturing (CIM)

FIGURE 7.11 ■ Computer-Integrated Manufacturing (CIM)

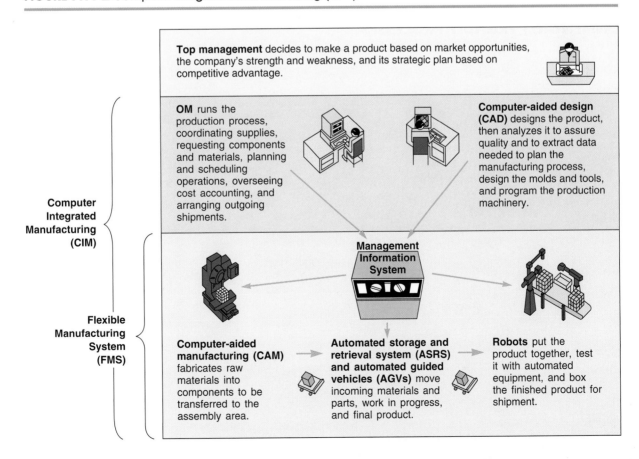

TECHNOLOGY IN SERVICES

PROCESS REENGINEERING

ENVIRONMENTALLY FRIENDLY PROCESSES

DISCUSSION QUESTIONS

1. What is process strategy?
2. What type of process is used for making each of the following products?
   - (a) beer
   - (b) wedding invitations
   - (c) automobiles
   - (d) paper
   - (e) "Big Macs"
   - (f) custom homes
   - (g) motorcycles
3. What is service blueprinting?
4. What is process reengineering?
5. What are the techniques to improve service productivity?
6. Name the four quadrants of the service process matrix. Discuss how the matrix is used to classify services into categories.
7. What is CIM?
8. What do we mean by a process control system and what are the typical elements in such systems?
9. Identify *manufacturing* firms that compete on each of the four processes shown in Figure 7.1 on page 7-2.
10. Identify the competitive advantage of each of the four firms identified in discussion question 9.
11. Identify *service* firms that compete on each of the four processes shown in Figure 7.1.
12. Identify the competitive advantage of each of the four firms identified in discussion question 11.
13. What are numerically controlled machines?
14. Describe briefly what an automatic identification system (AIS) is and how service organizations could use AIS to increase productivity and at the same time increase the variety of services offered.
15. Name some of the advances being made in technology that enhance production and productivity.
16. Explain what a flexible manufacturing system (FMS) is.
17. In what ways do CAD and FMS connect?

CRITICAL THINKING EXERCISE

For the sake of efficiency and lower costs, Premium Standard Farms of Princeton, Missouri, has turned pig production into a standardized product-focused process. Slaughterhouses have done this for a hundred years—but after the animal was dead. Doing it while the animal is alive is a relatively recent innovation. Here is how it works.

Impregnated female sows wait for 40 days in metal stalls so small that they cannot turn around. After an ultrasound test, they wait 67 days in a sim-

ilar stall until they give birth. Two weeks after delivering 10 or 11 piglets, the sows are moved back to breeding rooms for another cycle. After 3 years, the sow is slaughtered. Animal-welfare advocates say such confinement drives pigs crazy. Premium Standard replies that its hogs are in fact comfortable, arguing that only 1% die before Premium Standard wants them to.

Discuss the productivity and ethical implications of this industry and these two divergent opinions.

ACTIVE MODEL EXERCISE

This Active Model appears on your CD-ROM. It allows you to evaluate important elements in the crossover chart in Example 4 in your text.

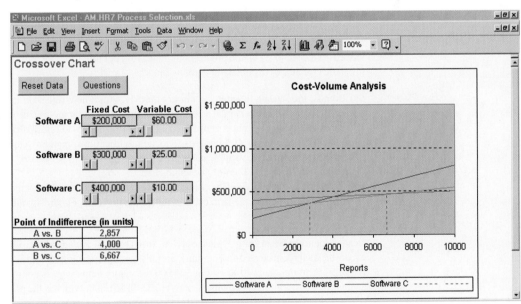

ACTIVE MODEL 7.1 ■

Crossover Chart Illustration of Example 4's Three Software Products

Questions

1. Suppose that Kleber Enterprises wants to lower the point of indifference between Software A and Software B to 2000 units. What would the fixed costs need to be for software B?
2. Examine the graph. If the expected volume is 1,500 reports, which process should be used?
3. Examine the graph. If the expected volume is 15,000 reports, which process should be used?
4. As the fixed costs for developing software B drop, what happens to the graph?

PROBLEMS

7.1   Prepare a flow diagram for one of the following:
a)   The registration process at a school.
b)   The process at the local car wash.
c)   A shoe shine.
d)   Some other process with the approval of the instructor.

7.2   Prepare a process chart for one of the activities in Problem 7.1.

7.3   Prepare a time-function map for one of the activities in Problem 7.1.

7.4   Prepare a service blueprint for one of the activities in Problem 7.1.

7.5   Meile Machine Shop, Inc., has a 1-year contract for the production of 200,000 gear housings for a new off-road vehicle. Owner Larry Meile hopes the contract will be extended and the volume increased next year. Meile has developed costs for three alternatives. They are general-purpose equipment (GPE), flexible manufacturing system (FMS), and expensive, but efficient, dedicated machine (DM). The cost data follow:

	GENERAL-PURPOSE EQUIPMENT (GPE)	FLEXIBLE MANUFACTURING SYSTEM (FMS)	DEDICATED MACHINE (DM)
Annual contracted units	300,000	300,000	300,000
Annual fixed cost	$100,000	$200,000	$500,000
Per unit variable cost	$ 15.00	$ 14.00	$ 13.00

Which process is best for this contract?

7.6   Using the data in Problem 7.5, determine the economical volume for each process.

7.7   Using the data in Problem 7.5, determine the best process for each of the following volumes: (1) 75,000, (2) 275,000, and (3) 375,000.

7.8   Refer to Problem 7.5. If a contract for the second and third years is pending, what are the implications for process selection?

7.9   Stan Fawcett's company is considering producing a gear assembly that it now purchases from Salt Lake Supply, Inc. Salt Lake Supply charges $4 per unit with a minimum order of 3,000 units. Stan estimates that it will cost $15,000 to set up the process and then $1.82 per unit for labor and materials. Either choice would have the same cost at approximately how many units?

7.10   Ski Boards, Inc., wants to enter the market quickly with a new finish on its ski boards. It has three choices: (a) refurbish the old equipment at a cost of $800, (b) make major modifications at the cost of $1,100, or (c) purchase new equipment at a net cost of $1,800. If the firm chooses to refurbish the equipment, materials and labor would be $1.10 per board. If it chooses to make modifications, materials and labor would be $0.70 per board. If it buys new equipment, variable costs are estimated to be $.40 per board.
a)   Graph the three total cost lines on the same chart.
b)   Which alternative should Ski Boards, Inc., choose if it thinks it could sell more than 3,000 boards.
c)   Which alternative should the firm use if it thinks the market for boards would be between 1,000 and 2,000?

7.11   Susan Meyer, owner/manager of Meyer's Motor Court in Key West, is considering outsourcing the daily room cleanup for her motel to Duffy's Maid Service. Susan rents an average of 50 rooms for each of 365 nights (365×50 equals the total rooms rented for the year). Susan's cost to clean a room is $12.50. The Duffy's Maid Service quote is $18.50 per room plus a fixed cost of $25,000 for sundry items such as uniforms with the motel's name. Susan's annual fixed cost for space, equipment, and supplies is $61,000. Which is the preferred process for Susan, and why?

7.12   Keith Whittingham, as manager of Designs by Whittingham, is upgrading his CAD software. The high performance software (HP) rents for $3,000 per month per workstation. The standard performance software (SP) rents for $2,000 per month per workstation. The productivity figures that he has available suggest that the HP software is faster for his kind of design. Therefore, with the HP software he will need five engineers and with the SP software he will need six. This translates into a variable cost of $200 per drawing for the HP system and $240 per drawing for the SP system. At his projected volume of 80 drawings per month, which system should he rent?

CASE STUDY

Rochester Manufacturing Corporation

Rochester Manufacturing Corporation (RMC) is considering moving some of its production from traditional numerically controlled machines to a flexible machining system (FMS). Its numerical control machines have been operating in a high-variety, low-volume, intermittent manner. Machine utilization, as near as it can determine, is hovering around 10%. The machine tool salespeople and a consulting firm want to put the machines together in an FMS. They believe that a $3,000,000 expenditure on machinery and the transfer machines will handle about 30% of RMC's work. There will, of course, be transition and start-up costs in addition to this.

The firm has not yet entered all its parts into a comprehensive group technology system, but believes that the 30% is a good estimate of products suitable for the FMS. This 30% should fit very nicely into a "family." A reduction, because of higher utilization, should take place in the number of pieces of machinery. The firm should be able to go from 15 to about 4 machines and personnel should go from 15 to perhaps as low as 3. Similarly, floor space reduction will go from 20,000 square feet to about 6,000. Throughput of orders should also improve with this family of parts being processed in 1 to 2 days rather than 7 to 10. Inventory reduction is estimated to yield a one-time $750,000 savings, and annual labor savings should be in the neighborhood of $300,000.

Although the projections all look very positive, an analysis of the project's return on investment showed it to be between 10% and 15% per year. The company has traditionally had an expectation that projects should yield well over 15% and have payback periods of substantially less than 5 years.

Discussion Questions

1. As a production manager for RMC, what do you recommend? Why?
2. Prepare a case by a conservative plant manager for maintaining the status quo until the returns are more obvious.
3. Prepare the case for an optimistic sales manager that you should move ahead with the FMS now.

VIDEO CASE STUDY

Process Strategy at Wheeled Coach

Wheeled Coach, based in Winter Park, Florida, is the world's largest manufacturer of ambulances. Working four 10-hour days, 350 employees make only custom-made ambulances: Virtually every vehicle is different. Wheeled Coach accommodates the marketplace by providing a wide variety of options and an engineering staff accustomed to innovation and custom design. Continuing growth, which now requires that more than 20 ambulances roll off the assembly line each week, makes process design a continuing challenge. Wheeled Coach's response has been to build a focused factory: Wheeled Coach builds nothing but ambulances. Within the focused factory, Wheeled Coach established work cells for every major module feeding an assembly line, including aluminum bodies, electrical wiring harnesses, interior cabinets, windows, painting, and upholstery.

Labor standards drive the schedule so that every work cell feeds the assembly line on schedule, just-in-time for installations. The chassis, usually that of a Ford truck, moves to a station at which the aluminum body is mounted. Then the vehicle is moved to painting. Following a custom paint job, it moves to the assembly line, where it will spend 7 days. During each of these 7 workdays, each work cell delivers its respective module to the appropriate position on the assembly line. During the first day, electrical wiring is installed; on the second day, the unit moves forward to the station at which cabinetry is delivered and installed, then to a window and lighting station, on to upholstery, to fit and finish, to further customizing, and finally to inspection and road testing. The *Global Company Profile* featuring Wheeled Coach (which opens Chapter 14) provides further details about this process.

Discussion Questions*

1. Why do you think major auto manufacturers do not build ambulances?
2. What is an alternative process strategy to the assembly line that Wheeled Coach currently uses?
3. Why is it more efficient for the work cells to prepare "modules" and deliver them to the assembly line than it would be to produce the component (e.g., interior upholstery) on the line?
4. How does Wheeled Coach determine what tasks are to be performed at each work station?

*You may wish to view this video case on your CD-ROM before addressing these questions.

Capacity Planning

Effective utilization of facilities is an important component of process efficiency and hence the operations manager's job. And effective utilization of facilities depends on both capacity being appropriate to demand (a long-run operations decision) and good short- and intermediate-range operations planning.

Capacity is the "throughput," or number of units a facility can hold, receive, store, or produce in a period of time. Operations managers must deal with the capacity design, effectiveness, utilization, and efficiency. Break-even analysis helps define the minimum necessary capacity. Decision trees provide expected monetary value, and net present value determines the discounted value of future cash flows.

BEFORE COMING TO CLASS, READ SUPPLEMENT 7 IN YOUR TEXT AND ANSWER THESE QUESTIONS.

1. Define capacity._____

_____

_____

2. What is effective capacity?_____

_____

_____

3. What are fixed and variable costs? _____

_____

_____

4. What is the purpose of net present value analysis? _____

_____

_____

5. What is meant by "break-even point"? _____

_____

_____

6. How do we define efficiency in regard to capacity? _____

_____

_____

CAPACITY

FIGURE S7.1 ■ Types of Planning over a Time Horizon

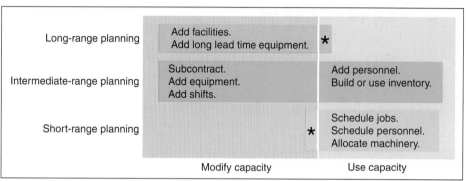

*Limited options exist.

Design Capacity

Effective Capacity

Utilization

Efficiency

Utilization = Actual output/Design capacity   (S7-1)

Efficiency = Actual output/Effective capacity   (S7-2)

Actual (or expected) output = (Effective capacity)(Efficiency)   (S7-3)

PRACTICE PROBLEM S7.1 ■ Utilization, Efficiency, and Output

The design capacity for engine repair in our company is 80 trucks per day. The effective capacity is 40 engines per day, and the actual output is 36 engines per day. Calculate the utilization and efficiency of the operation. If the efficiency for next month is expected to be 82%, what is the expected output?

Additional Practice Problem Space

Capacity Considerations

Managing Demand

CAPACITY PLANNING

FIGURE S7.4 ■ Approaches to Capacity Expansion

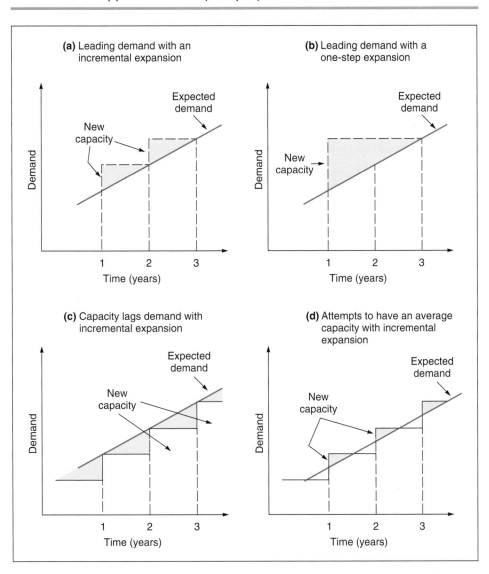

BREAK-EVEN ANALYSIS

$$\text{Break-even in units} = \frac{\text{Total fixed cost}}{\text{Price} - \text{Variable cost}} \qquad \text{(S7-4)}$$

$$\text{Break-even in dollars} = \frac{\text{Total fixed cost}}{1 - \dfrac{\text{Variable cost}}{\text{Selling price}}} \qquad \text{(S7-5)}$$

PRACTICE PROBLEM S7.2 ■ Break Even

Given: F = fixed cost = \$1,000
V = variable cost = \$2/unit
P = selling price = \$4/unit

Find the break-even point in dollars and in units.

PRACTICE PROBLEM S7.3 ■ Break-Even Chart

Develop a break-even chart for Practice Problem S7.2.

PRACTICE PROBLEM S7.4 ■ Break-Even

Jack's Grocery is manufacturing a "store brand" item that has a variable cost of $0.75 per unit and a selling price of $1.25 per unit. Fixed costs are $12,000. Current volume is 50,000 units. The grocery can substantially improve the product quality by adding a new piece of equipment at an additional fixed cost of $5,000. Variable cost would increase to $1, but volume should increase to 70,000 units due to the higher quality product. Should the company buy the new equipment?

PRACTICE PROBLEM S7.5 ■ Break-Even Points

What are the break-even points (dollars and units) for the two processes considered in Practice Problem S7.4?

PRACTICE PROBLEM S7.6 ■ Break-Even Chart

Develop a break-even chart for Practice Problem S7.4.

Additional Practice Problem Space

APPLYING DECISION TREES TO CAPACITY DECISIONS

Additional Practice Problem Space

STRATEGY-DRIVEN INVESTMENTS

Net Present Value

$$F = P(1 + i)^N \qquad \text{(S7-7)}$$

$$P = \frac{F}{(1 + i)^N} \qquad \text{(S7-8)}$$

$$P = \frac{F}{(1 + i)^N} = FX \qquad \text{(S7-9)}$$

where F = future value (such as $110.25 or $105)
  P = present value (such as $100.00)
  i = interest rate (such as .05)
  N = number of years (such as 1 year or 2 years)

TABLE S7.1 ■ Present Value of $1

YEAR	5%	6%	7%	8%	9%	10%	12%	14%
1	.952	.943	.935	.926	.917	.909	.893	.877
2	.907	.890	.873	.857	.842	.826	.797	.769
3	.864	.840	.816	.794	.772	.751	.712	.675
4	.823	.792	.763	.735	.708	.683	.636	.592
5	.784	.747	.713	.681	.650	.621	.567	.519
6	.746	.705	.666	.630	.596	.564	.507	.456
7	.711	.665	.623	.583	.547	.513	.452	.400
8	.677	.627	.582	.540	.502	.467	.404	.351
9	.645	.592	.544	.500	.460	.424	.361	.308
10	.614	.558	.508	.463	.422	.386	.322	.270
15	.481	.417	.362	.315	.275	.239	.183	.140
20	.377	.312	.258	.215	.178	.149	.104	.073

TABLE S7.2 ■ Present Value of an Annuity of $1

YEAR	5%	6%	7%	8%	9%	10%	12%	14%
1	.952	.943	.935	.926	.917	.909	.893	.877
2	1.859	1.833	1.808	1.783	1.759	1.736	1.690	1.647
3	2.723	2.673	2.624	2.577	2.531	2.487	2.402	2.322
4	3.546	3.465	3.387	3.312	3.240	3.170	3.037	2.914
5	4.329	4.212	4.100	3.993	3.890	3.791	3.605	3.433
6	5.076	4.917	4.766	4.623	4.486	4.355	4.111	3.889
7	5.786	5.582	5.389	5.206	5.033	4.868	4.564	4.288
8	6.463	6.210	5.971	5.747	5.535	5.335	4.968	4.639
9	7.108	6.802	6.515	6.247	5.985	5.759	5.328	4.946
10	7.722	7.360	7.024	6.710	6.418	6.145	5.650	5.216
15	10.380	9.712	9.108	8.559	8.060	7.606	6.811	6.142
20	12.462	11.470	10.594	9.818	9.128	8.514	7.469	6.623

PRACTICE PROBLEM S7.7 ■ Present Value

Good news! You are going to receive $6,000 in each of the next 5 years for sale of used machinery. In the meantime, a bank is willing to lend you the present value of the money at a discount of 10% per year. How much cash do you receive now?

DISCUSSION QUESTIONS

1. Distinguish between design capacity and effective capacity.
2. What are the assumptions of break-even analysis?
3. Where does the manager obtain data for break-even analysis?
4. What keeps plotted revenue data from falling on a straight line when doing break-even analysis?
5. Under what conditions would a firm want its capacity to lag demand? To lead demand?

6. Explain how net present value is an appropriate tool for comparing investments.
7. What is effective capacity?
8. What is efficiency?
9. How is actual, or expected, output computed?

ACTIVE MODEL EXERCISE

This Active Model appears on your CD-ROM. It allows you to evaluate important elements in a break-even analysis.

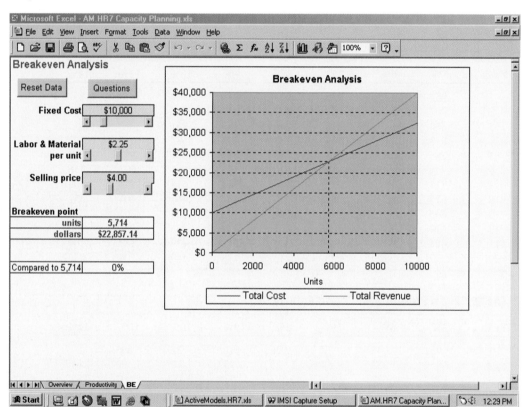

ACTIVE MODEL S7.2 ■

Break-even Analysis for Jimmy Stephens, Inc. Using Data in Example S3 in Your Text

Questions

1. Use the scrollbars to determine what happens to the break-even point as the fixed costs increase. Do the variable costs increase? Does the selling price increase?
2. What is the percentage increase (over 5,714) to the break-even point if the fixed costs increase by 10 percent to $11,000? If the variable costs increase by 10 percent to $2.48? If the price per unit increases by 10 percent to $4.40?
3. In order to cut the break-even point in half, by how much would the fixed costs have to decrease? The variable costs? How much would the selling price have to increase?

PROBLEMS*

· **S7.1**   If a plant was designed to produce 7,000 hammers per day, but is limited to making 6,000 hammers per day because of the time needed to change equipment between styles of hammers, what is the utilization?

*Note: **P** means the problem may be solved with POM for Windows; ✖ means the problem may be solved with Excel OM; and **P✖** means the problem may be solved with POM for Windows and/or Excel OM.

· S7.2   For the past month, the plant in Problem S7.1, which has an effective capacity of 6,500, has made only 4,500 hammers per day because of material delay, employee absences, and other problems. What is its efficiency?

· S7.3   If a plant has an effective capacity of 6,500 and an efficiency of 88%, what is the actual (planned) output?

· S7.4   A plant has an effective capacity of 900 units per day and produces 800 units per day with its product mix; what is its efficiency?

· S7.5   Material delays have routinely limited production of household sinks to 400 units per day. If the plant efficiency is 80%, what is the effective capacity?

: S7.6   What is the expected output for a plant with a design capacity of 108 chairs per day, if its effective capacity is 90 chairs and its efficiency is 90%?

· S7.7   A work center operates 2 shifts per day 5 days per week (8 hours per shift) and has 4 machines of equal capability. This is the effective capacity. If the work center has a system efficiency of 95%, what is the expected output in hours per week?

· S7.8   The effective capacity and efficiency for the next quarter at MMU Mfg. in Waco, Texas, for each of three departments are shown.

DEPARTMENT	EFFECTIVE CAPACITY	RECENT EFFICIENCY
Design	93,600	.95
Fabrication	156,000	1.03
Finishing	62,400	1.05

Compute the expected production for next quarter for each department.

Px S7.9   Eye Associates, which runs an optical lab, experienced substantial growth over the last decade. It purchased additional increments of lens-grinding equipment in relatively small units. Prior analysis of its data (since its growth has been steady and constant) suggests that regression analysis (as described in Chapter 4 in your text) is adequate to determine its capacity demands. Data for the past decade follow:

YEAR	1993	1994	1995	1996	1997	1998	1999	2000	2001	2002
Units Produced (in thousands)	15.0	15.5	16.25	16.75	16.9	17.24	17.5	17.3	17.75	18.1

a)   Determine the firm's capacity needs in units for 2003, 2005, and 2009.
b)   If each machine is capable of producing 2,500 lenses, how many machines should it expect to have in 2007?

· S7.10   Assume that in 2003, Eye Associates (Problem S7.9) has 8 machines, each capable of producing 2,500 lenses per year. However, the new and best machine then on the market has the capability of producing 5,000 per year.
a)   What is the status of capacity at the firm in the year 2009 if it buys the new and best machine in 2003?
b)   What is the status of capacity at the firm in the year 2009 if it buys in 2003 the standard machine with a capacity of 2,500?

: S7.11   Southeastern Oklahoma State University's business program has the facilities and faculty to handle an enrollment of 2,000 students per semester. However, in an effort to limit class sizes to a "reasonable" level (under 200, generally), Southeastern's dean, Tom Choi, placed a ceiling on enrollment of 1,500 students. Although there was ample demand for business courses last semester, conflicting schedules allowed only 1,450 students to take business courses. What are the utilization and efficiency of this system?

Px S7.12   Markland Manufacturing intends to increase capacity by overcoming a bottleneck operation through the addition of new equipment. Two vendors have presented proposals. The fixed costs for proposal A are $50,000, and for proposal B, $70,000. The variable cost for A is $12.00, and for B, $10.00. The revenue generated by each unit is $20.00.
a)   What is the break-even point in units for proposal A?
b)   What is the break-even point in units for proposal B?

Px S7.13   Using the data in Problem S7.12:
a)   What is the break-even point in dollars for proposal A if you add $10,000 installation to the fixed cost?
b)   What is the break-even point in dollars for proposal B if you add $10,000 installation to the fixed cost?

Px S7.14   Given the data in Problem S7.12, at what volume (units) of output would the two alternatives yield the same profit?

: S7.15   Janelle Heinke, the owner of Ha'Peppas!, is considering a new oven in which to bake the firm's signature dish, vegetarian pizza. Oven type A can handle 20 pizzas an hour. The fixed costs associated with oven A are $20,000 and the variable costs are $2.00 per pizza. Oven B is larger and can handle 40 pizzas an hour. The fixed costs associated with oven B are $30,000 and the variable costs are $1.25 per pizza. The pizzas sell for $14 each.

a)   What is the break-even point for each oven?
b)   If the owner expects to sell 9,000 pizzas, which oven should she purchase?
c)   If the owner expects to sell 12,000 pizzas, which oven should she purchase?
d)   At what volume should Janelle switch ovens?

Px . S7.16   Given the following data, calculate $BEP(x)$, $BEP(\$)$, and the profit at 100,000 units:

$$P = \$8/unit \quad V = \$4/unit \quad F = \$50,000$$

Px : S7.17   You are considering opening a copy service in the student union. You estimate your fixed cost at $15,000 and the variable cost of each copy sold at $.01. You expect the selling price to average $.05.

a)   What is the break-even point in dollars?
b)   What is the break-even point in units?

Px : S7.18   Dr. Aleda Roth, a prolific author, is considering starting her own publishing company. She will call it DSI Publishing, Inc. DSI's estimated costs are

Fixed	$250,000.00
Variable cost per book	$20.00
Selling price per book	$30.00

How many books must DSI sell to break even? What is its break-even point in dollars?

Px : S7.19   In addition to the costs in Problem S7.18, Dr. Roth wants to pay herself a salary of $75,000 per year.

a)   Now what is her break-even point in units?
b)   What is her break-even point in dollars?

Px : S7.20   An electronics firm is currently manufacturing an item that has a variable cost of $.50 per unit and a selling price of $1.00 per unit. Fixed costs are $14,000. Current volume is 30,000 units. The firm can substantially improve the product quality by adding a new piece of equipment at an additional fixed cost of $6,000. Variable cost would increase to $.60, but volume should jump to 50,000 units due to a higher-quality product. Should the company buy the new equipment?

Px : S7.21   The electronics firm in Problem S7.20 is now considering the new equipment and increasing the selling price to $1.10 per unit. With the higher-quality product, the new volume is expected to be 45,000 units. Under these circumstances, should the company purchase the new equipment and increase the selling price?

Px : S7.22   Zan Azlett and Angela Zesiger have joined forces to start A&Z Lettuce Products, a processor of packaged shredded lettuce for institutional use. Zan has years of food processing experience, and Angela has extensive commercial food preparation experience. The process will consist of opening crates of lettuce and then sorting, washing, slicing, preserving, and finally packaging the prepared lettuce. Together, with help from vendors, they feel they can adequately estimate demand, fixed costs, revenues, and variable cost per 5-pound bag of lettuce. They think a largely manual process will have monthly fixed costs of $37,500 and variable costs of $1.75 per bag. A more mechanized process will have fixed costs of $75,000 per month with variable costs of $1.25 per 5-pound bag. They expect to sell the shredded lettuce for $2.50 per 5-pound bag.

a)   What is the break-even quantity for the manual process?
b)   What is the revenue at the break-even quantity for the mechanized process?
c)   What is the break-even quantity for the mechanized process?
d)   What is the revenue at the break-even quantity?
e)   What is the monthly profit or loss of the *manual* process if they expect to sell 60,000 bags of lettuce per month?
f)   What is the monthly profit or loss of the *mechanized* process if they expect to sell 60,000 bags of lettuce per month?
g)   At what quantity would Zan and Angela be indifferent to the process selected?
h)   Over what range of demand would the *manual* process be preferred over the mechanized process? Over what range of demand would the *mechanized* process be preferred over the manual process?

: S7.23   Carter Manufacturing is currently producing a tape holder that has a variable cost of $0.75 per unit and a selling price of $2.00 per unit. Fixed costs are $20,000. Current volume is 40,000 units. The firm can produce a better product by adding a new piece of equipment to the process line. This equipment represents an increase of $5,000 in fixed cost. The variable cost would decrease $0.25 per unit. Volume for the new and improved product should rise to 50,000 units.

a)   Should the company invest in the new equipment?
b)   At what volume does the equipment choice change?
c)   At a volume of 15,000 units, which process should be used?

⋮ S7.24 As a prospective owner of a club known as the Red Rose, you are interested in determining the volume of sales dollars necessary for the coming year to reach the break-even point. You have decided to break down the sales for the club into four categories, the first category being beer. Your estimate of the beer sales is that 30,000 drinks will be served. The selling price for each unit will average $1.50; the cost is $.75. The second major category is meals, which you expect to be 10,000 units with an average price of $10.00 and a cost of $5.00. The third major category is desserts and wine, of which you also expect to sell 10,000 units, but with an average price of $2.50 per unit sold and a cost of $1.00 per unit. The final category is lunches and inexpensive sandwiches, which you expect to total 20,000 units at an average price of $6.25 with a food cost of $3.25. Your fixed cost (that is, rent, utilities, and so on) is $1,800 per month plus $2,000 per month for entertainment.

a) What is your break-even point in dollars per month?
b) What is the expected number of meals each day if you are open 360 days a year?

⋮ S7.25 Using the data in Problem S7.24, make the problem more realistic by adding labor cost (as a variable cost) at one-third the total cost of meals and sandwiches. Also add variable expenses (kitchen supplies, tablecloths, napkins, etc.) at 10% of cost for each category.

a) What is your break-even point?
b) If you expect to make an annual profit of $35,000 (before taxes) for your 12-hour days, what must your total sales be?

⋮ S7.26 As manager of the St. Cloud Theatre Company, you have decided that concession sales will support themselves. The following table provides the information you have been able to put together thus far:

ITEM	SELLING PRICE	VARIABLE COST	% OF REVENUE
Soft drink	$1.00	$ .65	25
Wine	1.75	.95	25
Coffee	1.00	.30	30
Candy	1.00	.30	20

Last year's manager, Jim Freeland, has advised you to be sure to add 10% of variable cost as a waste allowance for all categories.

You estimate labor cost to be $250.00 (5 booths with 3 people each). Even if nothing is sold, your labor cost will be $250.00, so you decide to consider this a fixed cost. Booth rental, which is a contractual cost at $50.00 for *each* booth per night, is also a fixed cost.

a) What is break-even volume per evening performance?
b) How much wine would you expect to sell at the break-even point?

P ⋮ S7.27 James Lawson's Bed and Breakfast, in a small historic Mississippi town, must decide how to subdivide (remodel) the large old home that will become its inn. There are three alternatives: Option A would modernize all baths and combine rooms, leaving the inn with four suites, each suitable for two to four adults. Option B would modernize only the second floor; the results would be six suites, four for two to four adults, two for two adults only. Option C (the status quo option) leaves all walls intact. In this case, there are eight rooms available, but only two are suitable for four adults, and four rooms will not have private baths. Below are the details of profit and demand patterns that will accompany each option.

	ANNUAL PROFIT UNDER VARIOUS DEMAND PATTERNS			
ALTERNATIVES	HIGH	p	AVERAGE	p
A (modernize all)	$90,000	.5	$25,000	.5
B (modernize 2nd)	$80,000	.4	$70,000	.6
C (status quo)	$60,000	.3	$55,000	.7

a) Draw the decision tree for Lawson
b) Which option has the highest expected value?

⋮ S7.28 As operations manager of Holz Furniture, you must make a decision about adding a line of rustic furniture. In discussing the possibilities with your sales manager, Steve Gilbert, you decide that there will definitely be a market and that your firm should enter that market. However, because rustic furniture has a different finish than your standard offering, you decide you need another process line. There is no doubt in your mind about the decision, and you are sure that you should have a second process. But you do question how large to make it. A large process line is going to cost $400,000; a small process line will cost $300,000. The question, therefore, is the demand for rustic furniture. After extensive discussion with Mr. Gilbert and Tim Ireland of Ireland Market Research, Inc., you determine that the best estimate you can make is that there is a two-out-of-three chance of profit from sales as large as $600,000 and a one-out-of-three chance as low as $300,000.

With a large process line, you could handle the high figure of $600,000. However, with a small process line you could not and would be forced to expand (at a cost of $150,000), after which time your profit from sales would be

$500,000 rather than the $600,000 because of the lost time in expanding the process. If you do not expand the small process, your profit from sales would be held to $400,000. If you build a small process and the demand is low, you can handle all of the demand.

Should you open a large or small process line?

P : S7.29   What is the net present value of an investment that costs $75,000, and has a salvage value of $45,000? The annual profit from the investment is $15,000 each year for 5 years. The cost of capital at this risk level is 12%.

P . S7.30   The initial cost of an investment is $65,000 and the cost of capital is 10%. The return is $16,000 per year for 8 years. What is the net present value?

P . S7.31   An investment will produce $2,000 three years from now. What is the amount worth today? That is, what is the present value if the interest rate is 9%?

P . S7.32   What is the present value of $5,600 when the interest rate is 8% and the return of $5,600 will not be received for 15 years?

: S7.33   Tim Smunt has been asked to evaluate two machines. After some investigation, he determines that they have the following costs. He is told to assume that
   a)   the life of each machine is 3 years, and
   b)   the company thinks it knows how to make 12% on investments no more risky than this one.

	MACHINE A	MACHINE B
Original cost	$10,000	$20,000
Labor per year	2,000	4,000
Maintenance per year	4,000	1,000
Salvage value	2,000	7,000

Determine, via the present value method, which machine Tim should recommend.

: S7.34   Your boss has told you to evaluate two ovens for Tink-the-Tinkers, a gourmet sandwich shop. After some questioning of vendors and receipt of specifications, you are assured that the ovens have the attributes and costs shown in the table below. The following two assumptions are appropriate:
   1)   The life of each machine is 5 years.
   2)   The company thinks it knows how to make 14% on investments no more risky than this one.

	THREE SMALL OVENS AT $1,250 EACH	TWO LARGE HIGH-QUALITY OVENS AT $2,500 EACH
Original cost	$3,750	$5,000
Labor per year in excess of larger models	$ 750 (total)	
Cleaning/maintenance	$ 750 ($250 each)	$ 400 ($200 each)
Salvage value	$ 750 ($250 each)	$1,000 ($500 each)

   a)   Determine via the present value method which machine to tell your boss to purchase.
   b)   What assumption are you making about the ovens?
   c)   What assumptions are you making in your methodology?

: S7.35   Consumer Products Corporation has a choice of three investments—A, B, and C. The following table gives the cost of each investment as well as the cash flows for each investment.

	INVESTMENT		
	A	B	C
COST:	$10,000	$12,000	$15,000
Income (cash flows)			
Year 1	4,000	10,000	6,000
Year 2	3,000	5,000	6,000
Year 3	6,000	3,000	6,000
Year 4	1,000	3,000	6,000
Year 5	7,000	3,000	6,000

Which investment is "best" based on the net present value criteria, if the cost of money is 9%?

INTERNET HOMEWORK PROBLEMS

See our Internet homepage at **www.prenhall.com/heizer** for these additional homework problems: S7.36 through S7.45.

CASE STUDY

Capacity Planning at Shouldice Hospital

Canada's Shouldice Hospital, shown in the photo in Chapter 5 in your text, is known worldwide for its specialty of hernia repairs. In fact, that is the only operation Shouldice performs, and it performs a great many of them. Over the past few decades, this 89-bed hospital has averaged 7,000 operations annually, with more than 250,000 hernia surgeries since 1945. Patients, coming from 80 different countries, are so loyal that as many as 1,500 per year attend the Hernia Reunion gala dinner, complete with free hernia inspection. Perhaps Shouldice's recurrence rate of only 1%, as opposed to 10% for general hospitals performing this surgery, is a major factor. About 1% of Shouldice's patients are themselves M.D.s.

A number of features in Shouldice's service delivery system contribute to its success: (1) it only accepts patients with uncomplicated external hernias and who are in good health; (2) patients are subject to early ambulation, which promotes healing; (3) its country club atmosphere, superior nursing staff, and built-in socializing make a surprisingly pleasant experience out of an inherently unpleasant medical procedure.

The Medical Facility

The medical facilities at Shouldice consist of five operating rooms, a patient recovery room, a laboratory, and six examination rooms. Shouldice performs, on average, 150 operations per week, with patients generally staying at the hospital for 3 days. Operations are performed only 5 days a week, but the remainder of the hospital is in operation continuously to attend to recovering patients.

An operation at Shouldice is performed by one of the 12 full-time surgeons. Surgeons generally take about 1 hour to prepare for and perform each hernia operation, and they operate on four patients per day.

The Surgery Procedure

All patients undergo a screening exam either by questionnaire or in person (if convenient) prior to setting a date for their operation. Patients then arrive at the clinic the afternoon before their surgery, receive a brief preoperative examination, and see an admissions clerk to complete paperwork. They are next directed to one of the two nurses

stations for blood and urine tests and then are shown to their rooms. Orientation begins at 5 P.M., followed by dinner in the dining room. Patients gather in the lounge area at 9:00 P.M. for tea and cookies.

On the day of the operation, the patient is administered a local anesthetic, leaving him alert and fully aware of the proceedings. At the conclusion of the operation, the patient is encouraged to walk from the operating table to a wheelchair, which is waiting to return him to his room. After a brief period of rest, he is encouraged to get up and start exercising. By 9 P.M. that day, he is in the lounge having cookies and tea, and talking with new, incoming patients.

The skin clips holding the incision together are loosened, and some are removed the next day. The remainder are removed the following morning just before the patient is discharged.

When Shouldice started, the average hospital stay for hernia surgery was 3 weeks. Today, some institutions push "same-day surgery" for a variety of reasons. Shouldice Hospital firmly believes that this is not in the best interests of the patients, and is committed to its 3-day process. Shouldice's post-op rehabilitation program is designed to enable the patient to resume normal activities with minimal interruption and discomfort.

The Plan for Expansion

Shouldice's management has been thinking of expanding the hospital's capacity to serve a considerable unsatisfied demand. The first option for expansion involves adding Saturday operations to the existing 5-day schedule. This would increase capacity by 20%. The second option is to add another floor of rooms to the hospital, increasing the number of beds by 50%. This would require more aggressive scheduling of the operating rooms.

Table S7.3 illustrates room occupancy for the existing system. Each row in the table follows the patients who checked in on a given day. The columns indicate the number of patients in the hospital on a given day. For example, the first row of the table shows that 30 people checked in on Monday and were in the hospital for Monday, Tuesday, and Wednesday. Summing the columns of the table for Wednesday indicates that there are 90 patients staying in the hospital that day.

The administrator is concerned about maintaining control over the quality of the service delivered. He thinks the facility is already

TABLE S7.3 ■ Shouldice Hospital's Operation, with 30 New Patients per Day[a]

	BEDS REQUIRED						
CHECK-IN DAY	MONDAY	TUESDAY	WEDNESDAY	THURSDAY	FRIDAY	SATURDAY	SUNDAY
Monday	30	30	30				
Tuesday		30	30	30			
Wednesday			30	30	30		
Thursday				30	30	30	
Friday							
Saturday							
Sunday	30	30	—	—	—	—	30
Total	60	90	90	90	60	30	30

[a]The actual number of beds at Shouldice Hospital is 89. Ninety is used to ease computations.

(continued)

achieving good utilization. The doctors and the staff are happy with their jobs, and the patients are satisfied with the service. Further expansion of capacity, he believes, might make it hard to maintain the same kind of working relationships and attitudes.

Discussion Questions

1. How well is the hospital currently utilizing its beds?
2. Develop a table to show the effects of adding operations on Saturday. Assume that 30 operations would still be performed each day. How would this affect the utilization of the bed capacity? Is this capacity sufficient for the additional patients?
3. If operations are performed only 5 days a week, 30 per day, what is the effect of increasing the number of beds by 50%?

How many operations could the hospital perform per day before running out of bed capacity? How well would the new resources be utilized relative to the current operation? Recalling the capacity of 12 surgeons and five operating rooms, could the hospital really perform this many operations? Why?

4. If adding bed capacity costs about $100,000 per bed, the average rate charged for the hernia surgery is $2,400, and surgeons are paid a flat $800 per operation, can Shouldice justify any expansion within a 5-year time period?

Source: Adopted from R. B. Chase, N. J. Aquilano, and F. R. Jacobs, *Production and Operations Management*, 9th ed. (Boston: Irwin-McGraw Hill, 2001): 371–372, using information on Shouldice Hospital found at www.shouldice.com/, January 2004.

Chapter 8

Location Strategies

Location may determine up to 10% of the total *cost* for an industrial firm. For the service, retail, or professional firm, location tends to be more critical in determining *revenue* than cost. In general, however, the objective of a location strategy is to maximize the benefit of location to the firm.

This chapter covers the factors that a firm should consider in the location decision and the techniques appropriate for that decision. For industrial firms, these issues include tangible costs such as transportation, energy, labor, raw material, and taxes, as well as intangible costs such as quality of education, government, labor, and quality of life. For service firms, issues such as competition, drawing area, purchasing power, parking, security, and rent are important.

BEFORE COMING TO CLASS, READ CHAPTER 8 IN YOUR TEXT AND ANSWER THESE QUESTIONS.

1. How does the industrial location decision differ from the service location decision? _____

2. What is meant by companies "clustering"? _____

3. Identify a dozen critical success factors that affect location decision at the country, regional, or site level._____

4. What is locational break-even analysis? _____

5. What is the objective of the location decision? _____

6. What is the center of gravity method and when is it used? _____

THE STRATEGIC IMPORTANCE OF LOCATION

FACTORS THAT AFFECT LOCATION DECISIONS

FIGURE 8.1 ■ Some Considerations and Factors That Affect
Location Decisions

Country Decision

1. Political risks, government rules, attitudes, incentives
2. Cultural and economic issues
3. Location of markets
4. Labor availability, attitudes, productivity, costs
5. Availability of supplies, communications, energy
6. Exchange rates and currency risk

Region/Community Decision

1. Corporate desires
2. Attractiveness of region (culture, taxes, climate, etc.)
3. Labor availability, costs, attitudes toward unions
4. Cost and availability of utilities
5. Environmental regulations of state and town
6. Government incentives
7. Proximity to raw materials and customers
8. Land/construction costs

Site Decision

1. Site size and cost
2. Air, rail, highway, waterway systems
3. Zoning restrictions
4. Nearness of services/supplies needed
5. Environmental impact issues

Labor Productivity

$$\frac{\text{Labor cost per day}}{\text{Productivity (that is, units per day)}} = \text{Labor cost per unit}$$

Exchange Rates

Costs

Attitudes

Proximity to Markets

Proximity to Suppliers

Clustering

METHODS OF EVALUATING LOCATION ALTERNATIVES

Major Location Evaluation Methods

1. Factor Rating Method

2. Locational Break-Even Analysis

3. Center of Gravity

4. Transportation Model

Factor Rating Method

Steps in the Factor Rating Method

1. _____

2. _____

3. _____

4. _____

5. _____

6. _____

PRACTICE PROBLEM 8.1 ■ Factor Rating Method

A major drug store chain wishes to build a new warehouse to serve the whole Midwest. At the moment, it is looking at three possible locations. The factors, weights, and ratings being considered are as follows:

		RATINGS		
FACTOR	WEIGHTS	PEORIA	DES MOINES	CHICAGO
Nearness to markets	20	4	7	5
Labor cost	5	8	8	4
Taxes	15	8	9	7
Nearness to suppliers	10	10	6	10

What city should it choose?

Additional Practice Problem Space

Locational Break-Even Analysis

• **Method of Cost-Volume Analysis Used for Industrial Locations**

Steps

1. _____

2. _____

3. _____

PRACTICE PROBLEM 8.2 ■ Break-Even Analysis

Balfour's is considering building a plant in one of three possible locations. They have estimated the following parameters for each location:

LOCATION	FIXED COST	VARIABLE COST
Waco, Texas	$300,000	$5.75
Tijuana, Mexico	$800,000	$2.75
Fayetteville, Arkansas	$100,000	$8.00

For what unit sales volume should they choose each location?

Total Location Cost Chart

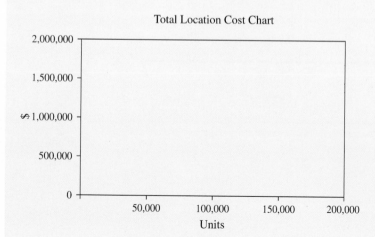

Additional Practice Problem Space

Center of Gravity Method

• **Finds Location of Single Distribution Center Serving Several Destinations**
• **Used Primarily for Services**
• **Considers location, Volume, and Shipping Distance**

$$x\text{-coordinate of the center of gravity} = \frac{\sum_i d_{ix} Q_i}{\sum_i Q_i} \tag{8-1}$$

$$y\text{-coordinate of the center of gravity} = \frac{\sum_i d_{iy} Q_i}{\sum_i Q_i} \tag{8-2}$$

where d_{ix} = x-coordinate of location i

d_{iy} = y-coordinate of location i

Q_i = Quantity of goods moved to or from location i

PRACTICE PROBLEM 8.3 ■ Center of Gravity Method

Our main distribution center in Phoenix, AZ, is due to be replaced with a much larger, more modern facility that can handle the tremendous needs that have developed with the city's growth. Fresh produce travels to the seven store locations several times a day, making site selection critical for efficient distribution. Using the data in the following table, determine the map coordinates for the proposed new distribution center.

STORE LOCATIONS	MAP COORDINATES (X, Y)	TRUCK ROUND TRIPS PER DAY
Mesa	(10,5)	3
Glendale	(3,8)	3
Camelback	(4,7)	2
Scottsdale	(15,10)	6
Apache Junction	(13,3)	5
Sun City	(1,12)	3
Pima	(5,5)	10

(continued)

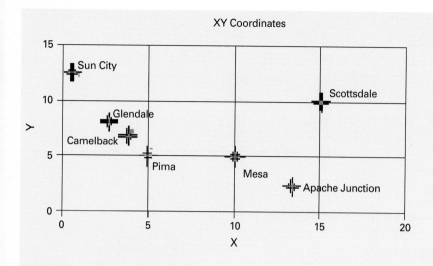

Additional Practice Problem Space

Transportation Model

• **Finds Amount to Be Shipped from Several Sources to Several Destinations**
• **Used Primarily for Industrial Locations**
• **Type of Linear Programming Model**

SERVICE LOCATION STRATEGY

TABLE 8.6 ■ Location Strategies—Service vs. Goods-Producing Organizations

SERVICE/RETAIL/PROFESSIONAL LOCATION	GOODS-PRODUCING LOCATION
REVENUE FOCUS	**COST FOCUS**
Volume/revenue	**Tangible costs**
Drawing area; purchasing power	Transportation cost of raw material
Competition; advertising/pricing	Shipment cost of finished goods
Physical quality	Energy and utility cost; labor; raw material; taxes; and so on
Parking/access; security/lighting; appearance/image	**Intangible and future costs**
Cost determinants	Attitude toward union
Rent	Quality of life
Management caliber	Education expenditures by state
Operation policies (hours, wage rates)	Quality of state and local government
TECHNIQUES	**TECHNIQUES**
Regression models to determine importance of various factors	Transportation method
Factor-rating method	Factor-rating method
Traffic counts	Locational break-even analysis
Demographic analysis of drawing area	Crossover charts
Purchasing power analysis of area	
Center-of-gravity method	
Geographic information systems	
ASSUMPTIONS	**ASSUMPTIONS**
Location is a major determinant of revenue	Location is a major determinant of cost
High customer-contact issues are critical	Most major costs can be identified explicitly for each site
Costs are relatively constant for a given area; therefore, the revenue function is critical	Low customer contact allows focus on the identifiable costs
	Intangible costs can be evaluated

DISCUSSION QUESTIONS

1. What is the key concept to FedEx's location competitive advantage? (See the *Global Company Profile* that begins Chapter 8 in your text.) Discuss.
2. Why do so many U.S. firms build facilities in other countries?
3. Why do so many foreign companies build facilities in the U.S.?
4. What is "clustering"?
5. How does factor weighting incorporate personal preference in location choices?
6. What are the advantages and disadvantages of a qualitative (as opposed to a quantitative) approach to location decision making?
7. Provide two examples of clustering in the service sector.
8. What are the major factors that firms consider when choosing a country in which to locate?
9. What factors affect region/community location decisions?
10. While most organizations may make the location decision infrequently, there are some organizations that make the decision quite regularly and often. Provide one or two examples. How might their approach to the location decision differ from the norm?
11. List those factors, other than globalization, that affect the location decision.

12. Explain the assumptions behind the center-of-gravity method. How can the model be used in a service facility location?
13. What are the three steps to locational break-even analysis?
14. An old location adage states, "Manufacturers locate near their resources, retailers locate near their customers." Discuss, with reference to the proximity-to-markets arguments covered in the text. Can you think of a counterexample in each case? Support your choices.
15. Why shouldn't low wage rates alone be sufficient to select a location?
16. List the techniques used by service organizations to select locations.
17. Contrast the location of a food distributor and a supermarket. (The distributor sends truckloads of food, meat, produce, etc., to the supermarket.) Show the relevant considerations (factors) they share; show those where they differ.
18. Elmer's Fudge Factory is planning to open 10 retail outlets in Oregon over the next 2 years. Identify (and weight) those factors relevant to the decision. Provide this list of factors and weights.

CRITICAL THINKING EXERCISE

In this chapter, we have discussed a number of location decisions. Consider another: United Airlines announced its competition to select a town for a new billion-dollar aircraft-repair base. The bidding for the prize of 7,000 jobs was fast and furious, with Orlando offering $154 million in incentives and Denver more than twice that amount. Kentucky's governor angrily rescinded Louisville's offer of $300 million, likening the bidding to "squeezing every drop of blood out of a turnip." What are the ethical, legal, and economic implications of such location bidding wars? Who pays for such giveaways? Are local citizens allowed to vote on offers made by their cities, counties, or states? Should there be limits on these incentives?

ACTIVE MODEL EXERCISE

This Active Model appears on your CD-ROM. It allows you to evaluate important elements in a center-of-gravity model.

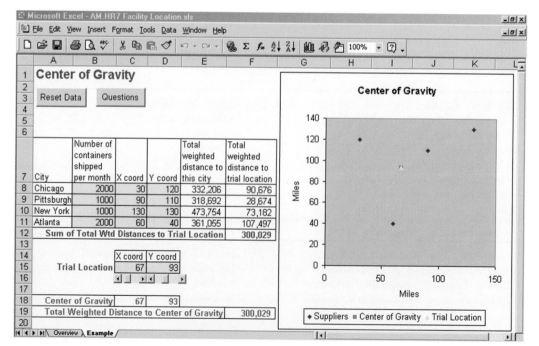

ACTIVE MODEL 8.1 ■

Center of Gravity Model Using Quain Department Store Data in Example 3 in Your Text

Questions

1. What is the total weighted distance from their current old and inadequate warehouse in Pittsburgh?
2. If they relocate their warehouse to the center of gravity, by how much will this reduce the total weighted shipping distance?
3. Observe the graph. If the number of shipments from New York doubles, how does this affect the center of gravity?
4. The center of gravity does not necessarily find the site with the minimum total weighted distance. Use the scrollbars to move the trial location and see if you can improve (lower) the distance.
5. If you have Solver set up in Excel, from Excel's main menu use Tools, Solver, Solve in order to see the best answer to the previous question.

PROBLEMS*

8.1 In Cambodia, six laborers, each making the equivalent of $3 per day, can produce 40 units per day. In China, 10 laborers, each making the equivalent of $2.00 per day, can produce 45 units. In Billings, Montana, two laborers, each making $60 per day, can make 100 units. Based on labor costs only, which location would be most economical to produce the item?

8.2 Refer to Problem 8.1. Shipping cost from Cambodia to Denver, Colorado, the final destination, is $1.50 per unit. Shipping cost from China to Denver is $1 per unit, while the shipping cost from Billings to Denver is $.25 per unit. Considering both labor and transportation costs, which is the most favorable production location?

8.3 You have been asked to analyze the bids for 200 polished disks used in solar panels. These bids have been submitted by three suppliers: Thailand Polishing, India Shine, and Sacramento Glow. Thailand Polishing has submitted a bid of 2,000 baht. India Shine has submitted a bid of 2,000 rupee. Sacramento Glow has submitted a bid of $200. You check with your local bank and find that $1 = 10 baht and $1 = 8 rupee. Which company should you choose?

8.4 Refer to Problem 8.3. If the final destination is New Delhi, India, and there is a 30% import tax, which firm should you choose?

8.5 Holiday Health, Inc., is opening a new spa. Three locations in the suburbs are being considered. The following table gives the factors for each site. At which site should Holiday open the new spa?

FACTOR	WEIGHT	MAITLAND	CRESTWOOD	NORTHSIDE MALL
Land space	.30	60	70	80
Land costs	.25	40	80	30
Traffic density	.20	50	80	60
Neighborhood income	.15	50	70	40
Zoning laws	.10	80	20	90

8.6 Karen Fowler owns the Rockey Mountain Coolers, a semiprofessional basketball team in Northern Colorado. She wishes to move the Coolers east to either Atlanta or Charlotte. The table below gives the factors that Karen thinks are important, their weights, and the scores for Atlanta and Charlotte. Which site should she select?

FACTOR	WEIGHT	ATLANTA	CHARLOTTE
Incentive	.4	80	60
Player satisfaction	.3	20	50
Sports interest	.2	40	90
Size of city	.1	70	30

8.7 Insurance Company of Latin America (ILA) is considering opening an office in the U.S. The two cities under consideration are Philadelphia and New York. The factor ratings (higher scores are better) for the two cities are given in the following table. In which city should ILA locate?

*Note: **P** means the problem may be solved with POM for Windows; ✗ means the problem may be solved with Excel OM; and **P✗** means the problem may be solved with POM for Windows and/or Excel OM.

FACTOR	WEIGHT	PHILADELPHIA	NEW YORK
Customer convenience	.25	70	80
Bank accessibility	.20	40	90
Computer support	.20	85	75
Rental costs	.15	90	55
Labor costs	.10	80	50
Taxes	.10	90	50

P⭐ : 8.8   Beth Spenser Retailers is attempting to decide on a location for a new retail outlet. At the moment, the firm has three alternatives—stay where it is but enlarge the facility; locate along the main street in nearby Newbury; or locate in a new shopping mall in Hyde Park. The company has selected the four factors listed in the following table as the basis for evaluation and has assigned weights as shown:

FACTOR	FACTOR DESCRIPTION	WEIGHT
1	Average community income	.30
2	Community growth potential	.15
3	Availability of public transportation	.20
4	Labor availability, attitude, and cost	.35

Spenser has rated each location for each factor, on a 100-point basis. These ratings are given below:

FACTOR	LOCATION		
	PRESENT LOCATION	NEWBURY	HYDE PARK
1	40	60	50
2	20	20	80
3	30	60	50
4	80	50	50

P⭐ : 8.9   A location analysis for Temponi Controls, a small manufacturer of parts for high-technology cable systems, has been narrowed down to four locations. Temponi will need to train assemblers, testers, and robotics maintainers in local training centers. Cecilia Temponi, the president, has asked each potential site to offer training programs, tax breaks, and other industrial incentives. The critical factors, their weights, and the ratings for each location are shown in the table below. High scores represent favorable values.

FACTOR	WEIGHT	LOCATION			
		AKRON, OH	BILOXI, MS	CARTHAGE, TX	DENVER, CO
Labor availability	.15	90	80	90	80
Technical school quality	.10	95	75	65	85
Operating cost	.30	80	85	95	85
Land and construction cost	.15	60	80	90	70
Industrial incentives	.20	90	75	85	60
Labor cost	.10	75	80	85	75

a) Compute the composite (weighted average) rating for each location.
b) Which site would you choose?
c) Would you reach the same conclusion if the weights for operating cost and labor cost were reversed? Recompute as necessary and explain.

P⭐ . 8.10   Consolidated Refineries, headquartered in Houston, must decide among three sites for the construction of a new oil-processing center. The firm has selected the six factors listed below as a basis for evaluation and has assigned rating weights from 1 to 5 on each factor.

FACTOR	FACTOR NAME	RATING WEIGHT
1	Proximity to port facilities	5
2	Power-source availability and cost	3
3	Workforce attitude and cost	4
4	Distance from Houston	2
5	Community desirability	2
6	Equipment suppliers in area	3

Management has rated each location for each factor on a 1 to 100 point basis.

FACTOR	LOCATION A	LOCATION B	LOCATION C
1	100	80	80
2	80	70	100
3	30	60	70
4	10	80	60
5	90	60	80
6	50	60	90

Which site will be recommended?

P_x: **8.11** A company is planning on expanding and building a new plant in one of three Southeast Asian countries. David Pentico, the manager charged with making the decision, has determined that five critical success factors (CSFs) can be used to evaluate the prospective countries. Pentico used a rating system of 1 (least desirable country) to 5 (most desirable) to evaluate each CSF. Which country should be selected for the new plant?

		CANDIDATE COUNTRY RATINGS		
CRITICAL SUCCESS FACTORS	WEIGHT	TAIWAN	THAILAND	SINGAPORE
Technology	0.2	4	5	1
Level of education	0.1	4	1	5
Political and legal aspects	0.4	1	3	3
Social and cultural aspects	0.1	4	2	3
Economic factors	0.2	3	3	2

P_x. **8.12** Thomas Green College is contemplating opening a European campus where students from the main campus could go to take courses for one of the four college years. At the moment it is considering five countries: Holland, Great Britain, Italy, Belgium, and Greece. The college wishes to consider eight factors in its decision. Each factor has an equal weight. The following table illustrates its assessment of each factor for each country (5 is best).

FACTOR	FACTOR DESCRIPTION	HOLLAND	GREAT BRITAIN	ITALY	BELGIUM	GREECE
1	Stability of government	5	5	3	5	4
2	Degree to which the population can converse in English	4	5	3	4	3
3	Stability of the monetary system	5	4	3	4	3
4	Communications infrastructure	4	5	3	4	3
5	Transportation infrastructure	5	5	3	5	3
6	Availability of historical/cultural sites	3	4	5	3	5
7	Import restrictions	4	4	3	4	4
8	Availability of suitable quarters	4	4	3	4	3

In which country should Thomas Green College choose to set up its European campus?

P_x. **8.13** How would the decision in Problem 8.12 change if the "degree to which the population can converse in English" was not an issue?

P_x: **8.14** An American consulting firm is planning to expand globally by opening a new office in one of four countries: Germany, Italy, Spain, or Greece. The chief partner entrusted with the decision, Cindy Ruppel, has identified eight critical success factors (CSFs) that she views as essential for the success of any consultancy. She used a rating system of 1 (least desirable country) to 5 (most desirable) to evaluate each CSF. Which country should be selected for the new office?

CRITICAL SUCCESS FACTORS	WEIGHT	CANDIDATE COUNTRY RATINGS			
		GERMANY	ITALY	SPAIN	GREECE
Level of education					
Number of consultants	.05	5	5	5	2
National literacy rate	.05	4	2	1	1
Political aspects					
Stability of government	0.2	5	5	5	2
Product liability laws	0.2	5	2	3	5
Environmental regulations	0.2	1	4	1	3
Social and cultural aspects					
Similarity in language	0.1	4	2	1	1
Acceptability of consultants	0.1	1	4	4	3
Economic factors					
Incentives	0.1	2	3	1	5

8.15   A British hospital chain wishes to make its first entry into the U.S. market by building a medical facility in the Midwest, a region with which its director, Doug Moodie, is comfortable because he got his medical degree at Northwestern University. After a preliminary analysis, four cities are chosen for further consideration. They are rated according to the factors shown below:

FACTOR	WEIGHT	CITY			
		CHICAGO	MILWAUKEE	MADISON	DETROIT
Costs	2.0	8	5	6	7
Need for a facility	1.5	4	9	8	4
Staff availability	1.0	7	6	4	7
Local incentives	0.5	8	6	5	9

a)   Which city should Moodie select?

b)   Assume a minimum score of 5 is now required for all factors. Which city should be chosen?

8.16   The fixed and variable costs for three potential manufacturing plant sites for a rattan chair weaver are shown below:

SITE	FIXED COST PER YEAR	VARIABLE COST PER UNIT
1	$ 500	$11
2	1,000	7
3	1,700	4

a)   Over what range of production is each location optimal?

b)   For a production of 200 units, which site is best?

8.17   Peter Billington Stereo, Inc., supplies car radios to auto manufacturers and is going to open a new plant. The company is undecided between Detroit and Dallas as the site. The fixed costs in Dallas are lower due to cheaper land costs, but the variable costs in Dallas are higher because shipping distances would increase. Given the following costs, perform an analysis of the volume over which each location is preferable.

	DALLAS	DETROIT
Fixed costs	$600,000	$800,000
Variable costs	$28/radio	$22/radio

8.18   Currently your company purchases welded brackets from a local supplier at a cost of $2.20 each. Your production supervisor has presented to you three alternatives for making the brackets in-house. Each alternative uses a different piece of equipment and different amounts of labor and materials. Alternative A would require the purchase of a piece of equipment costing $6,000 and would have variable costs of $.95 per bracket. Alternative B would use a piece of equipment costing $10,000, but variable costs would be lower at $.45 per bracket. Lastly, Alternative C would use the most expensive equipment at $12,000, and variable costs would be just $.30 per bracket. Over what range of demand would you select each alternative?

8.19   Hugh Leach Corp., a producer of machine tools, wants to move to a larger site. Two alternative locations have been identified: Bonham and McKinney. Bonham would have fixed costs of $800,000 per year and variable costs of $14,000 per standard unit produced. McKinney would have annual fixed costs of $920,000 and variable costs of $13,000 per standard unit. The finished items sell for $29,000 each.

a)   At what volume of output would the two locations have the same profit?

b)   For what range of output would Bonham be superior (have higher profits)?

c) For what range would McKinney be superior?

d) What is the relevance of break-even points for these cities?

8.20 The following table gives the map coordinates and the shipping loads for a set of cities that we wish to connect through a central "hub." Near which map coordinates should the hub be located?

CITY	MAP COORDINATE (x, y)	SHIPPING LOAD
A	(5, 10)	5
B	(6, 8)	10
C	(4, 9)	15
D	(9, 5)	5
E	(7, 9)	15
F	(3, 2)	10
G	(2, 6)	5

8.21 A chain of home health care firms in Louisiana needs to locate a central office from which to conduct internal audits and other periodic reviews of its facilities. These facilities are scattered throughout the state, as detailed in the table below. Each site, except for Houma, will be visited three times each year by a team of workers, who will drive from the central office to the site. Houma will be visited five times a year. What coordinates represent the distance-minimizing central location for this office? What other factors might influence the office location decision? Where would you place this office? Explain.

	MAP COORDINATES	
CITY	X	Y
Covington	9.2	3.5
Donaldsonville	7.3	2.5
Houma	7.8	1.4
Monroe	5.0	8.4
Natchitoches	2.8	6.5
New Iberia	5.5	2.4
Opelousas	5.0	3.6
Ruston	3.8	8.5

8.22 A small rural county has experienced unprecedented growth over the last 6 years, and as a result, the local school district built the new 500-student North Park Elementary School. The district has three older and smaller elementary schools: Washington, Jefferson, and Lincoln. Now the growth pressure is being felt at the secondary level. The school district would like to build a centrally located middle school to accommodate students and reduce busing costs. The older middle school is adjacent to the high school and will become part of the high school campus.

a) What are the coordinates of the central location?

b) What other factors should be considered before building a school?

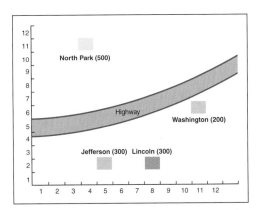

8.23 Todd's Video, a major video rental and TV sales chain headquartered in New Orleans, is about to open its first outlet in Mobile, Alabama, and wants to select a site that will place the new outlet in the center of Mobile's population base. Todd examines the seven census tracks in Mobile, plots the coordinates of the center of each from a map, and looks up the population base in each to use as a weighting. The information gathered appears in the following table. At what center-of-gravity coordinates should the new store be located?

CENSUS TRACT	POPULATION IN CENSUS TRACT	X, Y MAP COORDINATES
101	2,000	(25, 45)
102	5,000	(25, 25)
103	10,000	(55, 45)
104	7,000	(50, 20)
105	10,000	(80, 50)
106	20,000	(70, 20)
107	14,000	(90, 25)

8.24   Ramon Haynes owns an ambulance company that serves four hospitals in Claremont, California. Northwest Hospital has map coordinates of 20 West, 50 North. Northeast Hospital is located at 15 East, 30 North. Southwest Hospital is at 10 West, 40 South. Southeast Hospital is located on grid 25 East, 10 South. The average number of runs Haynes's service makes to each hospital is Northwest (60), Northeast (40), Southwest (50), and Southeast (100). Using the map grid system, determine where Haynes should place his offices in order to make them most centrally located.

8.25   The unification of Europe has brought about changes in airline regulation that dramatically affect major European carriers such as British International Air, SAS, KLM, Air France, Alitalia, and Swiss. With ambitious expansion plans, British International Air (BIA) has decided it needs a second service hub on the continent, to complement its large Heathrow (London) repair facility. The location selection is critical, and with the potential for 4,000 new skilled blue-collar jobs on the line, virtually every city in Western Europe is actively bidding for BIA's business.

After initial investigations by Holmes Miller, head of the Operations Department, BIA has narrowed the list to 9 cities. Each is then rated on 12 factors, with the table on the following page resulting.

a)   Help Miller rank the top three cities that BIA should consider as its new site for servicing aircraft.

b)   After further investigation, Miller decides that an existing set of hangar facilities for repairs is not nearly as important as earlier thought. If he lowers the weight of that factor to 30, does the ranking change?

c)   After Miller makes the change in part (b), Germany announces it has reconsidered its offer of financial incentives, with an additional 200-million euro package to entice BIA. Accordingly, BIA has raised Germany's rating to 10 on that factor. Is there any change in top rankings in part (b)?

Table for Problem 8.25

		LOCATION								
		ITALY			FRANCE			GERMANY		
FACTOR	IMPORTANCE WEIGHT	MILAN	ROME	GENOA	PARIS	LYON	NICE	MUNICH	BONN	BERLIN
Financial incentives	85	8	8	8	7	7	7	7	7	7
Skilled labor pool	80	4	6	5	9	9	7	10	8	9
Existing facility	70	5	3	2	9	6	5	9	9	2
Wage rates	70	9	8	9	4	6	6	4	5	5
Competition for jobs	70	7	3	8	2	8	7	4	8	9
Ease of air traffic access	65	5	4	6	2	8	8	4	8	9
Real estate cost	40	6	4	7	4	6	6	3	4	5
Communication links	25	6	7	6	9	9	9	10	9	8
Attractiveness to relocating executives	15	4	8	3	9	6	6	2	3	3
Political considerations	10	6	6	6	8	8	8	8	8	8
Expansion possibilities	10	10	2	8	1	5	4	4	5	6
Union strength	10	1	1	1	5	5	5	6	6	6

INTERNET HOMEWORK PROBLEMS

See our Internet homepage at **www.prenhall.com/heizer** for these additional homework problems: 8.26 through 8.34.

CASE STUDY

Southern Recreational Vehicle Company

In October 2002, top management of Southern Recreational Vehicle Company of St. Louis, Missouri, announced its plans to relocate its manufacturing and assembly operations by constructing a new plant in Ridgecrest, Mississippi. The firm, a major producer of pickup campers and camper trailers, had experienced 5 consecutive years of declining profits as a result of spiraling production costs. The costs of labor and raw materials had increased alarmingly, utility costs had gone up sharply, and taxes and transportation expenses had steadily

(continued)

climbed upward. In spite of increased sales, the company suffered its first net loss since operations were begun in 1982.

When management initially considered relocation, it closely scrutinized several geographic areas. Of primary importance to the relocation decision were the availability of adequate transportation facilities, state and municipal tax structures, an adequate labor supply, positive community attitudes, reasonable site costs, and financial inducements. Although several communities offered essentially the same incentives, the management of Southern Recreational Vehicle Company was favorably impressed by the efforts of the Mississippi Power and Light Company to attract "clean, labor-intensive" industry and the enthusiasm exhibited by state and local officials, who actively sought to bolster the state's economy by enticing manufacturing firms to locate within its boundaries.

Two weeks prior to the announcement, management of Southern Recreational Vehicle Company finalized its relocation plans. An existing building in Ridgecrest's industrial park was selected (the physical facility had previously housed a mobile home manufacturer that had gone bankrupt due to inadequate financing and poor management); initial recruiting was begun through the state employment office; and efforts to lease or sell the St. Louis property were initiated. Among the inducements offered Southern Recreational Vehicle Company to locate in Ridgecrest were

1. Exemption from county and municipal taxes for 5 years.
2. Free water and sewage services.
3. Construction of a second loading dock—free of cost—at the industrial site.
4. An agreement to issue $500,000 in industrial bonds for future expansion.
5. Public-financed training of workers in a local industrial trade school.

In addition to these inducements, other factors weighed heavily in the decision to locate in the small Mississippi town. Labor costs would be significantly less than those incurred in St. Louis; organized labor was not expected to be as powerful (Mississippi is a right-to-work state); and utility costs and taxes would be moderate. All in all, management of Southern Recreational Vehicle Company felt that its decision was sound.

On October 15, the following announcement was attached to each employee's paycheck:

To: Employees of Southern Recreational Vehicle Company

From: Gerald O'Brian, President

The Management of Southern Recreational Vehicle Company regretfully announces its plans to cease all manufacturing operations in St. Louis on December 31. Because of increased operating costs and the unreasonable demands forced upon the company by the union, it has become impossible to operate profitably. I sincerely appreciate the fine service that each of you has rendered to the company during the past years. If I can be of assistance in helping you find suitable employment with another firm, please let me know. Thank you again for your cooperation and past service.

Discussion Questions

1. Evaluate the inducements offered Southern Recreational Vehicle Company by community leaders in Ridgecrest, Mississippi.
2. What problems would a company experience in relocating its executives from a heavily populated industrialized area to a small rural town?
3. Evaluate the reasons cited by O'Brian for relocation. Are they justifiable?
4. What legal and ethical responsibilities does a firm have to its employees when a decision to cease operations is made?

Source: Reprinted by permission of Professor Jerry Kinard (Western Carolina University).

CASE STUDY

The Ambrose Distribution Center

The Ambrose family owns a small regional chain of retail stores. Their best-known products are audio CDs, concert DVDs, DVD players, and audio accessories. Currently, the family utilizes the services of an independent contractor to supply their stores by truck. The family is not completely satisfied with the timeliness and reliability of the contractor. The family has researched the issue of distribution centers, and has come to the conclusion that it will discontinue its contract with the trucking contractor, and go forward with its own distribution center (DC).

Coincidentally, the chain has 10 outlets—5 in Texas and 5 in Oklahoma. These outlets are located in 10 cities as shown in the table; also given are the annual tons of merchandise required at each outlet.

The family's research shows that there are two distinct capacity configurations for distribution centers: "small" and "large." The small version can support 5 retail outlets; the large can support 10. Annual fixed costs for the small are $2,000,000 each; each large has annual fixed costs of $3,600,000. The family's cost accountant treats variable costs as proportional to the amount of merchandise moved through a facility. Last year, that proportion was 35% of the value of merchandise. The organization recognizes that the other major cost is shipping—it must consider transportation costs of $2,00 per ton-mile. (A load of 40 tons moved 10 miles is 400 ton-miles.)

The locations are shown in the tables that follow. Each distance unit equals 40 miles.

	OKLAHOMA		
CITY	EAST-WEST DISTANCE X	NORTH-SOUTH DISTANCE Y	TONNAGE
Ada	9.7	3.5	600
Ardmore	9.0	2.4	300
Durant	10.1	2.1	250
McAlester	11.0	4.0	400
Norman	8.5	4.4	750

	TEXAS		
CITY	EAST-WEST DISTANCE X	NORTH-SOUTH DISTANCE Y	TONNAGE
Denton	9.0	0.7	200
Greenville	10.7	0.5	500
Paris	11.5	1.5	300
Sherman	9.8	1.4	600
Wichita Falls	6.9	1.9	550

(continued)

The family has contacted Robert Piland, a professor in Texas, to serve as its consultant on this project. It asked Professor Piland to answer several questions. Should the chain construct one large distribution center or two small ones? Where should the distribution center(s) be located? What will be the annual total costs associated with each choice? What considerations other than cost should be considered in making this decision?

Company analysts have done forecasts of growth and demand, and suggest that the 10 stores may become more alike in size in the future, and that each will need to be supplied with approximately 600 tons of merchandise per year. If this demand forecast is valid, would Piland's recommendation (one distribution center or two) be any different?

Discussion Question

Prepare Robert Piland's report to the Ambrose family.

Source: Professor Wayne Shell, Nicholls State University.

VIDEO CASE STUDY

Where to Place Hard Rock's Next Cafe

Some people would say that Oliver Munday, Hard Rock's vice president for cafe development, has the best job in the world. Travel the world to pick a country for Hard Rock's next cafe, select a city, and find the ideal site. It's true that selecting a site involves lots of incognito walking around, visiting nice restaurants, and drinking in bars. But that is not where Mr. Munday's work begins, nor where it ends. At the front end, selecting the country and city first involves a great deal of research. At the back end, Munday not only picks the final site and negotiates the deal, but then works with architects and planners, and stays with the project through the opening and first year's sales.

Munday is currently looking heavily into global expansion in Europe, Latin America, and Asia. "We've got to look at political risk, currency, and social norms—how does our brand fit into the country," he says. Once the country is selected, Munday focuses on the region and city. His research checklist is extensive.

Hard Rock's Standard Market Report (for off-shore sites)

A. Demographics (local, city, region, SMSA), with trend analysis
  1. Population of area
  2. Economic indicators
B. Visitor market, with trend analysis
  1. Tourists/business visitors
  2. Hotels
  3. Convention center
  4. Entertainment
  5. Sports
  6. Retail
C. Transportation
  1. Airport ◄———— sub-categories include:
  2. Rail   (a) age of airport,
  3. Road   (b) no. of passengers,
  4. Sea/river   (c) airlines,
                            (d) direct flights,
                            (e) hubs
D. Restaurants (a selection in key target market areas)
E. Nightclubs (a selection of clubs in key areas of target market)
F. Real estate market
G. Hard Rock Cafe comparable market analysis

Site location now tends to focus on the tremendous resurgence of "city centers," where nightlife tends to concentrate. That's what Munday selected in Moscow and Bogota, although in both locations he chose to find a local partner and franchise the operation. In these two political environments, "Hard Rock wouldn't dream of operating by ourselves," says Munday. The location decision also is at least a 10-to-15-year commitment by Hard Rock, which employs tools such as break-even analysis to help decide whether to purchase land and build, or to remodel an existing facility.

Discussion Questions*

1. From Munday's checklist, select any other four categories, such as population (A1), hotels (B2), or nightclubs (E), and provide three subcategories that should be evaluated. (See item C1 (airport) for a guide.)
2. Why is site selection more than just evaluating the best nightclubs and restaurants in a city?
3. Why does Hard Rock put such serious effort into its location analysis?
4. Under what conditions do you think Hard Rock prefers to franchise a cafe?

*You may wish to view this video case on your CD-ROM before answering the questions.

Source: Professors Barry Render (Rollins College), Jay Heizer (Texas Lutheran University), and Beverly Amer (Northern Arizona University).

Layout Strategy

Layouts make a substantial difference in operating efficiency. The six classic layout situations are (1) fixed position, (2) process oriented, (3) office, (4) retail, (5) warehouse, and (6) product oriented. A variety of techniques have been developed in attempts to solve these layout problems. Industrial firms focus on reducing material movement and assembly-line balancing. Retail firms focus on product exposure. Storage layouts focus on the optimum trade-off between storage costs and material handling costs.

Often the variables in the layout problem are so wide ranging and numerous as to preclude finding an optimal solution. For this reason, layout decisions, although having received substantial research effort, remain something of an art.

BEFORE COMING TO CLASS, READ CHAPTER 9 IN YOUR TEXT AND ANSWER THESE QUESTIONS.

1. What is the operations manager trying to achieve with process-oriented layout, and when is it used? _____

   _____

   _____

2. What is a product-oriented layout, and when is it used? _____

   _____

   _____

3. What is a work cell, and why do firms use it? _____

   _____

   _____

4. When are fixed-position layouts needed? _____

   _____

   _____

5. What is cross-docking? _____

   _____

   _____

6. What is random stocking? _____

THE STRATEGIC IMPORTANCE OF LAYOUT DECISIONS

TYPES OF LAYOUT

1. Fixed Position
2. Process Oriented
3. Office
4. Retail
5. Warehouse
6. Repetitive and Product Oriented

FIXED-POSITION LAYOUT

PROCESS-ORIENTED LAYOUT

$$\text{Minimize cost} = \sum_{i=1}^{n} \sum_{j=1}^{n} X_{ij} C_{ij} \qquad (9\text{-}1)$$

where n = total number of work centers or departments
i, j = individual departments
X_{ij} = number of loads moved from department i to department j
C_{ij} = cost to move a load between department i and department j

PRACTICE PROBLEM 9.1 ■ Process-Oriented Layout

As in most kitchens, the baking ovens in Lori's Kitchen in New Orleans are located in one area near the cooking burners. The refrigerators are located next to each other, as are the dishwashing facilities. A work area of tabletops is set aside for cutting, mixing, dough rolling, and assembling of final servings, although different table areas may be reserved for each of these functions.

Given the following interdepartmental activity matrix, develop an appropriate layout for Lori's Kitchen.

	INTERDEPARTMENTAL ACTIVITY MATRIX			
	COOKING BURNERS (A)	REFRIGERATORS (B)	DISHWASHING (C)	WORK AREA (D)
Cooking Burners (A)	—	7	193	12
Refrigerator (B)		—	4	82
Dishwashing (C)			—	222
Work Area (D)				—

The present layout is

A	B	C	D

with a distance of 10 feet between adjacent areas.
Computing the load × distance measure:

LOAD × DISTANCE		
A to B	7 × 10	70
A to C	193 × 20	3,860
A to D	12 × 30	360
B to C	4 × 10	40
B to D	82 × 20	1,640
C to D	222 × 10	2,220
Total		8,190

Develop a preferred layout. What is the sum of the loads × distance of your new layout?

Additional Practice Problem Space

Work Cells

FIGURE 9.8 ■ Improving Layouts by Moving to the Work Cell Concept

Note in both (a) and (b) that U-shaped work cells can reduce material and employee movement. The U shape may also reduce space requirements, enhance communication, cut the number of workers, and make inspection easier.

(a)

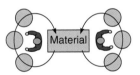

Current layout—workers in small closed areas. Cannot increase output without a third worker.

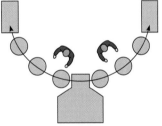

Improved layout—workers can assist each other. May be able to add a third worker.

(b)

Current layout—straight lines make it hard to balance tasks because workers may not be able to divide tasks evenly.

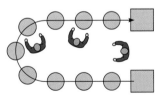

Improved layout—in U shape, workers have better access. Four workers were reduced to three.

Focused Work Center

Focused Factory

OFFICE LAYOUT

RETAIL LAYOUT

WAREHOUSING AND STORAGE LAYOUTS

Cross-Docking
Random Stocking
Customizing

REPETITIVE AND PRODUCT-ORIENTED LAYOUT

Fabrication Line
Assembly Line

FIGURE 9.11 ■ An Assembly-Line Layout

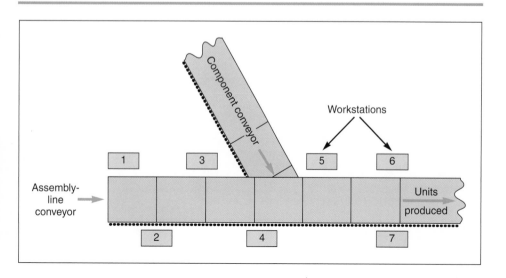

Assembly-Line Balancing

1. Cycle time $= \dfrac{\text{Production time available per day}}{\text{Units required per day}}$ (9-2)

2. Minimum number of workstations $= \dfrac{\sum\limits_{i=1}^{n} \text{Time for task } i}{\text{Cycle time}}$ (9-3)

3. Balance the Line Using a Technique in Table 9.4

TABLE 9.4 ■ Layout Heuristics That May Be Used to Assign Tasks to Work Stations in Assembly-Line Balancing

1. *Longest task (operation) time*	4. *Shortest task (operations) time*
2. *Most following tasks*	5. *Least number of following tasks*
3. *Ranked positional weight*	

PRACTICE PROBLEM 9.2 ■ Line Balancing

A firm must produce 40 units per day during an 8-hour workday. Tasks, times, and predecessor activities are as follows:

TASK	TIME (MINUTES)	PREDECESSOR(S)
A	2	—
B	2	A
C	8	—
D	6	C
E	3	B
F	10	D, E
G	4	F
H	3	G
Total	38 minutes	

Determine the cycle time and the appropriate number of workstations to produce the 40 units per day.

Efficiency

$$\text{Efficiency} = \frac{\Sigma \text{ task times}}{(\text{actual number of workstations}) \times (\text{assigned cycle time})} \qquad (9\text{-}4)$$

PRACTICE PROBLEM 9.3 ■ Efficiency

TASK ELEMENT	TIME (MINUTES)	ELEMENT PREDECESSOR
A	1	—
B	1	A
C	2	B
D	1	B
E	3	C, D
F	1	A
G	1	F
H	2	G
I	1	E, H

Given a cycle time of 4 minutes, develop an appropriate layout.

What is the efficiency of your layout?

Additional Practice Problem Space

Additional Practice Problem Space

DISCUSSION QUESTIONS

1. What are the six layout strategies presented in this chapter?
2. What are the three factors that complicate a fixed-position layout?
3. What are the advantages and disadvantages of process layout?
4. How would an analyst obtain data and determine the number of trips in:
   (a) a hospital?
   (b) a machine shop?
   (c) an auto-repair shop?
5. What are the advantages and disadvantages of product layout?
6. What are the four assumptions (or preconditions) of establishing layout for high-volume, low-variety products?
7. What are the three forms of work cells discussed in the textbook?
8. What are the advantages and disadvantages of work cells?
9. What are the requirements for a focused work center or focused factory to be appropriate?
10. What are the two major trends influencing office layout?
11. What layout variables would you consider particularly important in an office layout where computer programs are written?
12. What layout innovations have you noticed recently in retail establishments?
13. What are the variables that a manager can manipulate in a retail layout?
14. Visit a local supermarket and sketch its layout. What are your observations regarding departments and their locations?
15. What is random stocking?
16. What information is necessary for random stocking to work?
17. Explain the concept of cross-docking.
18. What is a heuristic? Name several that can be used in assembly-line balancing.

 CRITICAL THINKING EXERCISE

Supermarkets have seen great changes in the past decade, with many stores now including dry cleaners, video rentals, flower shops, bank branches, full bakeries, and other such services. But actual aisle layout in stores has changed very little in over 50 years. Many supermarkets have long unbroken aisles with high shelves. Some, like Leonard's Dairy Store in Norwalk, Connecticut, are designed so that it is almost impossible to turn around a shopping cart once a customer has entered an aisle. Controlling the flow of a shopper's route can mean increased exposure to high margin items and higher sales.

Discuss the features of the supermarkets at which you shop. Does the store break long aisles with "crossover" aisles or does it have shopping clusters? Why? What types of items occupy the "endcaps"? How does a product get itself positioned at an endcap? What other unique layout features are observed, and what are their advantages and disadvantages?

ACTIVE MODEL EXERCISE

This Active Model appears on your CD-ROM. It allows you to evaluate parameters in a process layout analysis. Active Model 9.1 contains a device for pairwise exchange of processes in rooms. There is a drop down box that tells the software which two processes to swap. There is a Swap button that will make the switch. If the

ACTIVE MODEL 9.1 ◾

Active Model 9.1
Process Layout Model
Using Walters Co. Data
in Example 1 in Your Text

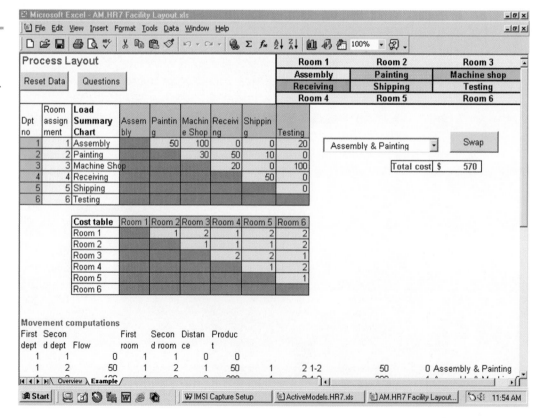

switch does not help then pressing the swap button a second time will place the two processes back into the rooms they were in before the swap.

Questions

1. What is the current total cost?
2. Assembly and Machine Shop have the highest degree of interaction. Would it be better to swap Assembly and Painting or Machine Shop and Painting in order to get Assembly and Machine Shop next to each other?
3. Use the swap button one swap at a time. If the swap helps, move to the next pair. If not, hit swap to put the departments back. What is the minimum total cost after all swaps have been tried?
4. Look at the two data tables and use the yellow shaded column to put processes in rooms. What room assignments lead to the minimum cost? What is this cost?

PROBLEMS*

9.1 Registration at Southern University has always been a time of emotion, commotion, and lines. Students must move among four stations to complete the trying semiannual process. Last semester's registration, held in the fieldhouse, is described in Figure 9.19. You can see, for example, that 450 students moved from the paperwork station (A) to advising (B), and 550 went directly from A to picking up their class cards (C). Graduate students, who for the most part had preregistered, proceeded directly from A to the station where registration is verified and payment collected (D). The layout used last semester is also shown in Figure 9.19. The registrar is preparing to set up this semester's stations and is anticipating similar numbers.

a) What is the "load × distance," or "movement cost," of the layout shown?

b) Provide an improved layout and compute its movement cost.

	Interstation Activity Mix			
	Pick up paperwork and forms	Advising station	Pick up class cards	Verification of status and payment
	(A)	(B)	(C)	(D)
Paperwork/forms (A)	---	450	550	50
Advising (B)	350	---	200	0
Class cards (C)	0	0	---	750
Verification/payment (D)	0	0	0	---

Existing Layout

A	B	C	D

|———30'———|———30'———|———30'———|

FIGURE 9.19 ■ Registration Flow of Students

9.2 David Jackson Enterprises, a machine shop, is planning to move to a new, larger location. The new building will be 60 feet long by 40 feet wide. Jackson envisions the building as having six distinct production areas, roughly equal in size. He feels strongly about safety and intends to have marked pathways throughout the building to facilitate the movement of people and materials. See the building schematic below. His foreman has completed a month-long study of the number of loads of material that have moved from one process to another in the current building. This information is contained in the flow matrix at the top of the next page. What is the appropriate layout of the new building?

*Note: **P** means the problem may be solved with POM for Windows; ✖ means the problem may be solved with Excel OM; and **P✖** means the problem may be solved with POM for Windows and/or Excel OM.

Flow Matrix between Production Processes

FROM \ TO	MATERIALS	WELDING	DRILLS	LATHES	GRINDERS	BENDERS
Materials	0	100	50	0	0	50
Welding	25	0	0	50	0	0
Drills	25	0	0	0	50	0
Lathes	0	25	0	0	20	0
Grinders	50	0	100	0	0	0
Benders	10	0	20	0	0	0

Building Schematic (with rooms 1–6)

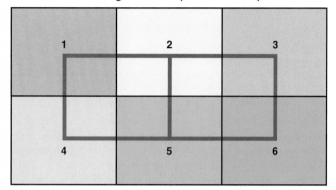

Distance between Areas (rooms)

	1	2	3	4	5	6
1		20	40	20	40	60
2			20	40	20	40
3				60	40	20
4					20	40
5						20
6						

P : 9.3   Six processes are to be laid out in six rooms along a long corridor at Tabitha McCuan Bookkeeping Service. The distance between adjacent work centers is 40 feet. The number of trips between work centers is given in the following table.

TRIPS BETWEEN ROOMS

FROM	To A	B	C	D	E	F
A		18	25	73	12	54
B			96	23	31	45
C				41	22	20
D					19	57
E						48
F						

a) Assign the processes to the rooms in a way that minimizes the total flow using a method that places rooms with highest flow adjacent to each other.

b) What assignment minimizes the total traffic flow?

P : 9.4   You have just been hired as the director of operations for Reid Chocolates, a purveyor of exceptionally fine candies. Reid Chocolates has two kitchen layouts under consideration for its recipe making and testing department. The strategy is to provide the best kitchen layout possible so that food scientists can devote their time and energy to product improvement, not wasted effort in the kitchen. You have been asked to evaluate these two kitchen layouts and to prepare a recommendation for your boss, Mr. Reid, so that he can proceed to place the contract for building the kitchens. (See Figure 9.20.)

P : 9.5   Reid Chocolates (see Problem 9.4) is considering a third layout, as shown below. Evaluate its effectiveness in trip-distance feet.

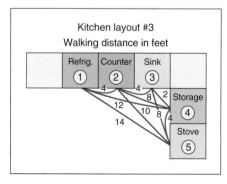

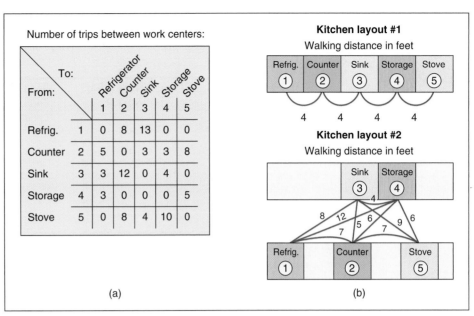

FIGURE 9.20 ■ Layout Options

P : **9.6** Reid Chocolates (see Problems 9.4 and 9.5) has yet two more layouts to consider.
a)   Layout #4 is shown below. What is the total trip distance?
b)   Layout #5, also below, has what total trip distance?

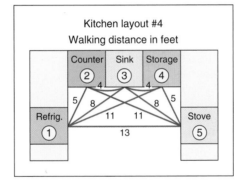

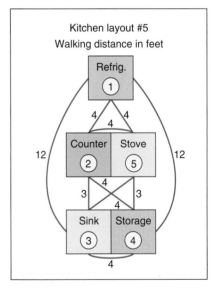

P : **9.7** The Temple Toy Company has decided to manufacture a new toy tractor, the production of which is broken into six steps. The demand for the tractor is 4,800 units per 40-hour workweek:

TASK	PERFORMANCE TIME (IN SECONDS)	PREDECESSORS
A	20	None
B	30	A
C	15	A
D	15	A
E	10	B, C
F	30	D, E

a)   Draw a precedence diagram of this operation.
b)   Given the demand, what is the cycle time for this operation?
c)   What is the theoretical minimum number of workstations?
d)   Assign tasks to workstations.
e)   What is the overall efficiency of the assembly line?

P :   **9.8**   South Carolina Furniture, Inc., produces all types of office furniture. The "Executive Secretary" is a chair that has been designed using ergonomics to provide comfort during long work hours. The chair sells for $130. There are 480 minutes available during the day, and the average daily demand has been 50 chairs. There are eight tasks.

TASK	PERFORMANCE TIME (MINUTES)	TASK MUST FOLLOW TASK LISTED BELOW
A	4	—
B	7	—
C	6	A, B
D	5	C
E	6	D
F	7	E
G	8	E
H	6	F, G

a)   Draw a precedence diagram of this operation.
b)   What is the cycle time for this operation?
c)   What is the minimum number of workstations?
d)   Assign tasks to workstations.
e)   What is the overall efficiency of the assembly line?

P :   **9.9**   The table below details the tasks required for Dallas-based T. Liscio Industries to manufacture a fully portable industrial vacuum cleaner. The times in the table are in minutes. Demand forecasts indicate a need to operate with a cycle time of 10 minutes.

ACTIVITY	ACTIVITY DESCRIPTION	IMMEDIATE PREDECESSORS	TIME
A	Attach wheels to tub	—	5
B	Attach motor to lid	—	1.5
C	Attach battery pack	B	3
D	Attach safety cutoff	C	4
E	Attach filters	B	3
F	Attach lid to tub	A, E	2
G	Assemble attachments	—	3
H	Function test	D, F, G	3.5
I	Final inspection	H	2
J	Packing	I	2

a)   Draw the appropriate network for this project.
b)   Which tasks are assigned to which workstation, and how much idle time is present?
c)   Discuss how this balance could be improved to 100%.

P :   **9.10**   Tailwind, Inc., produces high-quality but expensive training shoes for runners. The Tailwind shoe, which sells for $110, contains both gas- and liquid-filled compartments to provide more stability and better protection against knee, foot, and back injuries. Manufacturing the shoes requires 10 separate tasks. There are 400 minutes available for manufacturing the shoes in the plant each day. Daily demand is 60. The information for the tasks is as follows:

TASK	PERFORMANCE TIME (MINUTES)	TASK MUST FOLLOW TASK LISTED BELOW
A	1	—
B	3	A
C	2	B
D	4	B
E	1	C, D
F	3	A
G	2	F
H	5	G
I	1	E, H
J	3	I

Draw the precedence diagram. Assign tasks to the minimum feasible number of workstations according to the "greatest time remaining" decision rule. What is the efficiency of the process?

P : **9.11** Mach 10 is a one-person sailboat designed to be used in the ocean. Manufactured by Creative Leisure, Mach 10 can handle 40-mph winds and seas over 10 feet. The final assembly plant is in Cupertino, California. At this time, 200 minutes are available each day to manufacture Mach 10. The daily demand is 60 boats. Given the following information, draw the precedence diagram and assign tasks to the fewest workstations possible. What is the efficiency of the assembly line?

Task	Performance Time (Minutes)	Task Must Follow Task Listed Below
A	1	—
B	1	A
C	2	A
D	1	C
E	3	C
F	1	C
G	1	D, E, F
H	2	B
I	1	G, H

P : **9.12** Because of the expected high demand for Mach 10, Creative Leisure has decided to increase manufacturing time available to produce the Mach 10 (see Problem 9.11). If demand remained the same and 300 minutes were available each day, how many workstations would be needed? What would be the efficiency of the system? What would be the impact on the system if 400 minutes were available?

P : **9.13** If only 375 minutes were available each day (after allowances for personal fatigue and delay), what is the greatest number of Mach 10 sailboats Creative Leisure (see Problem 9.11) could produce in a day?

P : **9.14** Nearbeer Products, Inc., manufactures drinks that taste the same as a good draft beer but contain no alcohol. With changes in drinking laws and demographics, there has been an increased interest in Nearbeer Lite. It has fewer calories than regular beer, is less filling, and tastes great. The final packing operation requires 13 tasks. Nearbeer bottles Nearbeer Lite 5 hours a day, 5 days a week. Each week, there is a demand for 3,000 bottles of Nearbeer Lite. Given the following information, draw the precedence diagram. Assign tasks to the minimum feasible number of workstations according to the greatest time remaining decision rule. What is the efficiency of the process?

Data for Problems 9.14 and 9.15

Task	Performance Time (Minutes)	Task Must Follow Task Listed Below
A	0.1	—
B	0.1	A
C	0.1	B
D	0.2	B
E	0.1	B
F	0.2	C, D, E
G	0.1	A
H	0.1	G
I	0.2	H
J	0.1	I
K	0.2	F
L	0.2	J, K
M	0.1	L

P : **9.15** Nearbeer president Pete Nasta believes that weekly demand for Nearbeer Lite could explode (see Problem 9.14). How would the assembly line have to change if demand increased to 4,500?

P : **9.16** Suppose production requirements in Solved Problem 9.2 (see page 355) increase and require a reduction in cycle time from 8 minutes to 7 minutes. Balance the line once again using the new cycle time. Note that it is not possible to combine task times so as to group tasks into the minimum number of workstations. This condition occurs in actual balancing problems fairly often.

P : **9.17** Dr. Becky Mitchel, operations manager at Nesa Electronics, prides herself on excellent assembly-line balancing. She has been told that the firm needs to complete 96 instruments per 24-hour day. The assembly line activities are shown in the table at the top of the next page.

TASK	TIME (IN MINUTES)	PREDECESSORS
A	3	None
B	6	None
C	7	A
D	5	A, B
E	2	B
F	4	C
G	5	F
H	7	D, E
I	1	H
J	6	E
K	4	G, I, J
	50	

a) Draw the precedence diagram.
b) If the daily (24-hour) production rate is 96 units, what is the greatest possible cycle time?
c) If the cycle time after allowances is given as 10 minutes, what is the daily (24-hour) production rate?
d) With a 10-minute cycle time, what is the theoretical minimum number of stations with which the line can be balanced?
e) With a 10-minute cycle time and six workstations, what is the efficiency?
f) What is the total idle time per cycle with a 10-minute cycle time and six workstations?
g) What is the best work station assignment you can make without exceeding a 10-minute cycle time and what is its efficiency?

P : 9.18   Given the following data describing a line-balancing problem at Kate Moore's company, develop a solution allowing a cycle time of 3 minutes. What is the efficiency of that line? How many units can be produced in a 480-minute day?

TASK ELEMENT	TIME (MINUTES)	ELEMENT PREDECESSOR
A	1	—
B	1	A
C	2	B
D	1	B
E	3	C, D
F	1	A
G	1	F
H	2	G
I	1	E, H

: 9.19   The preinduction physical examination given by the U.S. Army involves the following seven activities:

ACTIVITY	AVERAGE TIME (MINUTES)
Medical history	10
Blood tests	8
Eye examination	5
Measurements (i.e., weight, height, blood pressure)	7
Medical examination	16
Psychological interview	12
Exit medical evaluation	10

These activities can be performed in any order, with two exceptions: Medical history must be taken first, and exit medical evaluation is last. At present, there are three paramedics and two physicians on duty during each shift. Only physicians can perform exit evaluations and conduct psychological interviews. Other activities can be carried out by either physicians or paramedics.

a) Develop a layout and balance the line. How many people can be processed per hour?
b) Which activity accounts for the current bottleneck?
c) If one more physician and one more paramedic can be placed on duty, how would you redraw the layout? What is the new throughput?

P : 9.20   As the McGuire Bicycle Co. of St. Louis completes plans for its new assembly line, it identifies 25 different tasks in the production process. VP of Operations Lou McGuire now faces the job of balancing the line. He lists precedences and provides time estimates for each step based on work-sampling techniques. His goal is to produce 1,000 bicycles per standard 40-hour workweek.

Task	Time (Seconds)	Precedence Tasks		Task	Time (Seconds)	Precedence Tasks
K3	60	—		E3	109	F3
K4	24	K3		D6	53	F4
K9	27	K3		D7	72	F9, E2, E3
J1	66	K3		D8	78	E3, D6
J2	22	K3		D9	37	D6
J3	3	—		C1	78	F7
G4	79	K4, K9		B3	72	D7, D8, D9, C1
G5	29	K9, J1		B5	108	C1
F3	32	J2		B7	18	B3
F4	92	J2		A1	52	B5
F7	21	J3		A2	72	B5
F9	126	G4		A3	114	B7, A1, A2
E2	18	G5, F3				

a) Balance this operation, using various heuristics. Which is best?
b) What happens if the firm can change to a 41-hour workweek?

 # INTERNET HOMEWORK PROBLEMS

See our Internet homepage at **www.prenhall.com/heizer** for these additional homework problems: 9.21 through 9.24.

CASE STUDY

State Automobile License Renewals

Henry Coupe, the manager of a metropolitan branch office of the state Department of Motor Vehicles, attempted to analyze the driver's license-renewal operations. He had to perform several steps. After examining the license-renewal process, he identified those steps and associated times required to perform each step, as shown in the following table:

State Automobile License-Renewals Process Times

Step	Average Time to Perform (Seconds)
1. Review renewal application for correctness	15
2. Process and record payment	30
3. Check file for violations and restrictions	60
4. Conduct eye test	40
5. Photograph applicant	20
6. Issue temporary license	30

Coupe found that each step was assigned to a different person. Each application was a separate process in the sequence shown above. He determined that his office should be prepared to accommodate a maximum demand of processing 120 renewal applicants per hour.

He observed that work was unevenly divided among clerks and that the clerk responsible for checking violations tended to shortcut

her task to keep up with the others. Long lines built up during the maximum-demand periods.

Coupe also found that steps 1 to 4 were handled by general clerks who were each paid $12 per hour. Step 5 was performed by a photographer paid $16 per hour. (Branch offices were charged $10 per hour for each camera to perform photography.) Step 6, issuing temporary licenses, was required by state policy to be handled by uniformed motor vehicle officers. Officers were paid $18 per hour but could be assigned to any job except photography.

A review of the jobs indicated that step 1, reviewing applications for correctness, had to be performed before any other step could be taken. Similarly, step 6, issuing temporary licenses, could not be performed until all the other steps were completed.

Henry Coupe was under severe pressure to increase productivity and reduce costs, but he was also told by the regional director that he must accommodate the demand for renewals. Otherwise, "heads would roll."

Discussion Questions

1. What is the maximum number of applications per hour that can be handled by the present configuration of the process?
2. How many applications can be processed per hour if a second clerk is added to check for violations?
3. Assuming the addition of one more clerk, what is the maximum number of applications the process can handle?
4. How would you suggest modifying the process in order to accommodate 120 applications per hour?

Source: Updated from a case by W. Earl Sasser, Paul R. Olson, and D. Daryl Wyckoff, *Management of Services Operations: Text, Cases, and Readings* (Boston: Allyn & Bacon).

VIDEO CASE STUDY

Facility Layout at Wheeled Coach

When President Bob Collins began his career at Wheeled Coach, the world's largest manufacturer of ambulances, there were only a handful of employees. Now the firm's Florida plant has a workforce of 350. The physical plant has also expanded, with offices, R&D, final assembly, and wiring, cabinetry, and upholstery work cells in one large building. Growth has forced the painting work cell into a separate building, aluminum fabrication and body installation into another, inspection and shipping into a fourth, and warehousing into yet another.

Like many growing companies, Wheeled Coach was not able to design its facility from scratch. And while management realizes that material-handling costs are a little higher than an ideal layout would provide, Collins is pleased with the way the facility has evolved and employees have adapted. The aluminum cutting work cell lies adjacent to body fabrication, which, in turn, is located next to the body-installation work cell. And while the vehicle must be driven across a street to one building for painting and then to another for final assembly, at least the ambulance is on wheels. Collins is also satisfied with the flexibility shown in design of the work cells. Cell construction is quite modular and can accommodate changes in product mix and volume. Additionally, work cells are typically small and movable, with many work benches and staging racks borne on wheels so that they can be easily rearranged and products transported to the assembly line.

Assembly-line balancing is one key problem facing Wheeled Coach and every other repetitive manufacturer. Produced on a schedule calling for four 10-hour work days per week, once an ambulance is on one of the six final assembly lines, it *must* move forward each day to the next workstation. Balancing just enough workers and tasks at each of the seven workstations is a never-ending challenge. Too many workers end up running into each other; too few can't finish an ambulance in 7 days. Constant shifting of design and mix and improved analysis has led to frequent changes.

Discussion Questions*

1. What analytical techniques are available to help a company like Wheeled Coach deal with layout problems?
2. What suggestions would you make to Bob Collins about his layout?
3. How would you measure the "efficiency" of this layout?

*You may wish to view this video case on your CD-ROM before addressing these questions.

Chapter 10

Human Resources and Job Design

Chapter Outline

"We hired workers and human beings came instead." Max Firsh's words ring very true to the operations manager because organizations do not function without human beings and do not function well without competent, motivated human beings. The objective of a human resource strategy is to design jobs and manage labor so that people are effectively and efficiently utilized.

This chapter discusses how operations managers can achieve an effective human resource strategy by effective labor planning, job design, a visual workplace, and labor standards to provide a competitive advantage.

BEFORE COMING TO CLASS, READ CHAPTER 10 IN YOUR TEXT AND ANSWER THESE QUESTIONS.

1. Identify the constraints on a human resource strategy. _____

_____

_____

2. How do job classifications and work rules limit an effective human resource strategy? _____

_____

_____

3. What are the advantages of labor specialization? _____

_____

_____

4. What are the advantages of job enrichment? _____

_____

_____

5. What is a process chart? _____

_____

_____

6. What are the core job characteristics as defined by Hackman and Oldham? _____

_____

HUMAN RESOURCE STRATEGY FOR COMPETITIVE ADVANTAGE

Objective of Human Resource Strategy

LABOR PLANNING

JOB DESIGN

Labor Specialization

Job Expansion

FIGURE 10.2 ■ An Example of Job Enlargement (*horizontal* job expansion) and Job Enrichment (*vertical* job expansion)

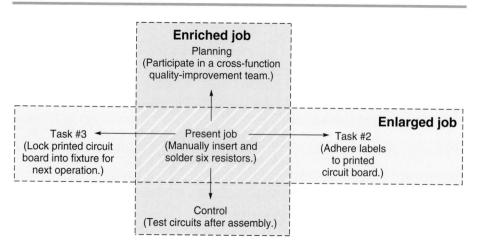

Psychological Components

Self-Directed Teams

FIGURE 10.3 ■ Job Design Continuum

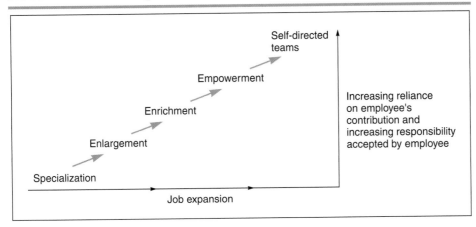

Motivation and Incentive Systems

Ergonomics and Work Methods

Ergonomics/Human Factors

Methods Analysis

Flow Diagrams and Process Charts

FIGURE 10.5 ■ Flow Diagram of Axle-Stand Production Line at Paddy Hopkirk Factory

(a) Old method; (b) new method; (c) process chart of axle-stand production using Paddy Hopkirk's new method (shown in b).

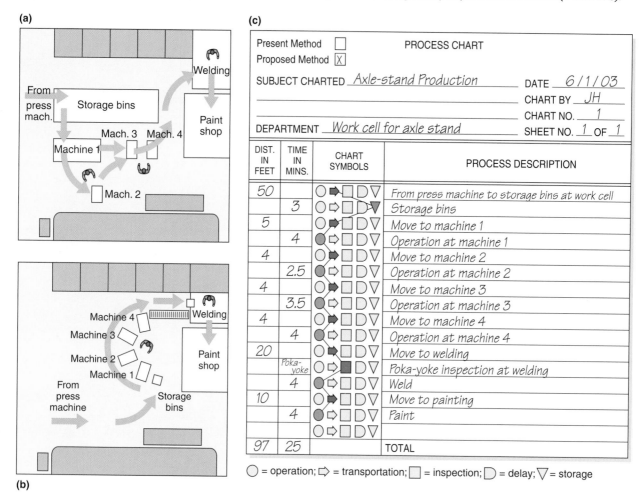

○ = operation; ⇨ = transportation; □ = inspection; ⬭ = delay; ▽ = storage

---

PRACTICE PROBLEM 10.1 ■ Process Chart for Sandwich

Develop a *process chart* for making a grilled cheese sandwich. Process charts should be quite detailed, containing all the required elements of the entire process. You should incorporate all the steps necessary for each part of the process of making the sandwich.

Additional Practice Problem Space

Activity and Operations Charts

FIGURE 10.6 ■ Activity Chart for Two-Person Crew Doing an Oil Change in 12 Minutes at Quick Car Lube

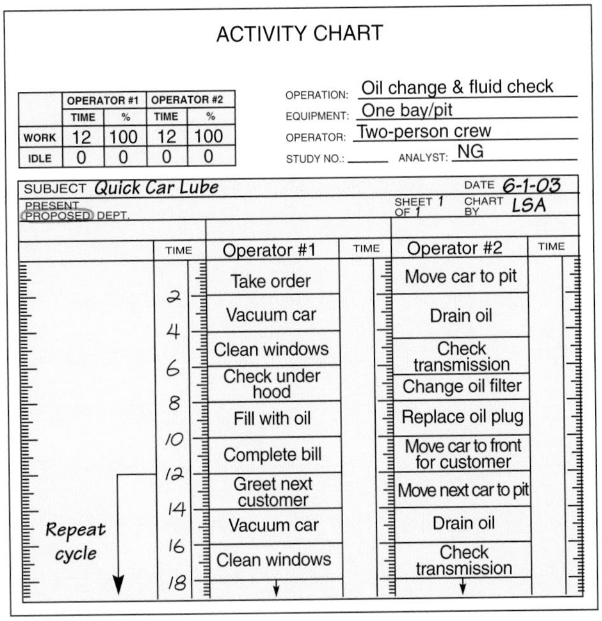

FIGURE 10.7 ■ Operation Chart (left-hand/right-hand chart) for Bolt-Washer Assembly

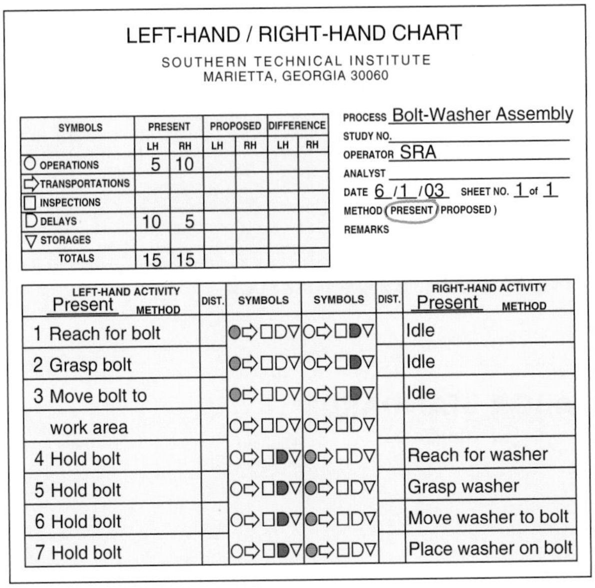

ACTIVITY CHART

	OPERATOR #1		OPERATOR #2	
	TIME	%	TIME	%
WORK	12	100	12	100
IDLE	0	0	0	0

OPERATION: Oil change & fluid check
EQUIPMENT: One bay/pit
OPERATOR: Two-person crew
STUDY NO.: _____ ANALYST: NG

SUBJECT *Quick Car Lube*　　DATE *6-1-03*
PRESENT (PROPOSED) DEPT.　　SHEET 1 OF 1　CHART BY *LSA*

TIME	Operator #1	TIME	Operator #2	TIME
2	Take order		Move car to pit	
4	Vacuum car		Drain oil	
6	Clean windows		Check transmission	
8	Check under hood		Change oil filter	
10	Fill with oil		Replace oil plug	
12	Complete bill		Move car to front for customer	
14	Greet next customer		Move next car to pit	
16	Vacuum car		Drain oil	
18	Clean windows		Check transmission	

Repeat cycle

LEFT-HAND / RIGHT-HAND CHART

SOUTHERN TECHNICAL INSTITUTE
MARIETTA, GEORGIA 30060

SYMBOLS	PRESENT		PROPOSED		DIFFERENCE	
	LH	RH	LH	RH	LH	RH
○ OPERATIONS	5	10				
⇨ TRANSPORTATIONS						
☐ INSPECTIONS						
D DELAYS	10	5				
▽ STORAGES						
TOTALS	15	15				

PROCESS Bolt-Washer Assembly
STUDY NO._____
OPERATOR SRA
ANALYST _____
DATE 6 /1 /03　SHEET NO. 1 of 1
METHOD (PRESENT/ PROPOSED)
REMARKS

LEFT-HAND ACTIVITY Present METHOD	DIST.	SYMBOLS	SYMBOLS	DIST.	RIGHT-HAND ACTIVITY Present METHOD
1 Reach for bolt		○⇨☐D▽	○⇨☐D▽		Idle
2 Grasp bolt		○⇨☐D▽	○⇨☐D▽		Idle
3 Move bolt to		○⇨☐D▽	○⇨☐D▽		Idle
work area		○⇨☐D▽	○⇨☐D▽		
4 Hold bolt		○⇨☐D▽	○⇨☐D▽		Reach for washer
5 Hold bolt		○⇨☐D▽	○⇨☐D▽		Grasp washer
6 Hold bolt		○⇨☐D▽	○⇨☐D▽		Move washer to bolt
7 Hold bolt		○⇨☐D▽	○⇨☐D▽		Place washer on bolt

PRACTICE PROBLEM 10.2 ■ Activity Chart for Laundry

Develop an *activity chart* for doing three loads of laundry. Activity charts should be quite detailed, containing all the required elements of the entire process and the utilization of required resources. For this exercise, assume you will have access to one washing machine and one dryer.

Additional Practice Problem Space

THE VISUAL WORKPLACE

LABOR STANDARDS

DISCUSSION QUESTIONS

1. How would you define a good quality of work life?
2. What are some of the worst jobs you know about? Why are they bad jobs? Why do people want these jobs?
3. If you were redesigning the jobs described in Question 2, what changes would you make? Are your changes realistic? Would they improve productivity (not just *production*, but *productivity*)?
4. Can you think of any jobs that push the man–machine interface to the limits of human capabilities?
5. What are the five core characteristics of a good job design?
6. What are the differences among job enrichment, job enlargement, job rotation, job specialization, and employee empowerment?
7. Define vertical job expansion and horizontal job expansion. Explain clearly how they differ.
8. Explain how job expansion can lead to higher accident rates.
9. Define ergonomics. Discuss the role of ergonomics in job design.
10. List the techniques available for carrying out methods analysis.
11. What are the constraints on human resource strategy as presented in the text.

CRITICAL THINKING EXERCISE

The situation at the Lordstown, Ohio, airbag manufacturer was getting sticky. A skilled technician and member of the safety committee, Sharon Lavoy, suggested that the line be shut down because of horrible fumes created as employees inserted a chemical sensor into each airbag. A new bonding agent for sealing the sensors, though safe after drying, was highly toxic as a liquid. Additionally, the union steward was questioning safety standards, suggesting that the bonding agent remained toxic while drying. A recently installed ventilation system made little difference in the odor, but all tests had shown the chemical parts per million to be below the OSHA standard of 100. Plant manager Steve Goodman had discussed the issue with health and safety manager Holly Malcolm, who advised that although the OSHA stan-

dard is 100 ppm, the American Conference of Governmental Industrial Hygienists' (ACGIH) standard is only 50. Goodman was also well aware that although the new employee-empowerment program was important, the automobile assembly plant 15 miles away needed the airbags now. The automaker had no airbags in stock and depended on JIT delivery from the Lordstown plant. Therefore, shutting down airbag assembly would also shut down the assembly plant. Lordstown's reputation and the jobs of its people depended on timely airbag delivery.

First, if you were Steve Goodman, what decision would you make? Justify your position as well as those of the union and Sharon Lavoy. Finally, propose a solution to deal with the very immediate problem.

 ## PROBLEMS

10.1 Make a process chart for changing the right rear tire on an automobile.

10.2 Draw an activity chart for a machine operator with the following operation. The relevant times are as follows:

Prepare mill for loading (cleaning, oiling, and so on)	.50 min.
Load mill	1.75 min.
Mill operating (cutting material)	2.25 min.
Unload mill	.75 min.

10.3 Draw an activity chart (a crew chart similar to Figure 10.6 on page 10-5) for a concert (for example, Britney Spears, Sheryl Crow, Bono, Bruce Springsteen) and determine how to put the concert together so the star has reasonable breaks. For instance, at what point is there an instrumental number, a visual effect, a duet, a dance moment, that allows the star to pause and rest physically or at least rest his or her voice? Do other members of the show have moments of pause or rest?

10.4 Make an operations chart of one of the following:
a) Putting a new eraser in (or on) a pencil.
b) Putting a paper clip on two pieces of paper.
c) Putting paper in a printer.

10.5 Develop a process chart for installing a new memory board in your personal computer.

10.6 For a job you have had, rate each of Hackman and Oldham's core job characteristics on a scale from 1 to 10. What is your total score? What about the job could have been changed to make you give it a higher score?

10.7 Using the data from Solved Problem 10.1 in your text, prepare an activity chart similar to the one in the solved problem but using only *four* crewmembers.

10.8 Using the data provided in Solved Problem 10.1 in the text, prepare an activity chart similar to the one in the solved problem. However, consider the fact that fuel will now be delivered at the rate of 1 1/2 gallons per second.

10.9   Draw an activity chart for changing the right rear tire on an automobile with:
  a)   Only one person working.
  b)   Two people working.

10.10   Draw an activity chart for washing the dishes in a double-sided sink. Two people participate, one washing, the other rinsing and drying. The rinser dries a batch of dishes from the drip rack as the washer fills the right sink with clean but unrinsed dishes. Then the rinser rinses the clean batch and places them on the drip rack. All dishes are stacked before being placed in the cabinets.

10.11   Your campus club is hosting a car wash. Due to demand, there are only going to be three people scheduled per wash line. So three people have to wash each vehicle. Design an activity chart for washing and drying a typical sedan. You must wash the wheels but ignore the cleaning of the interior because this part of the operation is done at a separate vacuum station.

10.12   Design a process chart for printing a short document on a laser printer at an office. Unknown to you, the printer in the hallway is out of paper. The paper is located in a supply room at the other end of the hall. You wish to make five stapled copies of the document once it is printed. The copier, located next to the printer, has a sorter but no stapler. How could you make the task more efficient with the existing equipment?

10.13   Make an operations chart for taping two 5-inch-by-4-inch pictures onto a piece of paper (letter size) in a portrait layout. (Each picture is part of a presentation that you will copy and hand out to participants.) The tape comes from a dispenser, and you have unlimited space on the top of your desk.

INTERNET HOMEWORK PROBLEMS

See our Internet homepage at **www.prenhall.com/heizer** for these additonal homework problems: 10.14 through 10.17.

CASE STUDY

Karstadt versus J.C. Penney

Andreas Drauschke and Angie Clark work comparable jobs for comparable pay at department stores in Berlin and suburban Washington, DC. But there is no comparison when it comes to the hours they put in.

Mr. Drauschke's job calls for a 37-hour week with 6 weeks' annual vacation. His store closes for the weekend at 2 P.M. on Saturday afternoon and stays open one evening each week—a new service in Germany that Mr. Drauschke detests. "I can't understand that people go shopping at night in America," says the 29-year-old, a supervisor at Karstadt, Germany's largest deparatment store chain. "Logically speaking, why should someone need to buy a bicycle at 8:30 P.M.?"

Mrs. Clark works at least 44 hours a week, including evening shifts and frequent Saturdays and Sundays. She often brings paperwork home with her, spends her days off scouting the competition, and never takes more than a week off at a time. "If I took any more, I'd feel like I was losing control," says the merchandising manager at J.C. Penney.

While Americans often marvel at German industriousness, a comparison of actual workloads explodes such national stereotypes. In manufacturing, for instance, the weekly U.S. average is 37.7 hours and rising; in Germany, it is 30 hours and has fallen steadily over recent decades. All German workers are guaranteed by law a minimum of 5 weeks' annual vacation.

The German department store workers also fiercely resist any incursions on their leisure hours, while many J.C. Penney employees work second jobs and rack up 60 hours a week. Long and irregular hours come at a price, however. Staff turnover at the German store is negligible; at J.C. Penney, it is 40% a year. Germans serve apprenticeships of 2 to 3 years and know their wares inside out. Workers at J.C. Penney receive training of 2 to 3 days. And it is economic necessity, more than any devotion to work for its own sake, that appears to motivate most of the American employees.

Mr. Drauschke has a much different view: Work hard when you're on the job and get out as fast as you can. A passionate gardener with a wife and young child, he has no interest in working beyond the 37 hours his contract mandates, even if it means more money. "Free time can't be paid for," he says.

The desire to keep hours short is an obsession in Germany—and a constant mission of its powerful unions. When Germany introduced Thursday night shopping in 1989, retail workers went on strike. And Mr. Drauschke finds it hard to staff the extra 2 hours on Thursday evening, even though the late shift is rewarded with an hour less overall on the job.

Mr. Drauschke, like other Germans, also finds the American habit of taking a second job inconceivable. "I already get home at 7. When should I work?" he asks. As for vacations, it is illegal—yes, illegal—for Germans to work at other jobs during vacations, a time that "is strictly for recovering," Mr. Drauschke explains.

At J.C. Penney, Mrs. Clark begins the workday at 8 A.M.. Though the store doesn't open until 10 A.M., she feels she needs the extra time to check floor displays and schedules. Most of the sales staff clock in at about 9 A.M. to set up registers and restock shelves—a sharp contrast to Karstadt, where salespeople come in just moments before the shop opens.

(continued)

Discussion Questions

1. How does the work culture in the U.S. differ from that in Germany?
2. What do you see as the basic advantages and disadvantages of each system?
3. If you were the top operations executive for an international department store chain with stores in both Germany and the U.S., what basic issues would you need to address regarding corporate human resources policies?
4. Are the retailing-employee issues different than other industries?
5. Under which system would you prefer to work?

Source: Adapted from R. W. Griffin and M. W. Pustay, *International Business: A Managerial Perspective*, Second Edition, (pages 761–762). © 1999 Addison Wesley Longman. Reproduced by permission of Addison Wesley Longman. All rights reserved.

CASE STUDY

The Fleet That Wanders

In March 2003, Bill Southard, owner of Southard Truck Lines, in Canyon, Texas, purchased a dozen new tractors from ARC Trucks.* His relations with his drivers have been excellent, but the new tractors are creating a problem. His drivers do not like them. They complain that the new tractors are hard to control on the highway; they "wander." By wandering, the drivers seem to mean the tractors take more work to control at highway speeds. Moreover, when the drivers have a choice, they choose the older tractors. Two drivers have even left the company and Southard believes that, instead of helping him keep good drivers, the new trucks have actually contributed to losing them. After many talks with the drivers, Southard concludes that the new tractors do indeed have a problem. He further believes that this situation has serious negative implications for the future of the firm. The new tractors are fully outfitted with the newest navigation features, as well as numerous expensive creature comforts. They get better gas mileage, should have lower maintenance costs, and have the latest antilocking brakes.

Because each tractor costs over $75,000, Southard's investment approaches a million dollars. He is desperately trying to improve his fleet performance by reducing maintenance and fuel costs. However, these improvements have not happened. Additionally, he wants to keep his drivers happy. This has not happened either. Consequently, Southard has had a series of talks with the manufacturer of the trucks.

The manufacturer, ARC Trucks of Denton, Texas, redesigned the front suspension for the trucks that Southard purchased. However, ARC insists that the new front end is great and operates without a problem. Southard finds out, however, that since he purchased his trucks, there have been further (though minor) changes in some front-suspension parts. ARC claims these changes are the normal product improvement that it makes as part of its policy of continuous product improvement.

Despite several strongly worded requests by Southard, ARC Trucks has refused to make any changes in the tractors Southard purchased. The new trucks do not seem to have a higher accident rate, but they do not have many miles on them either. No one has suggested there is a significant safety problem, but Bill's drivers are adamant that they have to work harder to keep the new tractors on the road. The result is Southard has new tractors spending much of their time sitting in the yard, while drivers use the old tractors. Southard's costs, therefore, are higher than they should be. He is considering court action, but legal counsel suggests that he document his case.

Discussion Questions

1. What suggestions do you have for Mr. Southard?
2. Having been exposed to introductory material about ergonomics, can you imagine an analytical approach to documenting the problems reported by the drivers?

*Large highway trucks are made up of two components; one, a tractor, which pulls the second, a trailer.

VIDEO CASE STUDY

Hard Rock's Human Resource Strategy*

Everyone—managers and hourly employees alike—who goes to work for Hard Rock Cafe takes Rock 101, an initial 2-day training class. There they receive their wallet-sized "Hard Rock Values" card which they carry at all times. The Hard Rock value system is to bring a fun, healthy, nurturing environment into the Hard Rock Cafe culture. This initial course and many other courses help employees develop both personally and professionally. The human resource department plays a critical role in any service organization, but at Hard Rock, with its "experience strategy," the human resource department takes on added importance.

Long before Jim Knight, manager of corporate training, begins the class, the human resource strategy of Hard Rock has had an impact. Hard Rock's strategic plan includes building a culture that allows for acceptance of substantial diversity and individuality. From a human resource perspective, this has the benefit of enlarging the pool of applicants as well as contributing to the Hard Rock culture.

Creating a work environment above and beyond a paycheck is a unique challenge. Outstanding pay and benefits are a start, but the key is to provide an environment that works for the employees. This includes benefits that start for part-timers who work at least 19 hours per week (while others in the industry start at 35 hours per week); a unique respect for individuality; continuing training; and a high level of internal promotions—some 60% of the managers are promoted from hourly employee ranks. The company's training is very specific, with job-oriented interactive CDs covering kitchen, retail, and front-of-the-house service. Outside volunteer work is especially encouraged to foster a bond between the workers, their community, and issues of importance to them.

Applicants also are screened on their interest in music and their ability to tell a story. Hard Rock builds on a hiring criterion of bright,

(continued)

positive-attitude, self-motivated individuals with an employee bill of rights and substantial employee empowerment. The result is a unique culture and work environment which, no doubt, contributes to the low turnover of hourly people—one-half the industry average.

The layout, memorabilia, music, and videos are important elements in the Hard Rock "experience," but it falls on the waiters and waitresses to make the experience come alive. They are particularly focused on providing an authentic and memorable dining experience. Like Southwest Airlines, Hard Rock is looking for people with a cause—people who like to serve. By succeeding with its human resource strategy, Hard Rock obtains a competitive advantage.

Discussion Questions†

1. What has Hard Rock done to lower employee turnover to one-half the industry average?
2. How does Hard Rock's human resource department support the company's overall strategy?
3. How would Hard Rock's value system work for automobile assembly line workers?

*Hard Rock Cafe's mission statement appears in Chapter 2 in Figure 2.2 in your text.

†Before answering these questions, you may wish to view this video case on your CD.

Source: Professors Barry Render (Rollins College), Jay Heizer (Texas Lutheran University), and Beverly Amer (Northern Arizona University).

Hard Rock Values

1. Innovate and create at every opportunity.
2. Encourage our employees to maximize their potential.
3. Love All—Serve All... treat every individual with respect.
4. Deliver exceptional quality... exceed expectations.
5. Ensure the long-term growth and success of our organization.
6. Save the Planet... actively participate in the well-being of our planet and its people.
7. Practice honesty, integrity and professionalism.

Supplement 10

Work Measurement

Supplement Outline

LABOR STANDARDS AND WORK MEASUREMENT

HISTORICAL EXPERIENCE

TIME STUDIES

PREDETERMINED TIME STANDARDS

WORK SAMPLING

Labor standards are required for efficient operations. They are needed for production planning, labor planning, costing, and evaluating performance. They can also be used as a basis for incentive systems. They are used in both the factory and the office. Standards may be established via historical data, time studies, predetermined time standards, and work sampling.

BEFORE COMING TO CLASS, READ SUPPLEMENT 10 IN YOUR TEXT AND ANSWER THESE QUESTIONS.

1. Why are labor standards important?_____

_____

_____

2. What is the normal time? _____

_____

_____

3. What does the term "allowance factor" mean? _____

_____

_____

4. What is a "classical stopwatch study"?_____

_____

_____

5. How did the Gilbreths set work standards? _____

_____

_____

6. What is a TMU, and what is its value? _____

_____

_____

LABOR STANDARDS AND WORK MEASUREMENT

1. Historical

2. Time Studies

3. Predetermined Time Standards

4. Work Sampling

HISTORICAL EXPERIENCE

TIME STUDIES

Eight Steps

1.

2.

3.

4.

5.

$$\text{Average observed cycle time} = \frac{\left(\begin{array}{c}\text{sum of the times recorded}\\\text{to perform each element}\end{array}\right)}{\text{number of cycles observed}} \qquad \text{(S10-1)}$$

6.

$$\text{Normal time} = (\text{average observed cycle time}) \times (\text{performance rating factor}) \qquad \text{(S10-2)}$$

7.

8.

$$\text{Standard time} = \frac{\text{total normal time}}{1 - \text{allowance factor}} \qquad \text{(S10-3)}$$

PRACTICE PROBLEM S10.1 ■ Normal and Standard Times

Carolyn Barrett, a marketing surveyor, takes an average of 10 minutes to complete a particular questionnaire. Carolyn's performance rating (pace) is 110%, and there is an allowance of 15%.

What is the normal time for completing this questionnaire?

What is the standard time for completing this questionnaire?

PRACTICE PROBLEM S10.2 ■ Additional Practice in Normal and Standard Times

Tom Leonard, of Leonard, Spitz, and Wareham, takes 3 hours and 25 minutes to write an end-of-month report. Tom is rated at 95% (work pace is 95%), and the office has a personal time allowance of 8%. There is no delay time or fatigue time.

What is the normal time for writing an end-of-month report?

What is the standard time for writing an end-of-month report?

PRACTICE PROBLEM S10.3 ■ Using Stopwatch Times

The two steps in preparing chocolate candy bars are molding and packaging. Personal fatigue and delay allowances are set at 15%. The molding machine operator is rated at 110%, and the packer is rated at 80%. Observed cycle times per batch are given as follows:

	OBSERVED CYCLE TIME IN MINUTES			
Task	1	2	3	4
Molding	26	30	29	31
Packing	45	50	35	30

Determine the normal and standard times for both tasks.

PRACTICE PROBLEM S10.4 ■ More Practice in Normal and Standard Times

A work-study sample of a manufacturing activity conducted over a 40-hour period shows that a worker with an 85% rating produced 12 parts. The worker's idle time was 10%, and the allowance factor was 12%.

Find the normal and standard times for this activity.

Additional Practice Problem Space

Sampling Error and Sample Size

$$\text{Required sample size} = n = \left(\frac{zs}{h\overline{x}} \right)^2 \tag{S10-4}$$

where h = accuracy level desired in percent of the job element, expressed as a decimal (5% = .05)

   z = number of standard deviations required for desired level of confidence (90% confidence = 1.65; see Table S10.1 or Appendix I for the more common z values)

   s = standard deviation of the initial sample

   $\overline{x}$ = mean of the initial sample

   n = required sample size

TABLE S10.1 ■ Common z Values

DESIRED CONFIDENCE (%)	z VALUE (STANDARD DEVIATION REQUIRED FOR DESIRED LEVEL OF CONFIDENCE)
90.0	1.65
95.0	1.96
95.45	2.00
99.0	2.58
99.73	3.00

PRACTICE PROBLEM S10.5 ■ Sample Size

Jim and Bob recently time-studied a janitorial task. From a sample of 75 observations, they computed an average cycle time of 15 minutes with a standard deviation of 2 minutes. Was their sample large enough that one can be 99% confident that the standard time is within 5% of the true value?

Additional Practice Problem Space

PREDETERMINED TIME STANDARDS

Therbligs

Time Measurement Units (TMUs)

FIGURE S10.2 ■ Sample MTM Table for GET and PLACE Motion

Time values are in TMUs.

GET and PLACE			DISTANCE RANGE IN IN.	<8	>8 <20	>20 <32
WEIGHT	CONDITIONS OF GET	PLACE ACCURACY	CODE	1	2	3
<2 LBS	EASY	APPROXIMATE	AA	20	35	50
		LOOSE	AB	30	45	60
		TIGHT	AC	40	55	70
	DIFFICULT	APPROXIMATE	AD	20	45	60
		LOOSE	AE	30	55	70
		TIGHT	AF	40	65	80
	HANDFUL	APPROXIMATE	AG	40	65	80
>2 LBS <18 LBS		APPROXIMATE	AH	25	45	55
		LOOSE	AJ	40	65	75
		TIGHT	AK	50	75	85
>18 LBS <45 LBS		APPROXIMATE	AL	90	106	115
		LOOSE	AM	95	120	130
		TIGHT	AN	120	145	160

PRACTICE PROBLEM S10.6 ■ MTM Calculations

Consider the following task broken down into 5 MTM elements:

	TMUs	CODE IN MTM BOOKS
Reach to tool box	14.2	R12D
Grasp a tool	3.5	BG1
Separate tool by pressing	10.6	AP2
Turn tool	3.5	T45S
Move and focus eyes	13.4	M12B

What is the total time for the task?

Additional Practice Problem Space

WORK SAMPLING

Five Steps

1. _____

2. _____

3. _____

4. _____

5. _____

$$n = \frac{z^2 p(1 - p)}{h^2}$$
(S10-7)

where n = required sample size

z = standard normal deviate for the desired confidence level

(z = 1 for 68% confidence, z = 2 for 95.45% confidence, and z = 3 for 99.73% confidence—
these values are obtained from Table S10.1 or the Normal Table in Appendix I)

p = estimated value of sample proportion (of time worker is observed busy
or idle)

h = acceptable error level, in percent

Additional Practice Problem Space

DISCUSSION QUESTIONS

1. Identify four ways in which labor standards are set.
2. Define normal time.
3. What are some of the uses to which labor standards are put?
4. As a new time-study engineer in your plant, you are engaged in studying an employee operating a drill press. Somewhat to your surprise, one of the first things you notice is that the operator is performing a lot of operations besides just drilling holes. Your problem is what to include in your time study. From the following examples, indicate how, as the individual responsible for labor standards in your plant, you would handle them.
   (a) Every so often, perhaps every 50 units or so, the drill press operator takes an extra-long look at the piece, which apparently is misshaped, and then typically throws it in the scrap barrel.
   (b) Approximately 1 out of 100 units has a rough edge and will not fit in the jig properly; therefore, the drill press operator picks up the piece, hits the lower right-hand edge with a file a few times, puts the file down, and returns to normal operation.
   (c) About every hour or so, the drill press operator stops to change the drill in the machine, even if he is in the middle of a job. (We can assume that the drill has become dull.)

5. What is the difference between "normal" and "standard" times?
6. What kind of work-pace change might you expect from an employee during a time study? Why?
7. How would you classify the following job elements? Are they personal fatigue or delay?
   (a) The operator stops to talk to you.
   (b) The operator lights up a cigarette.
   (c) The operator opens his lunch pail (it is not lunch time), removes an apple, and takes an occasional bite.
8. How do you classify the time for a drill press operator who is idle for a few minutes at the beginning of every job waiting for the setup man to complete the setup? Some of the setup time is used in going for stock, but the operator typically returns with stock before the setup man is finished with the setup.
9. How do you classify the time for a machine operator who, between every job and sometimes in the middle of jobs, turns off the machine and goes for stock?
10. The operator drops a part, which you pick up and hand to him. Does this make any difference in a time study? If so, how?
11. Describe Gilbreth's approach to setting work standards.

ACTIVE MODEL EXERCISE

This work sampling Active Model, using Example S5 in your text, displays the sample size required as a function of the proportion of time spent on a work activity. The scrollbars enable you to change the confidence or number of standard deviations. Alternatively, you may change the degree of allowable error, h, in order to determine the effects of this variable on sample size.

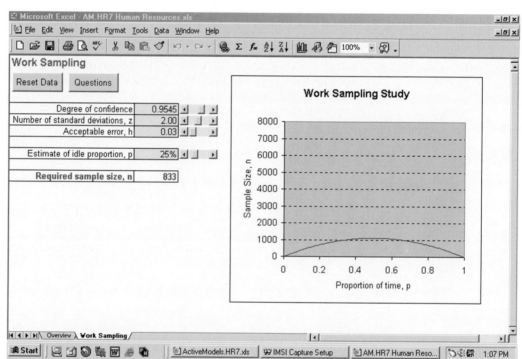

ACTIVE MODEL S10.1 ■

Work Sampling Analysis Using Data from Example S5 in Your Text

Questions

1. Scroll the mouse over the graph to determine what the sample size should be if $p = 30$ percent.
2. Based on the graph, what value of p requires the largest sample size?
3. Use the scrollbar to determine what happens to the sample size as the number of standard deviations, z, increases.
4. Use the scrollbar to determine what happens to the sample size as the acceptable error, h, increases.

PROBLEMS*

S10.1 An assembly-line employee had the following times, in seconds, for gluing three separate pieces together: 35, 33, 37, 34, 37, 56. What would you do next in attempting to determine the standard time for this operation?

P · S10.2 If a worker has times of 8.4, 8.6, 8.3, 8.5, 8.7, 8.5 and a performance rating of 110%, what is the normal time for this operation? Is the worker faster or slower than normal?

P · S10.3 If the worker in Problem S10.2 has a performance rating of 90%, what is the normal time for the operation? Is the worker faster or slower than normal?

P · S10.4 Refer to Problem S10.2. If the allowance factor is 15%, what is the standard time for this operation?

P · S10.5 Refer to Problem S10.2. If the allowance factor is 18% and the performance rating is now 90%, what is the standard time for this operation?

P · S10.6 A Northeast Airline gate agent, David Carhart, gives out seat assignments to ticketed passengers. He takes an average of 50 seconds per passenger and is rated 110% in performance. How long should a *typical* agent be expected to take to make seat assignments?

P · S10.7 After being observed many times, Marilyn Jones, a hospital lab analyst, had an average cycle time for blood tests of 12 minutes. Marilyn's performance rating is 105%. The hospital has a personal fatigue and delay allowance of 16%.
a) Find the normal time for this process.
b) Find the standard time for this blood test.

P · S10.8 Jell Lee Beans is famous for its boxed candies, which are sold primarily to businesses. About 30% of the candies are gift wrapped. One operator had the following observed times for gift wrapping in minutes: 2.2, 2.6, 2.3, 2.5, 2.4. If the operator has a performance rating of 105% and an allowance factor of 10%, what is the standard time for gift wrapping?

P · S10.9 After training, Shirley Benton, a computer technician, had an average cycle time for memory-chip tests of 12 seconds. Shirley's performance rating is 100%. The firm has a personal fatigue and delay allowance of 15%.
a) Find the normal time for this process.
b) Find the standard time for this process.

P : S10.10 Lissa Galbraith clocked the cycle time for welding a part onto truck doors at 5.3 minutes. The performance rating of the worker timed was estimated at 105%. Find the normal time for this operation.
Note: According to the local union contract, each welder is allowed 3 minutes of personal time per hour and 2 minutes of fatigue time per hour. Further, there should be an average delay allowance of 1 minute per hour. Compute the allowance factor and then find the standard time for the welding activity.

P · S10.11 The normal time for a particular task has been clocked at 25 minutes. If allowances are personal time: 5 minutes per hour; fatigue: 10 minutes per hour; and delay: 2 minutes per hour for set-up approval, then:
a) What is the allowance factor?
b) What is the standard time?

P : S10.12 A time study at the phone company has observed a job containing three elements. The times and ratings for 10 cycles are shown in the following table.

		OBSERVATIONS (MINUTES)									
ELEMENT	PERFORMANCE RATING (%)	1	2	3	4	5	6	7	8	9	10
1	85	.40	.45	.39	.48	.41	.50	.45	.39	.50	.40
2	88	1.5	1.7	1.9	1.7	1.8	1.6	1.8	1.8	2.0	2.1
3	90	3.8	3.4	3.0	4.8	4.0	4.2	3.5	3.6	3.7	4.3

a) Find the average observed time for each element.
b) Find the normal time for each element.
c) Assuming an allowance factor for 20% of job time, determine the standard time for this job.

Note: **P** means the problem may be solved with POM for Windows; ✘ means the problem may be solved with Excel OM; and **P✘** means the problem may be solved with POM for Windows and/or Excel OM.

P : S10.13   A hotel housekeeper was observed five times on each of four task elements shown in the table below. On the basis of these observations, find the standard time for the process. Assume a 10% allowance factor.

		OBSERVATIONS (MINUTES PER CYCLE)				
ELEMENT	PERFORMANCE RATING (%)	1	2	3	4	5
Check minibar	100	1.5	1.6	1.4	1.5	1.5
Make one bed	90	2.3	2.5	2.1	2.2	2.4
Vacuum floor	120	1.7	1.9	1.9	1.4	1.6
Clean Bath	100	3.5	3.6	3.6	3.6	3.2

P : S10.14   The Division of Continuing Education at Virginia College promotes a wide variety of executive-training courses for firms in the Arlington, Virginia, region. Division director Marilyn Helms believes that individually typed letters add a personal touch to marketing. To prepare letters for mailing, she conducts a time study of her secretaries. On the basis of the observations shown in the following table, she wishes to develop a time standard for the whole job.

   The college has an allowance factor of 12%. Helms decides to delete all unusual observations from the time study. What is the standard time?

	OBSERVATIONS (MINUTES)						PERFORMANCE
ELEMENT	1	2	3	4	5	6	RATING (%)
Typing letter	2.5	3.5	2.8	2.1	2.6	3.3	85
Typing envelope	.8	.8	.6	.8	3.1[a]	.7	100
Stuffing envelope	.4	.5	1.9[a]	.3	.6	.5	95
Sealing, sorting	1.0	2.9	.9	1.0	4.4	.9	125

[a]Disregard—secretary stopped to answer the phone.

P : S10.15   The results of a time study to perform a quality control test are shown in the table below. On the basis of these observations, determine the normal and standard time for the test, assuming a 23% allowance factor.

TASK ELEMENT	PERFORMANCE RATING (%)	OBSERVATIONS (MINUTES)				
		1	2	3	4	5
1	97	1.5	1.8	2.0	1.7	1.5
2	105	.6	.4	.7	3.7[a]	.5
3	86	.5	.4	.6	.4	.4
4	90	.6	.8	.7	.6	.7

[a]Disregard—employee is smoking a cigarette (included in personal time).

a)   What is the normal time?
b)   What is the standard time?

P : S10.16   Peter Billington, a loan processor, has been timed performing four work elements, with the results shown in the following table. The allowances for tasks such as this are personal, 7%; fatigue, 10%; and delay, 3%.

TASK ELEMENT	PERFORMANCE RATING (%)	OBSERVATIONS (MINUTES)				
		1	2	3	4	5
1	110	.5	.4	.6.	.4	.4
2	95	.6	.8	.7	.6	.7
3	90	.6	.4	.7	.5	.5
4	85	1.5	1.8	2.0	1.7	1.5

a)   What is the normal time?
b)   What is the standard time?

P : S10.17   Each year, Lord & Tailor, Ltd., sets up a gift-wrapping station to assist its customers with holiday shopping. Preliminary observations of one worker at the station produced the following sample time (in minutes per package): 3.5, 3.2, 4.1, 3.6, 3.9. Based on this small sample, what number of observations would be necessary to determine the true cycle time with a 95% confidence level and an accuracy of 5%?

P : **S10.18**   A time study of a factory worker has revealed an average observed time of 3.20 minutes, with a standard deviation of 1.28 minutes. These figures were based on a sample of 45 cycles observed. Is this sample adequate in size for the firm to be 99% confident that the standard time is within 5% of the true value? If not, what should be the proper number of observations?

P : **S10.19**   An analyst has taken 50 observations with an average time of 15 minutes and a standard deviation of 2.5 minutes. Is this number of observations sufficient to conclude with 99.5% confidence that the standard time is within 5% of its true value?

P : **S10.20**   Based on a careful work study in the Singhal Company, the results shown in the following table have been observed:

| | OBSERVATIONS (MINUTES) | | | | | PERFORMANCE |
ELEMENT	1	2	3	4	5	RATING (%)
Prepare daily reports	35	40	33	42	39	120
Photocopy results	12	10	36[a]	15	13	110
Label and package reports	3	3	5	5	4	90
Distribute reports	15	18	21	17	45[b]	85

[a]Photocopying machine broken; included as delay in the allowance factor.

[b]Power outage; included as delay in the allowance factor.

a)   Compute the normal time for each work element.
b)   If the allowance for this type of work is 15%, what is the standard time?
c)   How many observations are needed for a 95% confidence level within 5% accuracy? (*Hint:* Calculate the sample size of each element.)

P : **S10.21**   The Dubuque Cement Company packs 80-pound bags of concrete mix. Time-study data for the filling activity are shown in the following table. Because of the high physical demands of the job, the company's policy is a 23% allowance for workers. Compute the standard time for the bag-packing task. How many cycles are necessary for 99% confidence, within 5% accuracy?

| | OBSERVATIONS (SECONDS) | | | | | PERFORMANCE |
ELEMENT	1	2	3	4	5	RATING (%)
Grasp and place bag	8	9	8	11	7	110
Fill bag	36	41	39	35	112[a]	85
Seal bag	15	17	13	20	18	105
Place bag on conveyor	8	6	9	30[b]	35[b]	90

[a]Bag breaks open; included as delay in the allowance factor.

[b]Conveyor jams; included as delay in the allowance factor.

P : **S10.22**   Installing mufflers at the Stanley Garage in Golden, Colorado, involves five work elements. Linda Stanley has timed workers performing these tasks seven times, with the results shown in the following table.

| | OBSERVATIONS (MINUTES) | | | | | | | PERFORMANCE |
JOB ELEMENT	1	2	3	4	5	6	7	RATING (%)
1. Select correct mufflers	4	5	4	6	4	15[a]	4	110
2. Remove old muffler	6	8	7	6	7	6	7	90
3. Weld/install new muffler	15	14	14	12	15	16	13	105
4. Check/inspect work	3	4	24[a]	5	4	3	18[a]	100
5. Complete paperwork	5	6	8	—	7	6	7	130

[a]Employee has lengthy conversations with boss (not job related).

By agreement with her workers, Stanley allows a 10% fatigue factor and a 10% personal-time factor. To compute standard time for the work operation, Stanley excludes all observations that appear to be unusual or nonrecurring. She does not want an error of more than 5%.

a)   What is the standard time for the task?
b)   How many observations are needed to assure a 95% confidence level?

P · **S10.23**   Bank manager Art Hill wants to determine the percent of time that tellers are working and idle. He decides to use work sampling, and his initial estimate is that the tellers are idle 15% of the time. How many observations should Hill take in order to be 95.45% confident that the results will not be more than 4% away from the true result?

· **S10.24**   Supervisor Robert Hall wants to determine the percentage of time a machine in his area is idle. He decides to use work sampling, and his initial estimate is that the machine is idle 20% of the time. How many observations should Hall take in order to be 98% confident that the results will be less than 5% away from the true results?

· **S10.25**   A work sample taken over a 100-hour work month has produced the following results.

Units produced	300
Idle time (not part of task)	25%
Performance rating	110%
Allowance time	15%

What is the standard time for the job?

· **S10.26**   A random work sample of operators taken over a 160-hour work month at Tele-Marketing, Inc., has produced the following results. What is the percent of time spent working?

On phone with customer	858
Idle time	220
Personal time	85

· **S10.27**   A total of 300 observations of Bob Ramos, an assembly-line worker, were made over a 40-hour work week. The sample also showed that Bob was busy working (assembling the parts) during 250 observations. Find the percent of time Bob was working. If you want a confidence level of 95% and if 3% is an acceptable error, what size should the sample be? Was the sample size adequate?

· **S10.28**   Sharpening your pencil is an operation that may be divided into eight small elemental motions. In MTM terms, each element may be assigned a certain number of TMUs:

Reach 4 inches for the pencil	6 TMU
Grasp the pencil	2 TMU
Move the pencil 6 inches	10 TMU
Position the pencil	20 TMU
Insert the pencil into the sharpener	4 TMU
Sharpen the pencil	120 TMU
Disengage the pencil	10 TMU
Move the pencil 6 inches	10 TMU

What is the total normal time for sharpening one pencil? Convert your answer into minutes and seconds.

· **S10.29**   Supervisor Vic Sower at Huntsville Equipment Company is concerned that material is not arriving as promptly as needed at work cells. A new kanban system has been installed, but there seems to be some delay in getting the material moved to the work cells so that the job can begin promptly. Sower is interested in determining how much delay there is on the part of his highly paid machinists. Ideally the delay would be close to zero. He has asked his assistant to determine the delay factor among his 10 work cells. The assistant collects the data on a random basis over the next 2 weeks and determines that of the 1,200 observations, 105 were made while the operators were waiting for materials. What report does he give to Sower?

· **S10.30**   In the photo caption that begins the supplement in the text, Tim Nelson's job as an inspector for La-Z-Boy is discussed. Tim is expected to inspect 130 chairs per day.
 a)   If he works an 8-hour day, how many minutes is he allowed for each inspection (i.e., what is his "standard time")?
 b)   If he is allowed a 6% fatigue allowance, a 6% delay allowance, and 6% for personal time, what is the normal time that he is assumed to take to perform each inspection?

INTERNET HOMEWORK PROBLEMS

See our Internet homepage at **www.prenhall.com/heizer** for these additional homework problems: S10.31 through S10.38.

CASE STUDY

Jackson Manufacturing Company

Kathleen McFadden, vice president of operations at Jackson Manufacturing Company, has just received a request for quote (RFQ) from DeKalb Electric Supply for 400 units per week of a motor armature. The components are standard and either easy to work into the existing production schedule or readily available from established suppliers on a JIT basis. But there is some difference in assembly. Ms. McFadden has identified eight tasks that Jackson must perform in order to assemble the armature. Seven of these tasks are very similar to the ones performed by Jackson in the past; therefore, the cycle time and resulting labor standard of those tasks is known.

The eighth task, design of the new armature, requires performing a task that is very different from any performed previously, however. Kathleen has asked you to conduct a time study on the task in order to determine the standard time. Then an estimate can be made of the cost to assemble the armature. This information, combined with other cost data, will allow the firm to put together the information needed for the RFQ.

In order to determine a standard time for the task, an employee from an existing assembly station was trained in the new assembly process. Once proficient, the employee was then asked to perform the task 17 times so a standard could be determined. The actual times observed are:

1	2	3	4	5	6	7	8	9	10	11	12	13	14	15	16	17
2.05	1.92	2.01	1.89	1.77	1.80	1.86	1.83	1.93	1.96	1.95	2.05	1.79	1.82	1.85	1.85	1.99

The worker had a 115% performance rating. The task can be performed in a sitting position at a well-designed ergonomic workstation in an air-conditioned facility. Although the armature itself weighs 10.5 pounds, there is a carrier that holds it so that the operator need only rotate the armature. But the detail work remains high; therefore, the fatigue allowance will be 8%. The company has an established personal allowance of 6%. Delay should be very low. Previous studies of delay in this department average 2%. This standard is to use the same figure.

The workday is 7.5 hours, but operators are paid for 8 hours at an average of $12.50 per hour.

Discussion Questions

In your report to Ms. McFadden you realize you will want to address several factors:

1. How big should the sample be for a statistically accurate standard (at, say, the 99.73% confidence level and accuracy of 5%)?
2. Is the sample size adequate?
3. How many units should be produced at this workstation per day?
4. What is the cost per unit through this workstation in direct labor cost?

Source: Professor Hank Maddux, Sam Houston State University.

Supply-Chain Management

Chapter Outline

Most firms spend over 50% of their sales dollar on purchases. Because such a high percentage of an organization's costs are determined by purchasing, relationships with suppliers are critical. Indeed, as firms strive to increase their competitiveness via product customization, higher quality, cost reductions, and speed to market, they place added emphasis on the supply chain. The discipline that manages these relationships is known as *supply-chain management*.

The objective of supply-chain management is to build a chain of suppliers that focuses on maximizing value to the ultimate customer.

BEFORE COMING TO CLASS, READ CHAPTER 11 IN YOUR TEXT AND ANSWER THESE QUESTIONS.

1. Identify five supply-chain strategies._____

_____

_____

2. What is the "bullwhip" effect?_____

_____

_____

3. What factors contribute to the bullwhip effect?_____

_____

_____

4. Identify three negotiation strategies._____

_____

_____

5. What is outsourcing?_____

_____

_____

6. What is "Internet purchasing"?_____

_____

_____

THE STRATEGIC IMPORTANCE OF THE SUPPLY CHAIN

Supply-Chain Management

FIGURE 11.1 ■ The Supply Chain

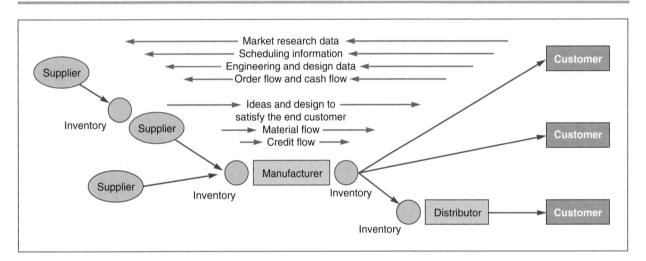

SUPPLY-CHAIN ECONOMICS

TABLE 11.3 ■ Dollars of Additional Sales Needed to Equal $1 Saved through the Supply Chain

PERCENT NET PROFIT OF FIRM	PERCENT OF SALES SPENT IN THE SUPPLY CHAIN						
	30%	40%	50%	60%	70%	80%	90%
2	$2.78	$3.23	$3.85	$4.76	$6.25	$9.09	$16.67
4	$2.70	$3.13	$3.70	$4.55	$5.88	$8.33	$14.29
6	$2.63	$3.03	$3.57	$4.35	$5.56	$7.69	$12.50
8	$2.56	$2.94	$3.45	$4.17	$5.26	$7.14	$11.11
10	$2.50	$2.86	$3.33	$4.00	$5.00	$6.67	$10.00

PRACTICE PROBLEM 11.1 ■ Supply-Chain Economics

Determine the sales necessary to equal a dollar of savings on purchases for a company that has a net profit of 6% and spends 70% of its revenues on purchases (using Table 11.3).

PRACTICE PROBLEM 11.2 ■ Supply-Chain Economics

Determine the sales necessary to equal a dollar of savings on purchases for a company that has a net profit of 4% and spends 40% of its revenues on purchases. (Use Table 11.3.)

Make or Buy

Outsourcing

SUPPLY-CHAIN STRATEGIES

1. Many Suppliers

2. Few Suppliers

3. Vertical Integration

4. Keiretsu Networks

5. Virtual Companies

FIGURE 11.2 ■ Vertical Integration Can Be Forward or Backward

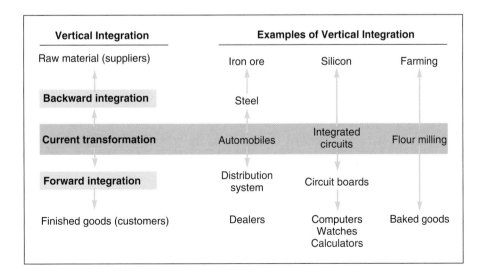

MANAGING THE SUPPLY CHAIN

Bullwhip Effect

Vendor Managing Inventory

Postponement

Channel Assembly

Drop Shipping

Blanket Orders

Standardization

Electronic Data Interchange (EDI)

INTERNET PURCHASING

VENDOR SELECTION

Vendor Evaluation

LOGISTICS MANAGEMENT

Distribution Systems: Trucking, Rail, Air, Water, and Pipelines

Shipping Costs

PRACTICE PROBLEM 11.3 ■ Shipping Costs

Phil Carter, president of Carter Computer Components Corp., has the option of shipping computer transformers from the company's Singapore plant via container ship or airfreight. The typical shipment has a value of $75,000. A container ship takes 24 days and costs $5,000; airfreight takes 1 day and costs $8,000. Holding cost is estimated to be 40% in either case. How should shipments be made?

Additional Practice Problem Space

BENCHMARKING SUPPLY-CHAIN MANAGEMENT

TABLE 11.5 ■ Supply-Chain Performance Compared

	TYPICAL FIRMS	BENCHMARK FIRMS
Administrative costs as percent of purchases	3.3%	.8%
Lead time (weeks)	15	8
Time spent placing an order	42 minutes	15 minutes
Percentage of late deliveries	33%	2%
Percentage of rejected material	1.5%	.0001%
Number of shortages per year	400	4

DISCUSSION QUESTIONS

1. Define supply-chain management.
2. What are the objectives of supply-chain management?
3. What is the objective of logistics management?
4. How do we distinguish between supply-chain management, purchasing, and logistics management?
5. What is vertical integration? Give examples of backward and forward integration.
6. What are three basic approaches to negotiations?
7. How does a traditional adversarial relationship with suppliers change when a firm makes a decision to move to a few suppliers?
8. What is the difference between postponement and channel assembly?
9. How does Wal-Mart use drop shipping?
10. What are blanket orders? How do they differ from invoiceless purchasing?
11. What can purchasing do to implement just-in-time deliveries?
12. What is e-procurement?
13. Both Brazil and Argentina have a strong labor union presence. What is the impact on unions in the VW approach to production described in the *Global Company Profile* that opens Chapter 11 in your text?

CRITICAL THINKING EXERCISE

What are the cultural impediments to establishing *keiretsu* networks in countries other than Japan? What would the antitrust division of the U.S. Department of Justice think of such arrangements? What would the European Union's position be on such arrangements? Find an example of a firm that has a *keiretsu* network and describe its effectiveness.

PROBLEMS

11.1 Choose a local establishment that is a member of a relatively large chain. From interviews with workers and information from the Internet, identify the elements of the supply chain. Determine whether the supply chain represents a low-cost, rapid response, or differentiation strategy (refer to Chapter 2 in your text). Are the supply chain characteristics significantly different from one product to another?

11.2 As purchasing agent for Woolsey Enterprises in Golden, Colorado, you ask your buyer to provide you with a ranking of "excellent," "good," "fair," or "poor" for a variety of characteristics for two potential vendors. You suggest that "Products" be weighted 40% and the other three categories be weighted 20% each. The buyer has returned the following ranking.

VENDOR RATING

Company	Excellent (4)	Good (3)	Fair (2)	Poor (1)
Financial Strength			K	D
Manufacturing Range			KD	
Research Facilities	K		D	
Geographical Locations		K	D	
Management		K	D	
Labor Relations			K	D
Trade Relations			KD	

Service	Excellent (4)	Good (3)	Fair (2)	Poor (1)
Deliveries on Time		KD		
Handling of Problems		KD		
Technical Assistance		K	D	

Products	Excellent (4)	Good (3)	Fair (2)	Poor (1)
Quality	KD			
Price			KD	
Packaging			KD	

Sales	Excellent (4)	Good (3)	Fair (2)	Poor (1)
Product Knowledge			D	K
Sales Calls			K	D
Sales Service		K	D	

DONNA INC. = D
KAY CORP. = K

Which of the two vendors would you select?

11.3 Using the data in Problem 11.2, assume that both Donna, Inc., and Kay Corp. are able to move all of their "poor" ratings to "fair." How would you then rank the two firms?

11.4 Develop a vendor-rating form that represents your comparison of the education offered by universities in which you considered (or are considering) enrolling. Fill in the necessary data, and identify the "best" choice. Are you attending that "best" choice? If not, why not?

11.5 Using sources from the Internet, identify some of the problems faced by a company of your choosing as it moves toward, or operates as, a virtual organization. Does its operating as a virtual organization simply exacerbate old problems, or does it create new ones?

11.6 Using Table 11.3 on page 11-2, determine the sales necessary to equal a dollar of savings on purchases for a company that has:
- a) A net profit of 4% and spends 40% of its revenue on purchases.
- b) A net profit of 6% and spends 80% of its revenue on purchases.

11.7 Using Table 11.3 on page 11-2, determine the sales necessary to equal a dollar of savings on purchases for a company that has:
- a) A net profit of 6% and spends 60% of its revenue on purchases.
- b) A net profit of 8% and spends 80% of its revenue on purchases.

11.8 Your options for shipping $100,000 of machine parts from Baltimore to Kuala Lumpur, Malaysia, are: (**a**) a ship that will take 30 days at a cost of $3,800, or (**b**) truck the parts to Los Angeles and then ship at a total cost of $4,800. The second option will take only 20 days. You are paid via a letter of credit the day the parts arrive. Your holding cost is estimated at 30% of the value per year.
- a) Which option is most economical?
- b) What customer issues are not included in the data presented above?

11.9 If you have a third option for the data in Problem 11.8 and it costs only $4,000 and also takes 20 days, what is your most economical plan?

11.10 Monczka-Trent Shipping is the logistics vendor for Handfield Manufacturing Co. in Ohio. Handfield has daily shipments of a power-steering pump from its Ohio plant to an auto assembly line in Alabama. The value of the standard shipment is $250,000. Monczka-Trent has two options: (1) its standard 2-day shipment or (2) a subcontractor who will team drive overnight with an effective delivery of 1 day. The extra driver costs $175. Handfield's holding cost is 35% annually for this kind of inventory.
- a) Which option is most economical?
- b) What production issues are not included in the data presented above?

INTERNET HOMEWORK PROBLEM

See our Internet homepage at **www.prenhall.com/heizer** for this additional homework problem: 11.11.

CASE STUDY

Dell's Supply Chain and the Impact of E-Commerce

Dell, the personal computer manufacturer highlighted in Chapter 7's *Global Company Profile* in your text, has long embraced the Internet and e-commerce in its supply chain. The figure at the bottom of this page shows Dell's unique e-commerce model.

Dell sells high-volume, low cost products directly to end users. Assembly begins immediately after receiving the customer order. Traditional PC manufacturers, in contrast, have previously assembled PCs ready for purchase at retail stores. Dell uses direct sales, primarily the Internet, to increase revenues by offering a virtually unlimited variety of PC configurations. Customers are allowed to select recommended PC configurations or customize them. Customization allows Dell to satisfy customers by giving them a product that is close to their specific requirements. Options are easy to display over the Internet and allow Dell to attract customers that value this choice. Dell also uses customized Web pages to enable large business customers to track past purchases and place orders consistent with their current needs. In addition, Dell constructs special Web pages for suppliers, allowing them to view orders for components they produce as well as current levels of inventory at Dell. This allows suppliers to plan based on customer demand and as a result reduces the bullwhip effect.

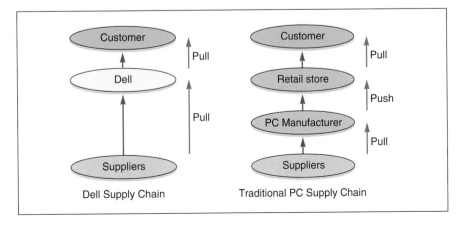

Dell Supply Chain

Traditional PC Supply Chain

Products in the PC industry have life cycles of only a few months. But PCs across different manufacturers are highly substitutable because they often have the same components. Thus a firm like Dell, which brings products to market faster than the competition, enjoys a huge early-to-market advantage. Competing firms that sell through distributors and retailers have to fill shelves at retailers before a product reaches the customer. Dell, in contrast, introduces a new product to customers over the Internet as soon as the first of that model is ready.

By using direct sales (phone and Internet) to sell PCs, Dell is able to eliminate distributor and retailer margins and increase its own margin. The direct sales model allows Dell customers to place orders at any time of the day from anywhere in the world and is much cheaper; retail stores have a huge array of additional costs because of their bricks and mortar model. Direct sales allow Dell to collect payment for its PCs in a matter of days after they are sold. However, Dell pays its suppliers according to the more traditional billing schedules. Given its low levels of inventory, Dell is able to operate its business with negative working capital because it manages to receive payment for its PCs an average of 5 days before it pays its suppliers for components. A PC supply chain that includes distributors and retailers finds it nearly impossible to achieve these results.

Dell's order processing, products, and assembly lines are designed such that all components on which customers are offered customization can be assembled in a matter of hours. This allows Dell to postpone assembly until after the customer order has been placed. As a result, Dell holds inventory in the form of components that are common across a wide variety of finished products. Postponement, component modularity, and tight scheduling allow low inventory and support mass customization. Dell maximizes the benefit of postponement by focusing on new PC models for which demand is hard to forecast.

PC manufacturers who sell via distributors and retailers find postponement virtually impossible. Therefore, traditional PC manu- facturers are often stuck with PC configurations that are not selling while simultaneously being out of the configurations that *are* selling. Dell, in contrast, is better able to match supply and demand.

Dell's e-commerce model results in higher shipping costs than selling through distributors and retailers, however. Dell sends individual PCs to customers from its factories. Because these shipments are small (often one or a few PCs), manufacturers selling through distributors and retailers ship with some economy of scale, using large truck shipments to warehouses and retailers, with the end user providing the last portion of delivery. The Dell supply chain's outbound transportation costs are higher, but relative to the price of a PC, transportation cost is low (typically 2% to 3%), and thus the impact on the overall cost is low.

Discussion Questions

1. Although it might seem at first glance that Dell, with its build-to-order model, is best equipped to benefit from e-commerce, a traditional PC manufacturer, selling through distributors and retailers, may also have a lot of gain from e-commerce. Why?
2. How has Dell exploited the advantage of the Internet to improve performance?
3. What is the main disadvantage of Dell selling PCs over the Internet?
4. How does Dell compete with a retailer who already has a PC in stock?
5. How does Dell's supply chain deal with the bullwhip effect?

Sources: Adapted from "Dell Branches Out," *Information Week* (August 26, 2002): 8–20, *Supply Chain Management*, S. Chopra and P. Meindl (Upper Saddle River, NJ: Prentice Hall, 2001), 399–402; and A. A. Thompson and J. E. Gamble, "Dell Computer Corporation: Strategy and Challenges for the 21st Century," *Cases in Strategic Management*, 12th ed. (New York: McGraw-Hill, 2001), C132–C173.

VIDEO CASE STUDY

Supply-Chain Management at Regal Marine

Like most manufacturers, Regal Marine finds that it must spend a huge portion of its revenue on purchases. Regal has also found that the better its suppliers understand its end users, the better are both the supplier's product and Regal's final product. As one of the 10 largest U.S. power boat manufacturers, Regal is trying to differentiate its products from the vast number of boats supplied by 300 other companies. Thus, the Orlando firm works closely with suppliers to ensure innovation, quality, and timely delivery.

Regal has done a number of things to drive down costs while driving up quality, responsiveness, and innovation. First, working on partnering relationships with suppliers ranging from providers of windshields to providers of instrument panel controls, Regal has brought timely innovation at reasonable cost to its product. Key vendors are so tightly linked with the company that they meet with designers to discuss material changes to be incorporated into new product designs.

Second, the company has joined about 15 other boat manufacturers in a purchasing group, known as American Boat Builders Association, to work with suppliers on reducing the costs of large purchases. Third, Regal is working with a number of local vendors to supply hardware and fasteners directly to the assembly line on a just-in-time basis. In some of these cases, Regal has worked out an arrangement with the vendor so that title does not transfer until parts are used by Regal. In other cases, title transfers when items are delivered to the property. This practice drives down total inventory and the costs associated with large-lot delivery.

Finally, Regal works with an Orlando personnel agency to outsource part of the recruiting and screening process for employees. In all of these cases, Regal is demonstrating innovative approaches to supply-chain management that help the firm and, ultimately, the end user. The *Global Company Profile* featuring Regal Marine (which opens Chapter 5 in your text) provides further background on Regal's operations.

Discussion Questions*

1. What other techniques might be used by Regal to improve supply-chain management?
2. What kind of response might members of the supply chain expect from Regal in response to their "partnering" in the supply chain?
3. Why is supply-chain management important to Regal?

*You may wish to view this case on your CD-ROM before answering the questions.

E-Commerce and Operations Management

Electronic commerce (e-commerce or e-business) is the use of computer networks to buy and sell products and services, and to exchange information. These high-speed networks span the globe and are not only fast but economical. Applications exist between firms, as well as between firms and their customers. Additionally, the technology is evident across business activities, from tracking consumer behavior in marketing functions, to collaboration on product design in production functions, to speeding transaction in accounting functions. E-commerce is about globalization, enhancing productivity, reaching new customers, and sharing knowledge for competitive advantage at the speed of electrons.

BEFORE COMING TO CLASS, READ SUPPLEMENT 11 IN YOUR TEXT AND ANSWER THESE QUESTIONS.

1. Define B2B, B2C, C2C, and C2B. _____

_____

_____

2. Identify six benefits of e-commerce. _____

_____

_____

3. Identify four limitations of e-commerce. _____

_____

_____

_____

4. What are three types of online catalogs? _____

_____

_____

5. What is Internet outsourcing? _____

_____

_____

6. What is a "pass-through facility"? _____

_____

_____

THE INTERNET

ELECTRONIC COMMERCE

FIGURE S11.1 ■ Types of E-Commerce Transactions

	Business	Consumer
Business	B2B GM/Ford/Daimler's Covisint Exchange	B2C Amazon, Dell, Netgrocer.com
Consumer	C2B Priceline, Travelocity	C2C eBay

ECONOMICS OF E-COMMERCE

PRODUCT DESIGN

E-PROCUREMENT

Online Catalogs

TABLE S11.3 ■ Internet Trading Exchanges

Health care products—set up by Johnson & Johnson, GE Medical Systems, Baxter International, Abbott Laboratories, and Medtronic Inc; called the Global Health Care Exchange (ghx.com).

Defense and aerospace products—created by Boeing, Raytheon, Lockheed-Martin, and Britain's BAE Systems; called the Aerospace and Defense Industry Trading Exchange (exostar.com).

Food, beverage, consumer products—set up by 49 leading food and beverage firms; called Transora (transora.com).

Retail goods—set up by Sears and France's Carrefour; called Global Net Xchange for retailers (gnx.com).

Steel and metal products—such as New View Technologies (exchange.e-steel.com) and Metal-Site (metalsite.com).

Hotels—created by Marriott and Hyatt, and later joined by Fairmont, Six Continents, and Club Corp: called Avendra (avendra.com) buys for 2,800 hotels.

RFQs

Internet Outsourcing

Online Auctions

INVENTORY TRACKING

E-commerce is supported by bar-code tracking of shipments. At each step of a journey, from initial pick-up to final destination, bar-codes are read and stored (left). Within seconds, this tracking information is available online to customers worldwide (right).

INVENTORY REDUCTION

SCHEDULING AND LOGISTICS IMPROVEMENTS

DISCUSSION QUESTIONS

1. Define e-commerce.
2. Explain the difference between B2B, B2C, C2C, and C2B e-commerce. Provide an example of each.
3. Why is e-commerce important in product design?
4. Explain each of the three versions of online catalogs.
5. What is the value of online auctions in e-commerce?
6. Explain how FedEx uses the Internet to meet requirements for quick and accurate delivery.
7. What economies are gained from e-commerce?
8. What are the benefits of e-commerce?
9. The Internet is revolutionizing the way companies do business. It may also increase the use of resources that are currently being underutilized. How can this happen? Provide some examples.
10. What types of services are being outsourced via the Internet?

PROBLEMS

S11.1   Using the Internet, find a consultant or software company that helps firms better manage their supply chains using e-commerce. Prepare a short report on the company, including the benefits it provides and the names of some of its clients.

S11.2   General Electric Information Services manages a community of tens of thousands of trading partners. Visit www.geis.com, then describe GE Global Exchange Services.

S11.3   Enter the www.peapod.com and www.netgrocer.com Web sites for electronic grocery shopping. Compare the services offered by these companies and recommend improvements in each.

S11.4   Visit the Web site for www.freemarkets.com (described in the *OM in Action* box). Explain its B2B e-commerce model.

S11.5   Use the Internet to find and explore the L.L. Bean Web site. What role does delivery logistics play in the firm's operations strategy? Does it have the added advantage of aiding Bean's marketing effort?

S11.6   The Internet should move many markets toward more open markets, perhaps with "perfect information." One of the characteristics of a perfect market is one where all information is readily available to all observers—customers and competitors alike. Under such conditions your suppliers, potential suppliers, and competitors would have substantial knowledge of your costs and selling prices. What are the implications of such knowledge on your supply chain?

S11.7   Use an online catalog to obtain the price of a small desk. Determine the dimensions and price.

CASE STUDY

E-Commerce at Amazon.com

Amazon started as an e-commerce book site and has now added music, toys, electronics, software, and home improvement equipment to its list of product offerings. As shown in the figure below, the Amazon supply chain is longer than that of a bookstore chain such as Borders or Barnes and Noble because of the presence of an additional intermediary—the distributor. The distributor margins in the Amazon supply chain can also be viewed as an increase in cost.

However, Amazon has exploited several opportunities on the Internet to attract customers and increase revenues. Amazon uses the Internet to attract customers by offering a huge resource of millions of books. A large physical bookstore, in contrast, carries fewer than 100,000 titles. Amazon also uses the Internet to customize service to the individual. Amazon's software allows it to develop and maintain customer relations by recommending books based on customer purchase history, sending reminders at holiday time, and permitting customers to review and comment on books. New titles are quickly introduced and made available online, whereas a brick-and-mortar bookstore chain must distribute and stock the titles prior to sale.

Amazon takes advantage of other Internet attributes: online ordering and 24-hour-a-day, 7-day-a-week availability. To this Amazon adds delivery to the customer's door.

Amazon uses e-commerce to lower inventory and facility costs, but processing costs and transportation costs increase. Amazon is able to decrease inventories by consolidating them in a few locations. A bookstore chain, on the other hand, must carry the title at every store. Amazon carries high-volume titles in inventory, but purchases low-volume titles from distributors in response to a customer order. This also tends to lower costs because the distributor is aggregating (consolidating) orders across bookstores in addition to Amazon.

E-commerce allows Amazon to lower facility costs because it does not need the retail infrastructure that a bookstore chain must have. Initially, Amazon did not have a warehouse and purchased all books from distributors. When demand volumes were low, the distributor was a more economical source. However, as demand grew, Amazon opened its own warehouses for high-volume books. Thus, Amazon's facility costs are growing but still remain lower than for a bookstore chain. Amazon does, however, incur higher order-processing costs than a bookstore chain. At a bookstore, the customer selects the books, and only cashiers are needed to receive payment. At

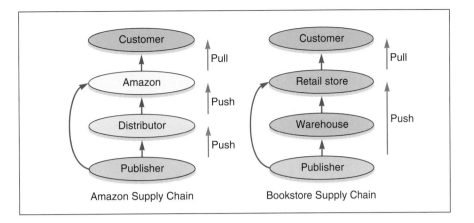

Amazon Supply Chain   Bookstore Supply Chain

Amazon, no cashiers are needed, but every order is picked from the warehouse and packed for delivery. For books that are received from distributors, additional handling at Amazon adds to the cost of processing orders.

Amazon's distribution incurs higher transportation costs than a retail store. Local bookstores do not have the cost of shipments to customers, as most customers take the books with them at the time of the sale. Amazon, in contrast, incurs this cost—which represents a significant fraction of the cost of a book (as high as 100% on an inexpensive book). As demand has grown, Amazon has opened six warehouses, with more than 3 million square feet, in an effort to get close to the customer, decrease transportation costs, and improve response time (see the *Global Company Profile* that opens Chapter 12 in your text).

Discussion Questions

1. What are the advantages and disadvantages of selling books over the Internet?
2. If books can be downloaded online, how will Amazon's business change?
3. What other products could Amazon sell that are downloadable?
4. What do traditional bookstores have to gain from setting up an e-commerce side to complement their retail stores?

Sources: Adapted from S. Chopra and P. Meindl, *Supply Chain Management* (Upper Saddle River, NJ: Prentice-Hall, 2001): 403–406; *New York Times* (January 21, 2002): C-3; and *APICS—The Performance Advantage* (May 2001): 34–38.

Inventory Management

Chapter Outline

Inventory represents a major investment for many firms. This investment is often larger than it should be because firms find it easier to have "just-in-case" inventory rather than "just-in-time" inventory. Inventories are of four types:

1. Raw material and purchased components
2. Work-in-process
3. Maintenance, repair, and operating (MRO)
4. Finished goods

This chapter discusses the inventory management topics of ABC analysis, record accuracy, and cycle counting. Three inventory models used to control independent demands are introduced: the EOQ model, the production order quantity model, and the quantity discount model.

BEFORE COMING TO CLASS, READ CHAPTER 12 IN YOUR TEXT AND ANSWER THESE QUESTIONS.

1. What is ABC analysis? _____

_____

2. What are the basic assumptions of the EOQ model? _____

_____

_____

3. What is the reorder point and how is it computed? _____

_____

4. How does the production order quantity model differ from the EOQ model? _____

_____

5. Explain the trade-off between holding costs and ordering costs in the EOQ model. _____

_____

FUNCTIONS AND TYPES OF INVENTORY

Four Types of Inventory

1. Raw material

2. Work-in-process

3. Maintenance, repair and operating (MRO)

4. Finished goods

INVENTORY MANAGEMENT

ABC Analysis

FIGURE 12.2 ■ Graphic Representation of ABC Analysis

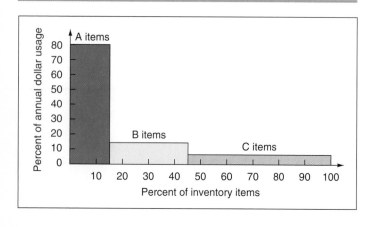

PRACTICE PROBLEM 12.1 ■ ABC

	ABC ANALYSIS	
STOCK NUMBER	ANNUAL $ VOLUME	PERCENT OF ANNUAL $ VOLUME
J24	12,500	46.2
R26	9,000	33.3
L02	3,200	11.8
M12	1,550	5.8
P33	620	2.3
T72	65	0.2
S67	53	0.2
Q47	32	0.1
V20	30	0.1
		100.0

What are the appropriate ABC groups of inventory items?

Additional Practice Problem Space

Inventory Accuracy and Cycle Counting

PRACTICE PROBLEM 12.2 ■ Cycle Counting

A firm has 1,000 "A" items (which it counts every week, i.e., 5 days), 4,000 "B" items (counted every 40 days), and 8,000 "C" items (counted every 100 days). How many items should be counted per day?

Service Inventory

INVENTORY MODELS

Independent vs. Dependent Demand

Holding Costs

TABLE 12.1 ■ Determining Inventory Holding Costs

CATEGORY	COST (AND RANGE) AS A PERCENT OF INVENTORY VALUE
Housing costs (building rent or depreciation, operating cost, taxes, insurance)	6% (3–10%)
Material handling costs (equipment lease or depreciation, power, operating cost)	3% (1–3.5%)
Labor cost	3% (3–5%)
Investment costs (borrowing costs, taxes, and insurance on inventory)	11% (6–24%)
Pilferage, scrap, and obsolescence	3% (2–5%)
Overall carrying cost	**26%**

Ordering and Setup Cost

MODELS FOR INDEPENDENT DEMAND: EOQ, PRODUCTION, AND QUANTITY DISCOUNT

ECONOMIC ORDER QUANTITY (EOQ)

Assumptions

1. _____

2. _____

3. _____

4. _____

5. _____

6. _____

Inventory Usage over Time

FIGURE 12.3 ■ Inventory Usage over Time

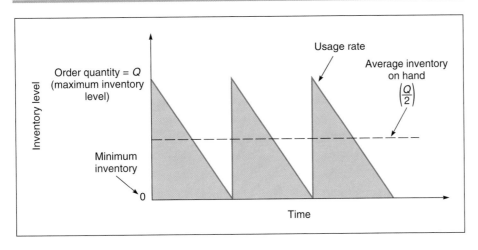

Minimizing Costs

FIGURE 12.4 ■ Total Cost as a Function of Order Quantity

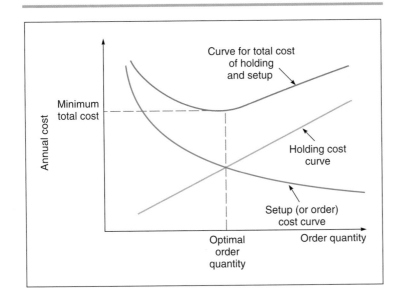

Definitions for the EOQ model

Q = Number of pieces per order

Q^* = Optimum number of pieces per order (EOQ)

D = Annual demand in units for the inventory item

S = Setup or ordering cost for each order

H = Holding or carrying cost per unit per year

Steps for Solving for Q*

1. _____

2. _____

3. _____

4. _____

EOQ Equation

$$Q^* = \sqrt{\frac{2DS}{H}}$$ (12-1)

PRACTICE PROBLEM 12.3 ■ EOQ

Assume you have a product with the following parameters:

Annual demand = 360 units

Holding cost per year = $1 per unit

Order cost = $100 per order

What is the EOQ for this product?

$$\text{Expected number of orders} = N = \frac{\text{Demand}}{\text{Order quantity}} = \frac{D}{Q^*}$$ (12-2)

$$\text{Expected time between orders} = T = \frac{\text{Number of working days per year}}{N}$$ (12-3)

PRACTICE PROBLEM 12.4 ■ Number of Orders/Time between Orders

Given the data from Practice Problem 12.3, and assuming a 300-day work year, how many orders should be processed per year? What is the expected time between orders?

Total Costs

Total annual cost = Setup cost + Holding cost $\hspace{4cm}$ (12-4)

$$TC = \frac{D}{Q}S + \frac{Q}{2}H \hspace{4cm} (12\text{-}5)$$

PRACTICE PROBLEM 12.5 ■ Total Costs

What is the total cost for the inventory policy used in Practice Problem 12.3?

Additional Practice Problem Space

Robust Model

PRACTICE PROBLEM 12.6 ■ Sensitivity

Based on the material from Practice Problems 12.3 to 12.5, what would cost be if the demand was actually higher than estimated (i.e., 500 units instead of 360 units), but the EOQ established in Practice Problem 12.3 is used? What will be the actual annual total cost?

Reorder Points

ROP= (Demand per day)(Lead time for a new order in days) = $d \times L$ (12-6)

FIGURE 12.5 ■ The Reorder Point (ROP) Curve

Q* is the optimum order quantity, and lead time represents the time between placing and receiving an order.

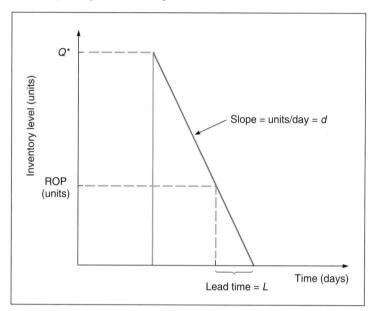

PRACTICE PROBLEM 12.7 ■ ROP

If demand for an item is 3 units per day, and delivery lead time is 15 days, what should we use for a simple reorder point?

Additional Practice Problem Space

PRODUCTION ORDER QUANTITY MODEL

Q = Number of pieces per order

H = Holding cost per unit per year

p = Daily production rate

d = Daily demand rate, or usage rate

t = Length of the production run in days

$$Q_p^* = \sqrt{\frac{2DS}{H[1-(d/p)]}} \qquad\qquad (12\text{-}7)$$

FIGURE 12.6 ■ Change in Inventory Levels over Time for the Production Model

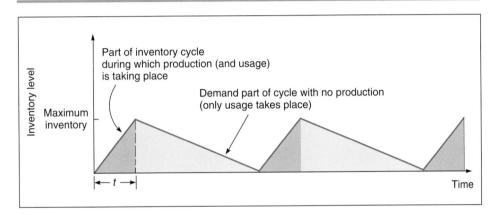

PRACTICE PROBLEM 12.8 ■ Production Order Quantity Model

Assume that our firm produces *Type C* fire extinguishers. We make 30,000 of these fire extinguishers per year. Each extinguisher requires one handle (assume a 300-day work year for daily usage rate purposes). Assume an annual carrying cost of $1.50 per handle, production setup cost of $150, and a daily production rate of 300. What is the optimal production order quantity?

Additional Practice Problem Space

QUANTITY DISCOUNT MODEL

Steps:

1. _____

2. _____

3. _____

4. _____

PRACTICE PROBLEM 12.9 ■ Quantity Discount

We use 1,000 electric drills per year in our production process. The ordering cost for these is $100 per order, and the carrying cost is assumed to be 40% of the per-unit cost. In orders of less than 120, drills cost $78 per unit; for orders of 120 or more, the cost drops to $50 per unit.

Should we take advantage of the quantity discount?

Additional Practice Problem Space

PROBABILISTIC MODELS

Safety Stock

$$ROP = d \times L + ss \qquad (12\text{-}11)$$

Annual stockout costs = the sum of the units short $\times$ the probability
$\times$ the stockout cost/unit $\times$ the number of orders per year $\qquad (12\text{-}12)$

PRACTICE PROBLEM 12.10 ■ Probabilistic Model

Litely Corp. sells 1,350 of its special decorator light switch per year and places orders for 300 of these switches at a time. Assuming no safety stocks, Litely estimates a 50% chance of no shortages in each cycle and the probability of shortages of 5, 10, and 15 units as 0.2, 0.15, and 0.15, respectively. The carrying cost per unit per year is calculated at $5, and the stockout cost is estimated at $6 ($3 lost profit per switch and another $3 loss of goodwills or future sales). What level of safety stock should Litely use for this product? (Consider safety stocks of 0, 5, 10, and 15 units.)

Additional Practice Problem Space

Service Level

$$ROP = \text{expected demand during lead time} + Z\sigma \qquad (12\text{-}13)$$

where Z = number of standard deviations
σ = standard deviation of lead time demand

$$\text{Safety stock} = Z\sigma \qquad (12\text{-}14)$$

PRACTICE PROBLEM 12.11 ■ Safety Stock

Presume that Litely (see Practice Problem 12.10) carries a modern white kitchen ceiling lamp that is quite popular. The anticipated demand during lead time can be approximated by a normal curve having a mean of 180 units and a standard deviation of 40 units. What safety stock should Litely carry to achieve a 95% service level?

FIXED-PERIOD (P) SYSTEMS

SUMMARY OF MODELS

TABLE 12.4 ■ Models for Independent Demand Summarized

Q = Number of pieces per order
EOQ = Optimum order quantity (Q^*)
D = Annual demand in units
S = Setup or ordering cost for each order
H = Holding or carrying cost per unit per year in dollars
p = Daily production rate
d = Daily demand rate

P = Price
I = Annual inventory carrying cost as a percentage of price
μ = Mean demand
σ = Standard deviation
x = Mean demand + Safety stock
Z = Standardized value under the normal curve

EOQ:

$$Q^* = \sqrt{\frac{2DS}{H}} \qquad (12\text{-}1)$$

Quantity discount EOQ model:

$$Q^* = \sqrt{\frac{2DS}{IP}} \qquad (12\text{-}10)$$

EOQ production order quantity model:

$$Q_p^* = \sqrt{\frac{2DS}{H[1 - (d/p)]}} \qquad (12\text{-}7)$$

Probability model:

$$\text{Safety stock} = Z\sigma = x - \mu \qquad (12\text{-}14)$$

Total cost for the EOQ and quantity discount EOQ models:

TC = Total cost

= Setup cost + Holding cost + Product cost

$$= \frac{D}{Q}S + \frac{Q}{2}H + PD \qquad (12\text{-}9)$$

DISCUSSION QUESTIONS

1. Describe the four types of inventory.
2. With the advent of low-cost computing, do you see alternatives to the popular ABC classifications?
3. What is the purpose of the ABC classification system?
4. Identify and explain the types of costs that are involved in an inventory system.
5. Explain the major assumptions of the basic EOQ model.
6. What is the relationship of the economic order quantity to demand? To the holding cost? To the setup cost?
7. Explain why it is not necessary to include product cost (price or price times quantity) in the EOQ model, but the quantity discount model requires this information.
8. What are the advantages of cycle counting?
9. What impact does a decrease in setup time have on EOQ?
10. When quantity discounts are offered, why is it not necessary to check discount points that are below the EOQ or points above the EOQ that are not discount points?

11. What is meant by *service level*?
12. Explain the following: All things being equal, the production inventory quantity will be larger than the economic order quantity.
13. Describe the difference between a fixed-quantity (Q) and a fixed-period (P) inventory system.
14. Explain what is meant by the expression "robust model." Specifically, what would you tell a manager who exclaimed, "Uh-oh, we're in trouble! The calculated EOQ is wrong, Actual demand is 10% greater than estimated."
15. What is "safety stock"? What does safety stock provide safety against?
16. When demand is not constant, the reorder point is a function of what four parameters?
17. How are inventory levels monitored in retail stores?
18. State a major advantage, and a major disadvantage, of a fixed-period (P) system.

CRITICAL THINKING EXERCISE

Wayne Hills Hospital in tiny Wayne, Nebraska, faces a problem common to large, urban hospitals as well as to small, remote ones like itself. That problem is deciding how much of each type of whole blood to keep in stock. Because blood is expensive and has a limited shelf life (up to 5 weeks under 1–6°C refrigeration), Wayne Hills naturally wants to keep its stock as low as possible. Unfortunately, past disasters such as a major tornado and a train wreck demon-strated that lives would be lost when not enough blood was available to handle massive needs. The hospital administrator wants to set an 85% service level based on demand over the past decade. Discuss the implications of this decision. What is the hospital's responsibility with regard to stocking lifesaving medicines with short shelf lives? How would you set the inventory level for a commodity such as blood?

ACTIVE MODEL EXERCISE

This Active Model explores the basics of a typical inventory decision and the sensitivity of the model to changes in demand and costs. It uses the data from Examples 3, 4, and 5 in your text.

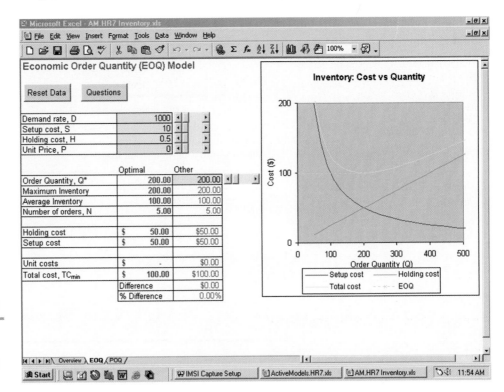

ACTIVE MODEL 12.1 ■

An EOQ Analysis of the Data in Examples 3, 4, and 5 (see your text) for Sharp, Inc.

Questions

1. What is the EOQ and what is the lowest total cost?
2. What is the annual cost of *carrying* inventory at the EOQ and the annual cost of *ordering* inventory at the EOQ of 200 units?
3. From the graph, what can you conclude about the relationship between the lowest total cost and the costs of ordering and carrying inventory?
4. How much does the total cost increase if the store manager orders 50 more hypodermics than the EOQ? 50 less hypodermics?
5. What happens to the EOQ and total cost when demand is doubled? When carrying cost is doubled?
6. Scroll through lower setup cost values and describe the changes to the graph. What happens to the EOQ?
7. Comment on the sensitivity of the EOQ model to errors in demand or cost estimates.

PROBLEMS*

 12.1 George Walker has compiled the following table of six items in inventory along with the unit cost and the annual demand in units.

IDENTIFICATION CODE	UNIT COST ($)	ANNUAL DEMAND IN UNITS
XX1	5.84	1,200
B66	5.40	1,110
3CPO	1.12	896
33CP	74.54	1,104
R2D2	2.00	1,110
RMS	2.08	961

Using ABC analysis, which item(s) should be carefully controlled using a quantitative inventory technique, and which item(s) should not be closely controlled?

 12.2 Boreki Enterprise has the following 10 items in inventory. Theodore Boreki asks you, a recent OM graduate, to divide these items into ABC classifications. What do you report back?

ITEM	ANNUAL DEMAND	COST/UNIT
A2	3,000	$ 50
B8	4,000	12
C7	1,500	45
D1	6,000	10
E9	1,000	20
F3	500	500
G2	300	1,500
H2	600	20
I5	1,750	10
J8	2,500	5

 12.3 McKenzie Services is considering using ABC analysis to focus attention on its most critical inventory items. A random sample of 20 items has been taken, and the dollar usages have already been calculated as shown below. Rank the items and assign them to an A, B, or C class. On the basis of this sample, does it appear that ABC analysis will help management identify the significant few items?

ITEM	DOLLAR USAGE	ITEM	DOLLAR USAGE
1	$ 9,200	11	$ 300
2	400	12	10,400
3	33,400	13	70,800
4	8,100	14	6,800
5	1,100	15	57,900
6	600	16	3,900
7	44,000	17	700
8	900	18	4,800
9	100	19	19,000
10	700	20	15,500

*Note: **P** means the problem may be solved with POM for Windows; ✕ means the problem may be solved with Excel OM; and **P✕** means the problem may be solved with POM for Windows and/or Excel OM.

12.4 Howard Electronics, a small manufacturer of electronic research equipment, has approximately 7,000 items in its inventory and has hired Joan Blasco-Paul to manage its inventory. Joan has determined that 10% of the items in inventory are A items, 35% are B items, and 55% are C items. She would like to set up a system in which all A items are counted monthly (every 20 working days), all B items are counted quarterly (every 60 working days), and all C items are counted semiannually (every 120 work days). How many items need to be counted each day?

P✘ · 12.5 William Beville's computer training school, in Richmond, stocks workbooks with the following characteristics:

$$\text{Demand } D = 19,500 \text{ units/year}$$
$$\text{Ordering cost } S = \$25/\text{order}$$
$$\text{Holding cost } H = \$4/\text{unit/year}$$

a) Calculate the EOQ for the workbooks. ᴜᴵ ᴵᴵ $EOQ = \sqrt{\dfrac{2DS}{H}}$
b) What are the annual holding costs for the workbooks?
c) What are the annual ordering costs? $EOQ = 243,750$

P✘ · 12.6 If $D = 8,000$ per month, $S = \$45$ per order, and $H = \$2$ per unit per month, what is the economic order quantity?

12.7 Henry Crouch's law office has traditionally ordered ink refills 60 units at a time. The firm estimates that carrying cost is 40% of the $10 unit cost and that annual demand is about 240 units per year. The assumptions of the basic EOQ model are thought to apply. For what value of ordering cost would its action be optimal?

P✘ · 12.8 Madeline Thimmes' Dream Store sells water beds and assorted supplies. Her best-selling bed has an annual demand of 400 units. Ordering cost is $40; holding cost is $5 per unit per year.

a) To minimize the total cost, how many units should be ordered each time an order is placed?
b) If the holding cost per unit were $6 instead of $5, what would the optimal order quantity be?

P✘ · 12.9 Southeastern Bell stocks a certain switch connector at its central warehouse for supplying field service offices. The yearly demand for these connectors is 15,000 units. Southeastern estimates its annual holding cost for this item to be $25 per unit. The cost to place and process an order from the supplier is $75. The company operates 300 days per year and the lead time to receive an order from the supplier is 8 working days.

a) Find the economic order quantity.
b) Find the annual holding costs. $D = 15,000$
c) Find the annual ordering costs. $H = 25/\text{unit}$
d) What is the reorder point? $\text{Lead Time} = 8 \text{ days}$
$S = 75$

12.10 Lead time for one of your fastest moving products is 21 days. Demand during this period averages 100 units per day. What would be an appropriate reorder point?

12.11 Annual demand for the notebook binders at Duncan's Stationery Shop is 10,000 units. Dana Duncan operates her business 300 days per year and finds that deliveries from her supplier generally take 5 working days. Calculate the reorder point for the notebook binders that she stocks.

P✘ : 12.12 Marilyn Hart is the purchasing agent for Central Valve Company, which sells industrial valves and fluid-control devices. One of Central's most popular valves is the Western, which has an annual demand of 4,000 units. The cost of each valve is $90, and the inventory carrying cost is $9. Marilyn has made a study of the costs involved in placing an order for any of the valves that Central stocks, and she has concluded that the average ordering cost is $25 per order. Furthermore, it takes about 5 working days for an order to arrive from the supplier. During this time, the demand per week for valves is approximately 80.

a) What is the economic order quantity?
b) What is the average inventory if the economic order quantity is used?
c) What is the optimal number of orders per year?
d) What is the optimal number of days between any two orders, assuming 250 working days per year?
e) What is the total annual inventory cost (carrying cost + order cost)?
f) What is the reorder point?

P✘ : 12.13 Joe Henry's machine shop uses 2,500 brackets during the course of a year. These brackets are purchased from a supplier 90 miles away. The following information is known about the brackets.

Annual demand:	2,500
Holding cost per bracket per year:	$1.50
Order cost per order:	$18.75
Lead time:	2 days
Working days per year:	250

a)   Given the above information, what would be the economic order quantity (EOQ)?
b)   Given the EOQ, what would be the average inventory? What would be the annual inventory holding cost?
c)   Given the EOQ, how many orders would be made each year? What would be the annual order cost?
d)   Given the EOQ, what is the total annual inventory cost?
e)   What is the time between orders?
f)   What is the reorder point (ROP)?

12.14   Marc Bove, of Bove Plumbing, uses 1,200 of a certain spare part that costs $25 for each order with an annual holding cost of $24.
a)   Calculate the total cost for order sizes of 25, 40, 50, 60, and 100.
b)   Identify the economic order quantity and consider the implications for making an error in calculating economic order quantity.

12.15   Patterson Electronics supplies microcomputer circuitry to a company that incorporates microprocessors into refrigerators and other home appliances. One of the components has an annual demand of 250 units, and this is constant throughout the year. Carrying cost is estimated to be $1 per unit per year, and the ordering cost is $20 per order.
a)   To minimize cost, how many units should be ordered each time an order is placed?
b)   How many orders per year are needed with the optimal policy?
c)   What is the average inventory if costs are minimized?
d)   Suppose that the ordering cost is not $20, and Patterson has been ordering 150 units each time an order is placed. For this order policy (of $Q = 150$) to be optimal, determine what the ordering cost would have to be.

12.16   Bruce Woodworth's company produces a product for which annual demand is 10,000. Because it operates 200 days per year, demand is about 50 per day. Daily production is 200 units. Holding costs are $1 per unit per year; setup costs are $200. If you wish to produce this product in batches, what size batch should be used?

12.17   Radovilsky Manufacturing Company, in Hayward, California, makes flashing lights for toys. The company operates its production facility 300 days per year. It has orders for about 12,000 flashing lights per year and has the capability of producing 100 per day. Setting up the light production costs $50. The cost of each light is $1. The holding cost is $0.10 per light per year.
a)   What is the optimal size of the production run?
b)   What is the average holding cost per year?
c)   What is the average setup cost per year?
d)   What is the total cost per year, including the cost of the lights?

12.18   Arthur Meiners is the production manager of Wheel-Rite, a small producer of metal parts. Wheel-Rite supplies Cal-Tex, a larger assembly company, with 10,000 wheel bearings each year. This order has been stable for some time. Setup cost for Wheel-Rite is $40, and holding cost is $.60 per wheel bearing per year. Wheel-Rite can produce 500 wheel bearings per day. Cal-Tex is a just-in-time manufacturer and requires that 50 bearings be shipped to it each business day.
a)   What is the optimum production quantity?
b)   What is the maximum number of wheel bearings that will be in inventory at Wheel-Rite?
c)   How many production runs of wheel bearings will Wheel-Rite have in a year?
d)   What is the total setup + holding cost for Wheel-Rite?

12.19   Cesar Rogo Computers, a Mississippi chain of computer hardware and software retail outlets, supplies both educational and commercial customers with memory and storage devices. It currently faces the following ordering decision relating to purchases of CD-ROMs:

$$D = 36,000 \text{ disks}$$
$$S = \$25$$
$$H = \$0.45$$
$$\text{Purchase price} = \$0.85$$
$$\text{Discount price} = \$0.82$$
$$\text{Quantity needed to qualify for the discount} = 6,000 \text{ disks}$$

Should the discount be taken?

12.20   McLeavey Manufacturing has a demand for 1,000 pumps each year. The cost of a pump is $50. It costs McLeavey $40 to place an order, and carrying cost is 25% of unit cost. If pumps are ordered in quantities of 200, McLeavey can get a 3% discount. Should McLeavey order 200 pumps at a time and take the 3% discount?

12.21   Wang Distributors has an annual demand for an airport metal detector of 1,400 units. The cost of a typical detector to Wang is $400. Carrying cost is estimated to be 20% of the unit cost, and the ordering cost is $25 per order. If Ping Wang, the owner, orders in quantities of 300 or more, he can get a 5% discount on the cost of the detectors. Should Wang take the quantity discount?

P : 12.22 The regular price of a DVD component is $20. On orders of 75 units or more, the price is discounted to $18.50. On orders of 100 units or more, the discount price is $15.75. At present, Sound Business, Inc., a manufacturer of high-fidelity components, has an inventory carrying cost of 5% per unit per year, and its ordering cost is $10. Annual demand is 45 components. What should Sound Business, Inc., do?

P : 12.23 Rocky Mountain Tire Center sells 20,000 tires of a particular type per year. The ordering cost for each order is $40, and the holding cost is 20% of the purchase price of the tires per year. The purchase price is $20 per tire if fewer than 500 tires are ordered, $18 per tire if more than 500 but fewer than 1,000 tires are ordered, and $17 per tire if 1,000 or more tires are ordered. How many tires should Rocky Mountain order each time it places an order?

P : 12.24 M. P. VanOyen Manufacturing has gone out on bid for a regulator component. Expected demand is 700 units per month. The item can be purchased from either Allen Manufacturing or Baker Manufacturing. Their price lists are shown below. Ordering cost is $50, and annual holding cost per unit is $5.

ALLEN MFG.		BAKER MFG.	
QUANTITY	UNIT PRICE	QUANTITY	UNIT PRICE
1–499	$16.00	1–399	$16.10
500–999	15.50	400–799	15.60
1,000+	15.00	800+	15.10

a) What is the economic order quantity?
b) Which supplier should be used? Why?
c) What is the optimal order quantity and total annual cost?

P : 12.25 Chris Sandvig Irrigation, Inc. has summarized the price list from four potential suppliers of an underground control valve. See the table below. Annual usage is 2,400 valves; order cost is $10 per order; and annual inventory holding costs are $3.33 per unit.

Which vendor should be selected and what order quantity is best if Sandvig Irrigation wants to minimize total cost?

VENDOR A		VENDOR B		VENDOR C		VENDOR D	
QUANTITY	PRICE	QUANTITY	PRICE	QUANTITY	PRICE	QUANTITY	PRICE
1–49	$35.00	1–74	$34.75	1–99	$34.50	1–199	$34.25
50–74	34.75	75–149	34.00	100–199	33.75	200–399	33.00
75–149	33.55	150–299	32.80	200–399	32.50	400+	31.00
150–299	32.35	300–499	31.60	400+	31.10		
300–499	31.15	500+	30.50				
500+	30.75						

P : 12.26 Emery Pharmaceutical uses an unstable chemical compound that must be kept in an environment where both temperature and humidity can be controlled. Emery uses 800 pounds per month of the chemical, estimates the holding cost to be 50% of the purchase price (because of spoilage), and estimates order costs to be $50 per order. Below are the cost schedules of two suppliers.

VENDOR 1		VENDOR 2	
QUANTITY	PRICE/LB	QUANTITY	PRICE/LB
1–499	$17.00	1–399	$17.10
500–999	16.75	400–799	16.85
1000+	16.50	800–1199	16.60
		1,200+	16.25

a) What is the economic order quantity for both suppliers?
b) What quantity should be ordered and which supplier should be used?
c) What is the total cost for the most economic order size?
d) What factor(s) should be considered besides total cost?

: 12.27 Barbara Flynn is in charge of maintaining hospital supplies at General Hospital. During the past year, the mean lead time demand for bandage BX-5 was 60 (and was normally distributed). Furthermore, the standard deviation for BX-5 was 7. Ms. Flynn would like to maintain a 90% service level.

a) What safety stock level do you recommend for BX-5?
b) What is the appropriate reorder point?

⋮ 12.28   Based on available information, lead time demand for CD-ROM drives averages 50 units (normally distributed), with a standard deviation of 5 drives. Management wants a 97% service level.
a)   What value of Z should be applied?
b)   How many drives should be carried as safety stock?
c)   What is the appropriate reorder point?

⋮ 12.29   Authentic Thai rattan chairs are delivered to Gary Schwartz's chain of retail stores, called The Kathmandu Shop, once a year. The reorder point, without safety stock, is 200 chairs. Carrying cost is $15 per unit per year, and the cost of a stockout is $70 per chair per year. Given the following demand probabilities during the reorder period, how much safety stock should be carried?

DEMAND DURING REORDER PERIOD	PROBABILITY
0	0.2
100	0.2
200	0.2
300	0.2
400	0.2

⋮ 12.30   Children's art sets are ordered once each year by Vicki Smith, Inc., and the reorder point, without safety stock (dL), is 100 art sets. Inventory carrying cost is $10 per set per year, and the cost of a stockout is $50 per set per year. Given the following demand probabilities during the reorder period, how much safety stock should be carried?

DEMAND DURING REORDER PERIOD	PROBABILITY
0	.1
50	.2
ROP → 100	.4
150	.2
200	.1
	1.0

⋮ 12.31   Mr. Beautiful, an organization that sells weight training sets, has an ordering cost of $40 for the BB-1 set. (BB-1 stands for Body Beautiful Number 1.) The carrying cost for BB-1 is $5 per set per year. To meet demand, Mr. Beautiful orders large quantities of BB-1 seven times a year. The stockout cost for BB-1 is estimated to be $50 per set. Over the past several years, Mr. Beautiful has observed the following demand during the lead time for BB-1:

DEMAND DURING LEAD TIME	PROBABILITY
40	.1
50	.2
60	.2
70	.2
80	.2
90	.1
	1.0

The reorder point for BB-1 is 60 sets. What level of safety stock should be maintained for BB-1?

⋮ 12.32   Kim Clark has asked you to help him determine the best ordering policy for a new product. The demand for the new product has been forecasted to be about 1,000 units annually. To help you get a handle on the carrying and ordering costs, Kim has given you the list of last year's costs. He thought that these costs might be appropriate for the new product.

COST FACTOR	COST ($)	COST FACTOR	COST ($)
Taxes for the warehouse	2,000	Warehouse supplies	280
Receiving and incoming inspection	1,500	Research and development	2,750
New product development	2,500	Purchasing salaries & wages	30,000
Acct. Dept. costs to pay invoices	500	Warehouse salaries & wages	12,800
Inventory insurance	600	Pilferage of inventory	800
Product advertising	800	Purchase order supplies	500
Spoilage	750	Inventory obsolescence	300
Sending purchasing orders	800	Purchasing Dept. overhead	1,000

He also told you that these data were compiled for 10,000 inventory items that were carried or held during the year. You have also determined that 200 orders were placed last year. Your job as a new operations management graduate is to help Kim determine the economic order quantity.

 12.33 Emarpy Appliance is a company which produces all kinds of major appliances. Bud Banis, the president of Emarpy, is concerned about the production policy for the company's best-selling refrigerator. The annual demand for this has been about 8,000 units each year, and this demand has been constant throughout the year. The production capacity is 200 units per day. Each time production starts, it costs the company $120 to move materials into place, reset the assembly line, and clean the equipment. The holding cost of a refrigerator is $50 per year. The current production plan calls for 400 refrigerators to be produced in each production run. Assume there are 250 working days per year.

a) What is the daily demand of this product?

b) If the company were to continue to produce 400 units each time production starts, how many days would production continue?

c) Under the current policy, how many production runs per year would be required? What would the annual setup cost be?

d) If the current policy continues, how many refrigerators would be in inventory when production stops? What would the average inventory level be?

e) If the company produces 400 refrigerators at a time, what would the total annual setup cost and holding cost be?

f) If Bud Banis wants to minimize the total annual inventory cost, how many refrigerators should be produced in each production run? How much would this save the company in inventory costs compared to the current policy of producing 400 in each production run?

12.34 Louisiana Power and Light orders utility poles on the first business day of each month from its supplier in Oregon. The target value is 40 poles in this P-system. It is time to order and there are 5 poles on hand. Because of a delayed shipment last month, 18 poles ordered earlier should arrive shortly. How many poles should be ordered now?

✿ INTERNET HOMEWORK PROBLEMS

See our Internet home page at **www.prenhall.com/heizer** for these additional homework problems: 12.35 through 12.47.

CASE STUDY

Southwestern University: (D)*

The recent success of Southwestern University's football program is causing SWU's president, Joel Wisner, more problems than he faced during the team's losing era in the early 1990s. For one thing, increasing game day attendance is squeezing the town of Stephenville, Texas, and the campus (see Southwestern University: B, in Chapter 4). Complaints are arising over parking, seating, concession prices, and even a shortage of programs at some games (see Southwestern University: C, in Chapter 6). Dr. Wisner once again turns to his stadium manager, Hank Maddux. This time he needs a guaranteed revenue stream to help fuel the stadium expansion. One source of income could easily be the high-profit game programs.

Selling for $5 each, programs are a tricky business. Under substantial pressure from Wisner, Maddux knows he has to ensure that costs are held to a minimum and contribution to the new expansion maximized. As a result, Maddux wants the programs for each game to be purchased economically. His inquiries have yielded two options. A local Stephenville printer, Sam Taylor of Quality Printing, has offered the following discount schedule for the programs and game inserts:

PROGRAMS		WEEKLY GAME DETAIL INSERTS	
10,000 to 30,000	$1.80 ea.	10,000 to 30,000	$.90 ea.
30,000 to 60,000	$1.70 ea.	30,000 to 60,000	$.85 ea.
60,000 to 250,000	$1.60 ea.	60,000 to 250,000	$.80 ea.
250,000 and up	$1.40 ea.	250,000 and up	$.70 ea.

As a second option, however, First Printing, owned by Michael Shader, an S.W.U. alumnus in Ft. Worth, will do the job for 10% less as a favor to help the athletic department. This option will mean sending a truck to Ft. Worth to pick up each order. Maddux estimates that the cost of each trip to Ft. Worth will be $200.

Maddux figures that the university's ordering/check-writing cost is about $100. His carrying cost is high because he lacks a good place to store the programs. He can't put them in the office, or store them down in the maintenance department, where they may get dirty and damaged. This means he will need to lease space in a storage area off-campus and transport them to and from the campus. He estimates annual holding costs at 50%.

Maddux's other major problem is he is never sure what the demand for programs will be. Sales vary from opponent to opponent, and how well the team is doing that year. However, he *does* know that running out is a very bad idea. This football team is not only expected to make money for SWU, but it is also entertainment. This means programs for all who want them. With the new facility, attendance could be 60,000 for each of the five home games. And two of every three people buy a program.

In addition to the programs, Maddux must purchase the inserts for each game. The inserts have information about the opposing team, photos of the expected starters, and recent game statistics. The purchasing issue is the same for inserts, except inserts will be purchased separately for each game and are a total loss after the game. The carrying cost, because inserts are to be delivered just as they are needed, should be nominal; he estimates 5%. The other costs and the same discount schedule apply, but the inserts only cost half as much because they are much smaller. First Printing will give the same 10% discount on the inserts.

Discussion Questions

1. With whom should Maddux place the order for the programs and how many should he order each time?
2. With whom should Maddux place the order for the inserts and how many should he order each time?
3. What is Maddux's total cost for programs with inserts for the season?
4. What other program management opportunities might Maddux pursue?

*This integrated case study runs throughout the text. Other issues facing Southwestern's football expansion include (A) managing the stadium project (Chapter 3); (B) forecasting game attendance (Chapter 4); (C) quality of facilities (Chapter 6); (E) scheduling of campus security officers/staff for game days (Chapter 13).

CASE STUDY

Mayo Medical Center

World-renowned Mayo Medical Center, located in Rochester, Minnesota, got a head start on inventory control when it began taking advantage of bar code technology in the late 1970s. Mayo developed a bar code–based tracking system that locates over 15,000 files circulating throughout the Rochester facility. Then, during the 1980s and 1990s, Mayo developed other bar code applications, tying them to the patient numbering system. These other bar code applications included the blood bank, the specimen laboratory, and patient bar code wristbands. More recently, Mayo has taken the leadership role in automating its handling of medical and surgical supplies, pharmaceuticals, office supplies, and dietary products.

Mayo's computer system allows staff throughout its medical system to order electronically. On the midnight shift, an employee goes to each supply room, scans supplies, and enters the data required to reestablish stock levels. These data are downloaded to a host computer where the current inventory data are reconciled. Supply requests are generated as a pick list at the inventory center. The order is picked and delivered the same day. When Mayo's system hits the reorder point, an order is created, transmitted to purchasing, and then sent electronically to the supplier. Mayo is able to provide a 98% fill level. The program has been successful at releasing patient care personnel from inventory activities as well as rapidly and economically bringing the product to the point of care. The inventory throughout the entire system has been reduced by $225,000.

Results such as these are found in other hospitals as well. One recent study of the industry found that prior to bar code–oriented inventory systems, hospitals could not account for as much as 20% of supply costs. However, with both pharmacy and nurses scanning the codes on every drug packet, syringe, and bandage used, that figure has now dropped to as low as 1%. When supplies account for a third of costs, which is the case for some hospitals, such reductions are significant. At the same time, these hospitals have reduced inventory investment to one-half of previous levels.

Bar code systems, with their inherent accuracy, provide a new tool for compiling, analyzing, and leveraging cost data. With accurate costs, hospitals are comfortable negotiating fixed-fee contracts. They are also able to use the information to save substantial sums on purchases such as hip and knee implants. Once orthopedic supply costs were identified and shared with physicians, the doctors at Mayo agreed to use the "best practices" at the lowest cost. The result was a net savings of a half million dollars a year.

Discussion Questions

1. What are the benefits of bar-coding inventory in a hospital environment?
2. What are the natural extensions of this type of inventory system within the hospital?
3. What are the natural extensions of this type of inventory system to the supply chain?
4. What are the benefits to patient, hospital, and supplier when such inventory systems are tied together through the Internet?

Sources: Deb Naves, "Materials Management Health Care," *IDSystems* (May 1997): 21–32; and the *Wall Street Journal* (June 10, 1997): A1, A6.

CASE STUDY

Sturdivant Sound Systems

Sturdivant Sound Systems manufactures and sells sound systems for both home and auto. All parts of the sound systems, with the exception of DVD players, are produced in the Rochester, New York, plant. DVD players used in the assembly of Sturdivant systems are purchased from Morris Electronics of Concord, New Hampshire.

Sturdivant purchasing agent Mary Kim submits a purchase requisition for DVD players once every 4 weeks. The company's annual requirements total 5,000 units (20 per working day), and the cost per unit is $60. (Sturdivant does not purchase in greater quantities because Morris Electronics does not offer quantity discounts.) Because Morris promises delivery within 1 week following receipt of a purchase requisition, rarely is there a shortage of DVD players. (Total time between date of order and date of receipt is 10 days.)

Associated with the purchase of each shipment are procurement costs. These costs, which amount to $20 per order, include the costs of preparing the requisition, inspecting and storing the delivered goods, updating inventory records, and issuing a voucher and a check for payment. In addition to procurement costs, Sturdivant incurs inventory carrying costs that include insurance, storage, handling, taxes, and so forth. These costs equal $6 per unit per year.

Beginning in August of this year, Sturdivant management will embark on a companywide cost-control program in an attempt to improve its profits. One area to be closely scrutinized for possible cost savings is inventory procurement.

Discussion Questions

1. Compute the optimal order quantity of DVD players.
2. Determine the appropriate reorder point (in units).
3. Compute the cost savings that the company will realize if it implements the optimal inventory procurement decision.
4. Should procurement costs be considered a linear function of the number of orders?

Source: Reprinted by permission of Professor Jerry Kinard, Western Carolina University.

VIDEO CASE STUDY

Inventory Control at Wheeled Coach

Controlling inventory is one of Wheeled Coach's toughest problems. Operating according to a strategy of mass customization and responsiveness, management knows that success is dependent on tight inventory control. Anything else results in an inability to deliver promptly, chaos on the assembly line, and a huge inventory investment. Wheeled Coach finds that almost 50% of the $40,000 to $100,000 cost of every vehicle is purchased materials. A large proportion of that 50% is in chassis (purchased from Ford), aluminum (from Reynolds Metal), and plywood used for flooring and cabinetry construction (from local suppliers). Wheeled Coach tracks these "A" inventory items quite carefully, maintaining tight security/control and ordering carefully so as to maximize quantity discounts while minimizing on-hand stock. Because of long lead times and scheduling needs at Reynolds, aluminum must actually be ordered as much as 8 months in advance.

In a crowded ambulance industry in which it is the only giant, its 45 competitors don't have the purchasing power to draw the same discounts as Wheeled Coach. But this competitive cost advantage cannot be taken lightly, according to President Bob Collins. "Cycle counting in our stockrooms is critical. No part can leave the locked stockrooms without appearing on a bill of materials."

Accurate bills of material (BOM) are a requirement if products are going to be built on time. Additionally, because of the custom nature of each vehicle, most orders are won only after a bidding process. Accurate BOMs are critical to cost estimation and the resulting bid. For these reasons, Collins was emphatic that Wheeled Coach maintain outstanding inventory control. The *Global Company Profile* featuring Wheeled Coach (which opens Chapter 14 in your text) provides further details about the ambulance inventory control and production process.

Discussion Questions*

1. Explain how Wheeled Coach implements ABC analysis.
2. If you were to take over as inventory control manager at Wheeled Coach, what additional policies and techniques would you initiate to ensure accurate inventory records?
3. How would you go about implementing these suggestions?

*You may wish to view this case on your CD-ROM before answering these questions.

Aggregate Planning

Chapter Outline

Aggregate planning is concerned with determining the quantity and timing of production for the intermediate future, often from 3 to 18 months ahead. Operations managers try to determine the best way to meet forecasted demand by adjusting production rates, labor levels, inventory levels, overtime work, subcontracting rates, and other controllable variables. Usually, the objective of aggregate planning is to minimize cost over the planning period. However, other strategic issues may be more important than low cost. These strategies may be to smooth employment levels, to drive down inventory levels, or to meet a high level of service.

This chapter describes the aggregate planning decision, shows how the aggregate plan fits into the overall planning process, and describes several techniques that managers use when developing an aggregate plan.

BEFORE COMING TO CLASS, READ CHAPTER 13 IN YOUR TEXT AND ANSWER THESE QUESTIONS.

1. What do we mean by "aggregate" in aggregate planning? _____

2. What is the charting (or graphical) method of aggregate planning? _____

3. What is the difference between a pure strategy and a mixed strategy? _____

4. What is a chase strategy? _____

5. How does the transportation method differ from the charting (graphical) method? _____

6. What is yield management, and in what industries is it popular? ____

THE PLANNING PROCESS AND THE NATURE OF AGGREGATE PLANNING

FIGURE 13.1 ■ Planning Tasks and Responsibilities

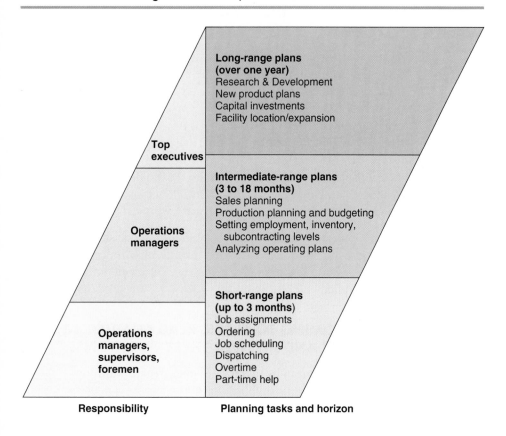

Disaggregation

Master Production Schedule

AGGREGATE PLANNING STRATEGIES

Capacity Options

1. _____
2. _____
3. _____
4. _____
5. _____

Demand Options

1. _____
2. _____
3. _____

Chase Strategy

Level Strategy

METHODS OF AGGREGATE PLANNING

Graphical and Charting Methods

Five Steps

1. _____
2. _____
3. _____
4. _____
5. _____

Additional Practice Problem Space

Transportation Method of Linear Programming

PRACTICE PROBLEM 13.1 ■ Transportation Model Approach

Set up the following problem in transportation format, and solve for the minimum cost plan.

	PERIOD		
	FEB.	MAR.	APR.
Demand	55	70	75
Capacity			
Regular	50	50	50
Overtime	5	5	5
Subcontract	12	12	10
Beginning inventory	10		
Costs			
Regular time		$60 per unit	
Overtime		$80 per unit	
Subcontract		$90 per unit	
Inventory carrying cost		$1 per unit per month	
Back order cost		$3 per unit per month	

Table with a few numbers filled in:

		Demand for				
		Feb.	Mar.	Apr.	Unused Capacity (dummy)	Total Capacity Available (supply)
February	Beginning inventory	0	1	2	0	10
	Regular time	60	61	62	0	50
	Overtime	80	81	82	0	5
	Subcontract	90	91	92	0	12
March	Regular time				0	
	Overtime				0	
	Subcontract				0	
April	Regular time				0	
	Overtime				0	
	Subcontract				0	
	Demand	55	70	75	9	209

Additional Practice Problem Space

Other Models

AGGREGATE PLANNING IN SERVICES

YIELD (OR REVENUE) MANAGEMENT

FIGURE 13.7 ■ Yield Management Matrix

	Price	
	Tend to be fixed	**Tend to be variable**
Predictable use	Quadrant 1: Movies Stadiums/arenas Convention centers Hotel meeting space	Quadrant 2: Hotels Airlines Rental cars Cruise lines
Unpredictable use	Quadrant 3: Restaurants Golf courses Internet service providers	Quadrant 4: Continuing care hospitals

(Duration of use)

DISCUSSION QUESTIONS

1. Define aggregate planning.
2. Explain what the term *aggregate* in "aggregate planning" means.
3. List the strategic objectives of aggregate planning. Which one of these is most often addressed by the quantitative techniques of aggregate planning? Which one of these is generally the most important?
4. Define chase strategy.
5. What is a pure strategy? Provide a few examples.
6. What is level scheduling? What is the basic philosophy underlying it?
7. Define mixed strategy. Why would a firm use a mixed strategy instead of a simple pure strategy?
8. What are the advantages and disadvantages of varying the size of the workforce to meet demand requirements each period?
9. Why are mathematical models not more widely used in aggregate planning?
10. How does aggregate planning in service differ from aggregate planning in manufacturing?
11. What is the relationship between the aggregate plan and the master production schedule?
12. Why are graphical aggregate planning methods useful?
13. What are major limitations of using the transportation method for aggregate planning?
14. How does "yield management" impact the aggregate plan?

CRITICAL THINKING EXERCISE

For the last several years you, the production manager responsible for scheduling, have been working toward a low-cost level aggregate production plan for Vaughan Enterprises. Vaughan Enterprises is an assembler of printed circuit boards primarily for the cell phone industry. After this morning's staff meeting, your boss and the major stockholder, Ben Vaughan, informed you that the company will be moving immediately to a just-in-time (JIT) system—from suppliers to Vaughan Enterprises' customers. In the discussion, Mr. Vaughan reminded you that this is the trend in the entire industry, and for Vaughan Enterprises to remain competitive, the effort must be successful. What are your concerns about the change?

ACTIVE MODEL EXERCISE

This Active Model contains a 6-month aggregate planning problem using a leveling strategy. You can use the scrollbars to adjust the base level of daily production during the month, the amount of daily overtime, and the amount of subcontracting. Note that the formulas are set up such that subcontracting is chosen before overtime since in the example the subcontracting cost per unit is less than the overtime cost per unit.

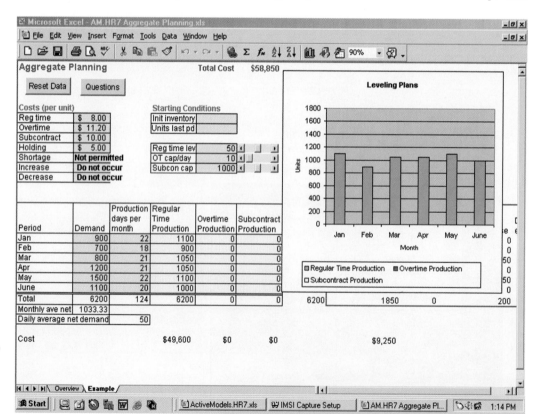

ACTIVE MODEL 13.1 ■

Analysis of Aggregate Plan 1 Using the Roofing Manufacturer Data in Example 2 in Your Text

Questions

1. Each worker makes five units per day. If the number of workers is reduced form 10 to 9, dropping the daily capacity, what happens to the cost?
2. What regular time level minimizes the total cost?
3. How low can the regular daily capacity get before overtime will be required?
4. How low can the regular daily capacity get before there will not be enough capacity to meet the demand?

PROBLEMS*

13.1 Develop another plan for the Mexican roofing manufacturer described in Examples 1 to 4 and Solved Problem 13.1 in your text. For this plan, plan 5, the firm wishes to maintain a constant workforce of six, using subcontracting to meet remaining demand. Is this plan preferable?

13.2 The same roofing manufacturer in Examples 1 to 4 and Solved Problem 13.1 in your text has yet a sixth plan. A constant workforce of seven is selected, with the remainder of demand filled by subcontracting. Is this a better plan?

13.3 The president of Hill Enterprises, Terri Hill, projects the firm's aggregate demand requirements over the next 8 months as follows:

Jan.	1,400	May	2,200
Feb.	1,600	June	2,200
Mar.	1,800	July	1,800
Apr.	1,800	Aug.	1,400

Her operations manager is considering a new plan, which begins in January with 200 units on hand and ends with zero inventory. Stockout cost of lost sales is $100 per unit. Inventory holding cost is $20 per unit per month. Ignore any idle-time costs. The plan is called plan A.

Plan A: Vary the workforce level to execute a "chase" strategy by producing the quantity demanded in the prior month. The December demand and rate of production are both 1,600 units per month. The cost of hiring additional workers is $5,000 per 100 units. The cost of laying off workers is $7,500 per 100 units. Evaluate this plan.

13.4 Using the information in Problem 13.3, develop plan B. Produce at a constant rate of 1,400 units per month, which will meet minimum demands. Then use subcontracting, with additional units at a premium price of $75 per unit. Evaluate this plan by computing the costs for January through August.

13.5 Hill is now considering plan C. Beginning inventory, stockout costs, and holding costs are provided in Problem 13.3.
   a) Plan C: Keep a stable workforce by maintaining a constant production rate equal to the average requirements and allow varying inventory levels.
   b) Plot the demand with a graph that also shows average requirements. Conduct your analysis for January through August.

13.6 Hill's operations manager (see Problems 13.3 through 13.5) is also considering two mixed strategies for January–August:
   Plan D: Keep the current workforce stable at producing 1,600 units per month. Permit a maximum of 20% overtime at an additional cost of $50 per unit. A warehouse now constrains the maximum allowable inventory on hand to 400 units or less.
   Plan E: Keep the current workforce, which is producing 1,600 units per month, and subcontract to meet the rest of the demand.
   Evaluate plans D and E.

13.7 Michael Carrigg, Inc., is a DVD manufacturer in need of an aggregate plan for July through December. The company has gathered the data shown in the table on the top of the next page.

*Note: **P** means the problem may be solved with POM for Windows; ✗ means the problem may be solved with Excel OM; and **P**✗ means the problem may be solved with POM for Windows and/or Excel OM.

COSTS		DEMAND	
Holding cost	$8/DVD/month	July	400
Subcontracting	$80/DVD	Aug.	500
Regular-time labor	$12/hour	Sept.	550
Overtime labor	$18/hour for hours above	Oct.	700
	8 hours/worker/day	Nov.	800
Hiring cost	$40/worker	Dec.	700
Layoff cost	$80/worker		

OTHER DATA	
Current workforce (June)	8 people
Labor-hours/DVD	4 hours
Workdays/month	20 days
Beginning inventory	150 DVDs
Ending inventory	0 DVDs

What will each of the two following strategies cost?

a) Vary the workforce so that exact production meets demand. Carrigg had eight workers on board in June.
b) Vary overtime only and use a constant workforce of eight.

13.8   You manage a consulting firm down the street form Michael Carrigg, Inc., and to get your foot in the door, you have told Mr. Carrigg (see Problem 13.7) that you can do a better job at aggregate planning than his current staff. He said, "Fine. You do that and you have a 1-year contract." You now have to make good on your boast using the data in Problem 13.7. If you develop a plan with back orders, which Mr. Carrigg doesn't like, be sure to include a $16-per-DVD-per-month cost.

13.9   Brooke Cashion, operations manager at Kansas Furniture, has received the following estimates of demand requirements:

July	Aug.	Sept.	Oct.	Nov.	Dec.
1,000	1,200	1,400	1,800	1,800	1,600

Assuming stockout costs for lost sales of $100, inventory carrying costs of $25 per unit per month, and zero ending inventory, evaluate these two plans on an *incremental* cost basis:

Plan A: Produce at a steady rate (equal to minimum requirements) of 1,000 units per month and subcontract additional units at a $60 per unit premium cost.

Plan B: Vary the workforce, which performs at a current production level of 1,300 units per month. The cost of hiring additional workers is $3,000 per 100 units produced. The cost of layoffs is $6,000 per 100 units cut back.

13.10   Brooke Cashion (see Problem 13.9) is considering two more mixed strategies. Using the data in Problem 13.9, compare plans C and D with plans A and B and make a recommendation.

Plan C: Keep the current workforce steady at a level producing 1,300 units per month. Subcontract the remainder to meet demand. Assume that 300 units remaining from June are available in July.

Plan D: Keep the current workforce at a level capable of producing 1,300 units per month. Permit a maximum of 20% overtime at a premium of $40 per unit. Assume that warehouse limitations permit no more than a 180-unit carryover from month to month. This plan means that any time inventories reach 180, the plant is kept idle. Idle time per unit is $60. Any additional needs are subcontracted at a cost of $60 per incremental unit.

13.11   K. Cunningham Health and Beauty Products has developed a new shampoo and you need to develop its aggregate schedule. The cost accounting department has supplied you the cost relevant to the aggregate plan and the marketing department has provided a four-quarter forecast. All are shown below.

QUARTER	FORECAST
1	1,400
2	1,200
3	1,500
4	1,300

COSTS	
Previous quarter's output	1,500 units
Beginning inventory	0 units
Stockout cost for backorders	$50 per unit
Inventory holding cost	$10 per unit for every unit held at the end of the quarter
Hiring workers	$40 per unit
Firing workers	$80 per unit
Unit cost	$30 per unit
Overtime	$15 extra per unit
Subcontracting	Not available

Your job is to develop an aggregate plan for the next four quarters.

a)   First, you try a chase plan by hiring and firing as necessary to hold down costs.
b)   Then you try a plan that holds employment steady.
c)   Which is the more economical plan for K. Cunningham Health and Beauty Products?

13.12   Tampa's Soda Pop, Inc., has a new fruit drink for which it has high hopes. Don Hammond, the production planner, has assembled the following cost data and demand forecast:

QUARTER	FORECAST
1	1,800
2	1,100
3	1,600
4	900

Previous quarter's output = 1,300 cases

Beginning inventory = 0 cases

Stockout cost = $150 per case

Inventory holding cost = $40 per case at end of quarter

Hiring employees = $40 per case

Terminating employees = $80 per case

Subcontracting cost = $60 per case

Unit cost on regular time = $30 per case

Overtime cost = $15 extra per case

Capacity on regular time = 1,800 cases per quarter

Don's job is to develop an aggregate plan. The three initial options he wants to evaluate are:

a)   Plan A: a chase strategy that hires and fires personnel as necessary to meet the forecast.
b)   Plan B: a level strategy.
c)   Plan C: a level strategy that produces 1,200 cases per quarter and meets the forecasted demand with inventory and subcontracting.
d)   Which strategy is the lowest-cost plan?
e)   If you are Don's boss, the VP for operations, which plan do you implement and why?

13.13   Scott Dustan's firm has developed the following supply, demand, cost, and inventory data. Allocate production capacity to meet demand at a minimum cost using the transportation method. What is the cost?

Supply Available

PERIOD	REGULAR TIME	OVERTIME	SUBCONTRACT	DEMAND FORECAST
1	30	10	5	40
2	35	12	5	50
3	30	10	5	40

Initial inventory	20 units
Regular-time cost per unit	$100
Overtime cost per unit	$150
Subcontract cost per unit	$200
Carrying cost per unit per month	$ 4

13.14   Haifa Instruments, an Israeli producer of portable kidney dialysis units and other medical products, develops a 4-month aggregate plan. Demand and capacity (in units) are forecast as follows:

CAPACITY SOURCE	MONTH 1	MONTH 2	MONTH 3	MONTH 4
Labor				
Regular time	235	255	290	300
Overtime	20	24	26	24
Subcontract	12	15	15	17
Demand	255	294	321	301

The cost of producing each dialysis unit is $985 on regular time, $1,310 on overtime, and $1,500 on a subcontract. Inventory carrying cost is $100 per unit per month. There is to be no beginning or ending inventory in stock. Set up a production plan that minimizes cost using the transportation method.

13.15   The production planning period for flat-screen monitors at Georgia's Fernandez Electronics, Inc., is 4 months. Cost data are as follows:

Regular-time cost per monitor	$ 70
Overtime cost per monitor	$110
Subcontract cost per monitor	$120
Carrying cost per monitor per month	$ 4

For each of the next 4 months, capacity and demand for flat-screen monitors are as follows:

	PERIOD			
	MONTH 1	MONTH 2	MONTH 3[a]	MONTH 4
Demand	2,000	2,500	1,500	2,100
Capacity				
Regular time	1,500	1,600	750	1,600
Overtime	400	400	200	400
Subcontract	600	600	600	600

[a]Factory closes for 2 weeks of vacation.

Fernandez Electronics expects to enter the planning period with 500 monitors in stock. Back ordering is not permitted (meaning, for example, that monitors produced in the second month cannot be used in the first month). Develop a production plan that minimizes costs using the transportation method.

P : 13.16   A large Omaha feed mill, Cohen and Render Processing, prepares its 6-month aggregate plan by forecasting demand for 50-pound bags of cattle feed as follows: January, 1,000 bags; February, 1,200; March, 1,250; April, 1,450; May, 1,400; and June, 1,400. The feed mill plans to begin the new year with no inventory left over from the previous year. It projects that capacity (during regular hours) for producing bags of feed will remain constant at 800 until the end of April, and then increase to 1,100 bags per month when a planned expansion is completed on May 1. Overtime capacity is set at 300 bags per month until the expansion, at which time it will increase to 400 bags per month. A friendly competitor in Sioux City, Iowa, is also available as a backup source to meet demand—but it insists on a firm contract and can provide only 500 bags total during the 6-month period. Develop a 6-month production plan for the feed mill using the transportation method.

Cost data are as follows:

Regular-time cost per bag (until April 30)	$12.00
Regular-time cost per bag (after May 1)	$11.00
Overtime cost per bag (during entire period)	$16.00
Cost of outside purchase per bag	$18.50
Carrying cost per bag per month	$ 1.00

P : 13.17   Lon Min has developed a specialized airtight vacuum bag to extend the freshness of seafood shipped to restaurants. He has put together the following demand cost data:

QUARTER	FORECAST (UNITS)	REGULAR TIME	OVER- TIME	SUB- CONTRACT
1	500	400	80	100
2	750	400	80	100
3	900	800	160	100
4	450	400	80	100

Initial inventory = 250 units
Regular time cost = $1.00/unit
Overtime cost = $1.50/unit
Subcontracting cost = $2.00/unit
Carrying cost = $0.20/unit/quarter
Back-order cost = $0.50/unit/quarter

a) Find the optimal plan using the transportation method.
b) What is the cost of the plan?
c) Does any regular time capacity go unused? If so, how much in which periods?
d) What is the extent of back ordering in units and dollars?

P : 13.18   José Martinez of El Paso has developed polished stainless steel parts for his Taco machine that makes it more of a "show piece" for display in Mexican restaurants. He has developed an 5-month aggregate plan. His forecast of capacity and demand follows:

	PERIOD				
	1	2	3	4	5
Demand	150	160	130	200	210
Capacity					
Regular	150	150	150	150	150
Overtime	20	20	10	10	10

Subcontracting: 100 units available over the 5-month period
Beginning inventory: 0 units
Ending inventory required: 20 units

COSTS	
Regular-time cost per unit	$100
Overtime cost per unit	$125
Subcontract cost per unit	$135
Inventory cost per unit per period	$ 3

Assume that back orders are not permitted.

13.19 Sean Fisher, owner of a Minnesota firm that manufactures display cabinets, develops an 8-month aggregate plan. Demand and capacity (in units) are forecast as follows:

CAPACITY SOURCE (UNITS)	JAN.	FEB.	MAR.	APR.	MAY	JUNE	JULY	AUG.
Regular time	235	255	290	300	300	290	300	290
Overtime	20	24	26	24	30	28	30	30
Subcontract	12	16	15	17	17	19	19	20
Demand	255	294	321	301	330	320	345	340

The cost of producing each unit is $1,000 on regular time, $1,300 on overtime, and $1,800 on a subcontract. Inventory carrying cost is $200 per unit per month. There is no beginning or ending inventory in stock and no back orders are permitted from period to period.

a) Set up a production plan that minimizes cost by producing exactly what the demand is each month. Let the workforce vary by using regular time first, then overtime, and then subcontracting. What is this plan's cost?

b) Through better planning, regular-time production can be set at exactly the same amount, 275 units, per month. Does this alter the solution?

c) If overtime costs rise from $1,300 to $1,400, will your answer to part (a) change? What if overtime costs they fall to $1,200?

13.20 Abernathy and Cohen is a small accounting firm, managed by Joseph Cohen since the retirement in 2002 of his partner Lionel Abernathy. Cohen and his 3 CPAs can together bill 640 hours per month. When Cohen or another accountant bills more than 160 hours per month, he or she gets an additional "overtime" pay of $62.50 for each of the extra hours: This is above and beyond the $5,000 salary each draws during the month. (Cohen draws the same base pay as his employees.) Cohen strongly discourages any CPA from working (billing) more than 240 hours in any given month. The demand for billable hours for the firm over the next 6 months is estimated below:

MONTH	ESTIMATE OF BILLABLE HOURS
Jan.	600
Feb.	500
Mar.	1,000
Apr.	1,200
May	650
June	590

Cohen has an agreement with his old partner that Lionel Abernathy will come in to help out during the busy tax season, if needed, for an hourly fee of $125. Cohen will not even consider laying off one of his colleagues in the case of a slow economy. He could, however, hire another CPA at the same salary as business dictates.

a) Develop an aggregate plan for the 6-month period.
b) Compute the cost of Cohen's plan of using overtime and Abernathy.
c) Should the firm remain as is, with a total of 4 CPAs?

13.21 Refer to the CPA firm in Problem 13.20. In planning for next year, Cohen estimates that billable hours will increase by 10% in each of the 6 months. He therefore proceeds to hire a fifth CPA. The same regular time, overtime, and outside consultant (i.e., Abernathy) costs still apply.

a) Develop the new aggregate plan and compute its costs.
b) Comment on the staffing level with 5 accountants. Was it a good decision to hire the additional accountant?

13.22 Southeastern Airlines' daily flight from Atlanta to Charlotte uses a Boeing 737, with all-coach seating for 120 people. In the past, the airline has priced every seat at $140 for the one-way flight. An average of 80 passengers are on each flight. The variable cost of a filled seat is $25. Laura Less, the new operations manager, has decided to try a yield revenue approach, with seats priced at $80 for early bookings and at $190 for bookings within 1 week of the flight. She estimates that the airline will sell 65 seats at the lower price and 35 at the higher price. Variable cost will not change. Which approach is preferable to Ms. Less?

INTERNET HOMEWORK PROBLEMS

See our Internet homepage at www.prenhall.com/heizer for these additional homework problems: 13.23 through 13.26.

CASE STUDY*

Southwestern University: (E)

With the rising demands of a successful football program, the campus police chief at Southwestern University, John Swearingen, wants to develop a 2-year plan that involves a request for additional resources.

The SWU department currently has 26 sworn officers. The size of the force has not changed over the past 15 years, but the following changes have prompted the chief to seek more resources:

- The size of the athletic program, especially football, has increased.
- The college has expanded geographically, with some new research facilities and laboratories now miles away from the main campus.
- Traffic and parking problems have increased.
- More portable, expensive computers with high theft potential are dispersed across the campus.
- Alcohol and drug problems have increased.
- The size of the surrounding community has doubled.
- The police need to spend more time on education and prevention programs.

The college is located in Stephenville, Texas, a small town about 30 miles southwest of the Dallas/Forth Worth metroplex. During the summer months, the student population is around 5,000. This number swells to 20,000 during fall and spring semesters. Thus demand for police and other services is significantly lower during the summer months. Demand for police services also varies by:

- Time of day (peak time is between 10 P.M. and 2 A.M.).
- Day of the week (weekends are the busiest).
- Weekend of the year (on football weekends, 50,000 extra people come to campus).
- Special events (check-in, checkout, commencement).

Football weekends are especially difficult to staff. Extra police services are typically needed from 8 A.M. to 5 P.M. on five football Saturdays. All 26 officers are called in to work double shifts. Over 40 law enforcement officers from surrounding locations are paid to come in on their own time, and a dozen state police lend a hand free of charge (when available). Twenty-five students and local residents are paid to work traffic and parking. During the last academic year (a 9-month period), overtime payments to campus police officers totaled over $120,000.

Other relevant data include the following:

- The average starting salary for a police officer is $28,000.
- Work-study and part-time students and local residents who help with traffic and parking are paid $9.00 an hour.
- Overtime is paid to police officers who work over 40 hours a week at the rate of $18.00 an hour. Extra officers who are hired part time from outside agencies also earn $18.00 an hour.
- There seems to be an unlimited supply of officers who will work for the college when needed for special events.
- With days off, vacations, and average sick leave considered, it takes five persons to cover one 24-hour, 7-day-a-week position.

The schedule of officers during fall and spring semesters is:

	WEEKDAYS	WEEKEND
First shift (7 A.M.–3 P.M.)	5	4
Second shift (3 P.M.–11 P.M.)	5	6
Third shift (11 P.M.–7 A.M.)	6	8

Staffing for football weekends and special events is *in addition to* the preceding schedule. Summer staffing is, on average, half that shown.

Swearingen thinks that his present staff is stretched to the limit. Fatigued officers are potential problems for the department and the community. In addition, neither time nor personnel has been set aside for crime prevention, safety, or health programs. Interactions of police officers with students, faculty, and staff are minimal and usually negative in nature. In light of these problems, the chief would like to request funding for four additional officers, two assigned to new programs and two to alleviate the overload on his current staff. He would also like to begin limiting overtime to 10 hours per week for each officer.

Discussion Questions

1. Which variations in demand for police services should be considered in an aggregate plan for resources? Which variations can be accomplished with short-term scheduling adjustments?
2. Evaluate the current staffing plan. What does it cost? Are 26 officers sufficient to handle the normal workload?
3. What would be the additional cost of the chief's proposal? How would you suggest that he justify his request?
4. How much does it currently cost the college to provide police services for football games? What would be the pros and cons of completely subcontracting this work to outside law enforcement agencies?
5. Propose other alternatives.

*This integrated case study runs throughout the text. Other issues facing Southwestern's football expansion include: (A) managing the stadium project (Chapter 3); (B) forecasting game attendance (Chapter 4); (C) quality of facilities (Chapter 6); (D) inventory planning of football programs (Chapter 12).

Source: Adapted from C. Haksever, B. Render, and R. Russell, *Service Management and Operations*, 2nd ed. (Upper Saddle River, NJ: Prentice Hall, 2000), 308–9. Reprinted by permission of Prentice Hall, Inc.

CASE STUDY

Andrew-Carter, Inc.

Andrew-Carter, Inc. (A-C), is a major Canadian producer and distributor of outdoor lighting fixtures. Its products are distributed throughout South and North America and have been in high demand for several years. The company operates three plants to manufacture fixtures and distribute them to five distribution centers (warehouses).

During the present global slowdown, A-C has seen a major drop in demand for its products, largely because the housing market has declined. Based on the forecast of interest rates, the head of operations feels that demand for housing and thus for A-C's products will remain depressed for the foreseeable future. A-C is considering closing one of its plants, as it is now operating with a forecast excess capacity of 34,000 units per week. The forecast weekly demands for the coming year are as follows:

Warehouse 1	9,000 units
Warehouse 2	13,000
Warehouse 3	11,000
Warehouse 4	15,000
Warehouse 5	8,000

Plant capacities, in units per week, are as follows:

Plant 1, regular time	27,000 units
Plant 1, on overtime	7,000
Plant 2, regular time	20,000
Plant 2, on overtime	5,000
Plant 3, regular time	25,000
Plant 3, on overtime	6,000

If A-C shuts down any plants, its weekly costs will change, because fixed costs will be lower for a nonoperating plant. Table 1 shows production costs at each plant, both variable at regular time and overtime, and fixed when operating and shut down. Table 2 shows distribution costs from each plant to each distribution center.

Discussion Questions

1. Evaluate the various configurations of operating and closed plants that will meet weekly demand. Determine which configuration minimizes total costs.
2. Discuss the implications of closing a plant.

TABLE 1 ■ Andrew-Carter, Inc., Variable Costs and Fixed Production Costs per Week

PLANT	VARIABLE COST (PER UNIT)	FIXED COST PER WEEK OPERATING	FIXED COST PER WEEK NOT OPERATING
1, regular time	$2.80	$14,000	$6,000
1, overtime	3.52		
2, regular time	2.78	12,000	5,000
2, overtime	3.48		
3, regular time	2.72	15,000	7,500
3, overtime	3.42		

TABLE 2 ■ Andrew-Carter, Inc., Distribution Costs per Unit

FROM PLANTS	TO DISTRIBUTION CENTERS W1	W2	W3	W4	W5
1	$.50	$.44	$.49	$.46	$.56
2	.40	.52	.50	.56	.57
3	.56	.53	.51	.54	.35

Source: Reprinted by permission of Professor Michael Ballot, University of the Pacific, Stockton, CA.

Chapter **14**

Material Requirements Planning (MRP) and ERP

Chapter Outline

The standard way to determine requirements for dependent demand is a material requirements planning (MRP) system. Dependent demand means that the demand for one item is related to the demand for another item. Once an item is scheduled, the demand for all of its components is known—they are *dependent* upon the scheduled item. For any item for which a schedule can be established, dependent techniques such as MRP are used.

MRP systems have evolved as a basis for enterprise resource planning (ERP) systems. ERP is an information system for identifying and planning for the enterprise-wide resources needed to purchase, make, ship, and account for customer orders.

BEFORE COMING TO CLASS, READ CHAPTER 14 IN YOUR TEXT AND ANSWER THESE QUESTIONS.

1. What is a master production schedule (MPS)? _____

_____

2. In a "make to order" (process focused) facility, what is scheduled? ___

_____

3. What are four ways to determine lot sizes in an MRP system? _____

_____

4. How is MRP used in a restaurant? _____

_____

5. What is MRP II? _____

_____

6. What is enterprise resource planning (ERP)? _____

_____

DEPENDENT INVENTORY MODEL REQUIREMENTS

1. Master Production Schedule (MPS)

2. Specification or Bill-of-Material

3. Inventory Available

4. Purchase Orders Outstanding

5. Lead Time

MRP STRUCTURE

FIGURE 14.5 ■ Structure of the MRP System

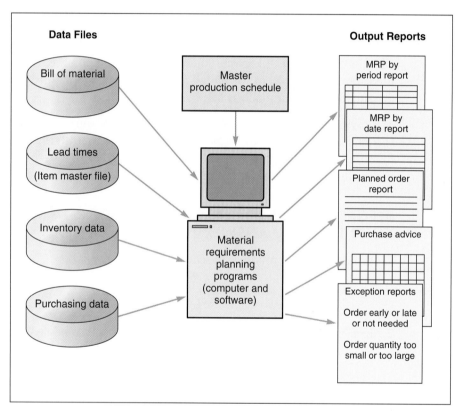

A Sample Product Structure Tree

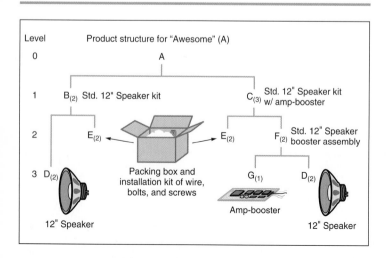

PRACTICE PROBLEM 14.1 ■ Material Structure Tree

The Hunicut and Hallock Corporation makes two versions of the same file cabinet: the TOL (top-of-the-line) five-drawer file cabinet and the HQ (high-quality) five-drawer file cabinet.

The TOL and HQ use the same cabinet frame and the same locking mechanism. The drawer assemblies are different, although both use the same drawer frame assembly. The drawer assemblies for the TOL cabinet use sliding assemblies that require *four* bearings per side, whereas the HQ sliding assemblies require *only two* bearings per side. (These bearings are identical for both cabinet types.) Hunicut and Hallock needs to assemble 100 TOL and 300 HQ file cabinets in week 10. No current stock exists.

Develop a material structure tree for the TOL and the HQ file cabinets.

PRACTICE PROBLEM 14.2 ■ Gross Material Requirements Plan

Develop a gross material requirements plan for the TOL and HQ cabinets in the previous example.

GROSS REQUIREMENTS PLAN

Week	1	2	3	4	5	6	7	8	9	10
TOL										
HQ										

PRACTICE PROBLEM 14.3 ■ Net Material Requirements Plan

Develop a net material requirements plan for the TOL and HQ file cabinets in the previous problems, assuming a current on-hand finished goods inventory of 100 TOL cabinets. The lead times are:

Painting and final assembly of both HQ and TOL require 2 weeks.
Both cabinet frames and lock assembly require 1 week for manufacturing.
Both drawer assemblies require 2 weeks for assembly.
Both sliding assemblies require 2 weeks for manufacturing.
Bearings require 2 weeks to arrive from supplier.

(see next page)

Answer Sheet for Practice Problem 14.3

| | | WEEK | | | | | | | | | | |
		1	2	3	4	5	6	7	8	9	10	LEAD TIME
TOL	Required date											weeks
	Order release date	None required; 100 in inventory										
HQ	Required date											weeks
	Order release date											
Cabinet frames and lock	Required date											week
	Order release date											
HQ drawer assembly	Required date											weeks
	Order release date											
Drawer frame	Required date											weeks
	Order release date											
HQ sliding assembly	Required date											weeks
	Order release date											
Bearings	Required date											weeks
	Order release date											

Scheduled receipts are:

	QUANTITY	IN WEEK
Cabinet frames and lock		
HQ drawer assembly		
Drawer frame assembly		
HQ sliding assembly		
Bearings		

MRP MANAGEMENT

MRP Dynamics

JIT

LOT-SIZING TECHNIQUES

1. Lot-for-Lot

PRACTICE PROBLEM 14.4 ■ Lot-for-Lot

If the TOL file cabinet has a gross material requirements plan as shown below and no inventory, and 2 weeks lead time is required for assembly, what are the order release dates and lot sizes when lot sizing is determined using lot-for-lot? Use a holding cost of $2 and a setup cost of $20, and assume no initial inventory.

GROSS MATERIAL REQUIREMENTS PLAN

Week	1	2	3	4	5	6	7	8	9	10
TOL			50		100		50			100

2. Economic Order Quantity

PRACTICE PROBLEM 14.5 ■ EOQ

If the TOL file cabinet has a gross material requirements plan as shown below and no inventory, and 2 weeks of lead time is required for assembly, what are the order release dates and lot sizes when lot sizing is determined by EOQ (economic order quantity)? Use a holding cost of $2 and a setup cost of $20, and assume no initial inventory.

GROSS MATERIAL REQUIREMENTS PLAN

Week	1	2	3	4	5	6	7	8	9	10
TOL			50		100		50			100

3. Part Period Balancing

PRACTICE PROBLEM 14.6 ■ Part Period Balancing

If the TOL file cabinet has a gross material requirements plan as shown below and no inventory, and 2 weeks of lead time is required for assembly, what are the order release dates and lot sizes when lot sizing is determined using PPB (part period balancing)? Use a holding cost of $2 and a setup cost of $20, and no initial inventory.

GROSS MATERIAL REQUIREMENTS PLAN

Week	1	2	3	4	5	6	7	8	9	10
TOL			50		100		50			100

4. Wagner-Whiten

EXTENSIONS OF MRP

1. Closed Loop

2. Capacity Planning

3. MRP II

MRP IN SERVICES

Restaurants

Hospitals

DISTRIBUTION RESOURCE PLANNING (DRP)

ENTERPRISE RESOURCE PLANNING (ERP)

Advantages of ERP

Disadvantages of ERP

DISCUSSION QUESTIONS

1. What is the difference between a *gross* requirements plan and a *net* requirements plan?
2. Once a material requirements plan (MRP) has been established, what other managerial applications might be found for the technique?
3. What are the similarities between MRP and DRP?
4. How does MRP II differ from MRP?
5. Which is the best lot-sizing policy for manufacturing organizations?
6. What impact does ignoring carrying cost in the allocation of stock in a DRP system have on lot sizes?
7. MRP is more than an inventory system; what additional capabilities does MRP possess?
8. What are the options for the production planner who has (a) scheduled more than capacity in a work center next week, but (b) a consistent lack of capacity in that work center?
9. Master schedules are expressed in three different ways depending on whether the process is continuous, a job shop, or repetitive. What are these three ways?
10. What functions of the firm affect an MRP system? How?
11. What is the rationale for (a) a phantom bill of material, (b) a planning bill of material, and (c) a pseudo bill of material?
12. Identify five specific requirements of an effective MRP system.
13. What are the typical benefits of ERP?
14. What are the distinctions between MRP, DRP, and ERP?
15. As an approach to inventory management, how does MRP differ from the approach taken in Chapter 12, dealing with economic order quantities (EOQ)?
16. What are the disadvantages of ERP?

CRITICAL THINKING EXERCISE

The very structure of MRP systems suggests fixed lead times. However, many firms have moved toward JIT and kanban techniques. What are the techniques, issues, and impact of adding JIT inventory and purchasing techniques to an organization that has MRP?

ACTIVE MODEL EXERCISE

We use Active Model 14.1 to demonstrate the effects of lot sizes (multiples) and minimum lot sizes.

Questions

1. Suppose that item B must be ordered in multiples of dozens. Which items are affected by this change?
2. Suppose that the minimum order quantity for item C is 200 units. Which items are affected by this change?

ACTIVE MODEL 14.1 ■

An Analysis of the MRP Model Used by Speaker Kits, Inc., in Examples 1– 3 in Your Text

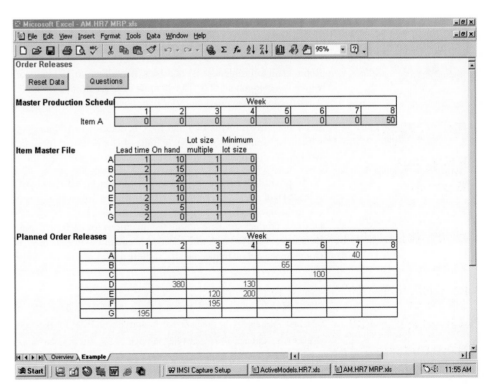

PROBLEMS*

· **14.1**   You have developed the following simple product structure of items needed for your gift bag for a rush party for prospective pledges in your organization. You forecast 200 attendees. Assume that there is no inventory on hand of any of the items. Explode the bill of material. (Subscripts indicate the number of units required.)

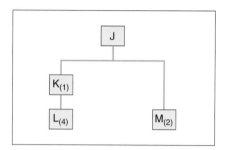

: **14.2**   You are expected to have the gift bags in Problem 14.1 ready at 5 P.M.. However, you need to personalize the items (monogrammed pens, note pads, literature from the printer, etc.). The lead time is 1 hour to assemble 200 Js once the other items are prepared. The other items will take a while as well. Given the volunteers you have, the other time estimates are item K (2 hours), item L (1 hour), and item M (4 hours). Develop a time-phased assembly plan to prepare the gift bags.

: **14.3**   The demand for subassembly S is 100 units in week 7. Each unit of S requires 1 unit of T and 2 units of U. Each unit of T requires 1 unit of V, 2 units of W, and 1 unit of X. Finally, each unit of U requires 2 units of Y and 3 units of Z. One firm manufactures all items. It takes 2 weeks to make S, 1 week to make T, 2 weeks to make U, 2 weeks to make V, 3 weeks to make W, 1 week to make X, 2 weeks to make Y, and 1 week to make Z.

   a)   Construct a product structure. Identify all levels, parents, and components.
   b)   Prepare a time-phased product structure.

14.4   Using the information in Problem 14.3, construct a gross material requirements plan.

14.5   Using the information in Problem 14.3, construct a net material requirements plan using the following on-hand inventory.

ITEM	ON-HAND INVENTORY	ITEM	ON-HAND INVENTORY
S	20	W	30
T	20	X	25
U	40	Y	240
V	30	Z	40

14.6   Refer again to Problems 14.3 and 14.4. In addition to 100 units of S, there is also a demand for 20 units of U, which is a component of S. The 20 units of U are needed for maintenance purposes. These units are needed in week 6. Modify the *gross material requirements plan* to reflect this change.

14.7   Refer again to Problems 14.3 and 14.5. In addition to 100 units of S, there is also a demand for 20 units of U, which is a component of S. The 20 units of U are needed for maintenance purposes. These units are needed in week 6. Modify the *net material requirements plan* to reflect this change.

: **14.8**   As the production planner for Adams-Ebert Products, Inc., you have been given a bill of material for a bracket that is made up of a base, two springs, and four clamps. The base is assembled from one clamp and two housings. Each clamp has one handle and one casting. Each housing has two bearings and one shaft. There is no inventory on hand.

   a)   Design a product structure noting the quantities for each item and show the low-level coding.
   b)   Determine the gross quantities needed of each item if you are to assemble 50 brackets.
   c)   Compute the net quantities needed if there are 25 of the base and 100 of the clamp in stock.

Note: **P** means the problem may be solved with POM for Windows; **X** means the problem may be solved with Excel OM; and **P X** means the problem may be solved with POM for Windows and/or Excel OM. Many of the exercises in this chapter (14.1 through 14.16 and 14.23 through 14.27) can be done on *Resource Manager for Excel,* a commercial system made available by User Solutions, Inc. Access to a trial version of the software and a set of notes for the user is available at www.usersolutions.com.

Lot Size	Lead Time (# of periods)	On Hand	Safety Stock	Allo-cated	Low-Level Code	Item ID		Period (week, day)							
								1	2	3	4	5	6	7	8
							Gross Requirements								
							Scheduled Receipts								
							Projected On Hand								
							Net Requirements								
							Planned Order Receipts								
							Planned Order Releases								
							Gross Requirements								
							Scheduled Receipts								
							Projected On Hand								
							Net Requirements								
							Planned Order Receipts								
							Planned Order Releases								
							Gross Requirements								
							Scheduled Receipts								
							Projected On Hand								
							Net Requirements								
							Planned Order Receipts								
							Planned Order Releases								
							Gross Requirements								
							Scheduled Receipts								
							Projected On Hand								
							Net Requirements								
							Planned Order Receipts								
							Planned Order Releases								
							Gross Requirements								
							Scheduled Receipts								
							Projected On Hand								
							Net Requirements								
							Planned Order Receipts								
							Planned Order Releases								

FIGURE 14.12 ■ MRP Form for Homework Problems in Chapter 14

For several problems in this chapter, a copy of the form in Figure 14.12 may be helpful.

14.9 Your boss at Adams-Ebert Products, Inc., has just provided you with the schedule and lead times for the bracket in Problem 14.8. The unit is to be prepared in week 10. The lead times for the components are bracket (1 week), base (1 week), spring (1 week), clamp (1 week), housing (2 weeks), handle (1 week), casting (3 weeks), bearing (1 week), and shaft (1 week).

a) Prepare the time-phased product structure for the bracket.
b) In what week do you need to start the castings?

14.10 a) Given the product structure and master production schedule (Figure 14.13), develop a gross requirements plan for all items.
b) Given the preceding product structure, master production schedule, and inventory status (Figure 14.13), develop a net materials requirements (planned order release) for all items.

14.11 Given the following product structure, master production schedule, and inventory status (Figure 14.14), (a) develop a gross requirements plan for Item C and (b) a net requirements plan for Item C.

14.12 Based on the following data (see Figure 14.14), complete a net material requirements schedule for all items (10 schedules in all).

14.13 Electro Fans has just received an order for one thousand 20-inch fans due week 7. Each fan consists of a housing assembly, two grills, a fan assembly, and an electrical unit. The housing assembly consists of a frame, two supports, and a handle. The fan assembly consists of a hub and five blades. The electrical unit consists of a motor, a switch, and a knob. The following table gives lead times, on-hand inventory, and scheduled receipts.

a) Construct a product structure.
b) Construct a time-phased product structure.
c) Prepare a net material requirements plan.

Master Production Schedule for X1

PERIOD	7	8	9	10	11	12
Gross requirements		50		20		100

ITEM	LEAD TIME	ON HAND		ITEM	LEAD TIME	ON HAND
X1	1	50		C	1	0
B1	2	20		D	1	0
B2	2	20		E	3	10
A1	1	5				

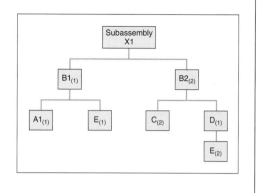

FIGURE 14.13 ■ Information for Problem 14.10

PERIOD	8	9	10	11	12
Gross requirements: A	100		50		150
Gross requirements: H		100		50	

ITEM	ON HAND	LEAD TIME		ITEM	ON HAND	LEAD TIME
A	0	1		F	75	2
B	100	2		G	75	1
C	50	2		H	0	1
D	50	1		J	100	2
E	75	2		K	100	2

FIGURE 14.14 ■ Information for Problems 14.11 and 14.12

FIGURE 14.15 ■

Information for Problems 14.14, 14.15 and 14.16

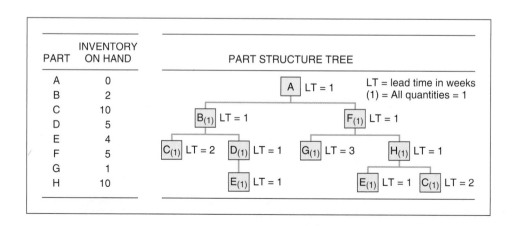

PART	INVENTORY ON HAND
A	0
B	2
C	10
D	5
E	4
F	5
G	1
H	10

PART STRUCTURE TREE

LT = lead time in weeks
(1) = All quantities = 1

Data Table for Problem 14.13

COMPONENT	LEAD TIME	ON HAND INVENTORY	LOT SIZE	SCHEDULED RECEIPT
20″ Fan	1	100	—	
Housing	1	100	—	
Frame	2	—	—	
Supports (2)	1	50	—	
Handle	1	400	—	
Grills (2)	2	200	—	
Fan Assembly	3	150	—	
Hub	1	—	—	
Blades (5)	2	—	100	
Electrical Unit	1	—	—	
Motor	1	—	—	
Switch	1	20	12	
Knob	1	—	25	200 knobs in week 2

14.14 A part structure, lead time (weeks), and on-hand quantities for product A are shown in Figure 14.15. From the information shown, generate

a) An indented bill of material for product A (see Figure 5.9 in Chapter 5 as an example of a BOM).

b) Net requirements for each part to produce 10 As in week 8 using lot-for-lot.

14.15 You are product planner for product A (in Problem 14.14). The field service manager, Al Trostel, has just called and told you that the requirements for B and F should each be increased by 10 units for his repair requirements in the field.

a) Prepare a list showing the quantity of each part required to produce the requirements for the service manager *and* the production request of 10.

b) What are the net requirements (the list in Part (a) less on-hand inventory)?

c) Prepare a net requirement plan by date for the new requirements (for both production and field service), assuming that the field service manager wants his 10 units of B and F in week 6 and the 10 production units in week 8.

14.16 You have just been notified via fax that the lead time for component G of product A (Problem 14.15) has been increased to 4 weeks.

a) Which items have changed and why?

b) What are the implications for the production plan?

c) As production planner, what can you do?

Data Table for Problems 14.17 through 14.19

Period	1	2	3	4	5	6	7	8	9	10	11	12
Gross requirements	30		40		30	70	20		10	80		50

Holding cost = $2.50/unit/week; setup cost = $150; lead time = 1 week; beginning inventory = 40.

14.17 Develop a lot-for-lot solution and calculate total relevant costs for the data in the table above.

14.18 Develop an EOQ solution and calculate total relevant costs for the data in the table above. Stockout costs equal $10 per unit.

14.19 Develop a PPB solution and calculate total relevant costs for the data in the table above.

14.20 Using the gross requirements schedule in Examples 4, 5, and 6 in the text, prepare an alternative ordering system that always orders 100 units the week prior to a shortage (a fixed order quantity of 100) with the same costs as in the example (setup at $100 each, holding at $1 per unit per period). What is the cost of this ordering system?

14.21 Using the gross requirements schedule in Examples 4, 5, and 6 in the text, prepare an alternative ordering system that orders every 3 weeks for 3 weeks ahead (a periodic order quantity). Use the same costs as in the example (setup at $100 each, holding at $1 per unit per period). What is the cost of this ordering system?

14.22 Using the gross requirements schedule in Examples 4, 5, and 6 in the text, prepare an alternative ordering system of your own design that uses the same cost as in the example (setup at $100 each, holding at $1 per unit per period). Can you do better than the costs shown in the text? What is the cost of your ordering system?

14.23   Beth Spenser, Inc., has received the following orders:

Period	1	2	3	4	5	6	7	8	9	10
Order size	0	40	30	40	10	70	40	10	30	60

The entire fabrication for these units is scheduled on one machine. There are 2,250 usable minutes in a week, and each unit will take 65 minutes to complete. Develop a capacity plan for the 10-week time period.

14.24   Reva Shader, Inc., has received the following orders:

Period	1	2	3	4	5	6	7	8	9	10
Order size	60	30	10	40	70	10	40	30	40	0

The entire fabrication for these units is scheduled on one machine. There are 2,250 usable minutes in a week, and each unit will take 65 minutes to complete. Develop a capacity plan for the 10-week time period.

14.25   As director of operations, you have recently installed a distribution requirements planning (DRP) system. The company has East Coast and West Coast warehouses, as well as a main factory warehouse in Omaha, Nebraska. You have just received the orders for the next planning period from the managers at each of the three facilities. Their reports are shown below and on the next page. The lead time to both the East and West Coast warehouses is 2 weeks, and there is a 1-week lead time to bring material to the factory warehouse. Shipments are in truckload quantities of 100 each. There is no initial inventory in the system. The factory is having trouble installing the level material work schedule and still has a lot size in multiples of 100.

Data for East Coast Warehouse

Period	1	2	3	4	5	6	7	8	9	10	11	12
Forecast requirements			40	100	80	70	20	25	70	80	30	50
Lead time = 2 weeks												

Data for West Coast Warehouse

Period	1	2	3	4	5	6	7	8	9	10
Forecast requirements		20	45	60	70	40	80	70	80	55
Lead time = 2 weeks										

Data for Factory Warehouse

Period	1	2	3	4	5	6	7	8	9	10
Forecast requirements			30	40	10	70	40	10	30	60
Lead time = 1 week										

a)   Show the plan for *receipt* of orders from the factory.
b)   If the factory requires 2 weeks to produce the merchandise, when must the orders be *released* to the factory?

14.26   Use the Web or other sources to:
a)   Find stories that highlight the advantages of an ERP system.
b)   Find stories that highlight the difficulties of purchasing, installing, or failure of an ERP system.

14.27   Use the Web or other sources to identify what an ERP vendor (SAP, PeopleSoft, Bann, Oracle, J. D. Edwards, IQMS, etc.) includes in these software modules:
a)   Customer Relationship Management.
b)   Supply Chain Management.
c)   Product Life Cycle Management.

 # INTERNET HOMEWORK PROBLEMS

See our Internet homepage at **www.prenhall.com/heizer** for these additional homework problems: 14.28 through 14.32.

CASE STUDY

Ikon's Attempt at ERP

Ikon Office Solutions is one of the world's leading office technology companies, with revenues exceeding $5 billion and operations in the U.S., Canada, Mexico, the United Kingdom, France, Germany, and Denmark. Ikon is pursing a growth strategy to move from what was more than 80 individually operating copier dealers to an integrated company twice that size in the next 4 years. Its goal is to provide total office technology solutions, ranging from copiers, digital printers, and document management services to systems integration, training, and other network technology services. The company has rapidly expanded its service capability with an aggressive acquisition effort that has included technology services and document management companies.

Given these objectives, the company seemed to need ERP software. A few years ago, it began a pilot project in the Northern California district to assess the possibility of using SAP's enterprise software applications companywide. Chief Information Officer David Gadra, who joined Ikon about a month after the pilot system was turned on, however, decided not to roll it out. Ikon will take a $25 million write-off on the cost of the pilot.

"There were a number of factors that made us decide this project was more challenging than beneficial for us," says Gadra. "When we added everything up—human factors, functionality gaps, and costs incurred—we decided our environment is ill-defined for SAP." Instead, Ikon is bringing all 13 of its regional operations onto a home-grown application system.

"I don't blame the consultants or SAP," he says. "We made errors on our side in estimating the amount of business change we'd have to make as part of this implementation."

The vast majority of the $25 million loss represents consultant fees; less than 10% went to pay for the software itself. At any given point in the project, Ikon was paying 40 to 50 outside consultants $300 an hour.

Ikon budgeted $12 million to get the system running. That cost came in at over $14 million, including $8 million paid to IBM for consulting.

A big reason the company decided to drop SAP was its conclusion that the software didn't sufficiently address the needs of a service company like Ikon, as opposed to manufacturers. For example, SAP didn't have an adequate feature for tracking service calls. Ikon also had great difficulty assembling an internal team of SAP experts. Ikon's costs were high because the firm relied heavily on consultants.

"I am extremely disappointed by Ikon's announcement," says SAP America president Jeremy Coote, describing Ikon's earlier pilot as on time and "extremely successful." Coote calls Ikon's decision to scrap the project "an example of what happens when you don't sell at the corporate level" as well as the divisional level. A newer version of SAP is to include a service management module.

Discussion Questions

1. What are the information needs at Ikon and what alternatives does Ikon have to meet these needs?
2. What are the advantages and disadvantages of ERP software in meeting these needs?
3. What risks did the company take in selecting SAP software for evaluation?
4. Why did Ikon cancel the SAP project?

Sources: Adapted from M. K. McGee, "Ikon Writes off $25M in Costs on SAP Project," *Information Week* (April 1997): 25; and J. R. Gordon and S. R. Gordon, *Information Systems: A Management Approach*, 2nd ed. (Fort Worth: Dryden Press, 1999): 182–183.

VIDEO CASE STUDY

MRP at Wheeled Coach

Wheeled Coach, the world's largest manufacturer of ambulances, builds thousands of different and constantly changing configurations of its products. The custom nature of its business means lots of options and special designs—and a potential scheduling and inventory nightmare. Wheeled Coach (a subsidiary of Collins Industries) addressed such problems, and succeeded in solving a lot of them, with an MRP system (described in the *Global Company Profile* that opens this chapter). As with most MRP installations, however, solving one set of problems uncovers a new set.

One of the new issues that had to be addressed by plant manager Lynn Whalen was newly discovered excess inventory. Managers discovered a substantial amount of inventory that was not called for in any finished products. Excess inventory was evident because of the new level of inventory accuracy required by the MRP system. The other reason was a new series of inventory reports generated by the IBM MAPICS MRP system purchased by Wheeled Coach. One of those reports indicates where items are used and is known as the

"Where Used" report. Interestingly, many inventory items were not called out on bills-of-material (BOMs) for any current products. In some cases, the reason some parts were in the stockroom remained a mystery.

The discovery of this excess inventory led to renewed efforts to ensure that the BOMs were accurate. With substantial work, BOM accuracy increased and the number of engineering change notices (ECNs) decreased. Similarly, purchase order accuracy, with regard to both part numbers and quantities ordered, was improved. Additionally, receiving department and stockroom accuracy went up, all helping to maintain schedule, costs, and ultimately, shipping dates and quality.

Eventually, Lynn Whalen concluded that the residual amounts of excess inventory were the result, at least in part, of rapid changes in ambulance design and technology. Another source was customer changes made after specifications had been determined and materials ordered. This latter excess occurs because, even though Wheeled Coach's own throughput time is only 17 days, many of the items that it purchases require much longer lead times. *(continued)*

Discussion Questions*

1. Why is accurate inventory such an important issue at Wheeled Coach?

2. What kind of a plan would you suggest for dealing with excess inventory at Wheeled Coach?

3. Be specific in your suggestions for reducing inventory and how to implement them.

*You may wish to view this case on your CD-ROM before answering the questions.

Chapter 15

Short-Term Scheduling

Chapter Outline

Scheduling involves the timing of operations to achieve the efficient movement of units through a system. This chapter addresses the issues of short-term scheduling in (1) process-focused, (2) repetitive, and (3) service environments. Process-focused facilities are production systems in which products are made to order; scheduling tasks in them is complex. There are several aspects and approaches to scheduling, loading, and sequencing of jobs, including Gantt charts, the assignment method of scheduling, priority rules, and Johnson's rule for sequencing.

Scheduling in service systems generally differs from scheduling in manufacturing systems. This leads to the use of appointment systems; first-come, first-served systems; and reservation systems, as well as to heuristics and linear programming approaches.

BEFORE COMING TO CLASS, READ CHAPTER 15 IN YOUR TEXT AND ANSWER THESE QUESTIONS.

1. Why is scheduling important? _____

_____

_____

2. How are Gantt charts used? _____

_____

_____

3. What is the "assignment method"? _____

_____

_____

4. Name five priority rules for sequencing. _____

_____

_____

5. Why is shortest processing time (SPT) such a popular rule? _____

_____

_____

6. What is a bottleneck? _____

_____

THE STRATEGIC IMPORTANCE OF SHORT-TERM SCHEDULING

FIGURE 15.1 ■ The Relationship between Capacity Planning, Aggregate Planning, Master Schedule, and Short-Term Scheduling

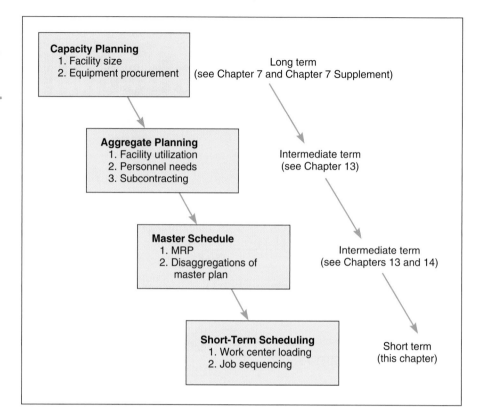

Capacity Planning
1. Facility size
2. Equipment procurement

Long term
(see Chapter 7 and Chapter 7 Supplement)

Aggregate Planning
1. Facility utilization
2. Personnel needs
3. Subcontracting

Intermediate term
(see Chapter 13)

Master Schedule
1. MRP
2. Disaggregations of master plan

Intermediate term
(see Chapters 13 and 14)

Short-Term Scheduling
1. Work center loading
2. Job sequencing

Short term
(this chapter)

SCHEDULING ISSUES

Forward Scheduling

Backward Scheduling

SCHEDULING PROCESS-FOCUSED WORK CENTERS

LOADING JOBS IN WORK CENTERS

Input–Output Control

Gantt Charts

FIGURE 15.3 ■ Gantt Load Chart for the Week of March 8

Work Center \ Day	Monday	Tuesday	Wednesday	Thursday	Friday
Metalworks	Job 349	✕		Job 350	
Mechanical		Job 349		Job 408	
Electronics	Job 408			Job 349	
Painting	Job 295		Job 408	✕	Job 349

▢ Processing   ▢ Unscheduled   ▨ Center not available (for example, maintenance time, repairs, shortages)

Assignment Method

Steps

1.

2.

3.

4.

PRACTICE PROBLEM 15.1 ■ Assignment Problem

Assume that Susan is a sorority pledge coordinator with four jobs and only three pledges. The table below gives the expected time for each pledge to do each job.

	JOB 1	JOB 2	JOB 3	JOB 4
Alice	4	9	3	8
Barbara	7	8	2	6
Jennifer	3	4	5	7

If Susan wishes to minimize the time taken, to whom should she assign which job?

Additional Practice Problem Space

SEQUENCING JOBS IN WORK CENTERS

Priority Rules:

FCFS

SPT

EDD

LPT

PRACTICE PROBLEM 15.2 ■ Job Shop Sequencing

A custom furniture shop has the following five jobs to be done, and the managers are unsure how to sequence them through the shop.

JOB	DAYS TO FINISH	DATE PROMISED (IN DAYS FROM TODAY)
A	2	5
B	8	8
C	6	12
D	4	10
E	1	4

Compare the effect of the scheduling methods (a) FCFS (first come, first served), (b) EDD (earliest due date), and (c) SPT (shortest processing time).

Additional Practice Problem Space

Critical Ratio Rule

$$CR = \frac{\text{Time remaining}}{\text{Workdays remaining}} = \frac{\text{Due date} - \text{Today's date}}{\text{Work (lead) time remaining}}$$

PRACTICE PROBLEM 15.3 ■ Critical Ratio Rule

A firm has the following six jobs waiting to be processed:

JOB	HOURS TO PROCESS	TIME DUE
#407	2	7
#281	8	16
#306	4	4
#429	10	17
#038	5	15
#998	12	18

Develop the appropriate sequencing for these jobs using the critical ratio criteria.

Additional Practice Problem Space

Scheduling N Jobs on Two Machines—Johnson's Rule

Four Steps

1.

2.

3.

4.

PRACTICE PROBLEM 15.4 ■ Johnson's Rule

Our furniture manufacturer has the following five jobs that must go through the two work centers, varnishing and painting.

JOB	HOURS REQUIRED	
	VARNISHING (CENTER 1)	PAINTING (CENTER 2)
R	4	5
S	17	7
T	14	12
U	9	2
V	11	6

What is the appropriate sequence for these jobs?

Additional Practice Problem Space

LIMITATIONS OF RULE-BASED DISPATCHING SYSTEMS

FINITE SCHEDULING

THEORY OF CONSTRAINTS

Five Steps:
1. Identify the Constraints
2. Develop a Plan for Overcoming Them
3. Focus Resources on Step 2
4. Offload Work or Expand Capability to Reduce Effects of Constraints
5. Start with New Constraints in Step 1

BOTTLENECK WORK CENTERS

Bottlenecks

REPETITIVE MANUFACTURING

Level Material Use

SCHEDULING FOR SERVICES

Cyclical Scheduling

DISCUSSION QUESTIONS

1. What is the overall objective of scheduling?
2. List the four criteria for determining the effectiveness of a *scheduling* decision. How do these criteria relate to the four criteria for *sequencing* decisions?
3. Describe what is meant by "loading" work centers. What are the two ways work centers can be loaded? What are two techniques used in loading?
4. Name five priority sequencing rules. Explain how each works to assign jobs.
5. What are the advantages and disadvantages of the shortest processing time (SPT) rule?
6. What is a due date?
7. Explain the terms "flow time" and "lateness."
8. Which shop-floor scheduling rule would you prefer to apply if you are the leader of the only team of experts charged with defusing several time bombs scattered throughout your building? You can see the bombs; they are of different types. You can tell how long each one will take to defuse. Discuss.
9. When is Johnson's rule best applied in job-shop scheduling?
10. State the four effectiveness measures for dispatching rules.
11. What are the steps of the assignment method of linear programming?
12. State the five-step process that serves as the basis of the theory of constraints.
13. What are the advantages of level material flow?
14. What are the techniques available to operations managers to deal with a bottleneck operation? Which of these does not increase throughput?
15. What is input–output control?

CRITICAL THINKING EXERCISE

Scheduling people to work the late, or "graveyard," shift is a problem in almost every 24-hour company. An article in the *Wall Street Journal* titled "Scheduling Workers Who Fall Asleep on the Job Is Not Easy" describes night-shift dilemmas at an oil refinery and a police department. Scheduling is also difficult for airlines that fly long routes, such as El Al Airline's popular 11-hour nonstop Tel Aviv to New York flight.

Select five companies that require night shifts and discuss how each can deal with its staffing requirements. What are the major issues in each that affect morale, productivity, alertness, and safety?

ACTIVE MODEL EXERCISE

This exercise, found on your CD-ROM, allows you to evaluate changes to input data in the job shop sequencing model.

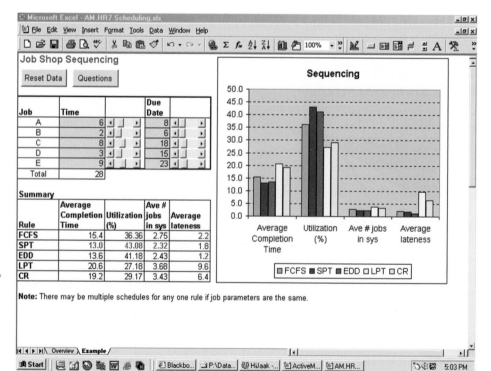

ACTIVE MODEL 15.1 ■

An Analysis of the
Sequencing of Jobs
Using the Example 5
Data of the
Architectural Firm in
Your Text

Questions

1. Which schedule (rule) minimizes the average completion time, maximizes the utilization, and minimizes the average number of jobs in the system for this example?
2. Use the scrollbar to change the processing time for job C and use the scrollbar to modify the due date for job C. Does the same rule always minimize the average completion time?
3. Which schedule (rule) minimizes the average lateness for this example?
4. Use the scrollbar to change the due date for job C. Does the same rule always minimize the average lateness?

PROBLEMS*

: 15.1 Ron Satterfield's excavation company has scheduled five jobs. Today, which is the end of day 7, Ron is reviewing the Gantt chart depicting these schedules.
- Job #151 was scheduled to begin on day 3 and to take 6 days. As of now, it is 1 day ahead of schedule.
- Job #177 was scheduled to begin on day 1 and take 4 days. It is currently on time.
- Job #179 was scheduled to start on day 7 and take 2 days. It actually got started on day 6 and is progressing according to plan.
- Job #211 was scheduled to begin on day 5, but missing equipment delayed it until day 6. It is progressing as expected and should take 3 days.
- Job #215 was scheduled to begin on day 4 and take 5 days. It got started on time but has since fallen behind 2 days.

Draw the Gantt chart as it looks to Ron.

: 15.2 First Printing and Copy Center has 4 more jobs to be scheduled, in addition to those shown in Example 3 in the chapter. Production scheduling personnel are reviewing the Gantt chart at the end of day 4.
- Job D was scheduled to begin early on day 2 and to end on the middle of day 9. As of now (the review point after day 4), it is 2 days ahead of schedule.
- Job E should begin on day 1 and end on day 3. It was on time.
- Job F was to begin on day 3, but maintenance forced a delay of $1\frac{1}{2}$ days. The job should now take 5 full days. It is now on schedule.
- Job G is a day behind schedule. It started at the beginning of day 2 and should require 6 days to complete.

Develop a Gantt schedule chart for First Printing and Copy Center.

P✗ . 15.3 The Orange Top Cab Company has a taxi waiting at each of four cabstands in Evanston, Illinois. Four customers have called and requested service. The distances, in miles, from the waiting taxis to the customers are given in the following table. Find the optimal assignment of taxis to customers so as to minimize total driving distances to the customers.

	CUSTOMER			
CAB SITE	A	B	C	D
Stand 1	7	3	4	8
Stand 2	5	4	6	5
Stand 3	6	7	9	6
Stand 4	8	6	7	4

P✗ . 15.4 Molly Riggs' medical testing company wishes to assign a set of jobs to a set of machines. The following table provides data as to the production of each machine when performing the specific job:

	MACHINE			
JOB	A	B	C	D
1	7	9	8	10
2	10	9	7	6
3	11	5	9	6
4	9	11	5	8

a) Determine the assignment of jobs to machines that will *maximize* total production.
b) What is the total production of your assignments?

P̶X̶ . 15.5   The Johnny Ho Manufacturing Company in Columbus, Ohio, is putting out four new electronic components. Each of Ho's four plants has the capacity to add one more product to its current line of electronic parts. The unit-manufacturing costs for producing the different parts at the four plants are shown in the accompanying table. How should Ho assign the new products to the plants to minimize manufacturing costs?

| | PLANT | | | |
ELECTRONIC COMPONENT	1	2	3	4
C53	$0.10	$0.12	$0.13	$0.11
C81	0.05	0.06	0.04	0.08
D5	0.32	0.40	0.31	0.30
D44	0.17	0.14	0.19	0.15

P̶X̶ : 15.6   Emilia Pawlowski, the scheduler at a small Pennsylvania plant, has six jobs that can be processed on any of six machines, with respective times as shown (in hours) below. Determine the allocation of jobs to machines that will result in minimum time.

| | MACHINE | | | | | |
JOB	1	2	3	4	5	6
A-52	60	22	34	42	30	60
A-53	22	52	16	32	18	48
A-56	29	16	58	28	22	55
A-59	42	32	28	46	15	30
A-60	30	18	25	15	45	42
A-61	50	48	57	30	44	60

P̶X̶ : 15.7   The Akron Police Department has five detective squads available for assignment to five open crime cases. The chief of detectives, Paul Kuzdrall, wishes to assign the squads so that the total time to conclude the cases is minimized. The average number of days, based on past performance, for each squad to complete each case is as follows:

| | CASE | | | | |
SQUAD	A	B	C	D	E
1	14	7	3	7	27
2	20	7	12	6	30
3	10	3	4	5	21
4	8	12	7	12	21
5	13	25	24	26	8

Each squad is composed of different types of specialists, and whereas one squad may be very effective in certain types of cases, it may be almost useless in others. Solve the problem by using the assignment method.

P̶X̶ . 15.8   The Gleaming Company has just developed a new dishwashing liquid and is preparing for a national television promotional campaign. The firm has decided to schedule a series of 1-minute commercials during the peak daytime audience viewing hours of 1:00 P.M. to 5:00 P.M. To reach the widest possible audience, Gleaming wants to schedule one commercial on each of four networks and have one commercial appear during each of the four 1-hour time blocks. The exposure ratings for each hour, representing the number of viewers per $1,000 spent, are presented in the accompanying table. Which network should be scheduled each hour in order to provide the maximum audience exposure?

| | NETWORKS | | | |
TIME	A	B	C	INDEPENDENT
1:00–2:00 P.M.	27.1	18.1	11.3	9.5
2:00–3:00 P.M.	18.9	15.5	17.1	10.6
3:00–4:00 P.M.	19.2	18.5	9.9	7.7
4:00–5:00 P.M.	11.5	21.4	16.8	12.8

P̶X̶ : 15.9   James Gross, chairman of the College of Oshkosh's business department, needs to assign professors to courses next semester. As a criterion for judging who should teach each course, Professor Gross reviews the past 2 years' teaching evaluations (which were filled out by students). Since each of the four professors taught each of the four courses at one time or another during the 2-year period, Gross is able to record a course rating for each instructor. These ratings are shown in the following table. Find the assignment of professors to courses to maximize the overall teaching rating.

	COURSE			
PROFESSOR	STATISTICS	MANAGEMENT	FINANCE	ECONOMICS
W. W. Fisher	90	65	95	40
D. Golhar	70	60	80	75
Z. Hug	85	40	80	60
N. K. Rustagi	55	80	65	55

P· : 15.10 The following jobs are waiting to be processed at the same machine center. Jobs are logged as they arrive:

JOB	DUE DATE	DURATION (DAYS)
A	313	8
B	312	16
C	325	40
D	314	5
E	314	3

In what sequence would the jobs be ranked according to the following decision rules: (1) FCFS, (2) EDD, (3) SPT, (4) LPT? All dates are specified as manufacturing planning calendar days. Assume that all jobs arrive on day 275. Which decision is best and why?

P . 15.11 Suppose that today is day 300 on the planning calendar and that we have not started any of the jobs given in Problem 15.10. Using the critical-ratio technique, in what sequence would you schedule these jobs?

P· : 15.12 An Alabama lumberyard has four jobs on order, as shown in the following table. Today is day 205 on the yard's schedule. In what sequence would the jobs be ranked according to the following decision rules:
- a) FCFS
- b) SPT
- c) LPT
- d) EDD
- e) Critical ratio

Which is best, and why? Which has the minimum lateness?

JOB	DUE DATE	REMAINING TIME IN DAYS
A	212	6
B	209	3
C	208	3
D	210	8

P· : 15.13 The following jobs are waiting to be processed at Rick Carlson's machine center. Carlson's machine center has a relatively long backlog and sets fresh schedules every 2 weeks, which do not disturb earlier schedules. Below are the jobs received during the previous 2 weeks. They are ready to be scheduled today, which is day 241. Job names refer to names of clients and contract numbers.

JOB	DATE JOB RECEIVED	PRODUCTION DAYS NEEDED	DATE JOB DUE
CX-01	225	25	270
BR-02	228	15	300
DE-06	230	35	320
SY-11	231	30	310
RG-05	235	40	360

- a) Complete the following table. (Show your supporting calculations.)
- b) Which dispatching rule has the best score for flow time?
- c) Which dispatching rule has the best score for utilization?
- d) Which dispatching rule has the best score for lateness?
- e) Which dispatching rule would you select? Support your decision.

DISPATCHING RULE	JOB SEQUENCE	FLOW TIME	UTILIZATION	AVERAGE NUMBER OF JOBS	AVERAGE LATENESS
EDD					
SPT					
LPT					

P⚹ : **15.14**   The following jobs are waiting to be processed at Julie Morel's machine center:

JOB	DATE ORDER RECEIVED	PRODUCTION DAYS NEEDED	DATE ORDER DUE
A	110	20	180
B	120	30	200
C	122	10	175
D	125	16	230
E	130	18	210

In what sequence would the jobs be ranked according to the following rules: (1) FCFS, (2) EDD, (3) SPT, (4) LPT? All dates are according to shop calendar days. Today on the planning calendar is day 130 and none of the jobs have been started or scheduled. Which rule is best?

P · **15.15**   Suppose that today is day 160 on the planning calendar and that we have not yet started any of the jobs in Problem 15.14. Using the critical-ratio technique, in what sequence would you schedule these jobs?

P : **15.16**   The following jobs are waiting to be processed at Pete Nesta's machine center. Today is day 250.

JOB	DATE JOB RECEIVED	PRODUCTION DAYS NEEDED	DATE JOB DUE
1	215	30	260
2	220	20	290
3	225	40	300
4	240	50	320
5	250	20	340

Using the critical-ratio scheduling rule, in what sequence would the jobs be processed?

P : **15.17**   The following set of seven jobs is to be processed through two work centers at George Heinrich's printing company. The sequence is first printing, then binding. Processing time at each of the work centers is shown below.

JOB	PRINTING (HOURS)	BINDING (HOURS)
T	15	3
U	7	9
V	4	10
W	7	6
X	10	9
Y	4	5
Z	7	8

a) What is the optimal sequence for these jobs to be scheduled?
b) Chart these jobs through the two work centers.
c) What is the total length of time of this optimal solution?

P : **15.18**   Six jobs are to be processed through a two-step operation. The first operation involves sanding, and the second involves painting. Processing times are as follows:

JOB	OPERATION 1 (HOURS)	OPERATION 2 (HOURS)
A	10	5
B	7	4
C	5	7
D	3	8
E	2	6
F	4	3

Determine a sequence that will minimize the total completion time for these jobs. Illustrate graphically.

P⚹ : **15.19**   NASA's astronaut crew currently includes 10 mission specialists who hold Ph.D.'s in either astrophysics or astromedicine. One of these specialists will be assigned to each of the 10 flights scheduled for the upcoming 9 months. Mission specialists are responsible for carrying out scientific and medical experiments in space or for launching, retrieving, or repairing satellites. The chief of astronaut personnel, a former crew member with three missions under his belt, must decide who should be assigned and trained for each of the very different missions. Clearly, astronauts with medical educations are more suited to missions involving biological or medical experiments, whereas those with engineering- or physics-oriented degrees are best suited to other types of missions. The chief assigns each astronaut a rating on a scale of 1 to 10 for each possible mission, with a 10 being a perfect match for the task at hand and a 1 being a mismatch. Only one specialist is assigned to each flight, and none is reassigned until all others have flown at least once.

	MISSION									
ASTRONAUT	JAN. 3	JAN. 27	FEB. 5	FEB. 26	MAR. 26	APR. 12	MAY 1	JUN. 9	AUG. 20	SEPT. 19
Chiang	9	7	2	1	10	9	8	9	2	6
Ittig	8	8	3	4	7	9	7	7	4	4
Malik	2	1	10	10	1	4	7	6	6	7
Moodie	4	4	10	9	9	9	1	2	3	4
Riddle	10	10	9	9	8	9	1	1	1	1
Sower	1	3	5	7	9	7	10	10	9	2
Sweeney	9	9	8	8	9	1	1	2	2	9
Temponi	3	2	7	6	4	3	9	7	7	9
Turner	5	4	5	9	10	10	5	4	9	8
Visich	10	10	9	7	6	7	5	4	8	8

a) Who should be assigned to which flight?

b) We have just been notified that Malik is getting married in February, and he has been granted a highly sought publicity tour in Europe that month. (He intends to take his wife and let the trip double as a honeymoon.) How does this change the final schedule?

c) Sweeney has complained that he was misrated on his January missions. Both ratings should be 10s, he claims to the chief, who agrees to recompute the schedule. Do any changes occur over the schedule set in part (b)?

d) What are the strengths and weaknesses of this approach to scheduling?

 # INTERNET HOMEWORK PROBLEMS

See our Internet homepage at **www.prenhall.com/heizer** for these additional homework problems: 15.20 through 15.25.

CASE STUDY

Payroll Planning, Inc.

Payroll Planning is a Boulder, Colorado, company that provides accounting services for small businesses. Small businesses either drop off their payroll records weekly, biweekly, or monthly or forward them electronically via the Internet. Payroll Planning then processes the records and issues the checks. The firm's main competitor is the nationally known company PayChex, Inc. The following table shows the processing times and types for jobs sent by Payroll Planning clients on Friday, May 1.

CLIENT	PROCESSING TYPE	TIME (IN MINUTES)
Allen Leather	Weekly	33
Art World	Biweekly	63
Beta Computing	Monthly	95
Colon Clinic	Monthly	87
Darrow Plumbing	Weekly	72
Denver Broncos	Weekly	15
Eden Roc Hotel	Monthly	26
Fink's Garage	Weekly	28
Golden Gloves	Weekly	47
Gunter's Guns	Weekly	32
Hug & Jordan	Weekly	24

CLIENT	PROCESSING TYPE	TIME (IN MINUTES)
Izenman Ads	Monthly	55
Jerry's Ice Cream	Weekly	31
Keystone Repairs	Weekly	33
Lifeblood, Inc.	Weekly	25
Lisa's Bakery	Weekly	48
Living Well	Biweekly	42
Mortician Supply Co.	Weekly	43
New Life Vitamins	Weekly	64
Owens & Marshal	Monthly	42
Philly Cheesedogs	Weekly	24
Quik Lube	Weekly	14
Rockin' Robin	Weekly	74
Sam's Sporting Goods	Monthly	110
Tennis n'More	Weekly	18
Tetris, Inc.	Weekly	13
Twins Emporium	Weekly	22
Valvoline Electric	Weekly	23
White's Dry Cleaner	Biweekly	64
Wilson & Jones	Monthly	88
Wings of S. F.	Weekly	8
Woodworth Auto	Monthly	76
Z.A.G. Inc.	Weekly	36
Zuesman Gym	Weekly	42

(continued)

When companies drop off or electronically transmit their records on time, Payroll Planning typically manages to get the checks printed on time. However, Payroll Planning has occasionally run into scheduling difficulties. The company feels that examining what has happened in the past will provide some insight into how to deal with similar situations in the future.

Payroll Planning sets due dates according to the type of customer. For monthly customers, the due date is 9:00 A.M.; for biweekly customers, the due date is noon; and for weekly customers, the due date is 3:00 P.M. All of the processing will begin on the third shift (at midnight) on the day that the records are due.

Payroll Planning has been using an "earliest due date" scheduling rule because this accords the highest priority to the monthly clients and the lowest priority to the weekly. If clients come in only once per month, there is less room for error (lateness) than if they use a weekly payroll. While Payroll Planning has been following this logic for the past decade, it wants to determine whether this is the best scheduling rule.

Discussion Question

1. Explore alternative scheduling possibilities for Payroll Planning.

Source: Reprinted by permission of Professors Howard J. Weiss and Mark E. Gershon, Temple University.

VIDEO CASE STUDY

Scheduling at Hard Rock Cafe

Whether it's scheduling nurses at Mayo Clinic, pilots at Southwest Airlines, classrooms at UCLA, or servers at a Hard Rock Cafe, it's clear that good scheduling is important. Proper schedules use an organization's assets (1) more effectively, by serving customers promptly, and (2) more efficiently, by lowering costs.

Hard Rock Cafe at Universal Studios, Orlando, is the world's largest restaurant, with 1,100 seats on two main levels. With typical turnover of employees in the restaurant industry at 80% to 100% per year, Hard Rock General Manager Ken Hoffman takes scheduling very seriously. Hoffman wants his 160 servers to be effective, but he also wants to treat them fairly. He has done so with scheduling software and flexibility that has increased productivity, while contributing to turnover that is half the industry average. His goal is to find the fine balance that gives employees financially productive daily work shifts, while at the same time, setting the schedule tight enough so as to not overstaff between lunch and dinner.

The weekly schedule begins with a sales forecast. "First, we examine last year's sales at the cafe for the same day of the week," says Hoffman. "Then we adjust our forecast for this year based on a variety of closely watched factors. For example, we call the Orlando Convention Bureau every week to see what major groups will be in town. Then we send two researchers out to check on the occupancy of nearby hotels. We watch closely to see what concerts are scheduled at Hard Rock Live—the 3,000-seat concert stage next door. From the forecast, we calculate how any people we need to have on duty each day for the kitchen, the bar, as hosts, and for table service."

Once Hard Rock determines the number of staff needed, servers submit request forms, which are fed into the software's linear programming mathematical model. Individuals are given priority rankings from 1 to 9 based on their seniority and how important they are to fill each day's schedule. Schedules are then posted by day and by workstation. Trades are handled between employees, who understand the value of each specific shift and station.

Hard Rock employees like the system, as does the general manager, since sales per manhour are rising and turnover is dropping.

Discussion Questions*

1. Name and justify several factors that Hoffman could use in forecasting weekly sales.
2. What can be done to lower turnover in large restaurants?
3. Why is seniority important in scheduling servers?
4. How does the schedule impact on productivity?

Source: Professors Barry Render, Rollins College; Jay Heizer, Texas Lutheran University; and Bev Amer, Northern Arizona University.

*You may wish to view this case on your CD-ROM before answering the questions.

Just-in-Time and Lean Production Systems

Just-in-time (JIT) and lean production are philosophies of continuous improvement. Lean production begins with a focus on customer desires, but both concepts focus on driving all waste out of the production process. Because waste is found in anything that does not add value, JIT and lean organizations are adding value more efficiently than other firms. Waste occurs when defects are produced within the production process or by outside suppliers. JIT and lean production attack wasted space because of a less-than-optimal layout; they attack wasted time because of poor scheduling; they attack waste in idle inventory; and they attack waste for poorly maintained machinery and equipment. The expectation is that committed, empowered employees work with committed management and suppliers to build systems that respond to customers with ever lower cost and higher quality.

BEFORE COMING TO CLASS, READ CHAPTER 16 IN YOUR TEXT AND ANSWER THESE QUESTIONS.

1. What is the difference between a "pull" system and a "push" system? __

2. What are the goals of JIT partnerships? _____

3. List several of the characteristics of JIT suppliers. _____

4. Why is JIT layout important? _____

5. Why is reducing inventory setup costs useful? _____

6. What is a kanban? _____

JUST-IN-TIME AND LEAN PRODUCTION

JIT

Lean Production

Pull System

Push System

SUPPLIERS

Goals of Partnerships

TABLE 16.2 ■ Characteristics of JIT Partnerships

SUPPLIERS

Few suppliers
Nearby suppliers
Repeat business with same suppliers
Analysis and support to enable desirable suppliers to become or to stay price competitive
Competitive bidding mostly limited to new purchases
Buyer resists vertical integration and subsequent wipeout of supplier business
Suppliers encouraged to extend JIT buying to their suppliers (second- and third-tier suppliers)

QUANTITIES

Steady output rate
Frequent deliveries in small-lot quantities
Long-term contract agreements
Minimal or no paperwork to release orders (use EDI or Internet)
Delivery quantities fixed for whole contract term
Little or no permissible overage or underage
Suppliers package in exact quantities
Suppliers reduce their production lot sizes

QUALITY

Minimal product specifications imposed on supplier
Help suppliers meet quality requirements
Close relationships between buyers' and suppliers' quality assurance people
Suppliers use poka-yoke and process control charts instead of lot-sampling inspection

SHIPPING

Scheduling of inbound freight
Gain control by use of company-owned or contract shipping and warehousing
Use of advanced shipping notice (ASN)

JIT LAYOUT

TABLE 16.3 ■ Layout Tactics

Build work cells for families of products
Minimize distance
Design little space for inventory
Improve employee communication
Use poka-yoke devices
Build flexible or movable equipment
Cross train workers to add flexibility

INVENTORY

TABLE 16.4 ■ JIT Inventory Tactics

Use a pull system to move inventory
Reduce lot size
Develop just-in-time delivery systems with suppliers
Deliver directly to point of use
Perform to schedule
Reduce setup time
Use group technology

FIGURE 16.2 ■ Frequent Orders Reduce Average Inventory

A lower order size increases the number of orders and total ordering cost, but reduces average inventory and total holding cost.

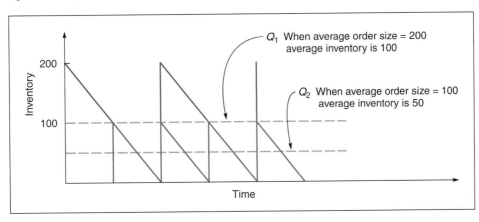

Production Order Quantity Model

$$Q^\star = \sqrt{\frac{2DS}{H[1-(d/p)]}}$$

(16-1)

where D = Annual demand
   S = Setup cost
   H = Holding cost
   d = Daily demand
   p = Daily production

Additional Practice Problem Space

SCHEDULING

TABLE 16.5 ■ JIT Scheduling Tactics

Communicate schedules to suppliers
Make level schedules
Freeze part of the schedule
Perform to schedule
Seek one-piece-make and one-piece-move
Eliminate waste
Produce in small lots
Use kanbans
Make each operation produce a perfect part

FIGURE 16.6 ■ Diagram of Outbound Stockpoint with Warning-Signal Marker

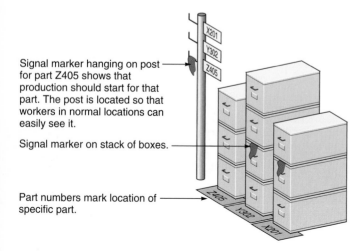

Signal marker hanging on post for part Z405 shows that production should start for that part. The post is located so that workers in normal locations can easily see it.

Signal marker on stack of boxes.

Part numbers mark location of specific part.

Level Schedules

Kanban

$$\text{Number of kanbans (containers)} = \frac{\text{Demand during lead time} + \text{Safety stock}}{\text{Size of container}}$$

PRACTICE PROBLEM 16.1 ■ Number of Kanbans

Bryant Electronics produces short runs of battery-powered pocket lanterns. As the new materials manager, you have been asked to reduce inventory by introducing a kanban system. After several hours of analysis, you have developed the following data for connectors used in one work cell. How many kanbans do you need for this connector?

Daily demand: 1,500 units
Production lead time: 1 day
Safety stock: 1 day
Kanban size: 250 units

PRACTICE PROBLEM 16.2 ■ Size and Number of Kanbans

Perkins Lighting managers wish to employ a kanban in their new floor lamp production system. For the floor lamp base, they have provided the following information:

Daily demand: 300 units (with 300 business days per year)
Holding cost: $20 per unit per year
Order cost: $10 per order
Lead time: 2 days
Safety stock: 600 units

Assuming that the size of the kanban is the EOQ, find the size of the kanban and the number of kanbans required.

QUALITY

TABLE 16.6 ■ JIT Quality Tactics

Use statistical process control
Empower employees
Build fail-safe methods (poka-yoke, checklists, etc.)
Provide immediate feedback

EMPLOYEE EMPOWERMENT

LEAN PRODUCTION

JIT IN SERVICES

DISCUSSION QUESTIONS

1. What is JIT?
2. What is a "lean producer"?
3. What is level scheduling?
4. Given the goals of JIT partnerships noted in the text, which do you think would be the hardest to accomplish?
5. JIT attempts to remove delays, which do not add value. How then does JIT cope with weather and its impact on crop harvest and transportation times?
6. What are three ways in which JIT and quality are related?
7. How does JIT contribute to competitive advantage?

8. What are the characteristics of just-in-time partnerships with respect to suppliers?
9. Discuss how the Japanese word for "card" has application in the study of JIT.
10. Standardized, reusable containers have fairly obvious benefits when shipping. What is the purpose of these devices within the plant?
11. Does JIT work in the service sector? Provide an illustration.
12. Which JIT techniques work in both the manufacturing *and* service sectors?

PROBLEMS*

16.1   Leblanc Electronics, Inc., in Nashville, produces short runs of custom airwave scanners for the defense industry. You have been asked by the owner, Larry Leblanc, to reduce inventory by introducing a kanban system. After several hours of analysis, you develop the following data for scanner connectors used in one work cell. How many kanbans do you need for this connector?

Daily demand	1,000 connectors
Demand during lead time	2 days
Safety stock	$\frac{1}{2}$ day
Kanban size	500 connectors

16.2   Chip Gillikin's company wants to establish kanbans to feed a newly established work cell. The following data has been provided. How many kanbans are needed?

Daily demand	250 units
Production lead time	$\frac{1}{2}$ day
Safety stock	$\frac{1}{4}$ day
Kanban size	50 units

 16.3   Mark Sibla Manufacturing, Inc., is moving to kanbans to support its telephone switching-board assembly lines. Determine the size of the kanban for subassemblies and the number of kanbans needed.

Setup cost = $30

Annual holding cost subassembly = $120 per subassembly

Daily production = 20 subassemblies

Annual usage = 2,500 (50 weeks × 5 days each × daily usage of 10 subassemblies)

Lead time = 16 days

Safety stock = 4 days' production of subassemblies.

 16.4   John Alexrod Motorcycle Corp. uses kanbans to support its transmission assembly line. Determine the size of the kanban for the mainshaft assembly and the number of kanbans needed.

Setup cost = $20

Annual holding cost of mainshaft assembly = $250 per unit

Daily production = 300 mainshafts

Annual usage = 20,000 (= 50 weeks × 5 days each × daily usage of 80 mainshafts)

Lead time = 3 days

Safety stock = $\frac{1}{2}$ day's production of mainshafts

Note: **P** means the problem may be solved with POM for Windows; ✗ means the problem may be solved with Excel OM; and **P**✗ means the problem may be solved with POM for Windows and/or Excel OM.

P. **16.5**   Discount-Mart, a major East Coast retailer, wants to determine the economic order quantity (see Chapter 12 for EOQ formulas) for its halogen lamps. It currently buys all halogen lamps from Specialty Lighting Manufacturers, in Atlanta. Annual demand is 2,000 lamps, ordering cost per order is $30, carrying cost per lamp is $12.
a)   What is the EOQ?
b)   What are the total annual costs of holding and ordering?
c)   How many orders should Discount-Mart place with Specialty Lighting per year?

P. **16.6**   Discount-Mart (see Problem 16.5), as part of its new JIT program, has signed a long-term contract with Specialty Lighting and will place orders electronically for its halogen lamps. Ordering costs will drop to $.50 per order, but Discount-Mart also reassessed its carrying costs and raised them to $20 per lamp.
a)   What is the new economic order quantity?
b)   How many orders will now be placed?
c)   What is the total annual cost with this policy?

16.7   How do your answers to Problems 16.5 and 16.6 provide insight into a JIT purchasing strategy?

16.8   Bill Penny has a repetitive manufacturing plant producing trailer hitches in Arlington, Texas. The plant has an average inventory turnover of only 12 times per year. He has, therefore, determined that he will reduce his component lot sizes. He has developed the following data for one component, the safety chain clip:

$$\text{Annual demand} = 31,200 \text{ units}$$
$$\text{Daily demand} = 120 \text{ units}$$
$$\text{Daily production} = 960 \text{ units}$$
$$\text{Desired lot size (1 hour of production)} = 120 \text{ units}$$
$$\text{Holding cost per unit per year} = \$12$$
$$\text{Setup labor cost per hour} = \$20$$

How many minutes of setup time should he have his plant manager aim for regarding this component?

16.9   Given the following information about a product, at Phyllis Simon's firm, what is the appropriate setup time?

$$\text{Annual demand} = 39,000 \text{ units}$$
$$\text{Daily demand} = 150 \text{ units}$$
$$\text{Daily production} = 1,000 \text{ units}$$
$$\text{Desired lot size (1 hour of production)} = 150 \text{ units}$$
$$\text{Holding cost per unit per year} = \$10$$
$$\text{Setup labor cost per hour} = \$40$$

16.10   Rick Wing has a repetitive manufacturing plant producing automobile steering wheels. Use the following data to prepare for a reduced lot size. The firm uses a work year of 305 days.

Annual demand for steering wheels	30,500
Daily demand	100
Daily production	800
Desired lot size (2 hours of production)	200
Holding cost per unit per year	$10

a)   What is the setup cost, based on the desired lot size?
b)   What is the setup time, based on $40 per hour setup labor?

INTERNET HOMEWORK PROBLEMS

See our Internet home page at **www.prenhall.com/heizer** for these additional homework problems: 16.11 and 16.12.

CASE STUDY

Mutual Insurance Company of Iowa

Mutual Insurance Company of Iowa (MICI) has a major insurance office facility located in Des Moines, Iowa. The Des Moines office is responsible for processing all of MICI's insurance claims for the entire nation. The company's sales have experienced rapid growth during the last year, and as expected, record levels in claims followed. Over 2,500 forms for claims a day are now flowing into the office for processing. Unfortunately, fewer than 2,500 forms a day are flowing out. The total time to process a claim, from the time it arrives to the time a check is mailed, has gone from 10 days to 10 weeks. As a result, some customers are threatening legal action. Sally Cook, the manager of Claims Processing, is particularly distressed as she knows that a claim seldom requires more than 3 hours of actual work. Under the current administrative procedures, human resources limitations, and facility constraints, there appear to be no easy fixes for the problem. But clearly, something must be done, as the workload has overwhelmed the existing system.

MICI management wants aggressive, but economical, action taken to fix the problem. Ms. Cook has decided to try a JIT approach to claim processing. With support from her bosses, and as a temporary fix, Cook has brought in part-time personnel from MICI sales divisions across the country to help. They are to work down the claims backlog while a new JIT system is installed.

Meanwhile, Claims Processing managers and employees are to be trained in JIT principles. With JIT principles firmly in mind, managers will redesign jobs to move responsibilities for quality control activities to each employee, holding them responsible for quality work and any necessary corrections. Cook will also initiate worker-training programs that explain the entire claim processing flow, as well as provide comprehensive training on each step in the process. Data entry skills will also be taught to both employees and managers in an effort to fix responsibility for data accuracy on the processor rather than data entry clerks. Additionally, emphasis will be placed on cross training to enable workers within departments to process a variety of customer claim applications in their entirety.

Cook and her supervisors are also reexamining the insurance and claim forms currently in use. They want to see if standardization of forms will cut processing time, reduce data entry time, and cut work-in-process.

They hope the changes will also save training time. Making changes in work methods and worker skills leads logically to a need for change in the layout of the Claims Processing Department. This potential change represents a major move from the departmental layout of the past, and will be a costly step. To help ensure the successful implementation of this phase of the changeover, Cook established a team made up of supervisors, employees, and an outside office layout consultant. She also had the team visit the Kawasaki motor cycle plant in Lincoln, Nebraska, to observe their use of work cells to aid JIT.

The team concluded that a change in the office facilities is necessary to successfully implement and integrate JIT concepts at MICI. The team believes it should revise the layout of the operation and work methods to bring them in line with "group technology cell" layouts. An example of the current departmental layout and claim processing flow pattern is presented in Figure 16.8. As can be seen in this figure, customer claims arrive for processing at the facility and flow through a series of offices and departments to eventually complete the claim process. While the arrangement of the offices and

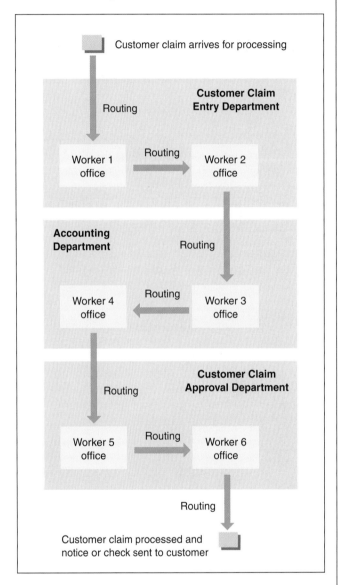

FIGURE 16.8 ■

Claims Processing Department Layout

workers in Figure 16.8 is typical, the entire facility actually operates 20 additional flows, each consisting of the same three departments. However, not all of the 20 flows are configured the same. The number of employees, for example, varies depending on the claim form requirements (larger claims have to be approved by more people). So while all forms must pass through the same three departments (Customer Claim Entry, Accounting, and Customer Claim Approval), the number of workers for each claim may vary from two to four. For this reason, the MICI facility currently maintains a staff of over 180 office workers just to process and route claims. All of these people work for Ms. Cook.

(continued)

Discussion Questions

1. Identify the attributes you would expect the Claims Processing Department at MICI to have once the new JIT system is in place.
2. What would the restructured cell layout for claim processing in Figure 16.8 look like? Draw it.
3. What assumptions are you making about personnel and equipment in the new group technology cell layout?

4. How will the new JIT oriented system benefit the MICI operation? Explain.

Source: Adapted from Marc J. Schniederjans, *Topics in Just-in-Time Management*, pp. 283–285. Reprinted by permission of Prentice-Hall, Inc., Upper Saddle River, NJ.

CASE STUDY

JIT after the Fire

World-renowned Toyota Motor Company has a worldwide presence, with Toyota's investment in North America alone exceeding $12 billion in 10 manufacturing plants. Toyota is at the forefront of lean firms and a showcase of JIT. Executives from all over the world make the journey to Toyota to see how JIT works.

But early one Saturday morning in February, a fire roared through the huge Aisin Seiki plant in Kariya, Japan. The fire incinerated the main source of crucial brake valves that Toyota buys from Aisin and uses in most of its cars. Aisin has long been a supplier of the critical brake-fluid-proportioning valves (P-valves), supplying 99% of Toyota's requirement for the valve. About 80% of Aisin's total output goes to Toyota. As the smoke cleared, the extent of the disaster was clear—most of the 506 special machines used to manufacture the P-valves were useless. A few might be repaired in 2 weeks, but most would need to be replaced—and the lead time was 6 weeks. Both Aisin and Toyota had been operating at full capacity.

Consistent with JIT practices, Toyota maintained only a 4-hour supply of the valve. And there were few of the valves in the closely knit network that constituted Toyota's supply chain. Depending on a single source and holding little inventory is a risk, but it also keeps Toyota lean and its costs low. The Toyota plants in Japan build 14,000 cars a day. Without that valve, production would come to a rapid halt. Moreover, Toyota production managers were dismayed to find they needed 200 variations of the P-valve.

Consistent with the *keiretsu* networks that are typical of Japan's manufacturing sector, Toyota holds 23% of Aisin's stock and Aisin's president is Kanshiro Toyoda of the Toyoda family that founded the automaker. Kosuke Ikebuchi, a Toyota senior managing director, was tracked down at 8 A.M. at a golf course clubhouse and given the bad news.

Discussion Questions

1. If you are Mr. Ikebuchi, what do you do?
2. What does this experience tell you (and Aisin and Toyota) about just-in-time?
3. If you are in charge of DaimlerChrysler's JIT supplies the morning of September 11, 2001, what action do you take?

Sources: Case is based on material in: the *Wall Street Journal* (September 13, 2001): B3, (May 8, 1997): A1, A5, and (September 24, 2001); B1, B4; and *Harvard Business Review* (September–October 1999): 97–106.

Maintenance and Reliability

Chapter Outline

High facility utilization, tight scheduling, low inventory, and consistent quality demand reliable systems. Variability in a system means inefficient use of plant, equipment, and human resources. Managers reduce variability and achieve effective and efficient operations by improving reliability and maintenance. Successful operations managers adopt a practice known as total productive maintenance (TPM). The objective of TPM is to maintain the capability of the system while controlling costs.

BEFORE COMING TO CLASS, READ CHAPTER 17 IN YOUR TEXT AND ANSWER THESE QUESTIONS.

1. What are two tactics for improving reliability? _____

_____

_____

2. What are two tactics for improving maintenance? _____

_____

_____

3. Define *mean time between failures* (MTBF). _____

_____

_____

4. How do we provide redundancy in a system? _____

_____

_____

5. What is meant by *total productive maintenance* (TPM)? _____

_____

_____

6. What is preventive maintenance? _____

_____

_____

THE STRATEGIC IMPORTANCE OF MAINTENANCE AND RELIABILITY

Maintenance

Tactic of Implementing Preventive Maintenance

Tactic of Increasing Repair Capability/Speed

Reliability

Tactic of Improving Individual Components

Tactic of Providing Redundancy

RELIABILITY

$$R_s = R_1 \times R_2 \times R_3 \times \ldots \times R_n \qquad\qquad (17\text{-}1)$$

where R_1 = reliability of component 1

R_2 = reliability of component 2

FIGURE 17.2 ■ Overall System Reliability as a Function of Number of Components and Component Reliability with Components in a Series

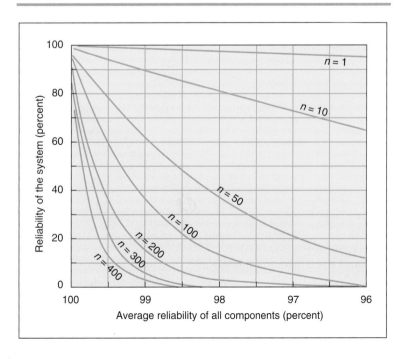

$$FR(\%) = \frac{\text{Number of failures}}{\text{Number of units tested}} \times 100\% \qquad (17\text{-}2)$$

$$FR(N) = \frac{\text{Number of failures}}{\text{Number of unit-hours of operating time}} \qquad (17\text{-}3)$$

$$MTBF = \frac{1}{FR(N)} \qquad (17\text{-}4)$$

PRACTICE PROBLEM 17.1 ■ Reliability

California Instruments, Inc., produces 3,000 computer chips per day. Three hundred are tested for a period of 500 operating hours each. During the test, six failed: two after 50 hours, two at 100 hours, one at 300 hours, and one at 400 hours.

Find FR(%) and FR(N).

PRACTICE PROBLEM 17.2 ■ Reliablity

If 300 of the chips from Practice Problem 17.1 are used in building a mainframe computer, how many failures of the computer can be expected per month?

Additional Practice Problem Space

Redundancy

PRACTICE PROBLEM 17.3 ■ Reliablity

Find the reliability of this system:

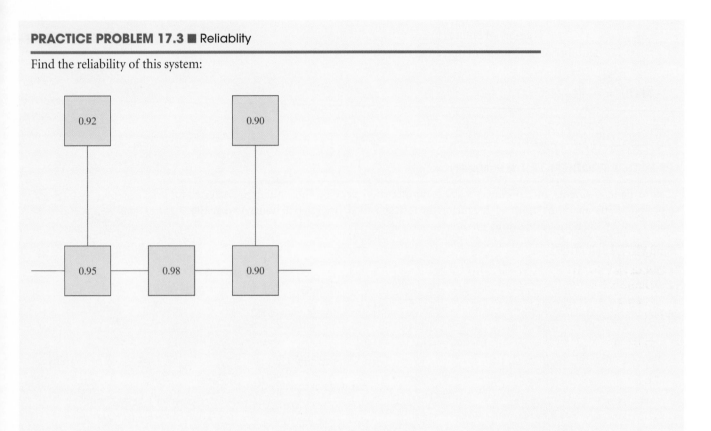

MAINTENANCE

Preventive Maintenance

Breakdown Maintenance

FIGURE 17.4 ■ Maintenance Costs

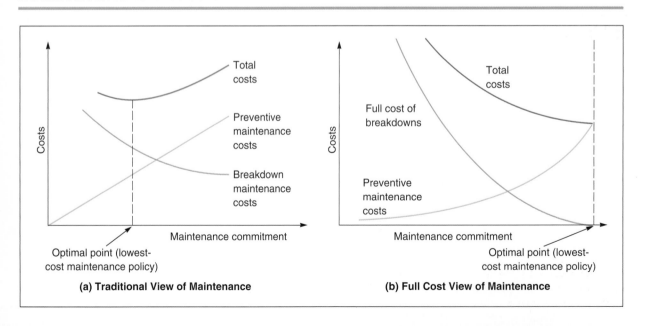

(a) Traditional View of Maintenance   (b) Full Cost View of Maintenance

PRACTICE PROBLEM 17.4 ■ Expected Breakdown Cost

Given the following probabilities, calculate the expected breakdown cost.

NUMBER OF BREAKDOWNS	DAILY FREQUENCY
0	3
1	2
2	2
3	3

Assume a cost of $10 per breakdown.

Additional Practice Problem Space

TOTAL PRODUCTIVE MAINTENANCE

TECHNIQUES FOR ESTABLISHING MAINTENANCE POLICIES

DISCUSSION QUESTIONS

1. What is the objective of maintenance and reliability?
2. How does one identify a candidate for preventive maintenance?
3. Explain the notion of "infant mortality" in the context of product reliability.
4. Why is simulation often an appropriate technique for maintenance problems?
5. What is the trade-off between operator-performed maintenance versus supplier-performed maintenance?
6. How can a manager evaluate the effectiveness of the maintenance function?

7. How does machine design contribute to either increasing or alleviating the maintenance problem?
8. What roles can information technology play in the maintenance function?
9. During an argument as to the merits of preventive maintenance at Windsor Printers, the company owner asked, "Why fix it before it breaks?" How would you, as the director of maintenance, respond?
10. Will preventive maintenance eliminate *all* breakdowns?

CRITICAL THINKING EXERCISE

When a McDonnell Douglas DC-10 crashed over Iowa, a subsequent investigation suggested that the plane's hydraulic systems may not provide enough protection. The DC-10 has three separate hydraulic systems, all of which failed when an engine exploded. The engine threw off shreds of metal that severed two of the lines, and the third line required power from the demolished engine that was no longer available. The DC-10, unlike other commercial jets, has no shutoff valves that might have stemmed the flow of hydraulic fluid. Lockheed's similar L-1011 trijet has four hydraulic systems. A McDonnell Douglas VP said at the time, "You can always be extreme and not have a practical airplane. You can be perfectly safe and never get off the ground." Discuss the pros and cons of McDonnell's position. How might you design a reliability experiment? What has since happened to the McDonnell Douglas Corporation?

ACTIVE MODEL EXERCISE

In this Active Model, you may evaluate various elements of a reliability system with redundancy.

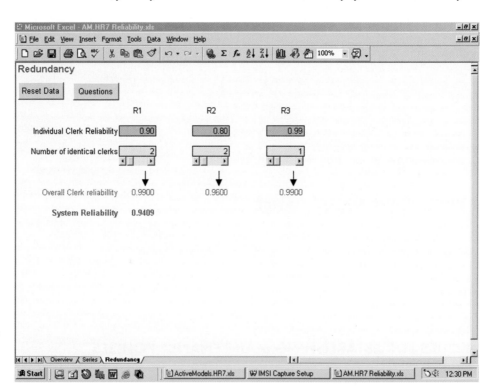

ACTIVE MODEL 17.2 ■

Redundancy at National Bank, using Example 3 Data in Your Text

Questions

1. If one additional clerk were available, which would be the best place to add this clerk?
2. What is the minimum number of total clerks that need to be added in order to achieve a system reliability of 99%?

PROBLEMS*

· **17.1** The Beta II computer's electronic processing unit contains 50 components in series. The average reliability of each component is 99.0%. Using Figure 17.2, determine the overall reliability of the processing unit.

· **17.2** A testing process at Boeing Aircraft has 400 components in series. The average reliability of each component is 99.5%. Use Figure 17.2 to find the overall reliability of the whole testing process?

· **17.3** What are the *expected* number of yearly breakdowns for the power generator at Orlando Utilities that has exhibited the following data over the past 20 years?

Number of breakdowns		0	1	2	3	4	5	6
Number of years in which breakdown occurred		2	2	5	4	5	2	0

· **17.4** Each breakdown of a graphic plotter table at Airbus Industries costs $50. Find the expected daily breakdown cost given the following data:

Number of breakdowns	0	1	2	3	4
Daily breakdown probability	.1	.2	.4	.2	.1

P : **17.5** A new aircraft control system is being designed which must be 98% reliable. This system consists of three components in series. If all three of the components are to have the same level of reliability, what level of reliability is required?

: **17.6** Robert Klassan Manufacturing, a medical equipment manufacturer, has subjected 100 heart pacemakers to 5,000 hours of testing. Halfway through the testing, 5 pacemakers failed. What was the failure rate in terms of the following:
a) Percent of failures?
b) Number of failures per unit-hour?
c) Number of failures per unit-year?
d) If 1,100 people receive pacemaker implants, how many units can we expect to fail during the following 1 year?

P : **17.7** What is the reliability of the following production process? $R_1 = 0.95$, $R_2 = 0.90$, $R_3 = 0.98$.

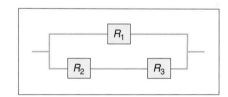

P : **17.8** You have a system composed of four components in series. The reliability of each component is .95. What is the reliability of the system?

P : **17.9** What is the reliability of bank loans being processed accurately if each of the 5 clerks shown below has the reliability shown?

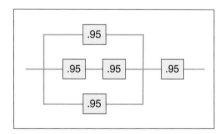

P : **17.10** Merrill Kim Sharp has a system composed of three components in parallel. The components have the following reliabilities:

$$R_1 = 0.90, \qquad R_2 = 0.95, \qquad R_3 = 0.85$$

What is the reliability of the system? (*Hint:* See Example 3.)

*Note: **P** means the problem may be solved with POM for Windows.

P · 17.11   A medical control system has three components in series with individual reliabilities (R_1, R_2, R_3) as shown:

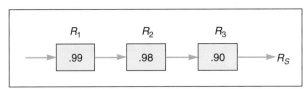

What is the reliability of the system?

P : 17.12 a)   What is the reliability of the system shown below?

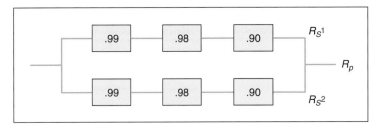

b)   How much has reliability improved if the medical control system shown in Problem 17.11 changed to the redundant parallel system shown here?

P : 17.13   Assume that for cardiac bypass surgery, 85% of patients survive the surgery, 95% survive the recovery period after surgery, 80% are able to make the lifestyle changes needed to extend their survival to 1 year or more, and only 10% of those who do not make the lifestyle changes survive more than a year. What is the likelihood that a given patient will survive more than a year?

P : 17.14   Your design team has proposed the following system with component reliabilities as indicated: What is the reliability of the system?

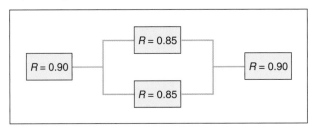

: 17.15   The maintenance department at Mechanical Dynamics has presented you with the following failure curve. What does it suggest?

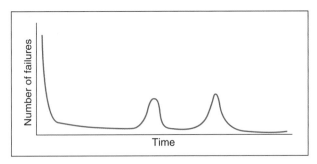

P : 17.16   Rick Wing, salesperson for Wave Soldering Systems, Inc. (WSSI), has provided you with a proposal for improving the temperature control on your present machine. The machine uses a hot-air knife to cleanly remove excess solder from printed circuit boards; this is a great concept, but the hot-air temperature control lacks reliability. According to Wing, engineers at WSSI have improved the reliability of the critical temperature controls. The new system still has the four sensitive integrated circuits controlling the temperature, but the new machine has a backup for each. The four integrated circuits have reliabilities of .90, .92, .94, and .96. The four backup circuits all have a reliability of .90.

a)   What is the reliability of the new temperature controller?

b)   If you pay a premium, Wing says he can improve all four of the backup units to .93. What is the reliability of this option?

17.17 What is the expected number of breakdowns per year for a machine on which we have the following data?

Number of breakdowns	0	1	2	3	4	5
Number of years in which breakdowns occurred	4	3	1	5	5	0

P : 17.18 As VP for operations at Krause Engineering, you must decide which product design below, A or B, has the higher reliability? B is designed with "back-up" units for components R_3 and R_4. What is the reliability of each design?

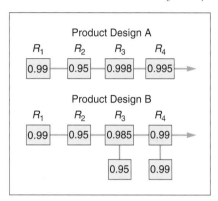

17.19 A typical retail transaction consists of several smaller parts, which can be considered components subject to failure. A list of such components might include:

COMPONENT	DESCRIPTION	DEFINITION OF FAILURE
1	Find product in proper size, color, etc.	Can't find product
2	Enter cashier line	No lines open; lines too long; line experiencing difficulty
3	Scan product UPC for name, price, etc.	Won't scan; item not on file; scans incorrect name or price
4	Calculate purchase total	Wrong weight; wrong extension; wrong data entry; wrong tax
5	Make payment	Customer lacks cash; check not acceptable; credit card refused
6	Make change	Makes change incorrectly
7	Bag merchandise	Damages merchandise while bagging; bag splits
8	Conclude transaction and exit	No receipt; unfriendly, rude, or aloof clerk

Let the eight probabilities of success be .92, .94, .99, .99, .98, .97, .95, and .96. What is the reliability of the system, that is, the probability that there will be a satisfied customer? If you were the store manager, what do you think should be an acceptable value for this probability? Which components would be good candidates for backup, which for redesign?

 # INTERNET HOMEWORK PROBLEMS

See our Internet homepage at **www.prenhall.com/heizer** for these additional homework problems: 7-20 through 7-24.

CASE STUDY

Worldwide Chemical Company

Jack Smith wiped the perspiration from his face. It was another scorching-hot summer day, and one of the four process refrigeration units was down. The units were critical to the operation of Worldwide Chemical Company's Fibers Plant, which produces synthetic fibers and polymer flake for a global market.

Before long, Al Henson, the day-shift production superintendent, was on the intercom, shouting his familiar proclamation that *(continued)* "heads would roll" if the unit was not back on-line within the hour. However, Jack Smith, the maintenance superintendent, had heard it all before—nothing ever happened as a result of Henson's temper tantrums. "Serves him right," he thought. "Henson is uncooperative when we want to perform scheduled maintenance, so it doesn't get done and equipment goes down."

At that moment, however, Henson was genuinely furious over the impact that the breakdown would have on his process yield figures. Meeting with plant manager Beth Conner, he was charging that all the maintenance department did was "sit around" and play cards like firemen waiting for an alarm to send them to a three-alarm blaze across town. The "fix-it" approach to maintenance was costing the plant throughput that was vital to meeting standard costs and avoiding serious variances. Foreign competitors were delivering high-quality fibers in less time and at lower prices. Conner had already been called on the carpet at corporate headquarters over output levels that were significantly below the budgeted numbers. The business cycle contained predictable seasonal variations. That meant building inventories that would be carried for months, tying up scarce capital, a characteristic of most continuous processes. Monthly shipments would look bad. Year-to-date shipments would look even worse because of machine breakdowns and lost output to date. Conner knew that something had to be done to develop machine reliability. Capacity on demand was needed to respond to growing foreign competition. Unreliable production equipment was jeopardizing the company's TQM effort by causing process variations that affected both first-quality product yields and on-time deliveries, but no one seemed to have the answer to the problem of machine breakdowns.

The maintenance department operated much like a fire department, rushing to a breakdown with a swarm of mechanics, some who disassembled the machine while others pored over wiring schematics and still others hunted for spare parts in the maintenance warehouse. Eventually, they would have the machine back up, though sometimes only after working through the night to get the production line going again. Maintenance had always been done this way. However, with new competitors, machine reliability had suddenly become a major barrier to competing successfully.

Rumors of a plant closing were beginning to circulate and morale was suffering, making good performance that much more difficult. Beth Conner knew she needed solutions if the plant had any chance of survival.

Discussion Questions

1. Can Smith and Hensen do anything to improve performance?
2. Is there an alternative to the current operations approach of the maintenance department?
3. How could production make up for lost output resulting from scheduled maintenance?
4. How could maintenance mechanics be better utilized?
5. Is there any way to know when a machine breakdown is probable?

Source: Patrick Owings, under the supervision of Professor Marilyn M. Helms, University of Tennessee at Chattanooga.

Quantitative Module A

Decision-Making Tools

Module Outline

Every day operations managers make hundreds of decisions that alter the lives of customers, employees, and owners. These managers need to make those decisions in a logical, coherent way and with the right tools. Those tools include decision tables and decision trees, which we will discuss in this module. To understand these two tools we will also examine (1) states of nature and probabilities that provide the environment of decisions and (2) decision alternatives and decision criteria.

BEFORE COMING TO CLASS, READ MODULE A IN YOUR TEXT AND ANSWER THESE QUESTIONS.

1. What are *states of nature*? _____
_____
_____

2. What is decision making under risk? _____
_____
_____

3. What is *expected monetary value* (EMV)? _____
_____
_____

4. What is expected value of perfect information (EVPI)? _____
_____
_____

5. What do we mean by expected value under certainty? _____
_____
_____

6. What is a maximax decision criterion? _____
_____
_____

THE DECISION PROCESS IN OPERATIONS

Six Steps

1. Define the Problem

2. Develop Objectives

3. Develop a Model

4. Evaluate Alternative Solutions

5. Select the Best Alternative

6. Implement the Decision

FUNDAMENTALS OF DECISION MAKING

Alternatives

States of Nature

DECISION TABLES

Additional Practice Problem Space

Decision Making under Uncertainty

1. Maximax

2. Maximin

3. Equally Likely

Decision Making under Risk

Expected Monetary Value (EMV)

EMV (Alternative i) = (Payoff of 1st state of nature)
$\qquad$ × (Probability of 1st state of nature)

$\qquad$ + (Payoff of 2nd state of nature)
$\qquad$ × (Probability of 2nd state of nature)

$\qquad$ + ··· + (Payoff of last state of nature)
$\qquad$ × (Probability of last state of nature)

Decision Making under Certainty

Expected Value of Perfect Information (EVPI)

Expected value under certainty = (Best outcome or consequence for 1st state of nature)
$\qquad$ × (Probability of 1st state of nature)

$\qquad$ + (Best outcome for 2nd state of nature)
$\qquad$ × (Probability of 2nd state of nature)

$\qquad$ + ··· + (Best outcome for last state of nature)
$\qquad$ × (Probability of last state of nature)

Additional Practice Problem Space

DECISION TREES

Five Steps

1. Define the Problem

2. Draw the Tree

3. Assign Probabilities

4. Estimate Payoffs

5. Compute EMVs by Working Right to Left

PRACTICE PROBLEM A.1 ■ Decision Tree

Bascomb's Candy is considering the introduction of a new line of products. In order to produce the new line, the bakery is considering either a major or minor renovation of the current plant. The market for the new line of products could be either favorable or unfavorable. Bascomb's Candy has the option of not developing the new product line. Develop the appropriate decision tree.

PRACTICE PROBLEM A.2 ■ EMVs

With major renovation at Bascomb's Candy (see Practice Problem A.1), the payoff from a favorable market is $100,000 and from an unfavorable market it is −$90,000. With minor renovation, the payoff from a favorable market is $40,000 and from an unfavorable market it is −$20,000. Assuming that a favorable market and an unfavorable market are equally likely, solve the decision tree.

PRACTICE PROBLEM A.3 ■ EVPI

Jeff Heyl, the owner of Bascomb's Candy (Practice Problems A.1 and A.2), realizes that he should get more information before making his final decision. He decides to contract with a market research firm to conduct a market survey. How much should Jeff be willing to pay for accurate information (i.e., what the expected value of perfect information [EVPI] is)?

Additional Practice Problem Space

DISCUSSION QUESTIONS

1. Identify the six steps in the decision process.
2. Give an example of a good decision you made that resulted in a bad outcome. Also give an example of a bad decision you made that had a good outcome. Why was each decision good or bad?
3. What is the *equally likely* decision model?
4. Discuss the differences between decision making under certainty, under risk, and under uncertainty.
5. What is a decision tree?
6. Explain how decision trees might be used in several of the 10 OM decisions.
7. What is the expected value of perfect information?
8. What is the expected value under certainty?
9. Identify the five steps in analyzing a problem using a decision tree.
10. Why are the maximax and maximin strategies considered to be optimistic and pessimistic, respectively?
11. The expected value criterion is considered to be the rational criterion on which to base a decision. Is this really true? Is it rational to consider risk?
12. When are decision trees most useful?

PROBLEMS*

A.1   Given the following conditional value table, determine the appropriate decision under uncertainty using:
a)   Maximax.
b)   Maximin.
c)   Equally likely.

	STATES OF NATURE		
ALTERNATIVES	VERY FAVORABLE MARKET	AVERAGE MARKET	UNFAVORABLE MARKET
Build new plant	$350,000	$240,000	−$300,000
Subcontract	$180,000	$ 90,000	−$ 20,000
Overtime	$110,000	$ 60,000	−$ 10,000
Do nothing	$ 0	$ 0	$ 0

A.2   Even though independent gasoline stations have been having a difficult time, Susan Helms has been thinking about starting her own independent gasoline station. Susan's problem is to decide how large her station should be. The annual returns will depend on both the size of her station and a number of marketing factors related to the oil industry and demand for gasoline. After a careful analysis, Susan developed the following table:

SIZE OF FIRST STATION	GOOD MARKET ($)	FAIR MARKET ($)	POOR MARKET ($)
Small	50,000	20,000	−10,000
Medium	80,000	30,000	−20,000
Large	100,000	30,000	−40,000
Very large	300,000	25,000	−160,000

For example, if Susan constructs a small station and the market is good, she will realize a profit of $50,000.
a)   Develop a decision table for this decision.
b)   What is the maximax decision?
c)   What is the maximin decision?
d)   What is the equally likely decision?

A.3   Clay Whybark, a soft-drink vendor at Hard Rock Cafe's annual Rockfest, created a table of conditional values for the various alternatives (stocking decision) and states of nature (size of crowd):

	STATES OF NATURE (DEMAND)		
ALTERNATIVES	BIG	AVERAGE	SMALL
Large Stock	$22,000	$12,000	−$2,000
Average Stock	$14,000	$10,000	$6,000
Small Stock	$ 9,000	$ 8,000	$4,000

Note: **P** means the problem may be solved with POM for Windows; ✖ means the problem may be solved with Excel OM; and **P✖** means the problem may be solved with POM for Windows and/or Excel OM.

If the probabilities associated with the states of nature are 0.3 for a big demand, 0.5 for an average demand, and 0.2 for a small demand, determine the alternative that provides Clay Whybark the greatest expected monetary value (EMV).

P𝕏 . A.4   For Problem A.3, compute the expected value of perfect information (EVPI).

P𝕏 . A.5   Bill Ruch, Inc., is considering building a sensitive new airport scanning device. Managers believe that there is a probability of 0.4 that the ATR Co. will come out with a competitive product. If Ruch adds an assembly line for the product and ATR Co. does not follow with a competitive product, Ruch's expected profit is $40,000; if Ruch adds an assembly line and ATR follows suit, Ruch still expects $10,000 profit. If Ruch adds a new plant addition and ATR does not produce a competitive product, Ruch expects a profit of $600,000; if ATR does compete for this market, Ruch expects a loss of $100,000.
    Determine the EMV of each decision.

P𝕏 . A.6   For Problem A.5, compute the expected value of perfect information.

P𝕏 . A.7   The following payoff table provides profits based on various possible decision alternatives and various levels of demand at Reed Wickman's software firm:

	DEMAND	
	LOW	HIGH
Alternative 1	$10,000	$30,000
Alternative 2	$ 5,000	$40,000
Alternative 3	−$ 2,000	$50,000

The probability of low demand is 0.4, whereas the probability of high demand is 0.6.
a) What is the highest possible expected monetary value?
b) What is the expected value under certainty?
c) Calculate the expected value of perfect information for this situation.

P𝕏 . A.8   Leah Johnson, director of Legal Services of Brookline, wants to increase capacity to provide free legal advice but must decide whether to do so by hiring another full-time lawyer or by using part-time lawyers. The table below shows the expected *costs* of the two options for three possible demand levels:

ALTERNATIVES	STATES OF NATURE		
	LOW DEMAND	MEDIUM DEMAND	HIGH DEMAND
Hire full-time	$300	$500	$ 700
Hire part-time	$ 0	$350	$1,000
Probabilities	.2	.5	.3

Using expected value, what should Ms. Johnson do?

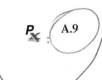

P𝕏 : A.9   Chung Manufacturing is considering the introduction of a family of new products. Long-term demand for the product group is somewhat predictable, so the manufacturer must be concerned with the risk of choosing a process that is inappropriate. Chen Chung is VP of operations. He can choose among batch manufacturing, custom manufacturing, or he can invest in group technology. Chen won't be able to forecast demand accurately until after he makes the process choice. Demand will be classified into four compartments: poor, fair, good, and excellent. The table below indicates the payoffs (profits) associated with each process/demand combination, as well as the probabilities of each long-term demand level.

	POOR	FAIR	GOOD	EXCELLENT
Probability	.1	.4	.3	.2
Batch	−$ 200,000	$1,000,000	$1,200,000	$1,300,000
Custom	$ 100,000	$ 300,000	$ 700,000	$ 800,000
Group technology	−$1,000,000	−$ 500,000	$ 500,000	$2,000,000 ᵢ mil

a) Based on expected value, what choice offers the greatest gain?
b) What would Chen Chung be willing to pay for a forecast that would accurately determine the level of demand in the future?

P𝕏 . A.10   Jacqueline Johnson's company is considering expansion of its current facility to meet increasing demand. If demand is high in the future, a major expansion would result in an additional profit of $800,000, but if demand is low there would be a loss of $500,000. If demand is high, a minor expansion will result in an increase in profits of

$200,000, but if demand is low, there is a loss of $100,000. The company has the option of not expanding. If there is a 50% chance demand will be high, what should the company do to maximize long-run average profits?

A.11 The University of Dallas bookstore stocks textbooks in preparation for sales each semester. It normally relies on departmental forecasts and preregistration records to determine how many copies of a text are needed. Preregistration shows 90 operations management students enrolled, but bookstore manager Curtis Ketterman has second thoughts, based on his intuition and some historical evidence. Curtis believes that the distribution of sales may range from 70 to 90 units, according to the following probability model:

Demand	70	75	80	85	90
Probability	.15	.30	.30	.20	.05

This textbook costs the bookstore $82 and sells for $112. Any unsold copies can be returned to the publisher, less a restocking fee and shipping, for a net refund of $36.
a) Construct the table of conditional profits.
b) How many copies should the bookstore stock in order to achieve highest expected value?

A.12 Joseph Cheese Company is a small manufacturer of several different cheese products. One product is a cheese spread sold to retail outlets. Susan Joseph must decide how many cases of cheese spread to manufacture each month. The probability that demand will be 6 cases is .1, for 7 cases it is .3, for 8 cases it is .5, and for 9 cases it is .1. The cost of every case is $45, and the price Susan gets for each case is $95. Unfortunately, any cases not sold by the end of the month are of no value as a result of spoilage. How many cases should Susan manufacture each month?

P : A.13 Ronald Lau, chief engineer at South Dakota Electronics, has to decide whether to build a new state-of-the-art processing facility. If the new facility works, the company could realize a profit of $200,000. If it fails, South Dakota Electronics could lose $180,000. At this time, Lau estimates a 60% chance that the new process will fail.
　The other option is to build a pilot plant and then decide whether to build a complete facility. The pilot plant would cost $10,000 to build. Lau estimates a fifty-fifty chance that the pilot plant will work. If the pilot plant works, there is a 90% probability that the complete plant, if it is built, will also work. If the pilot plant does not work, there is only a 20% chance that the complete project (if it is constructed) will work. Lau faces a dilemma. Should he build the plant? Should he build the pilot project and then make a decision? Help Lau by analyzing this problem.

A.14 Karen Villagomez, president of Wright Industries, is considering whether to build a manufacturing plant in the Ozarks. Her decision is summarized in the following table:

ALTERNATIVES	FAVORABLE MARKET	UNFAVORABLE MARKET
Build large plant	$400,000	−$300,000
Build small plant	$ 80,000	−$ 10,000
Don't build	$ 0	$ 0
Market probabilities	0.4	0.6

a) Construct a decision tree.
b) Determine the best strategy using expected monetary value (EMV).
c) What is the expected value of perfect information (EVPI)?

P · A.15 Deborah Kellogg buys breathalyzer test sets for the Denver Police Department. The quality of the test sets from her two suppliers is indicated in the following table:

PERCENT DEFECTIVE	PROBABILITY FOR LOOMBA TECHNOLOGY	PROBABILITY FOR STEWART-DOUGLAS ENTERPRISES
1	.70	.30
3	.20	.30
5	.10	.40

For example, the probability of getting a batch of tests that are 1% defective from Loomba Technology is .70. Because Kellogg orders 10,000 tests per order, this would mean that there is a .7 probability of getting 100 defective tests out of the 10,000 tests if Loomba Technology is used to fill the order. A defective breathalyzer test set can be repaired for $.50. Although the quality of the second supplier, Stewart-Douglas Enterprises, is lower, it will sell an order of 10,000 test sets for $37 less than Loomba.
a) Develop a decision tree.
b) Which supplier should Kellogg use?

P : **A.16** Deborah Hollwager, a concessionaire for the Des Moines ballpark, has developed a table of conditional values for the various alternatives (stocking decision) and states of nature (size of crowd).

	STATES OF NATURE (SIZE OF CROWD)		
ALTERNATIVES	**LARGE**	**AVERAGE**	**SMALL**
Large inventory	$20,000	$10,000	−$2,000
Average inventory	$15,000	$12,000	$6,000
Small inventory	$ 9,000	$ 6,000	$5,000

If the probabilities associated with the states of nature are 0.3 for a large crowd, 0.5 for an average crowd, and 0.2 for a small crowd, determine:
a) The alternative that provides the greatest expected monetary value (EMV).
b) The expected value of perfect information (EVPI).

P . **A.17** Joseph Biggs owns his own Sno-Cone business and lives 30 miles from a California beach resort. The sale of Sno-Cones is highly dependent on his location and on the weather. At the resort, his profit will be $120 per day in fair weather, $10 per day in bad weather. At home, his profit will be $70 in fair weather and $55 in bad weather. Assume that on any particular day, the weather service suggest a 40% chance of foul weather.
a) Construct Joseph's decision tree.
b) What decision is recommended by the expected value criterion?

P **A.18** Kenneth Boyer is considering opening a bicycle shop in North Chicago. Boyer enjoys biking, but this is to be a business endeavor from which he expects to make a living. He can open a small shop, a large shop, or no shop at all. Because there will be a 5-year lease on the building that Boyer is thinking about using, he wants to make sure he makes the correct decision. Boyer is also thinking about hiring his old marketing professor to conduct a marketing research study to see if there is a market for his services. The results of such a study could be either favorable or unfavorable. Develop a decision tree for Boyer.

: **A.19** Kenneth Boyer (of Problem A.18) has done some analysis of his bicycle shop decision. If he builds a large shop, he will earn $60,000 if the market is favorable; he will lose $40,000 if the market is unfavorable. A small shop will return a $30,000 profit with a favorable market and a $10,000 loss if the market is unfavorable. At the present time, he believes that there is a fifty-fifty chance of a favorable market. His former marketing professor, Y. L. Yang, will charge him $5,000 for the market research. He has estimated that there is a .6 probability that the market survey will be favorable. Furthermore, there is a .9 probability that the market will be favorable given a favorable outcome of the study. However, Yang has warned Boyer that there is a probability of only .12 of a favorable market if the marketing research results are not favorable. Expand the decision tree of Problem A.18 to help Boyer decide what to do.

· **A.20** Dick Holliday is not sure what he should do. He can build either a large video rental section or a small one in his drugstore. He can also gather additional information or simply do nothing. If he gathers additional information, the results could suggest either a favorable or an unfavorable market, but it would cost him $3,000 to gather the information. Holliday believes that there is a fifty-fifty chance that the information will be favorable. If the rental market is favorable, Holliday will earn $15,000 with a large section or $5,000 with a small. With an unfavorable video-rental market, however, Holliday could lose $20,000 with a large section or $10,000 with a small section. Without gathering additional information, Holliday estimates that the probability of a favorable rental market is .7. A favorable report from the study would increase the probability of a favorable rental market to .9. Furthermore, an unfavorable report from the additional information would decrease the probability of a favorable rental market to .4. Of course, Holliday could forget all of these numbers and do nothing. What is your advice to Holliday?

P . **A.21** Problem A.8 dealt with a decision facing Legal Services of Brookline. Using the data in that problem, provide:
a) The appropriate decision tree showing payoffs and probabilities.
b) The best alternative using expected monetary value (EMV).

P : **A.22** Using the data in Problem A.2, develop a decision tree and determine the best decision based on the highest expected monetary value. Assume that each outcome is equally likely.

P : **A.23** Louisiana is busy designing new lottery "scratch-off" games. In the latest game, Bayou Boondoggle, the player is instructed to scratch off one spot: A, B, or C. A can reveal "Loser, " "Win $1," or "Win $50." B can reveal "Loser" or "Take a Second Chance." C can reveal "Loser" or "Win $500." On the second chance, the player is instructed to scratch off D or E. D can reveal "Loser" or "Win $1." E can reveal "Loser" or "Win $10." The probabilities at A are .9, .09, and .01. The probabilities at B are .8 and .2. The probabilities at C are .999 and .001. The probabilities at D are .5 and .5. Finally, the probabilities at E are .95 and .05. Draw the decision tree that represents this scenario. Use proper symbols and label all branches clearly. Calculate the expected value of this game.

INTERNET HOMEWORK PROBLEMS

See our Internet homepage at www.prenhall.com/heizer for these additional homework problems: A.24 through A.31.

CASE STUDY

Tom Tucker's Liver Transplant

Tom Tucker, a robust 50-year-old executive living in the northern suburbs of St. Paul, has been diagnosed by a University of Minnesota internist as having a decaying liver. Although he is otherwise healthy, Tucker's liver problem could prove fatal if left untreated.

Firm research data are not yet available to predict the likelihood of survival for a man of Tucker's age and condition without surgery. However, based on her own experience and recent medical journal articles, the internist tells him that if he elects to avoid surgical treatment of the liver problem, chances of survival would be approximately as follows: only a 60% chance of living 1 year, a 20% chance of surviving for 2 years, a 10% chance for 5 years, and a 10% chance

of living to age 58. She places his probability of survival beyond age 58 without a liver transplant to be extremely low.

The transplant operation, however, is a serious surgical procedure. Five percent of patients die during the operation or its recovery stage, with an additional 45% dying during the first year. Twenty percent survive for 5 years, 13% survive for 10 years, and 8%, 5%, and 4% survive, respectively, for 15, 20, and 25 years.

Discussion Questions

1. Do you think that Tucker should select the transplant operation?
2. What other factors might be considered?

CASE STUDY

Ski Right Corp.

After retiring as a physician, Bob Guthrie became an avid downhill skier on the steep slopes of the Utah Rocky Mountains. As an amateur inventor, Bob was always looking for something new. With the recent deaths of several celebrity skiers, Bob knew he could use his creative mind to make skiing safer and his bank account larger. He knew that many deaths on the slopes were caused by head injuries. Although ski helmets have been on the market for some time, most skiers considered them boring and basically ugly. As a physician, Bob knew that some type of new ski helmet was the answer.

Bob's biggest challenge was to invent a helmet that was attractive, safe, and fun to wear. Multiple colors and using the latest fashion designs would be musts. After years of skiing, Bob knew that many skiers believed that how you looked on the slopes was more important than how you skied. His helmets would have to look good and fit in with current fashion trends. But attractive helmets were not enough. Bob had to make the helmets fun and useful. The name of the new ski helmet, Ski Right, was sure to be a winner. If Bob could come up with a good idea, he believed that there was a 20% chance that the market for the Ski Right helmet would be excellent. The chance of a good market should be 40%. Bob also knew that the market for his helmet could be only average (30% chance) or even poor (10% chance).

The idea of how to make ski helmets fun and useful came to Bob on a gondola ride to the top of a mountain. A busy executive on the gondola ride was on his cell phone trying to complete a complicated merger. When the executive got off the gondola, he dropped the phone and it was crushed by the gondola mechanism. Bob decided that his new ski helmet would have a built-in cell phone and an AM/FM stereo radio. All of the electronics could be operated by a control pad worn on a skier's arm or leg.

Bob decided to try a small pilot project for Ski Right. He enjoyed being retired and didn't want a failure to cause him to go back to work. After some research, Bob found Progressive Products (PP). The company was willing to be a partner in developing the Ski Right and sharing any profits. If the market were excellent, Bob would net $5,000 per month. With a good market, Bob would net $2,000. An average market would result in a loss of $2,000, and a poor market would mean Bob would be out $5,000 per month.

Another option for Bob was to have Leadville Barts (LB) make the helmet. The company had extensive experience in making bicycle helmets. Progressive would then take the helmets made by Leadville Barts and do the rest. Bob had a greater risk. He estimated that he could lose $10,000 per month in a poor market or $4,000 in an average market. A good market for Ski Right would result in $6,000 profit for Bob, while an excellent market would mean a $12,000 profit per month.

A third option for Bob was to use TalRad (TR), a radio company in Tallahassee, Florida. TalRad had extensive experience in making military radios. Leadville Barts could make the helmets, and Progressive Products could do the rest of production and distribution. Again, Bob would be taking on greater risk. A poor market would mean a $15,000 loss per month, while an average market would mean a $10,000 loss. A good market would result in a net profit of $7,000 for Bob. An excellent market would return $13,000 per month.

Bob could also have Celestial Cellular (CC) develop the cell phones. Thus, another option was to have Celestial make the phones and have Progressive do the rest of the production and distribution. Because the cell phone was the most expensive component of the helmet, Bob could lose $30,000 per month in a poor market. He could lose $20,000 in an average market. If the market were good or excellent, Bob would see a net profit of $10,000 or $30,000 per month, respectively.

Bob's final option was to forget about Progressive Products entirely. He could use Leadville Barts to make the helmets, Celestial Cellular to make the phones, and TalRad to make the AM/FM stereo radios. Bob could then hire some friends to assemble everything and market the finished Ski Right helmets. With this final alternative, Bob could realize a net profit of $55,000 a month in an excellent market. Even if the market were just good, Bob would net $20,000. An average market, however, would mean a loss of $35,000. If the market were poor Bob would lose $60,000 per month.

Discussion Questions

1. What do you recommend?
2. Compute the expected value of perfect information.
3. Was Bob completely logical in how he approached this decision problem?

Source: B. Render, R. M. Stair, and M. Hanna, *Quantitative Analysis for Management*, 8th ed. Upper Saddle River, N.J.: Prentice Hall (2003). Reprinted by permission of Prentice Hall, Inc.

Linear Programming

Module Outline

Linear programming (LP) is a widely used mathematical tool that can help operations managers plan and make the decisions necessary to allocate resources. The technique requires the development of a mathematical objective function that defines the quantity to be maximized or minimized and the development of constraint equations that limit the degree to which resources are available.

LP problems with two variables can be solved graphically, while larger problems are solved with a technique known as the simplex method. Both types of problems can be solved by hand or by computer. Large LP problems are typically solved by computer.

BEFORE COMING TO CLASS, READ MODULE B IN YOUR TEXT AND ANSWER THESE QUESTIONS.

1. What is an *objective function?* _____

_____

_____

2. What are *constraints?* _____

_____

_____

3. What is meant by a *feasible region?* _____

_____

_____

4. What is the *corner point method?* _____

_____

_____

5. What is an *iso profit line?* _____

_____

_____

6. What are the limitations of the graphical method of linear programming? _____

_____

_____

REQUIREMENTS OF A LINEAR PROGRAMMING PROBLEM

1. Objective

2. Constraints

3. Alternatives

4. Linear

FORMULATING LINEAR PROGRAMMING PROBLEMS

GRAPHICAL SOLUTION TO A LINEAR PROGRAMMING PROBLEM

Decision Variables

Objective Function

Constraints

Feasible Region

Iso-Profit Line Method

Corner Point Method

PRACTICE PROBLEM B.1 ■ Maximization Problem

Chad's Pottery Barn has enough clay to make 24 small vases or 6 large vases. He has only enough of a special glazing compound to glaze 16 of the small vases or 8 of the large vases. Let X_1 = the number of small vases and X_2 = the number of large vases. The smaller vases sell for \$3 each, and the larger vases would bring \$9 each.

a. Formulate the problem.
b. Solve the problem graphically.

Additional Practice Problem Space

SENSITIVITY ANALYSIS

Changes in the Right-Hand Side Values

Shadow Price

Changes in the Objective Function Coefficients

Sample Excel Sensitivity Analysis Output (Using Text Example)

PROGRAM B.1 ■ Sensitivity Analysis for Shader Electronics Using Excel's Solver

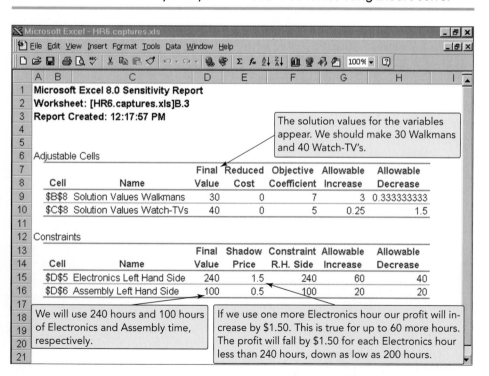

SOLVING MINIMIZATION PROBLEMS

PRACTICE PROBLEM B.2 ■ Minimization Problem

A fabric firm has received an order for cloth specified to contain at least 45 pounds of cotton and 25 pounds of silk. The cloth can be woven out of any suitable mix of two yarns, A and B. They contain the proportions of cotton and silk (by weight) as shown in the following table:

	COTTON	SILK
A	30%	50%
B	60%	10%

Material A costs $3 per pound, and B costs $2 per pound. What quantities (pounds) of A and B yarns should be used to minimize the cost of this order?

Additional Practice Problem Space

LINEAR PROGRAMMING APPLICATIONS

Production Mix

Diet Problem

Production Scheduling

Labor Scheduling

Additional Practice Problem Space

THE SIMPLEX METHOD OF LP

• See CD-ROM Tutorial 3 for extended discussion

DISCUSSION QUESTIONS

1. List at least four applications of linear programming problems.
2. What is a "corner point"? Explain why solutions to linear programming problems focus on corner points.
3. Define the feasible region of a graphical LP problem. What is a feasible solution?
4. Each linear programming problem that has a feasible region has an infinite number of solutions. Explain.
5. Under what circumstances is the objective function more important than the constraints in a linear programming model?
6. Under what circumstances are the constraints more important than the objective function in a linear programming model?
7. Why is the diet problem, in practice, applicable for animals but not for people?
8. How many feasible solutions are there in a linear program? Which ones do we need to examine to find the optimal solution?

9. Define shadow price (or dual).
10. Explain how to use the iso-cost line in a graphical minimization problem.
11. Compare how the corner-point and iso-profit line methods work for solving graphical problems.
12. Where a constraint crosses the vertical or horizontal axis, the quantity is fairly obvious. How does one go about finding the quantity coordinates where two constraints cross, not at an axis?
13. Suppose a linear programming (maximation) problem has been solved and that the optimal value of the objective function is $300. Suppose an additonal constraint is added to this problem. Explain how this might affect each of the following:
    (a) The feasible region.
    (b) The optimal value of the objective function.

ACTIVE MODEL EXERCISE

The Active Model describes the Shader Electronics Example maximization problem (see your text) with two less-than-or-equal-to constraints. You can use the scrollbars to change any of the 8 numbers in the example or to move the isoprofit line.

ACTIVE MODEL B.1 ■

Analysis of the Shader Electronics Example Data in Your Text

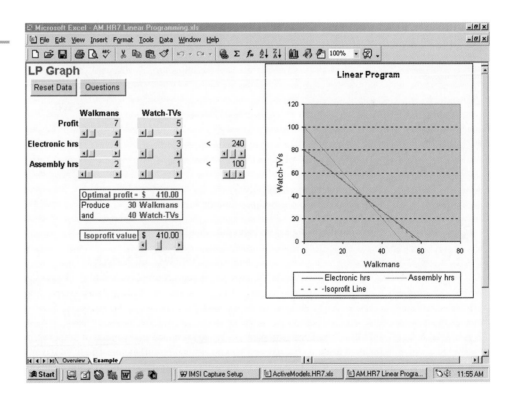

Questions

1. By how much does the profit on Walkmans need to rise to make it the only product manufactured?
2. By how much does the profit on Walkmans need to fall to stop manufacturing it?
3. What happens to the profit as the number of assembly hours increases by 1 hour at a time? For how many hours is this true?
4. What happens if we can reduce the electronics time for Watch-TVs to 2.5 hours?

PROBLEMS*

P. B.1   Solve the following linear programming problem graphically:

$$\text{Maximize} \quad Z = 4X + 6Y$$
$$\text{Subject to:} \quad X + 2Y \le 8$$
$$5X + 4Y \le 20$$
$$X, Y \le 0$$

P. B.2   Solve the following linear programming problem graphically.

$$\text{Maximize} \quad Z = X + 10Y$$
$$\text{Subject to:} \quad 4X + 3Y \le 36$$
$$2X + 4Y \le 40$$
$$Y \ge 3$$
$$X, Y \ge 0$$

P. B.3   Graphically analyze the following problem:

$$\text{Maximize profit} = \$4X_1 + \$6X_2$$
$$\text{Subject to:} \quad 1X_1 + 2X_2 \le 8$$
$$6X_1 + 4X_2 \le 24$$

a)   What is the optimal solution?
b)   If the first constraint is altered to $1X_1 + 3X_2 \le 8$, does the feasible region or optimal solution change?

P. B.4   Consider the following linear programming problem:

$$\text{Maximize} \quad Z = 30X_1 + 10X_2$$
$$\text{Subject to:} \quad 3X_1 + X_2 \le 300$$
$$X_1 + X_2 \le 200$$
$$X_1 \quad \le 100$$
$$X_2 \ge 50$$
$$X_1 - X_2 \le 0$$
$$X_1, X_2 \ge 0$$

a)   Solve the problem graphically.
b)   Is there more than one optimal solution? Explain.

P. B.5   Solve the following LP problem graphically:

$$\text{Minimize} \quad Z = 24X + 15Y$$
$$\text{Subject to:} \quad 7X + 11Y \ge 77$$
$$16X + 4Y \ge 80$$
$$X, Y \ge 0$$

P. B.6   Ed Silver Dog Food Company wishes to introduce a new brand of dog biscuits composed of chicken- and liver-flavored biscuits that meet certain nutritional requirements. The liver-flavored biscuits contain 1 unit of nutrient A and 2 units of nutrient B; the chicken-flavored biscuits contain 1 unit of nutrient A and 4 units of nutrient B. According to federal requirements, there must be at least 40 units of nutrient A and 60 units of nutrient B in a package of the new mix. In addition, the company has decided that there can be no more than 15 liver-flavored biscuits in a package. If it costs 1¢ to make 1 liver-flavored biscuit and 2¢ to make 1 chicken-flavored, what is the optimal product mix for a package of the biscuits in order to minimize the firm's cost?

a)   Formulate this as a linear programming problem.
b)   Solve this problem graphically, giving the optimal values of all variables.
c)   What is the total cost of a package of dog biscuits using the optimal mix?

*Note: **P** means the problem may be solved with POM for Windows; ✗ means the problem may be solved with Excel; and **P✗** means the problem may be solved with POM for Windows and/or Excel. Recall that Excel OM does not have an LP module because the *LP Solver* is built into Excel.

P . **B.7**   The Electrocomp Corporation manufactures two electrical products: air conditioners and large fans. The assembly process for each is similar in that both require a certain amount of wiring and drilling. Each air conditioner takes 3 hours of wiring and 2 hours of drilling. Each fan must go through 2 hours of wiring and 1 hour of drilling. During the next production period, 240 hours of wiring time are available and up to 140 hours of drilling time may be used. Each air conditioner sold yields a profit of $25. Each fan assembled may be sold for a $15 profit.

Formulate and solve this LP production-mix situation, and find the best combination of air conditioners and fans that yields the highest profit.

P . **B.8**   The Anne Riddick Tub Company manufactures two lines of bathtubs, called model A and model B. Every tub requires blending a certain amount of steel and zinc; the company has available a total of 25,000 lb of steel and 6,000 lb of zinc. Each model A bathtub requires a mixture of 125 lb of steel and 20 lb of zinc, and each yields a profit of $90. Each model B tub requires 100 lb of steel and 30 lb of zinc and can be sold for a profit of $70.

Find by graphical linear programming the best production mix of bathtubs.

P . **B.9**   The Grand Valley Company, run by the J. Motwani family, produces two products: bed mattresses and box springs. A prior contract requires that the firm produce at least 30 mattresses or box springs, in any combination, per week. In addition, union labor agreements demand that stitching machines be kept running at least 40 hours per week, which is one production period. Each box spring takes 2 hours of stitching time, while each mattress takes 1 hour on the machine. Each mattress produced costs $20; each box spring costs $24.

a)   Formulate this problem so as to minimize total production costs.
b)   Solve graphically.

P . **B.10**   MSA Computer Corporation manufactures two models of minicomputers, the Alpha 4 and the Beta 5. The firm employs 5 technicians, working 160 hours each per month, on its assembly line. Management insists that full employment (that is, *all* 160 hours of time) be maintained for each worker during next month's operations. It requires 20 labor-hours to assemble each Alpha 4 computer and 25 labor-hours to assemble each Beta 5 model. MSA wants to see at least 10 Alpha 4s and at least 15 Beta 5s produced during the production period. Alpha 4s generate a $1,200 profit per unit, and Betas yield $1,800 each.

Determine the most profitable number of each model of minicomputer to produce during the coming month.

P . **B.11**   The Sweet Smell Fertilizer Company markets bags of manure labeled "not less than 60 lb dry weight." The packaged manure is a combination of compost and sewage wastes. To provide good-quality fertilizer, each bag should contain at least 30 lb of compost but no more than 40 lb of sewage. Each pound of compost costs Sweet Smell 5¢ and each pound of sewage costs 4¢. Use a graphical LP method to determine the least-cost blend of compost and sewage in each bag.

P . **B.12**   Consider Krista Christenson's following linear programming formulation:

$$\text{Minimize cost} = \$1X_1 + \$2X_2$$
$$\text{Subject to:} \quad X_1 + 3X_2 \geq 90$$
$$8X_1 + 2X_2 \geq 160$$
$$3X_1 + 2X_2 \geq 120$$
$$X_2 \leq 70$$

a)   Graphically illustrate the feasible region and apply the iso-cost line procedure to indicate to Krista which corner point produces the optimal solution.
b)   What is the cost of this solution?

B.13   The LP relationships that follow were formulated by Jeffrey Rummel at the Connecticut Chemical Company. Which ones are invalid for use in a linear programming problem, and why?

$$\text{Maximize} = 6X_1 + \tfrac{1}{2} X_1X_2 + 5X_3$$
$$\text{Subject to:} \quad 4X_1X_2 + 2X_3 \quad \leq 70$$
$$7.9X_1 - 4X_2 \quad \geq 15.6$$
$$3X_1 + 3X_2 + 3X_3 \geq 21$$
$$19X_2 - \tfrac{1}{3} X_3 = 17$$
$$-X_1 - X_2 + 4X_3 = 5$$
$$4X_1 + 2X_2 + 3\sqrt{X_3} \leq 80$$

B.14 Kalyan Singhal Corp. makes three products, and it has three machines available as resources as given in the following LP problem:

$$\text{Maximize contribution} = 4X_1 + 4X_2 + 7X_3$$
$$\text{Subject to:} \quad 1X_1 + 7X_2 + 4X_3 \le 100 \text{ (hours on machine 1)}$$
$$2X_1 + 1X_2 + 7X_3 \le 110 \text{ (hours on machine 2)}$$
$$8X_1 + 4X_2 + 1X_3 \le 100 \text{ (hours on machine 3)}$$

a) Determine the optimal solution using LP software.
b) Is there unused time available on any of the machines with the optimal solution?
c) What would it be worth to the firm to make an additional hour of time available on the third machine?
d) How much would the firm's profit increase if an extra 10 hours of time were made available on the second machine at no extra cost?

B.15 Consider the following LP problem developed at Jason Treat's San Antonio optical scanning firm:

$$\text{Maximize profit} = \$1X_1 + \$1X_2$$
$$\text{Subject to:} \quad 2X_1 + 1X_2 \le 100$$
$$1X_1 + 2X_2 \le 100$$

a) What is the optimal solution to this problem? Solve it graphically.
b) If a technical breakthrough occurred that raised the profit per unit of X_1 to $3, would this affect the optimal solution?
c) Instead of an increase in the profit coefficient X_1, to $3, suppose that profit was overestimated and should only have been $1.25. Does this change the optimal solution?

B.16 The Arden County, Maryland, superintendent of education is responsible for assigning students to the three high schools in his county. He recognizes the need to bus a certain number of students, for several sectors of the county are beyond walking distance to a school. The superintendent partitions the county into five geographic sectors as he attempts to establish a plan that will minimize the total number of student miles traveled by bus. He also recognizes that if a student happens to live in a certain sector and is assigned to the high school in that sector, there is no need to bus him because he can walk to school. The three schools are located in sectors B, C, and E.

The accompanying table reflects the number of high-school-age students living in each sector and the distance in miles from each sector to each school.

	DISTANCE TO SCHOOL			
SECTOR	SCHOOL IN SECTOR B	SCHOOL IN SECTOR C	SCHOOL IN SECTOR E	NUMBER OF STUDENTS
A	5	8	6	700
B	0	4	12	500
C	4	0	7	100
D	7	2	5	800
E	12	7	0	400
				2,500

Each high school has a capacity of 900 students.
a) Set up the objective function and constraints of this problem using linear programming so that the total number of student miles traveled by bus is minimized.
b) Solve the problem.

B.17 The National Credit Union has $250,000 available to invest in a 12-month commitment. The money can be placed in Treasury notes yielding an 8% return or in municipal bonds at an average rate of return of 9%. Credit union regulations require diversification to the extent that at least 50% of the investment be placed in Treasury notes. Because of defaults in such municipalities as Cleveland and New York, it is decided that no more than 40% of the investment be placed in bonds. How much should the National Credit Union invest in each security so as to maximize its return on investment?

B.18 Boston's famous Robert Swan Restaurant is open 24 hours a day. Servers report for duty at 3 A.M., 7 A.M., 11 A.M., 3 P.M., 7 P.M., or 11 P.M., and each works an 8-hour shift. The following table shows the minimum number of workers needed during the 6 periods into which the day is divided.

PERIOD	TIME	NUMBER OF SERVERS REQUIRED
1	3 A.M.–7 A.M.	3
2	7 A.M.–11 A.M.	12
3	11 A.M.–3 P.M.	16
4	3 P.M.–7 P.M.	9
5	7 P.M.–11 P.M.	11
6	11 P.M.–3 A.M.	4

Swan's scheduling problem is to determine how many servers should report for work at the start of each time period in order to minimize the total staff required for one day's operation. (*Hint:* Let X_i equal the number of servers beginning work in time period i, where $i = 1, 2, 3, 4, 5, 6$.)

B.19 A craftsman named Paul Vaupel builds two kinds of birdhouses, one for wrens and a second for bluebirds. Each wren birdhouse takes 4 hours of labor and 4 units of lumber. Each bluebird house requires 2 hours of labor and 12 units of lumber. The craftsman has available 60 hours of labor and 120 units of lumber. Wren houses yield a profit of $6 each and bluebird houses yield a profit of $15 each.

a) Write out the objective and constraints.
b) Solve graphically.

B.20 Each coffee table produced by Robert West Designers nets the firm a profit of $9. Each bookcase yields a $12 profit. West's firm is small and its resources limited. During any given production period (of 1 week), 10 gallons of varnish and 12 lengths of high-quality redwood are available. Each coffee table requires approximately 1 gallon of varnish and 1 length of redwood. Each bookcase takes 1 gallon of varnish and 2 lengths of wood.

Formulate West's production-mix decision as a linear programming problem, and solve. How many tables and bookcases should be produced each week? What will the maximum profit be?

B.21 Graph the following LP problem:

$$\text{Maximize profit} = \$3X_1 + \$2X_2$$
$$\text{Subject to:} \quad 2X_1 + 1X_2 \le 150$$
$$2X_1 + 3X_2 \le 300$$

a) What is the optimal solution?
b) Does the optimal solution change if the profit per unit of X_1 changes to $4.50?
c) What happens if the profit function should have been $3X_1 + \$3X_2$?

B.22 Solve the following linear programming problem graphically.

$$\text{Minimize cost} = 4X_1 + 5X_2$$
$$\text{Subject to:} \quad X_1 + 2X_2 \ge 80$$
$$3X_1 + X_2 \ge 75$$
$$X_1, X_2 \ge 0$$

B.23 DeBruzzi Distributors packages and distributes industrial supplies. A standard shipment can be packaged in a class A container, a class K container, or a class T container. A single class A container yields a profit of $9; a class K container, a profit of $7; and a class T container, a profit of $15. Each shipment prepared requires a certain amount of packing material and a certain amount of time.

Resources Needed per Standard Shipment

CLASS OF CONTAINER	PACKING MATERIAL (POUNDS)	PACKING TIME (HOURS)
A	2	2
K	1	6
T	3	4
Total amount of resource available each week	130 pounds	240 hours

John DeBruzzi, head of the firm, must decide the optimal number of each class of container to pack each week. He is bound by the previously mentioned resource restrictions but also decides that he must keep his 6 full-time packers employed all 240 hours (6 workers × 40 hours) each week.

Formulate and solve this problem using LP software.

P . **B.24**   Using the data from Problem B.7 and LP software:

a) Determine the range within which the unit profit contribution of an air conditioner must fall for the current solution to remain optimal.

b) What is the shadow price for the wiring constraint?

P : **B.25**   The Denver advertising agency promoting the new Breem dishwashing detergent wants to get the best exposure possible for the product within the $100,000 advertising budget ceiling placed on it. To do so, the agency needs to decide how much of the budget to spend on each of its two most effective media: (1) television spots during the afternoon hours and (2) large ads in the city's Sunday newspaper. Each television spot costs $3,000; each Sunday newspaper ad costs $1,250. The expected exposure, based on industry ratings, is 35,000 viewers for each TV commercial and 20,000 readers for each newspaper advertisement. The agency director, Deborah Kellogg, knows from experience that it is important to use both media in order to reach the broadest spectrum of potential Breem customers. She decides that at least 5 but no more than 25 television spots should be ordered, and that at least 10 newspaper ads should be contracted. How many times should each of the two media be used to obtain maximum exposure while staying within the budget? Use the graphical method to solve.

P : **B.26**   Catherine Reynolds Manufacturing has three factories (1, 2, and 3) and three warehouses (A, B, and C). The following table shows the shipping costs between each factory and warehouse, the factory manufacturing capabilities (in thousands), and the warehouse capacities (in thousands).

a) Write the objective function and the constraint in equations. Let X_{1A} = 1,000s of units shipped from factory 1 to warehouse A, and so on.

b) Solve by computer.

To FROM	WAREHOUSE A	WAREHOUSE B	WAREHOUSE C	PRODUCTION CAPABILITY
FACTORY 1	$ 6	$ 5	$ 3	6
FACTORY 2	$ 8	$10	$ 8	8
FACTORY 3	$11	$14	$18	10
CAPACITY	7	12	5	

P : **B.27**   The seasonal yield of olives in a Piraeus, Greece, vineyard is greatly influenced by a process of branch pruning. If olive trees are pruned every 2 weeks, output is increased. The pruning process, however, requires considerably more labor than permitting the olives to grow on their own and results in a smaller-size olive. It also, though, permits olive trees to be spaced closer together. The yield of 1 barrel of olives by pruning requires 5 hours of labor and 1 acre of land. The production of a barrel of olives by the normal process requires only 2 labor-hours but takes 2 acres of land. An olive grower has 250 hours of labor available and a total of 150 acres for growing. Because of the olive size difference, a barrel of olives produced on pruned trees sells for $20, whereas a barrel of regular olives has a market price of $30. The grower has determined that because of uncertain demand, no more than 40 barrels of pruned olives should be produced. Use graphical LP to find:

a) The maximum possible profit.

b) The best combination of barrels of pruned and regular olives.

c) The number of acres that the olive grower should devote to each growing process.

P : **B.28**   New Orleans's Mt. Sinai Hospital is a large, private, 600-bed facility complete with laboratories, operating rooms, and X-ray equipment. In seeking to increase revenues, Mt. Sinai's administration has decided to make a 90-bed addition on a portion of adjacent land currently used for staff parking. The administrators feel that the labs, operating rooms, and X-ray department are not being fully utilized at present and do not need to be expanded to handle additional patients. The addition of 90 beds, however, involves deciding how many beds should be allocated to the medical staff (for medical patients) and how many to the surgical staff (for surgical patients).

The hospital's accounting and medical records departments have provided the following pertinent information. The average hospital stay for a medical patient is 8 days, and the average medical patient generates $2,280 in revenues. The average surgical patient is in the hospital 5 days and generates $1,515 in revenues. The laboratory is capable of handling 15,000 tests per year more than it *was* handling. The average medical patient requires 3.1 lab tests, the average surgical patient 2.6 lab tests. Furthermore, the average medical patient uses 1 X ray, the average surgical patient 2 X rays. If the hospital were expanded by 90 beds, the X-ray department could handle up to 7,000 X rays without significant additional cost. Finally, the administration estimates that up to 2,800 additional operations could be performed in existing operating-room facilities. Medical patients, of course, require no surgery, whereas each surgical patient generally has one surgery performed.

Formulate this problem so as to determine how many medical beds and how many surgical beds should be added in order to maximize revenues. Assume that the hospital is open 365 days per year.

P $\times$: **B.29**

Charles Watts Electronics manufactures the following six peripheral devices used in computers especially designed for jet fighter planes: internal modems, external modems, graphics circuit boards, floppy disk drives, hard disk drives, and memory expansion boards. Each of these technical products requires time, in minutes, on three types of electronic testing equipment as shown in the following table:

	INTERNAL MODEM	EXTERNAL MODEM	CIRCUIT BOARD	FLOPPY DRIVES	HARD DRIVES	MEMORY BOARDS
Test device 1	7	3	12	6	18	17
Test device 2	2	5	3	2	15	17
Test device 3	5	1	3	2	9	2

The first two test devices are available 120 hours per week. The third (device 3) requires more preventive maintenance and may be used only 100 hours each week. The market for all six computer components is vast, and Watts Electronics believes that it can sell as many units of each product as it can manufacture. The table that follows summarizes the revenues and material costs for each product:

DEVICE	REVENUE PER UNIT SOLD ($)	MATERIAL COST PER UNIT ($)
Internal modem	200	35
External modem	120	25
Graphics circuit board	180	40
Floppy disk drive	130	45
Hard disk drive	430	170
Memory expansion board	260	60

In addition, variable labor costs are $15 per hour for test device 1, $12 per hour for test device 2, and $18 per hour for test device 3. Watts Electronics wants to maximize its profits.

a) Formulate this problem as an LP model.
b) Solve the problem by computer. What is the best product mix?
c) What is the value of an additional minute of time per week on test device 1? Test device 2? Test device 3? Should Watts Electronics add more test device time? If so, on which equipment?

P $\times$: **B.30**

Rachel Yang, campus dietitian for a small Illinois college, is responsible for formulating a nutritious meal plan for students. For an evening meal, she feels that the following five meal-content requirements should be met: (1) between 900 and 1,500 calories; (2) at least 4 milligrams of iron; (3) no more than 50 grams of fat; (4) at least 26 grams of protein; and (5) no more than 50 grams of carbohydrates. On a particular day, Rachel's food stock includes seven items that can be prepared and served for supper to meet these requirements. The cost per pound for each food item and its contribution to each of the five nutritional requirements are given in the accompanying table:

	TABLE OF FOOD VALUES[a] AND COSTS					
FOOD ITEM	CALORIES/ POUND	IRON (MG/LB)	FAT (GM/LB)	PROTEIN (GM/LB)	CARBOHYDRATES (GM/LB)	COST/ POUND ($)
Milk	295	0.2	16	16	22	0.60
Ground Meat	1,216	0.2	96	81	0	2.35
Chicken	394	4.3	9	74	0	1.15
Fish	358	3.2	0.5	83	0	2.25
Beans	128	3.2	0.8	7	28	0.58
Spinach	118	14.1	1.4	14	19	1.17
Potatoes	279	2.2	0.5	8	63	0.33

[a]From C. F. Church and H. N. Church, Bowes and Church's *Food Values of Portions Commonly Used*, 12th ed. Philadelphia: J. B. Lippincott, 1975.

What combination and amounts of food items will provide the nutrition Rachel requires at the least total food cost?

a) Formulate as an LP problem.
b) What is the cost per meal?
c) Is this a well-balanced diet?
d) How sensitive is the solution to price changes in milk, ground meat, fish, and chicken?

INTERNET HOMEWORK PROBLEMS

See our Internet homepage at www.prenhall.com/heizer for these additional homework problems: B.31 through B.40.

CASE STUDY

Golding Landscaping and Plants, Inc.

Kenneth and Patricia Golding spent a career as a husband-and-wife real estate investment partnership in Washington, DC. When they finally retired to a 25-acre farm in northern Virginia's Fairfax County, they became ardent amateur gardeners. Kenneth planted shrubs and fruit trees, and Patricia spent her hours potting all sizes of plants. When the volume of shrubs and plants reached the point that the Goldings began to think of their hobby in a serious vein, they built a greenhouse adjacent to their home and installed heating and watering systems.

By 2002, the Goldings realized their retirement from real estate had really only led to a second career—in the plant and shrub business—and they filed for a Virginia business license. Within a matter of months, they asked their attorney to file incorporation documents and formed the firm Golding Landscaping and Plants, Inc.

Early in the new business's existence, Kenneth Golding recognized the need for a high-quality commercial fertilizer that he could blend himself, both for sale and for his own nursery. His goal was to keep his costs to a minimum while producing a top-notch product that was especially suited to the northern Virginia climate.

Working with chemists at George Mason University, Golding blended "Golding-Grow." It consists of four chemical compounds, C-30, C-92, D-21, and E-11. The cost per pound for each compound is indicated in the following table:

CHEMICAL COMPOUND	COST PER POUND
C-30	$.12
C-92	.09
D-21	.11
E-11	.04

The specifications for Golding-Grow are established as:

a. Chemical E-11 must comprise at least 15% of the blend.
b. C-92 and C-30 must together constitute at least 45% of the blend.
c. D-21 and C-92 can together constitute no more than 30% of the blend.
d. Golding-Grow is packaged and sold in 50-lb bags.

Discussion Questions

1. Formulate an LP problem to determine what blend of the four chemicals will allow Golding to minimize the cost of a 50-lb bag of the fertilizer.
2. Solve to find the best solution.

Source: From *Quantitative Analysis for Management* 8/e by Barry Render, Ralph Stair, and Michael Hanna, p. 283. Copyright © 2003. Reprinted by permission of Prentice Hall, Inc., Upper Saddle River, NJ.

Transportation Models

Module Outline

The transportation method finds the least cost means of shipping supplies from several *origins* to several *destinations*. Origin points (sources of supply) can be factories, warehouses, or any other points from which goods are shipped. Destinations are any points that receive goods.

Use of the transportation method requires (1) origin points with the supply for a given time period at each, (2) destination points with the demand for a given time period at each, and (3) the cost of shipping one unit from each origin point to each destination point.

These problems can be solved by hand and by computer.

BEFORE COMING TO CLASS, READ MODULE C IN YOUR TEXT AND ANSWER THESE QUESTIONS.

1. What is the objective in a transportation problem? _____

_____

_____

2. What is the northwest-corner rule? _____

_____

3. What is the stepping-stone method?_____

_____

_____

4. What happens when the quantity being supplied does not equal the quantity required?_____

_____

_____

5. What are dummy sources or dummy destinations? _____

_____

_____

6. What is meant by degeneracy in a transportation problem? _____

_____

_____

TRANSPORTATION MODELING

Origins

Destinations

Need to Know

1. Origins and supply at each
2. Destinations and demand at each
3. Cost of shipping 1 unit from each origin to each destination

DEVELOPING AN INITIAL SOLUTION

Northwest-Corner Rule

Steps

1. _____

2. _____

3. _____

The Intuitive Lowest-Cost Method

Steps

1. _____

2. _____

3. _____

4. _____

THE STEPPING-STONE METHOD

Steps

1. _____

2. _____

3. _____

4. _____

5. _____

PRACTICE PROBLEM C.1 ■ Shipping Allocations

John Galt Shipping wishes to ship a product that is made at two different factories to three different warehouses. The company produces 18 units at Factory A and 22 units at Factory B. It needs 10 units in Warehouse 1, 20 units in Warehouse 2, and 10 units in Warehouse 3. Per-unit transportation costs are shown in the following table. How many units should be shipped from each factory to each warehouse?

	WAREHOUSE 1	WAREHOUSE 2	WAREHOUSE 3
Plant A	$4	$2	$3
Plant B	$3	$2	$1

Additional Practice Problem Space

SPECIAL ISSUES IN MODELING

Demand Not Equal to Supply

Dummy Sources

Dummy Destinations

PRACTICE PROBLEM C.2 ■ Unbalanced Problem

Assume that in Practice Problem C.1 the demand at each warehouse is increased by 4 units. How many units now should be shipped from each factory to each warehouse?

Additional Practice Problem Space

Degeneracy

Rule about Shipping Routes

The number of occupied squares in any solution is equal to the number of rows in the table plus the number of columns minus 1. If not, degeneracy exists.

DISCUSSION QUESTIONS

1. What are the three information needs of the transportation model?
2. What are the steps in the intuitive lowest-cost method?
3. Identify the three "steps" in the northwest-corner rule.
4. How do you know when an optimal solution has been reached?
5. Which starting technique generally gives a better initial solution, and why?
6. The more sources and destinations there are for a transportation problem, the smaller the percentage of all cells that will be used in the optimal solution. Explain.
7. All of the transportation examples appear to apply to long distances. Is it possible for the transportation model to apply on a much smaller scale, for example, within the departments of a store or the offices of a building? Discuss; create an example or prove the application impossible.

8. Develop a *northeast*-corner rule and explain how it would work. Set up an initial solution for the Arizona Plumbing problem analyzed in Example C1 in your text.
9. What is meant by an unbalanced transportation problem, and how would you balance it?
10. How many cells must all solutions use?
11. Explain the significance of a negative improvement index in a transportation-minimizing problem.
12. How can the transportation method address production costs in addition to transportation costs?
13. Explain what is meant by the term "degeneracy" within the context of transportation modeling.

PROBLEMS*

 . C.1   Find an initial solution to the following transportation problem.
a)   Use the northwest-corner method.
b)   Use the intuitive lowest-cost approach.
c)   What is the total cost of each method?

FROM	To			SUPPLY
	LOS ANGELES	CALGARY	PANAMA CITY	
MEXICO CITY	$ 6	$18	$ 8	100
DETROIT	$17	$13	$19	60
OTTAWA	$20	$10	$24	40
DEMAND	50	80	70	

. C.2   Using the stepping-stone method, find the optimal solution to Problem C.1. Compute the total cost.

. C.3   a)   Use the northwest-corner method to find an initial feasible solution to the following problem. What must you do before beginning the solution steps?
b)   Use the intuitive lowest-cost approach to find an initial feasible solution. Which is better?

FROM	To			SUPPLY
	A	B	C	
X	$10	$18	$12	100
Y	$17	$13	$ 9	50
Z	$20	$18	$14	75
DEMAND	50	80	70	

. C.4   Find the optimal solution to Problem C.3 using the stepping-stone method.

. C.5   Whitlock Air Conditioning manufactures room air conditioners at plants in Houston, Phoenix, and Memphis. These are sent to regional distributors in Dallas, Atlanta, and Denver. The shipping costs vary, and the company would like to find the least-cost way to meet the demands at each of the distribution centers.

*Note: **P** means the problem may be solved with POM for Windows; ✗ means the problem may be solved with Excel OM; and **P**✗ means the problem may be solved with POM for Windows and/or Excel OM.

Dallas needs to receive 800 air conditioners per month, Atlanta needs 600, and Denver needs 200. Houston has 850 air conditioners available each month, Phoenix has 650, and Memphis has 300. The shipping cost per unit from Houston to Dallas is $8, to Atlanta $12, and to Denver $10.The cost per unit from Phoenix to Dallas is $10, to Atlanta $14, and to Denver $9. The cost per unit from Memphis to Dallas is $11, to Atlanta $8, and to Denver $12. How many units should Hanna Whitlock ship from each plant to each regional distribution center? What is the total cost for this? (Note that a "dummy" destination is needed to balance the problem.)

C.6 The following table is the result of one or more iterations:

From \ To	1	2	3	Capacity
A	40 (cost 30)	(cost 30)	10 (cost 5)	50
B	(cost 10)	30 (cost 10)	(cost 10)	30
C	(cost 20)	30 (cost 10)	45 (cost 25)	75
Demand	40	60	55	155

a) Complete the next iteration using the stepping-stone method.
b) Calculate the "total cost" incurred if your results were to be accepted as the final solution.

C.7 The three blood banks in Franklin County are coordinated through a central office that facilitates blood delivery to four hospitals in the region. The cost to ship a standard container of blood from each bank to each hospital is shown in the table below. Also given are the biweekly number of containers available at each bank and the biweekly number of containers of blood needed at each hospital. How many shipments should be made biweekly from each blood bank to each hospital so that total shipment costs are minimized?

FROM	HOSP. 1	HOSP. 2	HOSP. 3	HOSP. 4	SUPPLY
BANK 1	$ 8	$ 9	$11	$16	50
BANK 2	$12	$ 7	$ 5	$ 8	80
BANK 3	$14	$10	$ 6	$ 7	120
DEMAND	90	70	40	50	250

C.8 In Solved Problem C.1 (in your text), Williams Auto Top Carriers proposed opening a new plant in either New Orleans or Houston. Management found that the total system cost (of production plus distribution) would be $20,000 for the New Orleans site. What would be the total cost if Williams opened a plant in Houston? At which of the two proposed locations (New Orleans or Houston) should Williams open the new facility?

C.9 For the Karen-Reifsteck Corp. data below, find the starting solution and initial cost using the northwest-corner method. What must you do to balance this problem?

FROM	W	X	Y	Z	SUPPLY
A	$132	$116	$250	$110	220
B	$220	$230	$180	$178	300
C	$152	$173	$196	$164	435
DEMAND	160	120	200	230	

P✗ : **C.10**   The Danielle Walsh Clothing Group owns factories in three towns (W, Y, and Z), which distribute to three Walsh retail dress shops in three other cities. (A, B, and C). The following table summarizes factory availabilities, projected store demands, and unit shipping costs:

Walsh Clothing Group

From \ To	Dress Shop A	Dress Shop B	Dress Shop C	Factory availability
Factory W	$4	$3	$3	35
Factory Y	$6	$7	$6	50
Factory Z	$8	$2	$5	50
Store demand	30	65	40	135

a)   Complete the analysis, determining the optimal solution for shipping at the Walsh Clothing Group.
b)   How do you know if it is optimal or not?

P✗ : **C.11**   Consider the following transportation problem at Frank Timoney Enterprises in Clifton Park, NY.

	To			
FROM	**DESTINATION A**	**DESTINATION B**	**DESTINATION C**	**SUPPLY**
SOURCE 1	$8	$9	$4	72
SOURCE 2	$5	$6	$8	38
SOURCE 3	$7	$9	$6	46
SOURCE 4	$5	$3	$7	19
DEMAND	110	34	31	175

a)   Find an initial solution using the northwest-corner rule. What special condition exists?
b)   Explain how you will proceed to solve the problem.
c)   What is the optimal solution?

P✗ : **C.12**   Bell Mill Works (BMW) ships French doors to three building-supply houses from mills in Mountpelier, Nixon, and Oak Ridge. Determine the best shipment schedule for BMW from the data provided by Kelly Bell, the traffic manager at BMW. Use the northwest-corner starting procedure and the stepping-stone method. Refer to the following table. (*Note:* You may face a degenerate solution in one of your iterations.)

Bell Mill Works

From \ To	Supply House 1	Supply House 2	Supply House 3	Mill capacity (in tons)
Mountpelier	$3	$3	$2	25
Nixon	$4	$2	$3	40
Oak Ridge	$3	$2	$3	30
Supply house demand (in tons)	30	30	35	95

P✗ : **C.13**   Captain Cabell Corp. manufacturers fishing equipment. Currently, the company has a plant in Los Angeles and a plant in New Orleans. David Cabell, the firm's owner, is deciding where to build a new plant—Philadelphia or Seattle. Use the table on the following page to find the total shipping costs for each potential site. Which should Cabell select?

	WAREHOUSE			
PLANT	PITTSBURGH	ST. LOUIS	DENVER	CAPACITY
LOS ANGELES	$100	$75	$50	150
NEW ORLEANS	$ 80	$60	$90	225
PHILADELPHIA	$ 40	$50	$90	350
SEATTLE	$110	$70	$30	350
DEMAND	200	100	400	

C.14 Susan Helms Manufacturing Co. has hired you to evaluate its shipping costs. The table below shows present demand, capacity, and freight costs between each factory and each warehouse. Find the shipping pattern with the lowest cost.

Susan Helms Manufacturing Data

From \ To	Warehouse 1	Warehouse 2	Warehouse 3	Warehouse 4	Plant capacity
Factory 1	4	7	10	12	2,000
Factory 2	7	5	8	11	2,500
Factory 3	9	8	6	9	2,200
Warehouse demand	1,000	2,000	2,000	1,200	6,700 / 6,200

C.15 Drew Rosen Corp. is considering adding a fourth plant to its three existing facilities in Decatur, Minneapolis, and Carbondale. Both St. Louis and East St. Louis are being considered. Evaluating only the transportation costs per unit as shown in the table below, decide which site is best.

	FROM EXISTING PLANTS			
TO	DECATUR	MINNEAPOLIS	CARBONDALE	DEMAND
BLUE EARTH	$20	$17	$21	250
CIRO	$25	$27	$20	200
DES MOINES	$22	$25	$22	350
CAPACITY	300	200	150	

	FROM PROPOSED PLANTS	
TO	EAST ST. LOUIS	ST. LOUIS
BLUE EARTH	$29	$27
CIRO	$30	$28
DES MOINES	$30	$31
CAPACITY	150	150

C.16 Using the data from Problem C.15 and the unit production costs in the following table, show which locations yield the lowest cost.

LOCATION	PRODUCTION COSTS ($)
Decatur	$50
Minneapolis	60
Carbondale	70
East St. Louis	40
St. Louis	50

C.17 Duffy Pharmaceuticals enjoys a dominant position in the southeast U.S., with over 800 discount retail outlets. These stores are served by twice-weekly deliveries from Duffy's 16 warehouses, which are in turn supplied daily by 7 factories that manufacture about 70% of all of the chain's products.

It is clear to Marcie Wademan, VP operations, that an additional warehouse is desperately needed to handle growth and backlogs. Three cities, Mobile, Tampa, and Huntsville, are under final consideration. The following table illustrates the current and proposed factory/warehouse capacities/demands and shipping costs per average box of supplies.

a) Based on shipping costs only, which city should be selected for the new warehouse?
b) One study shows that Ocala's capacity can increase to 500 boxes per day. Would this affect your decision in part (a)?
c) Because of a new intrastate shipping agreement, rates for shipping from each factory in Florida to each warehouse in Florida drop by $1 per carton. How does this factor affect your answer to parts (a) and (b)?

Table for Problem C.17

FACTORY	ATLANTA, GA	NEW ORLEANS, LA	JACKSON, MS	BIRMINGHAM, AL	MONTGOMERY, AL	RALEIGH, NC	ASHEVILLE, NC	COLUMBIA, SC	CAPACITY (CARTONS PER DAY)
Valdosta, GA	$3	$5	$4	$3	$4	$6	$8	$8	500
Ocala, FL	4	6	5	5	6	7	6	7	300
Augusta, GA	1	4	3	2	2	6	7	8	400
Stuart, FL	3	5	2	6	6	5	5	6	200
Biloxi, MS	4	1	4	3	3	8	9	10	600
Starkville, MS	3	3	1	2	2	6	5	6	400
Durham, NC	4	8	8	7	7	2	2	2	500
Requirements (cartons/day)	150	250	50	150	100	200	150	300	

FACTORY	ORLANDO, FL	MIAMI, FL	JACKSONVILLE, FL	WILMINGTON, NC	CHARLOTTE, NC	MOBILE, AL	TAMPA, FL	HUNTSVILLE, AL	CAPACITY (CARTONS PER DAY)
Valdosta, GA	$9	$10	$8	$8	$11	$4	$6	$3	500
Ocala, FL	2	3	2	6	7	5	2	5	300
Augusta, GA	7	9	6	8	9	3	5	2	400
Stuart, FL	2	2	3	5	5	6	3	5	200
Biloxi, MS	7	13	9	8	8	2	6	3	600
Starkville, MS	6	8	7	7	8	3	6	2	400
Durham, NC	6	8	5	1	2	8	7	8	500
Requirements (cartons/day)	250	300	300	100	150	300	300	300	

INTERNET HOMEWORK PROBLEMS

See our Internet homepage at www.prenhall.com/heizer for these additional homework problems: C.18 through C.22.

CASE STUDY

Custom Vans, Inc.

Custom Vans, Inc., specializes in converting standard vans into campers. Depending on the amount of work and customizing to be done, the customizing could cost less than $1,000 to over $5,000. In less than 4 years, Tony Rizzo was able to expand his small operation in Gary, Indiana, to other major outlets in Chicago, Milwaukee, Minneapolis, and Detroit.

Innovation was the major factor in Tony's success in converting a small van shop into one of the largest and most profitable custom van operations in the Midwest. Tony seemed to have a special ability to design and develop unique features and devices that were always in high demand by van owners. An example was Shower-Rific, which was developed by Tony only 6 months after Custom Vans, Inc., was started. These small showers were completely self-contained, and they could be placed in almost any type of van and in a number of different locations within a van. Shower-Rific was made of fiberglass, and contained towel racks, built-in soap and shampoo holders, and a unique plastic door. Each Shower-Rific took 2 gallons of fiberglass and 3 hours of labor to manufacture.

(continued)

Most of the Shower-Rifics were manufactured in Gary in the same warehouse where Custom Vans, Inc., was founded. The manufacturing plant in Gary could produce 300 Shower-Rifics in a month, but this capacity never seemed to be enough. Custom Van shops in all locations were complaining about not getting enough Shower-Rifics, and because Minneapolis was farther away from Gary than the other locations, Tony was always inclined to ship Shower-Rifics to the other locations before Minneapolis. This infuriated the manager of Custom Vans at Minneapolis, and after many heated discussions, Tony decided to start another manufacturing plant for Shower-Rifics at Fort Wayne, Indiana. The manufacturing plant at Fort Wayne could produce 150 Shower-Rifics per month.

The manufacturing plant at Fort Wayne was still not able to meet current demand for Shower-Rifics, and Tony knew that the demand for his unique camper shower would grow rapidly in the next year. After consulting with his lawyer and banker, Tony concluded that he should open two new manufacturing plants as soon as possible. Each plant would have the same capacity as the Fort Wayne manufacturing plant. An initial investigation into possible manufacturing locations was made, and Tony decided that the two new plants should be located in Detroit, Michigan; Rockford, Illinois; or Madison, Wisconsin. Tony knew that selecting the best location for the two new manufacturing plants would be difficult. Transportation costs and demands for the various locations would be important considerations.

The Chicago shop was managed by Bill Burch. This shop was one of the first established by Tony, and it continued to outperform the other locations. The manufacturing plant at Gary was supplying 200 Shower-Rifics each month, although Bill knew that the demand for the showers in Chicago was 300 units. The transportation cost per unit from Gary was $10, and although the transportation cost from Fort Wayne was double that amount, Bill was always pleading with Tony to get an additional 50 units from the Fort Wayne manufacturer. The two additional manufacturing plants would certainly be able to supply Bill with the additional 100 showers he needed. The transportation costs would, of course, vary, depending on which two locations Tony picked. The transportation cost per shower would be $30 from Detroit, $5 from Rockford, and $10 from Madison.

Wilma Jackson, manager of the Custom Van shop in Milwaukee, was the most upset about not getting an adequate supply of showers. She had a demand for 100 units, and at the present time, she was only getting half of this demand from the Fort Wayne manufacturing plant. She could not understand why Tony didn't ship her all 100 units from Gary. The transportation cost per unit from Gary was only $20, while the transportation cost from Fort Wayne was $30. Wilma was hoping that Tony would select Madison for one of the manufacturing locations. She would be able to get all of the showers needed, and the transportation cost per unit would only be $5. If not Madison, a new plant in Rockford would be able to supply her total needs, but the transportation cost per unit would be twice as much as it would be from Madison. Because the transportation cost per unit from Detroit would be $40, Wilma speculated that even if Detroit became one of the new plants, she would not be getting any units from Detroit.

Custom Vans, Inc., of Minneapolis was managed by Tom Poanski. He was getting 100 showers from the Gary plant. Demand was 150 units. Tom faced the highest transportation costs of all locations. The transportation cost from Gary was $40 per unit. It would cost $10 more if showers were sent from the Fort Wayne location. Tom was hoping that Detroit would not be one of the new plants, as the transportation cost would be $60 per unit. Rockford and Madison would have a cost of $30 and $25, respectively, to ship one shower to Minneapolis.

The Detroit shop's position was similar to Milwaukee's—only getting half of the demand each month. The 100 units that Detroit did receive came directly from the Fort Wayne plant. The transportation cost was only $15 per unit from Fort Wayne, while it was $25 from Gary. Dick Lopez, manager of Custom Vans, Inc., of Detroit, placed the probability of having one of the new plants in Detroit fairly high. The factory would be located across town, and the transportation cost would be only $5 per unit. He could get 150 showers from the new plant in Detroit and the other 50 showers from Fort Wayne. Even if Detroit was not selected, the other two locations were not intolerable. Rockford had a transportation cost per unit of $35, and Madison had a transportation cost of $40.

Tony pondered the dilemma of locating the two new plants for several weeks before deciding to call a meeting of all the managers of the van shops. The decision was complicated, but the objective was clear—to minimize total costs. The meeting was held in Gary, and everyone was present except Wilma.

Tony: Thank you for coming. As you know, I have decided to open two new plants at Rockford, Madison, or Detroit. The two locations, of course, will change our shipping practices, and I sincerely hope that they will supply you with the Shower-Rifics that you have been wanting. I know you could have sold more units, and I want you to know that I am sorry for this situation.

Dick: Tony, I have given this situation a lot of consideration, and I feel strongly that at least one of the new plants should be located in Detroit. As you know, I am now only getting half of the showers that I need. My brother, Leon, is very interested in running the plant, and I know he would do a good job.

Tom: Dick, I am sure that Leon could do a good job, and I know how difficult it has been since the recent layoffs by the auto industry. Nevertheless, we should be considering total costs and not personalities. I believe that the new plants should be located in Madison and Rockford. I am farther away from the other plants than any other shop, and these locations would significantly reduce transportation costs.

Dick: That may be true, but there are other factors. Detroit has one of the largest suppliers of fiberglass, and I have checked prices. A new plant in Detroit would be able to purchase fiberglass for $2 per gallon less than any of the other existing or proposed plants.

Tom: At Madison, we have an excellent labor force. This is due primarily to the large number of students attending the University of Madison. These students are hard workers, and they will work for $1 less per hour than the other locations that we are considering.

Bill: Calm down, you two. It is obvious that we will not be able to satisfy everyone in locating the new plants. Therefore, I would like to suggest that we vote on the two best locations.

Tony: I don't think that voting would be a good idea. Wilma was not able to attend, and we should be looking at all of these factors together in some type of logical fashion.

Discussion Question

Where would you locate the two new plants? Why?

Source: From *Managerial Decision Modeling with Spreadsheets* by B. Render, R. M. Stair, and R. Balakrishnan pp. 202–203. Copyright © 2003. Reprinted by permission of Prentice Hall, Inc., Upper Saddle River, NJ.

Quantitative Module D

Waiting-Line Models

Module Outline

CHARACTERISTICS OF A WAITING-LINE SYSTEM

QUEUING COSTS

THE VARIETY OF QUEUING MODELS

OTHER QUEUING APPROACHES

DISCUSSION QUESTIONS

ACTIVE MODEL EXERCISE

PROBLEMS

INTERNET HOMEWORK PROBLEMS

CASE STUDIES: NEW ENGLAND CASTINGS; THE WINTER PARK HOTEL

Waiting lines, generally called queues, are a common occurrence in the life of an operations manager. Indeed, waiting lines are a common occurrence in the lives of most of us. Queues can be found at shipping and loading docks in factories and at service counters in post offices, banks, and your neighborhood supermarket. Therefore, operations managers need to understand them. Conveniently, many common queues can be analyzed with some straightforward equations.

This module will introduce and explain four common types of queuing models.

BEFORE COMING TO CLASS, READ MODULE D IN YOUR TEXT AND ANSWER THESE QUESTIONS.

1. Name six places where queues can be found. _____

_____

_____

2. What are the assumptions of the four queuing models described in this module? _____

_____

_____

_____

3. In the basic queuing model (the M/M/1 model), arrivals are assumed to be what type of statistical distribution? _____

_____

4. In the basic queuing model (the M/M/1 model), service times are assumed to be what type of statistical distribution? _____

_____

5. What are some of the measures of a queue's performance? _____

_____

_____

6. How are queues analyzed when standard queuing models are not adequate? _____

CHARACTERISTICS OF A WAITING-LINE SYSTEM

FIGURE D.1 ■ Three Parts of a Waiting Line, or Queuing System, at Dave's Car Wash

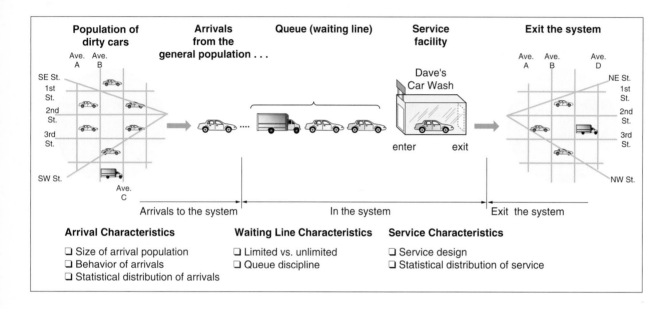

Arrival Characteristics

1. Size of Arrival Population

2. Pattern of Arrivals

Poisson distribution often applies.

$$P(x) = \frac{e^{-\lambda}\lambda^x}{x!} \quad \text{for } x = 0, 1, 2, 3, 4, \ldots \tag{D-1}$$

where $P(x)$ = probability of x arrivals
$\quad\quad\quad x$ = number of arrivals per unit of time
$\quad\quad\quad \lambda$ = average arrival rate
$\quad\quad\quad e$ = 2.7183 (which is the base of the natural logarithms)

3. Behavior of Arrivals

FIGURE D.2 ■ Two Examples of the Poisson Distribution for Arrival Times

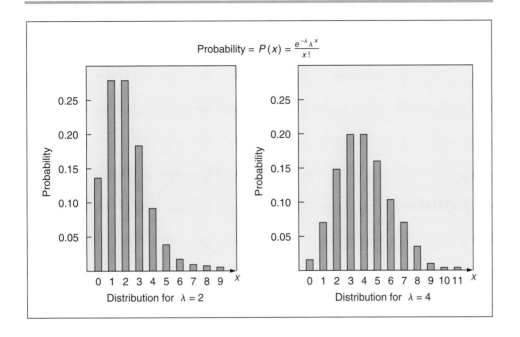

$$\text{Probability} = P(x) = \frac{e^{-\lambda}\lambda^x}{x!}$$

Distribution for $\lambda = 2$

Distribution for $\lambda = 4$

Waiting Line Characteristics

Service Characteristics

Basic Designs

1. **Single Channel**
2. **Multiple Channel**
3. **Single Phase**
4. **Multiphase**

Service Time Distribution

Negative exponential probability distribution often applies.

FIGURE D.4 ■ Two Examples of the Negative Exponential Distribution for Service Times

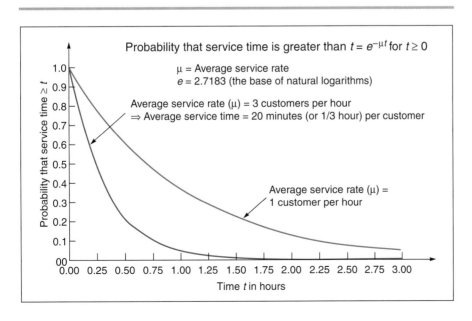

Probability that service time is greater than $t = e^{-\mu t}$ for $t \geq 0$

μ = Average service rate
e = 2.7183 (the base of natural logarithms)

Average service rate (μ) = 3 customers per hour
$\Rightarrow$ Average service time = 20 minutes (or 1/3 hour) per customer

Average service rate (μ) = 1 customer per hour

Time t in hours

Seven Performance Measures

1. Average time that each customer or object spends in the queue.
2. Average queue length.
3. Average time that each customer spends in the system (waiting time plus service time).
4. Average number of customers in the system.
5. Probability that the service facility will be idle.
6. Utilization factor for the system.
7. Probability of a specific number of customers in the system.

QUEUING COSTS

THE VARIETY OF QUEUING MODELS

Model A: M/M/1

Assumptions

1. _____
2. _____
3. _____
4. _____
5. _____
6. _____

TABLE D.3 ■ Queuing Formulas for Model A: Simple System, Also Called M/M/1

λ = mean number of arrivals per time period

μ = mean number of people or items served per time period

L_s = average number of units (customers) in the system (waiting and being served)

$$= \frac{\lambda}{\mu - \lambda}$$

W_s = Average time a unit spends in the system (waiting time plus service time)

$$= \frac{1}{\mu - \lambda}$$

L_q = Average number of units waiting in the queue

$$= \frac{\lambda^2}{\mu(\mu - \lambda)}$$

W_q = Average time a unit spends waiting in the queue

$$= \frac{\lambda}{\mu(\mu - \lambda)}$$

ρ = Utilization factor for the system

$$= \frac{\lambda}{\mu}$$

P_0 = Probability of 0 units in the system (that is, the service unit is idle)

$$= 1 - \frac{\lambda}{\mu}$$

$P_{n>k}$ = Probability of more than k units in the system, where n is the number of units in the system

$$= \left(\frac{\lambda}{\mu}\right)^{k+1}$$

PRACTICE PROBLEM D.1 ■ Basic Single-Channel Model

A new shopping mall is considering setting up an information desk manned by one employee. Based on information obtained from similar information desks, it is believed that people will arrive at the desk at a rate of 20 per hour. It takes an average of 2 minutes to answer a question. It is assumed that the arrivals follow a Poisson distribution and answer times are exponentially distributed.

a. Find the probability that the employee is idle.
b. Find the proportion of the time that the employee is busy.
c. Find the average number of people receiving and waiting to receive some information.
d. Find the average number of people waiting in line to get some information.
e. Find the average time a person seeking information spends in the system.
f. Find the expected time a person spends just waiting in line to have a question answered (time in the queue).

PRACTICE PROBLEM D.2 ■ Costs in Practice Problem D.1

Assume that the information desk employee in Practice Problem D.1 earns $5 per hour. The cost of waiting time, in terms of customer unhappiness with the mall, is $12 per hour of time spent waiting in line. Find the total expected costs over an 8-hour day.

Additional Practice Problem Space

Model B: M/M/S

TABLE D.4 ■ Queuing Formulas for Model B: Multichannel System, Also Called M/M/S

M = number of channels open
λ = average arrival rate
μ = average service rate at each channel

The probability that there are zero people or units in the system is

$$P_0 = \frac{1}{\left[\displaystyle\sum_{n=0}^{M-1} \frac{1}{n!}\left(\frac{\lambda}{\mu}\right)^n\right] + \frac{1}{M!}\left(\frac{\lambda}{\mu}\right)^M \frac{M\mu}{M\mu - \lambda}} \quad \text{for } M\mu > \lambda$$

The average number of people or units in the system is

$$L_s = \frac{\lambda\mu(\lambda/\mu)^M}{(M-1)!(M\mu - \lambda)^2} P_0 + \frac{\lambda}{\mu}$$

The average time a unit spends in the waiting line or being serviced (namely, in the system) is

$$W_s = \frac{\mu(\lambda/\mu)^M}{(M-1)!(M\mu - \lambda)^2} P_0 + \frac{1}{\mu} = \frac{L_s}{\lambda}$$

The average number of people or units in line waiting for service is

$$L_q = L_s - \frac{\lambda}{\mu}$$

The average time a person or unit spends in the queue waiting for service is

$$W_q = W_s - \frac{1}{\mu} = \frac{L_q}{\lambda}$$

PRACTICE PROBLEM D.3 ■ Adding a Second Employee to Practice Problem D.1

The shopping mall has decided to investigate the use of two employees on the information desk.

a. Find the proportion of the time the employees will be idle.
b. Find the average number of people waiting in this system.
c. Find the expected time a person spends waiting in this system.
d. Assuming the same salary level and waiting costs as in Practice Problem D.2, find the total expected costs over an 8-hour day.

Additional Practice Problem Space

Model C: M/D/1

TABLE D.5 ■ Queuing Formulas for Model C: Constant Service,
                 Also Called M/D/1

Average length of queue: $L_q = \dfrac{\lambda^2}{2\mu(\mu - \lambda)}$

Average waiting time in queue: $W_q = \dfrac{\lambda}{2\mu(\mu - \lambda)}$

Average number of customers in system: $L_s = L_q + \dfrac{\lambda}{\mu}$

Average waiting time in system: $W_s = W_q + \dfrac{1}{\mu}$

PRACTICE PROBLEM D.4 ■ Constant Service Time Model

Three students arrive per minute at a coffee machine that dispenses exactly 4 cups per minute at a constant rate. Describe the system parameters.

Additional Practice Problem Space

Model D: Limited Population

TABLE D.6 ■ Queuing Formulas and Notation for Model D: Limited Population Formulas

Service factor: $X = \dfrac{T}{T + U}$

Average number running: $J = NF(1 - X)$

Average number waiting: $L = N(1 - F)$

Average number being serviced: $H = FNX$

Average waiting time: $W = \dfrac{L(T + U)}{N - L} = \dfrac{T(1 - F)}{XF}$

Number of population: $N = J + L + H$

NOTATION

D = probability that a unit will have to wait in queue
F = efficiency factor
H = average number of units being served
J = average number of units not in queue or in service bay
L = average number of units waiting for service
M = number of service channels

N = number of potential customers
T = average service time
U = average time between unit service requirements
W = average time a unit waits in line
X = service factor

PRACTICE PROBLEM D.5 ■ Limited Population Model

A repairperson at a local metal working shop services the shop's 5 drill presses. Service time averages 10 minutes and is exponentially distributed. Machines break down after an average of 70 minutes of operation (following a Poisson distribution). Describe the major system characteristics.

OTHER QUEUING APPROACHES

DISCUSSION QUESTIONS

1. Name the three parts of a typical queuing system.
2. When designing a waiting line system, what "qualitative" concerns need to be considered?
3. Name the three factors that govern the structure of "arrivals" in a queuing system.
4. State the seven common measures of queuing system performance.
5. State the assumptions of the "basic" queuing model (Model A or M/M/1).
6. Is it good or bad to operate a supermarket bakery system on a strict first-come, first-served basis? Why?
7. Describe what is meant by the waiting-line terms "balk" and "renege." Provide an example of each.
8. Which is larger, W_s or W_q? Explain.
9. Briefly describe three situations in which the first-in, first-out (FIFO) discipline rule is not applicable in queuing analysis.
10. Describe the behavior of a waiting line where $\lambda > \mu$. Use both analysis and intuition.
11. Discuss the likely outcome of a waiting line system where $\mu > \lambda$, but only by a tiny amount. (For example, $\mu = 4.1$, $\lambda = 4$).

12. Provide examples of four situations in which there is a limited, or finite, waiting line.
13. What are the components of the following queuing systems? Draw and explain the configuration of each.
    (a) Barbershop.
    (b) Car wash.
    (c) Laundromat.
    (d) Small grocery store.
14. Do doctors' offices generally have random arrival rates for patients? Are service times random? Under what circumstances might service times be constant?
15. What happens if two single-channel systems have the same mean arrival and service rates, but the service time is constant in one and exponential in the other?
16. What dollar value do you place on yourself per hour that you spend waiting in lines? What value do your classmates place on themselves? Why do they differ?

ACTIVE MODEL EXERCISE

In this active model example, we can examine the relationship between arrival and service rates, and costs and the number of servers. The first two inputs to the model are arrival and service rates in customers per hour. The average time between arrivals and service time is also displayed: but do not change these two numbers, which are shaded in pink.

ACTIVE MODEL D.2 ■

An Analysis of the Golden Muffler Shop (Examples D1–D3 in Your Text) with Cost as a Variable

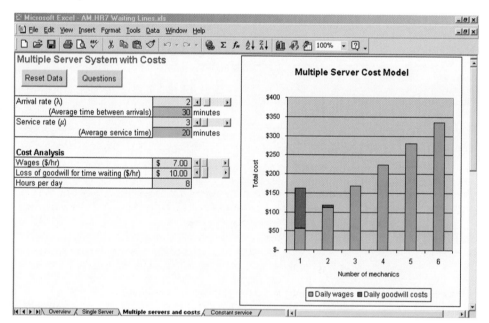

Questions

1. What number of mechanics yields the lowest total daily cost? What is the minimum total daily cost?
2. Use the scrollbar on the arrival rate. What would the arrival rate need to be in order that a third mechanic would be required?
3. Use the scrollbar on the goodwill cost and determine the range of goodwill costs for which you would have exactly 1 mechanic. Two mechanics?
4. How high would the wage rate need to be in order to make 1 mechanic the least costly option?
5. If a second mechanic is added, is it less costly to have the 2 mechanics working separately or to have the 2 mechanics work as a single team with a service rate that is twice as fast?

PROUBLEMS*

P✗ . D.1 Customers arrive at Derek Thibodeau's Styling Shop at a rate of 3 per hour, distributed in a Poisson fashion. Derek can perform haircuts at a rate of 5 per hour, distributed exponentially.
a) Find the average number of customers waiting for haircuts.
b) Find the average number of customers in the shop.
c) Find the average time a customer waits until it is his or her turn.
d) Find the average time a customer spends in the shop.
e) Find the percentage of time that Derek is busy.

P✗ . D.2 There is only one copying machine in the student lounge of the business school. Students arrive at the rate of $\lambda = 40$ per hour (according to a Poisson distribution). Copying takes an average of 40 seconds, or $\mu = 90$ per hour (according to an exponential distribution). Compute the following:
a) The percentage of time that the machine is used.
b) The average length of the queue.
c) The average number of students in the system.
d) The average time spent waiting in the queue.
e) The average time in the system.

P✗ . D.3 Glen Schmidt owns and manages a chili dog and soft drink stand near the Georgeville campus. While Glen can service 30 customers per hour on the average (μ), he only gets 20 customers per hour (λ). Because Glen could wait on 50% more customers than actually visit his stand, it doesn't make sense to him that he should have any waiting lines.
    Glen hires you to examine the situation and to determine some characteristics of his queue. After looking into the problem, you find it follows the six conditions for a single-channel waiting line (as seen in Model A, the M/M/1 model). What are your findings?

P✗ . D.4 Sam Certo, a Longwood vet, is running a rabies vaccination clinic for dogs at the local grade school. Sam can "shoot" a dog every 3 minutes. It is estimated that the dogs will arrive independently and randomly throughout the day at a rate of one dog every 6 minutes according to a Poisson distribution. Also assume that Sam's shooting times are exponentially distributed. Compute the following:
a) The probability that Sam is idle.
b) The proportion of the time that Sam is busy.
c) The average number of dogs being vaccinated and waiting to be vaccinated.
d) The average number of dogs waiting to be vaccinated.
e) The average time a dog waits before getting vaccinated.
f) The average amount of time a dog spends waiting in line and being vaccinated.

P✗ : **D.5** Brett Holmes' distribution center has 6 receiving docks. Trucks arrive at the rate of 4 per hour in a Poisson distribution. Receiving dock personnel take a mean of 12 minutes to unload each truck, following a negative exponential distribution.
a) What is the probability that a truck cannot find an available dock open?
b) What is the probability that all 6 docks are full?
c) What is the average time a truck is in the system (waiting plus service)?

P✗ . D.6 Calls arrive at James Hamann's hotel switchboard at a rate of 2 per minute. The average time to handle each is 20 seconds. There is only one switchboard operator at the current time. The Poisson and exponential distributions appear to be relevant in this situation.
a) What is the probability that the operator is busy?
b) What is the average time that a caller must wait before reaching the operator?
c) What is the average number of calls waiting to be answered?

P✗ : **D.7** Automobiles arrive at the drive-through window at the downtown Urbana, Illinois, post office at the rate of 4 every 10 minutes. The average service time is 2 minutes. The Poisson distribution is appropriate for the arrival rate and service times are exponentially distributed.
a) What is the average time a car is in the system?
b) What is the average number of cars in the system?
c) What is the average number of cars waiting to receive service?
d) What is the average number of cars in line behind the customer receiving service?
e) What is probability that there are no cars at the window?
f) What percentage of the time is the postal clerk busy?
g) What is the probability that there are exactly 2 cars in the system?

Note: **P** means the problem may be solved with POM for Windows; ✗ means the problem may be solved with Excel OM; and **P✗** means the problem may be solved with POM for Windows and/or Excel OM.

Px . **D.8**   The Moira Tarpy Electronics Corporation retains a service crew to repair machine breakdowns that occur on an average of $\lambda = 3$ per day (approximately Poisson in nature). The crew can service an average of $\mu = 8$ machines per day, with a repair time distribution that resembles the exponential distribution.

a)   What is the utilization rate of this service system?
b)   What is the average downtime for a broken machine?
c)   How many machines are waiting to be serviced at any given time?
d)   What is the probability that more than one machine is in the system? The probability that more than two are broken and waiting to be repaired or being serviced? More than three? More than four?

Px :   **D.9**   Zimmerman's Bank is the only bank in the small town of St. Thomas. On a typical Friday, an average of 10 customers per hour arrive at the bank to transact business. There is one teller at the bank, and the average time required to transact business is 4 minutes. It is assumed that service times may be described by the exponential distribution. A single line would be used, and the customer at the front of the line would go to the first available bank teller. If a single teller is used, find:

a)   The average time in the line.
b)   The average number in the line.
c)   The average time in the system.
d)   The average number in the system.
e)   The probability that the bank is empty.
f)   Zimmerman is considering adding a second teller (who would work at the same rate as the first) to reduce the waiting time for customers. She assumes that this will cut the waiting time in half. If a second teller is added, find the new answers to parts (a) to (e) above.

Px :   **D.10**   Nadine Skinner manages a Columbus, Ohio, movie theater complex called Cinema I, II, III, and IV. Each of the four auditoriums plays a different film; the schedule staggers starting times to avoid the large crowds that would occur if all four movies started at the same time. The theater has a single ticket booth and a cashier who can maintain an average service rate of 280 patrons per hour. Service times are assumed to follow an exponential distribution. Arrivals on a normally active day are Poisson-distributed and average 210 per hour.

  In order to determine the efficiency of the current ticket operation, Nadine wishes to examine several queue-operating characteristics.

a)   Find the average number of moviegoers waiting in line to purchase a ticket.
b)   What percentage of the time is the cashier busy?
c)   What is the average time that a customer spends in the system?
d)   What is the average time spent waiting in line to get to the ticket window?
e)   What is the probability that there are more than two people in the system? More than three people? More than four?

Px :   **D.11**   Bill Youngdahl has been collecting data at the TU student grill. He has found that, between 5:00 P.M. and 7:00 P.M., students arrive at the grill at a rate of 25 per hour (Poisson distributed) and service time takes an average of 2 minutes (exponential distribution). There is only 1 server, who can work on only 1 order at a time.

a)   What is the average number of students in line?
b)   What is the average time a student is in the grill area?
c)   Suppose that a second server can be added to team up with the first (and, in effect, act as one faster server). This would reduce the average service time to 90 seconds. How would this affect the average time a student is in the grill area?
d)   Suppose a second server is added and the 2 servers act independently, with *each* taking an average of 2 minutes. What would be the average time a student is in the system?

Px :   **D.12**   The wheat harvesting season in the American Midwest is short, and farmers deliver their truckloads of wheat to a giant central storage bin within a 2-week span. Because of this, wheat-filled trucks waiting to unload and return to the fields have been known to back up for a block at the receiving bin. The central bin is owned cooperatively, and it is to every farmer's benefit to make the unloading/storage process as efficient as possible. The cost of grain deterioration caused by unloading delays and the cost of truck rental and idle driver time are significant concerns to the cooperative members. Although farmers have difficulty quantifying crop damage, it is easy to assign a waiting and unloading cost for truck and driver of $18 per hour. During the 2-week harvest season, the storage bin is open and operated 16 hours per day, 7 days per week, and can unload 35 trucks per hour according to an exponential distribution. Full trucks arrive all day long (during the hours the bin is open) at a rate of about 30 per hour, following a Poisson pattern.

  To help the cooperative get a handle on the problem of lost time while trucks are waiting in line or unloading at the bin, find the following:

a)   The average number of trucks in the unloading system.
b)   The average time per truck in the system.
c)   The utilization rate for the bin area.
d)   The probability that there are more than three trucks in the system at any given time.

e) The total daily cost to the farmers of having their trucks tied up in the unloading process.

f) As mentioned, the cooperative uses the storage bin heavily only 2 weeks per year. Farmers estimate that enlarging the bin would cut unloading costs by 50% next year. It will cost $9,000 to do so during the off-season. Would it be worth the expense to enlarge the storage area?

P⊁ : D.13 Radovilsky's Department Store in Haywood, California, maintains a successful catalog sales department in which a clerk takes orders by telephone. If the clerk is occupied on one line, incoming phone calls to the catalog department are answered automatically by a recording machine and asked to wait. As soon as the clerk is free, the party who has waited the longest is transferred and serviced first. Calls come in at a rate of about 12 per hour. The clerk can take an order in an average of 4 minutes. Calls tend to follow a Poisson distribution, and service times tend to be exponential.

The cost of the clerk is $10 per hour, but because of lost goodwill and sales, Radovilsky's loses about $25 per hour of customer time spent waiting for the clerk to take an order.

a) What is the average time that catalog customers must wait before their calls are transferred to the order clerk?

b) What is the average number of callers waiting to place an order?

c) Radovilsky's is considering adding a second clerk to take calls. The store's cost would be the same $10 per hour. Should it hire another clerk? Explain your decision.

P⊁ . D.14 Customers arrive at an automated coffee-vending machine at a rate of four per minute, following a Poisson distribution. The coffee machine dispenses cups of coffee at a constant time of 10 seconds.

a) What is the average number of people waiting in line?

b) What is the average number in the system?

c) How long does the average person wait in line before receiving service?

P⊁ : D.15 The typical subway station in Washington, DC, has six turnstiles, each of which can be controlled by the station manager to be used for either entrance or exit control—but never for both. The manager must decide at different times of the day how many turnstiles to use for entering passengers and how many to use for exiting passengers.

At the George Washington University (GWU) Station, passengers enter the station at a rate of about 84 per minute between the hours of 7 A.M. and 9 A.M. Passengers exiting trains at the stop reach the exit turnstile area at a rate of about 48 per minute during the same morning rush hours. Each turnstile can allow an average of 30 passengers per minute to enter or exit. Arrival and service times have been thought to follow Poisson and exponential distributions, respectively. Assume riders form a common queue at both entry and exit turnstile areas and proceed to the first empty turnstile.

The GWU station manager, Ernie Forman, does not want the average passenger at his station to have to wait in a turnstile line for more than 6 seconds, nor does he want more than 8 people in any queue at any average time.

a) How many turnstiles should be opened in each direction every morning?

b) Discuss the assumptions underlying the solution of this problem using queuing theory.

P⊁ : D.16 Melissa Steffen's Car Wash takes a constant time of 4.5 minutes in its automated car wash cycle. Autos arrive following a Poisson distribution at the rate of 10 per hour. Melissa wants to know:

a) The average waiting time in line.

b) The average length of the line.

P⊁ : D.17 Brent Sheppard's cabinet-making shop, in Memphis, has five tools that automate the drilling of holes for the installation of hinges. These machines need setting up for each order of cabinets. The orders appear to follow the Poisson distribution, averaging 3 per day. There is a single technician for setting these machines. His service times are exponential, averaging 2 hours each.

a) What is the service factor for this system?

b) What is the average number of these machines in service?

c) What impact on machines in service would there be if a second technician were available?

P⊁ : D.18 Two technicians, working separately, monitor a group of 5 computers that run an automated manufacturing facility. It takes an average of 15 minutes (exponentially distributed) to adjust a computer that develops a problem. Computers run for an average of 85 minutes (Poisson-distributed) without requiring adjustments. Determine the following:

a) The average number of computers waiting for adjustment.

b) The average number being adjusted.

c) The average number of computers not in working order.

P⊁ : D.19 One mechanic services 5 drilling machines for a steel plate manufacturer. Machines break down on an average of once every 6 working days, and breakdowns tend to follow a Poisson distribution. The mechanic can handle an average of one repair job per day. Repairs follow an exponential distribution.

a) On the average, how many machines are waiting for service?

b) On the average, how many drills are in running order?

c) How much would waiting time be reduced if a second mechanic were hired?

: **D.20**   The administrator at a large hospital emergency room faces the problem of providing treatment for patients who arrive at different rates during the day. There are 4 doctors available to treat patients when needed. If not needed, they can be assigned other responsibilities (such as doing lab tests, reports, X-ray diagnoses) or else rescheduled to work at other hours.

It is important to provide quick and responsive treatment, and the administrator feels that, on the average, patients should not have to sit in the waiting area for more than 5 minutes before being seen by a doctor. Patients are treated on a first-come, first-served basis and see the first available doctor after waiting in the queue. The arrival pattern for a typical day is as follows:

TIME	ARRIVAL RATE
9 A.M.–3 P.M.	6 patients/hour
3 P.M.–8 P.M.	4 patients/hour
8 P.M.–midnight	12 patients/hour

Arrivals follow a Poisson distribution, and treatment times, 12 minutes on the average, follow the exponential pattern.

How many doctors should be on duty during each period in order to maintain the level of patient care expected?

: **D.21**   The Chattanooga Furniture store gets an average of 50 customers per shift. Marilyn Helms, the manager, wants to calculate whether she should hire 1, 2, 3, or 4 salespeople. She has determined that average waiting times will be 7 minutes with one salesperson, 4 minutes with two salespeople, 3 minutes with three salespeople, and 2 minutes with four salespeople. She has estimated the cost per minute that customers wait at $1. The cost per salesperson per shift (including fringe benefits) is $70.

How many salespeople should be hired?

: **D.22**   Gather real arrival and service data from somewhere on campus or some other locale (perhaps a bank, barbershop, car wash, fast-food restaurant, etc.). Then address the following questions:

a)   Determine the distributions of the arrivals and the service times (plot both).
b)   Did the arrivals or the services follow the distributions discussed in the text? (Plot these distributions on the same graph as your raw data.)
c)   What queuing model did your "real" queue follow?
d)   Determine the average length of the queue.
e)   Determine the average number of customers in the system.

INTERNET HOMEWORK PROBLEMS

See our Internet homepage at www.prenhall.com/heizer for these additional homework problems: D.23 through D.31.

CASE STUDY

New England Castings

For over 75 years, New England Castings, Inc. (NECI), has manufactured wood stoves for home use. In recent years, with increasing energy prices, president George Mathison has seen sales triple. This dramatic increase has made it difficult for George to maintain quality in all of his wood stoves and related products.

Unlike other companies manufacturing wood stoves, NECI is *only* in the business of making stoves and stove-related products. Its major products are the Warmglo I, the Warmglo II, the Warmglo III, and the Warmglo IV. The Warmglo I is the smallest wood stove, with a heat output of 30,000 BTUs, and the Warmglo IV is the largest, with a heat output of 60,000 BTUs.

The Warmglo III outsold all other models by a wide margin. Its heat output and available accessories were ideal for the typical home. The Warmglo III also had a number of other outstanding features that made it one of the most attractive and heat-efficient stoves on the market. These features, along with the accessories, resulted in expanding sales and prompted George to build a new factory to manufacture the Warmglo III model. An overview diagram of the factory is shown in Figure D.6.

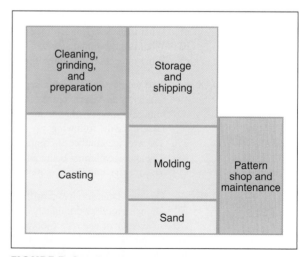

FIGURE D.6 ■ Overview of Factory

The new foundry used the latest equipment, including a new Disamatic that helped in manufacturing stove parts. Regardless of new equipment or procedures, casting operations have remained basically unchanged for hundreds of years. To begin with, a wooden pattern is made for every cast-iron piece in the stove. The wooden pattern is an exact duplicate of the cast-iron piece that is to be manufactured. All NECI patterns are made by Precision Patterns, Inc., and are stored in the pattern shop and maintenance room. Next, a specially formulated sand is molded around the wooden pattern. There can be two or more sand molds for each pattern. Mixing the sand and making the molds is done in the molding room. When the wooden pattern is removed, the resulting sand molds form a negative image of the desired casting. Next, molds are transported to the casting room, where molten iron is poured into them and allowed to cool. When the iron has solidified, molds are moved into the cleaning, grinding, and preparation room, where they are dumped into large vibrators that shake most of the sand from the casting. The rough castings are then subjected to both sandblasting to remove the rest of the sand and grinding to finish some of their surfaces. Castings are then painted with a special heat-resistant paint, assembled into workable stoves, and inspected for manufacturing defects that may have gone undetected. Finally, finished stoves are moved to storage and shipping, where they are packaged and transported to the appropriate locations.

At present, the pattern shop and the maintenance department are located in the same room. One large counter is used by both maintenance personnel, who store tools and parts; and sand molders, who need various patterns for the molding operation. Pete Nawler and Bob Dillman, who work behind the counter, can service a total of 10 people per hour (about 5 per hour each). On the average, 4 people from maintenance and 3 from molding arrive at the counter each hour. People from molding and maintenance departments arrive randomly, and to be served, they form a single line.

Pete and Bob have always had a policy of first-come, first-served. Because of the location of the pattern shop and maintenance department, it takes about 3 minutes for an individual from the maintenance department to walk to the pattern and maintenance room, and it takes about 1 minute for an individual to walk from the molding department to the pattern and maintenance room.

After observing the operation of the pattern shop and maintenance room for several weeks, George decided to make some

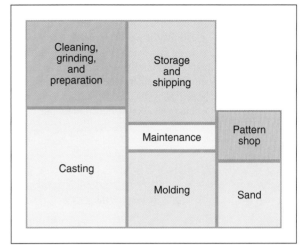

FIGURE D.7 ■ Overview of Factory after Changes

changes to the factory layout. An overview of these changes appears in Figure D.7.

Separating the maintenance shop from the pattern shop had a number of advantages. It would take people from the maintenance department only 1 minute instead of 3 to get to the new maintenance room. Using motion and time studies, George was also able to determine that improving the layout of the maintenance room would allow Bob to serve 6 people from the maintenance department per hour; improving the layout of the pattern department would allow Pete to serve 7 people from the molding shop per hour.

Discussion Questions

1. How much time would the new layout save?
2. If maintenance personnel were paid $9.50 per hour and molding personnel were paid $11.75 per hour, how much could be saved per hour with the new factory layout?
3. Should George have made the change in layout?

Source: From *Quantitative Analysis for Management*, 8/e, by B. Render, R. Stair, and M. Hanna, pp. 596–598. Copyright © 2003. Reprinted by permission of Prentice Hall, Inc., Upper Saddle River, NJ.

CASE STUDY

The Winter Park Hotel

Donna Shader, manager of the Winter Park Hotel, is considering how to restructure the front desk to reach an optimum level of staff efficiency and guest service. At present, the hotel has five clerks on duty, each with a separate waiting line, during peak check-in time of 3:00 P.M. to 5:00 P.M. Observation of arrivals during this period shows that an average of 90 guests arrive each hour (although there is no upward limit on the number that could arrive at any given time). It takes an average of 3 minutes for the front-desk clerk to register each guest.

Ms. Shader is considering three plans for improving guest service by reducing the length of time that guests spend waiting in line. The first proposal would designate one employee as a quick-service clerk for guests registering under corporate accounts, a market segment that fills about 30% of all occupied rooms. Because corporate guests are preregistered, their registration takes just 2 minutes. With these guests separated from the rest of the clientele, the average time for registering a typical guest would climb to 3.4 minutes. Under this plan, noncorporate guests would choose any of the remaining four lines.

The second plan is to implement a single-line system. All guests could form a single waiting line to be served by whichever of five clerks became available. This option would require sufficient lobby space for what could be a substantial queue.

The use of an automatic teller machine (ATM) for check-ins is the basis of the third proposal. This ATM would provide about the same service rate as would a clerk. Because initial use of this technol-

(continued)

ogy might be minimal, Shader estimates that 20% of customers, primarily frequent guests, would be willing to use the machines. (This might be a conservative estimate if guests perceive direct benefits from using the ATM, as bank customers do. Citibank reports that some 95% of its Manhattan customers use its ATMs.) Ms. Shader would set up a single queue for customers who prefer human check-in clerks. This line would be served by the five clerks, although Shader is hopeful that the ATM machine will allow a reduction to four.

Discussion Questions

1. Determine the average amount of time that a guest spends checking in. How would this change under each of the stated options?
2. Which option do you recommend?

Source: From *Quantitative Analysis for Management*, 8/e, by B. Render, R. Stair, and M. Hanna, p. 598. Copyright © 2003. Reprinted by permission of Prentice Hall, Inc., Upper Saddle River, NJ.

Learning Curves

Module Outline

LEARNING CURVES IN SERVICES AND MANUFACTURING

APPLYING THE LEARNING CURVE

STRATEGIC IMPLICATIONS OF LEARNING CURVES

LIMITATIONS OF LEARNING CURVES

DISCUSSION QUESTIONS

ACTIVE MODEL EXERCISE

PROBLEMS

INTERNET HOMEWORK PROBLEMS

CASE STUDY: SMT'S NEGOTIATION WITH IBM

Most of us get better with practice. So do most processes. As firms and employees perform a task repeatedly, they learn how to perform those tasks more efficiently. We call this the learning curve.

The learning curve has application to (1) labor time, (2) purchased components, and (3) strategic decisions regarding costs and pricing.

The learning curve is based on a doubling of similar production units. That is, when production doubles, the decrease in time per unit determines the learning curve.

BEFORE COMING TO CLASS, READ MODULE E IN YOUR TEXT AND ANSWER THESE QUESTIONS.

1. What is the basic assumption of learning curves? _____

_____

_____

2. How is the learning curve used within an organization? _____

_____

_____

3. How is the learning curve applied to suppliers? _____

_____

_____

4. How is the learning curve used for strategic decisions? _____

_____

_____

5. What three ways can learning curves be calculated? _____

_____

_____

6. Explain the "doubling concept" of learning curves. _____

_____

_____

LEARNING CURVES IN SERVICES AND MANUFACTURING

Doubling Concept

$$T \times L^n = \text{Time required for the } n\text{th unit} \qquad (E\text{-}1)$$

where T = unit cost or unit time of the first unit
L = learning curve rate
n = number of times T is doubled

APPLYING THE LEARNING CURVE

Arithmetic Approach

Logarithmic Approach

$$T_N = T_1(N^b) \qquad (E\text{-}2)$$

where T_N = time for the Nth unit
T_1 = hours to produce the first unit
b = (log of the learning rate)/(log 2) = slope of the learning curve

Learning Curve Coefficient Approach

$$T_N = T_1 C \qquad (E\text{-}3)$$

where T_N = number of labor-hours required to produce the Nth unit
T_1 = number of labor-hours required to produce the first unit
C = learning-curve coefficient found in Table E.3

TABLE E.3 ■ Learning-Curve Coefficients, where Coefficient = $N^{(\log\ of\ learning\ rate/\log\ 2)}$

UNIT NUMBER (N)	70% UNIT TIME	70% TOTAL TIME	75% UNIT TIME	75% TOTAL TIME	80% UNIT TIME	80% TOTAL TIME	85% UNIT TIME	85% TOTAL TIME	90% UNIT TIME	90% TOTAL TIME
1	1.000	1.000	1.000	1.000	1.000	1.000	1.000	1.000	1.000	1.000
2	.700	1.700	.750	1.750	.800	1.800	.850	1.850	.900	1.900
3	.568	2.268	.634	2.384	.702	2.502	.773	2.623	.846	2.746
4	.490	2.758	.562	2.946	.640	3.142	.723	3.345	.810	3.556
5	.437	3.195	.513	3.459	.596	3.738	.686	4.031	.783	4.339
6	.398	3.593	.475	3.934	.562	4.299	.657	4.688	.762	5.101
7	.367	3.960	.446	4.380	.534	4.834	.634	5.322	.744	5.845
8	.343	4.303	.422	4.802	.512	5.346	.614	5.936	.729	6.574
9	.323	4.626	.402	5.204	.493	5.839	.597	6.533	.716	7.290
10	.306	4.932	.385	5.589	.477	6.315	.583	7.116	.705	7.994
11	.291	5.223	.370	5.958	.462	6.777	.570	7.686	.695	8.689
12	.278	5.501	.357	6.315	.449	7.227	.558	8.244	.685	9.374
13	.267	5.769	.345	6.660	.438	7.665	.548	8.792	.677	10.052
14	.257	6.026	.334	6.994	.428	8.092	.539	9.331	.670	10.721
15	.248	6.274	.325	7.319	.418	8.511	.530	9.861	.663	11.384
16	.240	6.514	.316	7.635	.410	8.920	.522	10.383	.656	12.040
17	.233	6.747	.309	7.944	.402	9.322	.515	10.898	.650	12.690
18	.226	6.973	.301	8.245	.394	9.716	.508	11.405	.644	13.334
19	.220	7.192	.295	8.540	.388	10.104	.501	11.907	.639	13.974
20	.214	7.407	.288	8.828	.381	10.485	.495	12.402	.634	14.608
25	.191	8.404	.263	10.191	.355	12.309	.470	14.801	.613	17.713
30	.174	9.305	.244	11.446	.335	14.020	.450	17.091	.596	20.727
35	.160	10.133	.229	12.618	.318	15.643	.434	19.294	.583	23.666
40	.150	10.902	.216	13.723	.305	17.193	.421	21.425	.571	26.543
45	.141	11.625	.206	14.773	.294	18.684	.410	23.500	.561	29.366
50	.134	12.307	.197	15.776	.284	20.122	.400	25.513	.552	32.142

PRACTICE PROBLEM E.1 ■ Learning Curve

The initial external tank for NASA's Space Shuttle took 400 hours of labor to produce. The learning rate is 80%. How long will the twentieth tank take?

Additional Practice Problem Space

PRACTICE PROBLEM E.2 ■ Learning Curve Costs

An operation has a 90% learning curve, and the first unit produced took 28 minutes. The labor cost is $20 per hour.

    a. How long will the second unit take?
    b. How much should the second unit cost?

PRACTICE PROBLEM E.3 ■ Cumulative Values

Using the data from Practice Problem E.1, how long will it take to produce all 20 tanks?

Additional Practice Problem Space

STRATEGIC IMPLICATIONS OF LEARNING CURVES

LIMITATIONS OF LEARNING CURVES

DISCUSSION QUESTIONS

1. What are some of the limitations to the use of learning curves?
2. Identify three applications of the learning curve.
3. What are the approaches to solving learning-curve problems?
4. Refer to Example E2 in your text: What are the implications for Great Lakes, Inc., if the engineering department wants to change the engine in the third and subsequent tugboats that the firm purchases?

5. Why isn't the learning-curve concept as applicable in a high-volume assembly line as it is in most other human activities?
6. What are the elements that can disrupt the learning curve?
7. Explain the concept of the "doubling" effect in learning curves.
8. What techniques can a firm use to move to a steeper learning curve?

ACTIVE MODEL EXERCISE

This Active Model, found on your CD-ROM, allows you to evaluate important elements in the learning curve model described in Examples E2 and E3 in the text. You may change any input parameter in a green colored cell.

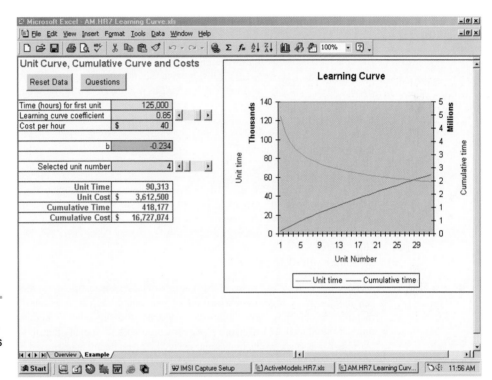

ACTIVE MODEL E.2 ■

Great Lakes, Inc. Learning Curve Analysis of Boats, Using Examples E2 and E3 Data in Your Text

Questions

1. If the learning is not as good as expected and rises to 90%, how much will the 4th boat cost?
2. What should the learning coefficient be to keep the total cost of the first 4 boats below $16,000,000?
3. How many boats need to be produced before the cost of an individual boat is below $4,000,000?
4. How many boats need to be produced before the *average* cost of an individual boat is below $4,000,000?

PROBLEMS*

 E.1
Jennifer Lucking, an IRS auditor, took 45 minutes to process her first tax return. The IRS uses an 85% learning curve. How long will the
a) second return take?
b) fourth return take?
c) eighth return take?

*Note: **P** means the problem may be solved with POM for Windows; ✕ means the problem may be solved with Excel OM; and **P✕** means the problem may be solved with POM for Windows and/or Excel OM.

P⊠ . E.2   Seton Hall Trucking Co. just hired Annette Bratcher to verify daily invoices and accounts payable. She took 9 hours and 23 minutes to complete her task on the first day. Prior employees in this job have tended to follow a 90% learning curve. How long will the task take at the end of

   a) the second day?
   b) the fourth day?
   c) the eighth day?
   d) the sixteenth day?

P⊠ . E.3   If Professor Donna Conroy takes 15 minutes to grade the first exam, and follows an 80% learning curve, how long will it take her

   a) to grade the twenty-fifth exam?
   b) to grade the first 10 exams?

P⊠ . E.4   If it took 563 minutes to complete a hospital's first cornea transplant, and the hospital uses a 90% learning rate, what is the cumulative time to complete

   a) the first 3 transplants?
   b) the first 6 transplants?
   c) the first 8 transplants?
   d) the first 16 transplants?

P⊠ : E.5   Beth Zion Hospital has received initial certification from the state of California to become a center for liver transplants. The hospital, however, must complete its first 18 transplants under great scrutiny and at no cost to the patients. The very first transplant, just completed, required 30 hours. On the basis of research at the hospital, Beth Zion estimates that it will have an 80% learning curve. Estimate the time it will take to complete

   a) the fifth liver transplant.
   b) all of the first 5 transplants.
   c) the eighteenth transplant.
   d) all 18 transplants.

P⊠ : E.6   Refer to Problem E.5. Beth Zion Hospital has just been informed that only the first 10 transplants must be performed at the hospital's expense. The cost per hour of surgery is estimated to be $5,000. Again, the learning rate is 80% and the first surgery took 30 hours.

   a) How long will the tenth surgery take?
   b) How much will the tenth surgery cost?
   c) How much will all 10 cost the hospital?

P⊠ . E.7   Manceville Air has just produced the first unit of a large industrial compressor that incorporated new technology in the control circuits and a new internal venting system. The first unit took 112 hours of labor to manufacture. The company knows from past experience that this labor content will decrease significantly as more units are produced. In reviewing past production data, it appears that the company has experienced a 90% learning curve when producing similar designs. The company is interested in estimating the total time to complete the next 7 units. Your job as the production cost estimator is to prepare the estimate.

P⊠ . E.8   Candice Cotton, a student at San Diego State University, bought six bookcases for her dorm room. Each required unpacking of parts and assembly, which included some nailing and bolting. Candice completed the first bookcase in 5 hours and the second in 4 hours.

   a) What is her learning rate?
   b) Assuming the same rate continues, how long will the third bookcase take?
   c) The fourth, fifth, and sixth cases?
   d) All six cases?

P⊠ : E.9   Professor Mary Beth Marrs took 6 hours to prepare the first lecture in a new course. Traditionally, she has experienced a 90% learning factor. How much time should it take her to prepare the fifteenth lecture?

P⊠ . E.10   The first vending machine that M. D'Allessandro, Inc., assembled took 80 labor-hours. Estimate how long the fourth machine will require for each of the following learning rates:

   a) 95%
   b) 87%
   c) 72%

P⊠ . E.11   Kevin-Glynn Systems is installing networks for Advantage Insurance. The first installation took 46 man-hours to complete. Estimate how long the fourth and the eighth installations will take for each of the following learning rates:

   a) 92%
   b) 84%
   c) 77%

P_X : **E.12** Baltimore Assessment Center screens and trains employees for a computer assembly firm in Towson, Maryland. The progress of all trainees is tracked and those not showing the proper progress are moved to less demanding programs. By the tenth repetition trainees must be able to complete the assembly task in 1 hour or less. Torri Olson-Alves has just spent 5 hours on the fourth unit and 4 hours completing her eighth unit, while another trainee, Kate Derrick, took 4 hours on the third and 3 hours on the sixth unit. Should you encourage either or both of the trainees to continue? Why?

P_X : **E.13** The better students at Baltimore Assessment Center (see Problem E.12) have an 80% learning curve and can do a task in 20 minutes after just six times. You would like to weed out the weak students sooner and decide to evaluate them after the third unit. How long should the third unit take?

P_X : **E.14** Sarah Davis, the purchasing agent for Northeast Airlines, is interested in determining what she can expect to pay for airplane number 4 if the third plane took 20,000 hours to produce. What would Davis expect to pay for plane number 5? Number 6? Use an 85% learning curve and a $40-per-hour labor charge.

P_X : **E.15** Using the data from Problem E.14, how long will it take to complete the twelfth plane? The fifteenth plane? How long will it take to complete planes 12 through 15 inclusive? At $40 per hour, what can Davis, as purchasing agent, expect to pay for all 4 planes?

P_X : **E.16** Dynamic RAM Corp. produces semiconductors and has a learning curve of .7. The price per bit is 100 millicents when the volume is $.7 \times 10^{12}$ bits. What is the expected price at 1.4×10^{12} bits? What is the expected price at 89.6×10^{12} bits?

P_X : **E.17** Central Power owns 25 small power generating plants. It has contracted with Genco Services to overhaul the power turbines of each of the plants. The number of hours that Genco billed Central to complete the third turbine was 460. Central pays Genco $60 per hour for its services. As the maintenance manager for Central, you are trying to estimate the cost of overhauling the fourth turbine. How much would you expect to pay for the overhaul of number 5 and number 6? All the turbines are similar and an 80% learning curve is appropriate.

P_X : **E.18** It takes 28,718 hours to produce the eighth locomotive at a large French manufacturing firm. If the learning factor is 80%, how long does it take to produce the tenth locomotive?

P_X : **E.19** Eric Krassow's firm is about to bid on a new radar system. Although the product uses new technology, Krassow believes that a learning rate of 75% is appropriate. The first unit is expected to take 700 hours, and the contract is for 40 units.
a) What is the total amount of hours to build the 40 units?
b) What is the average time to build each of the 40 units?
c) Assume that a worker works 2,080 hours per year. How many workers should be assigned to this contract to complete it in a year?

P_X : **E.20** As the estimator for Doug Greive Enterprises, your job is to prepare an estimate for a potential customer service contract. The contract is for the service of diesel locomotive cylinder heads. The shop has done some of these in the past on a sporadic basis. The time required to service each cylinder head has been exactly 4 hours, and similar work has been accomplished at an 85% learning curve. The customer wants you to quote in batches of 12 and 20.
a) Prepare the quote.
b) After preparing the quote, you find a labor ticket for this customer for five locomotive cylinder heads. From the notations on the labor ticket, you conclude that the fifth unit took 2.5 hours. What do you conclude about the learning curve and your quote?

P_X : **E.21** Carolyn Ghazi-Tehrani and James Misenti are teammates at a discount store; their new job is assembling swing sets for customers. Assembly of a swing set has a learning rate of 90%. They forgot to time their effort on the first swing set, but spent 4 hours on the second set. They have six more sets to do. Determine approximately how much time will be (was) required for
a) the first unit.
b) the eighth unit.
c) all eight units.

: **E.22** Kelly-Lambing, Inc., a builder of government-contracted small ships, has a steady work force of 10 very skilled craftspeople. These workers can supply 2,500 labor-hours each per year. Kelly-Lambing is about to undertake a new contract, building a new style of boat. The first boat is expected to take 6,000 hours to complete. The firm thinks that 90% is the expected learning rate.
a) What is the firm's "capacity" to make these boats—that is, how many units can the firm make in 1 year?
b) If the operations manager can increase the learning rate to 85% instead of 90%, how many units can the firm make?

P : **E.23**   Fargo Production has contracted with Johnson Services to overhaul the 25 robots at its plant. All the robots are similar and an 80% learning curve is appropriate. The number of hours that Johnson billed Fargo to complete the third robot overhaul was 460. Fargo pays $60 per hour for its services. Fargo wants to estimate the following:

a)   How many hours will it take to overhaul the 13th robot?

b)   The fifteenth robot?

c)   How long will it take to complete robots 10 through 15 inclusive?

d)   As the person who manages the costs for overhauling all equipment, what is your estimate of the cost of the entire contract for overhauling all 25 robots?

E.24   You are considering building a plane for training pilots. You believe there is a market for 50 of these planes, which will have a top speed of 400 kn and an empty weight of 10,000 lb. You will need one test plane. Use the NASA Web site (**www.jsc.nasa.gov/bu2/airframe.html**) to determine the total cost and engineering cost of building all 50 planes.

E.25   Using the log-log graph below, answer the following questions:

a)   What are the implications for management if it has forecast its cost on the optimum line?

b)   What could be causing the fluctuations above the optimum line?

c)   If management forecast the tenth unit on the optimum line, what was that forecast in hours?

d)   If management built the tenth unit as indicated by the actual line, how many hours did it take?

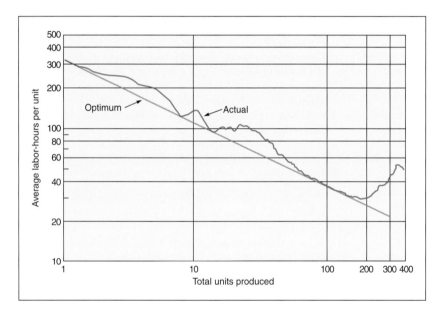

INTERNET HOMEWORK PROBLEMS

See our Internet homepage at **www.prenhall.com/heizer** for these additional homework problems: E.26 through E.33.

CASE STUDY

SMT's Negotiation with IBM

SMT and one other, much larger company were asked by IBM to bid on 80 more units of a particular computer product. The RFQ (request for quote) asked that the overall bid be broken down to show the hourly rate, the parts and materials component in the price, and any charges for subcontracted services. SMT quoted $1.62 million and supplied the cost breakdown as requested. The second company submitted only one total figure, $5 million, with no cost breakdown. The decision was made to negotiate with SMT.

The IBM negotiating team included two purchasing managers and two cost engineers. One cost engineer had developed manufac-

turing cost estimates for every component, working from engineering drawings and cost-data books that he had built up from previous experience and that contained time factors, both setup and run times, for a large variety of operations. He estimated materials costs by working both from data supplied by the IBM corporate purchasing staff and from purchasing journals. He visited SMT facilities to see the tooling available so that he would know what processes were being used. He assumed that there would be perfect conditions and trained operators, and he developed cost estimates for the 158th unit (previous orders were for 25, 15, and 38 units). He added 5% for scrap-and-flow loss; 2% for the use of temporary tools, jigs, and fixtures; 5% for quality control; and 9% for purchasing burden. Then, using an 85% learning curve, he backed up his costs to get an estimate for the first unit. He next checked the data on hours and materials for the 25, 15, and 38 units already made and found that his estimate for the first unit was within 4% of actual cost. His check, however, had indicated a 90% learning-curve effect on hours per unit.

In the negotiations, SMT was represented by one of the two owners of the business, two engineers, and one cost estimator. The sessions opened with a discussion of learning curves. The IBM cost estimator demonstrated that SMT had in fact been operating on a 90% learning curve. But, he argued, it should be possible to move to an 85% curve, given the longer runs, reduced setup time, and increased continuity of workers on the job that would be possible with an order for 80 units. The owner agreed with this analysis and was willing to reduce his price by 4%.

However, as each operation in the manufacturing process was discussed, it became clear that some IBM cost estimates were too low because certain crating and shipping expenses had been overlooked. These oversights were minor, however, and in the following discussions, the two parties arrived at a common understanding of specifications and reached agreements on the costs of each manufacturing operation.

At this point, SMT representatives expressed great concern about the possibility of inflation in material costs. The IBM negotiators volunteered to include a form of price escalation in the contract, as previously agreed among themselves. IBM representatives suggested that if overall material costs changed by more than 10%, the price could be adjusted accordingly. However, if one party took the initiative to have the price revised, the other could require an analysis of *all* parts and materials invoices in arriving at the new price.

Another concern of the SMT representatives was that a large amount of overtime and subcontracting would be required to meet IBM's specified delivery schedule. IBM negotiators thought that a relaxation in the delivery schedule might be possible if a price concession could be obtained. In response, the SMT team offered a 5% discount, and this was accepted. As a result of these negotiations, the SMT price was reduced almost 20% below its original bid price.

In a subsequent meeting called to negotiate the prices of certain pipes to be used in the system, it became apparent to an IBM cost estimator that SMT representatives had seriously underestimated their costs. He pointed out this apparent error because he could not understand why SMT had quoted such a low figure. He wanted to be sure that SMT was using the correct manufacturing process. In any case, if SMT estimators had made a mistake, it should be noted. It was IBM's policy to seek a fair price both for itself and for its suppliers. IBM procurement managers believed that if a vendor was losing money on a job, there would be a tendency to cut corners. In addition, the IBM negotiator felt that by pointing out the error, he generated some goodwill that would help in future sessions.

Discussion Questions

1. What are the advantages and disadvantages to IBM and SMT from this approach?
2. How does SMT's proposed learning rate compare with that of other companies?
3. What are the limitations of the learning curve in this case?

Source: Adapted from E. Raymond Corey, *Procurement Management: Strategy, Organization, and Decision Making* (New York: Van Nostrand Reinhold).

Quantitative Module F

Simulation

Module Outline

Simulation is an attempt to duplicate the significant features of a real system by building a mathematical model. The model is then used to understand and evaluate the real world system. The major advantage of mathematical simulation is that the real system need not be touched until an understanding and evaluation of the system has been accomplished.

Although simulation models can be developed manually, simulation by computer is a more realistic approach. The Monte Carlo technique uses random numbers to represent variables such as demand in inventory systems or arrivals and service times in a drive-through restaurant.

BEFORE COMING TO CLASS, READ MODULE F IN YOUR TEXT AND ANSWER THESE QUESTIONS.

1. Identify some applications of mathematical simulation. _____

_____

_____

2. What are six advantages of simulation? _____

_____

_____

3. Name three disadvantages of simulation. _____

_____

_____

4. What is meant by Monte Carlo simulation? _____

_____

_____

5. What is a random-number generator? _____

_____

_____

6. What computer languages are used for commercial simulations? ____

_____

_____

WHAT IS SIMULATION?

1. Imitate Real-World Situation Mathematically

2. Study Its Properties

3. Take Action Based on Simulation

FIGURE F.1 ■ The Process of Simulation

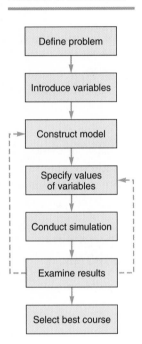

ADVANTAGES AND DISADVANTAGES OF SIMULATION

MONTE CARLO SIMULATION

Five Steps

1. Setting up a probability distribution for important variables.

2. Building a cumulative probability distribution for each variable.

3. Establishing an interval of random numbers for each variable.

4. Generating random numbers.

5. Actually simulating a series of trials.

SIMULATION OF A QUEUING PROBLEM

PRACTICE PROBLEM F.1 ■ Queuing Simulation

The time between arrivals at a drive-through window of Kirby's Fast Food follows the distribution given in the following table. The service time distribution is also given in the table. Use the random numbers provided to simulate the activities of the first five arrivals. Assume that the window opens at 11:00 A.M. and that the first arrival after this is based on the first interarrival time.

TIME BETWEEN ARRIVALS	PROBABILITY		SERVICE TIME	PROBABILITY
1	0.2		1	0.3
2	0.3		2	0.5
3	0.3		3	0.2
4	0.2			

Random numbers for arrivals: 14, 74, 27, 03; Random numbers for service times: 88, 32, 36, 24

What time does the fourth customer leave the system?

SIMULATION AND INVENTORY ANALYSIS

PRACTICE PROBLEM F.2 ■ Inventory Simulation

Average daily sales of a product are 8 units. The actual number of units each day is 7, 8, or 9, with probabilities 0.3, 0.4, and 0.3, respectively. The lead time for delivery of this product averages 4 days, although the time may be 3, 4, or 5 days with probabilities 0.2, 0.6, and 0.2, respectively. The company plans to place an order when the inventory level drops to 32 units (based on average demand and lead time). The beginning inventory is 32. The following random numbers have been generated:

Set 1: 60, 87, 46, 63, 50, 76, 11, 04, 97, 96, 65

Set 2: 52, 78, 13, 06, 99, 98, 80, 09, 67, 89, 45

Use Set 1 to generate lead times, and use Set 2 to simulate daily demand. Simulate two ordering periods, and determine how often the company runs out of stock before the shipment arrives.

Assume an order quantity of 32.

Additional Practice Problem Space

TABLE F.4 ■ Table of Random Numbers

52	06	50	88	53	30	10	47	99	37	66	91	35	32	00	84	57	07
37	63	28	02	74	35	24	03	29	60	74	85	90	73	59	55	17	60
82	57	68	28	05	94	03	11	27	79	90	87	92	41	09	25	36	77
69	02	36	49	71	99	32	10	75	21	95	90	94	38	97	71	72	49
98	94	90	36	06	78	23	67	89	85	29	21	25	73	69	34	85	76
96	52	62	87	49	56	59	23	78	71	72	90	57	01	98	57	31	95
33	69	27	21	11	60	95	89	68	48	17	89	34	09	93	50	44	51
50	33	50	95	13	44	34	62	64	39	55	29	30	64	49	44	30	16
88	32	18	50	62	57	34	56	62	31	15	40	90	34	51	95	26	14
90	30	36	24	69	82	51	74	30	35	36	85	01	55	92	64	09	85
50	48	61	18	85	23	08	54	17	12	80	69	24	84	92	16	49	59
27	88	21	62	69	64	48	31	12	73	02	68	00	16	16	46	13	85
45	14	46	32	13	49	66	62	74	41	86	98	92	98	84	54	33	40
81	02	01	78	82	74	97	37	45	31	94	99	42	49	27	64	89	42
66	83	14	74	27	76	03	33	11	97	59	81	72	00	64	61	13	52
74	05	81	82	93	09	96	33	52	78	13	06	28	30	94	23	37	39
30	34	87	01	74	11	46	82	59	94	25	34	32	23	17	01	58	73
59	55	72	33	62	13	74	68	22	44	42	09	32	46	71	79	45	89
67	09	80	98	99	25	77	50	03	32	36	63	65	75	94	19	95	88
60	77	46	63	71	69	44	22	03	85	14	48	69	13	30	50	33	24
60	08	19	29	36	72	30	27	50	64	85	72	75	29	87	05	75	01
80	45	86	99	02	34	87	08	86	84	49	76	24	08	01	86	29	11
53	84	49	63	26	65	72	84	85	63	26	02	75	26	92	62	40	67
69	84	12	94	51	36	17	02	15	29	16	52	56	43	26	22	08	62
37	77	13	10	02	18	31	19	32	85	31	94	81	43	31	58	33	51

THE ROLE OF COMPUTERS IN SIMULATION

DISCUSSION QUESTIONS

1. State, in order, the seven steps an operations manager should perform when using simulation to analyze a problem.
2. List the advantages of simulation.
3. List the disadvantages of simulation.
4. Explain the difference between *simulated* average demand and *expected* average demand.
5. What is the role of random numbers in a Monte Carlo simulation?
6. Why might the results of a simulation differ each time you make a run?
7. What is Monte Carlo simulation? What principles underlie its use, and what steps are followed in applying it?
8. List six ways that simulation can be used in business.
9. Why is simulation such a widely used technique?

10. What are the advantages of special-purpose simulation languages?
11. In the simulation of an order policy for drills at Simkin's hardware (Example F3 in your text), would the results (of Table F.10) change significantly if a longer period were simulated? Why is the 10-day simulation valid or invalid?
12. Why is a computer necessary in conducting a real-world simulation?
13. Why might a manager be forced to use simulation instead of an analytical model in dealing with a problem of
    (a) inventory order policy?
    (b) ships docking in a port to unload?
    (c) bank-teller service windows?
    (d) the U.S. economy?

PROBLEMS*

The problems that follow involve simulations that can be done by hand. However, to obtain accurate and meaningful results, long periods must be simulated. This task is usually handled by a computer. If you are able to program some of the problems in Excel or a computer language with which you are familiar, we suggest you try to do so. If not, the hand simulations will still help you understand the simulation process.

F.1 The daily demand for tuna sandwiches at a Roosevelt University cafeteria vending machine is either 8, 9, 10, or 11, with probabilities 0.4, 0.3, 0.2, or 0.1, respectively. Assume the following random numbers have been generated: 09, 55, 73, 67, 53, 59, 04, 23, 88, and 84. Using these numbers, generate daily sandwich sales for 10 days.

F.2 The number of machine breakdowns per day at Kristen Hodge's factory is either 0, 1, or 2, with probabilities 0.5, 0.3, or 0.2, respectively. The following random numbers have been generated: 13, 14, 02, 18, 31, 19, 32, 85, 31, and 94. Use these numbers to generate the number of breakdowns for 10 consecutive days. What proportion of these days had at least 1 breakdown?

F.3 The table below shows the partial results of a Monte Carlo simulation. Assume that the simulation began at 8:00 A.M. and there is only one server.

CUSTOMER NUMBER	ARRIVAL TIME	SERVICE TIME
1	8:01	6
2	8:06	7
3	8:09	8
4	8:15	6
5	8:20	6

a) When does service begin for customer number 3?
b) When will customer number 5 leave?
c) What is the average waiting time in line?
d) What is the average time in the system?

F.4 Barbara Flynn sells papers at a newspaper stand for $.35. The papers cost her $.25, giving her a $.10 profit on each one she sells. From past experience Barbara knows that
a) 20% of the time she sells 100 papers.
b) 20% of the time she sells 150 papers.
c) 30% of the time she sells 200 papers.
d) 30% of the time she sells 250 papers.
Assuming that Barbara believes the cost of a lost sale to be $.05 and any unsold papers cost her $.25, simulate her profit outlook over 5 days if she orders 200 papers for each of the 5 days. Use the following random numbers: 52, 06, 50, 88, and 53.

*Note: **P** means the problem may be solved with POM for Windows; ✖ means the problem may be solved with Excel; and **P✖** means the problem may be solved with POM for Windows and/or Excel. Note that Excel OM does not include a simulation module because Excel already has built-in simulation capabilities.

Pₓ . F.5 Children's Hospital is studying the number of emergency surgery kits that it uses on weekends. Over the las weekends the number of kits used is as follows:

NUMBER OF KITS	FREQUENCY
4	4
5	6
6	10
7	12
8	8

The following random numbers have been generated: 11, 52, 59, 22, 03, 03, 50, 86, 85, 15, 32, 47. Simulate 12 nights of emergency kit usage. What is the average number of kits used during these 12 nights?

× : F.6 Susan Sherer's grocery store has noted the following figures with regard to the number of people who arrive at the store's three checkout stands and the time it takes to check them out:

ARRIVALS/MIN.	FREQUENCY
0	.3
1	.5
2	.2

SERVICE TIME IN MIN.	FREQUENCY
1	.1
2	.3
3	.4
4	.2

Simulate the utilization of the three checkout stands over 5 minutes, using the following random numbers: 07, 60, 77, 49, 76, 95, 51, 16, and 14. Record the results at the end of the 5-minute period. Start at time = 0.

Pₓ . F.7 A warehouse manager at Mary Beth Marrs Corp. needs to simulate the demand placed on a product which does not fit standard models. The concept being measured is "demand during lead time," where both lead time and daily demand are variable. The historical record for this product, along with the cumulative distribution, appear below. Random numbers have been generated to simulate the next 5 order cycles; they are 91, 45, 37, 65, and 51. What are the five demand values? What is their average?

DEMAND DURING LEAD TIME	PROBABILITY	CUMULATIVE PROBABILITY
100	.01	.01
120	.15	.16
140	.30	.46
160	.15	.61
180	.04	.65
200	.10	.75
220	.25	1.00

× : F.8 The time between arrivals at the drive-through window of Barry Harmon's fast-food restaurant follows the distribution given below. The service-time distribution is also given. Use the random numbers provided to simulate the activity of the first 4 arrivals. Assume that the window opens at 11:00 A.M. and that the first arrival occurs afterward, based on the first interarrival time generated.

TIME BETWEEN ARRIVALS	PROBABILITY	SERVICE TIME	PROBABILITY
1	.2	1	.3
2	.3	2	.5
3	.3	3	.2
4	.2		

Random numbers for arrivals: 14, 74, 27, 03
Random numbers for service times: 88, 32, 36, 24

At what time does the fourth customer leave the system?

F.9   Phantom Controls monitors and repairs control circuit boxes on elevators installed in multistory buildings in downtown Chicago. The company has the contract for 108 buildings. When a box malfunctions, Phantom installs a new one and rebuilds the failed unit in its repair facility located in Gary, Indiana. The data for failed boxes over the last 2 years is shown in the following table:

NUMBER OF FAILED BOXES PER MONTH	PROBABILITY
0	.10
1	.14
2	.26
3	.20
4	.18
5	.12

Simulate 2 years (24 months) of operation for Phantom and determine the average number of failed boxes per month from the simulation. Was it common to have fewer than 7 failures over 3 months of operation? (Start your simulation at the top of the 10th column of Table F.4 in your text and on page F-5 of this Lecture Guide, $RN = 37$, and go down in the table.)

F.10   The number of cars arriving at Wayne Froelich's Car Wash during the last 200 hours of operation is observed to be the following:

NUMBER OF CARS ARRIVING	FREQUENCY
3 or fewer	0
4	20
5	30
6	50
7	60
8	40
9 or more	0
	200

a)   Set up a probability and cumulative-probability distribution for the variable of car arrivals.
b)   Establish random-number intervals for the variable.
c)   Simulate 15 hours of car arrivals and compute the average number of arrivals per hour. Select the random numbers needed from column 1, Table F.4 in your text and on page F-5 of this Lecture Guide, beginning with the digits 52.

F.11   Leonard Presby's newsstand uses naive forecasting to order tomorrow's papers. The number of newspapers ordered corresponds to the previous day's demands. Today's demand for papers was 22. Presby buys the newspaper for $.20 and sells them for $.50. Whenever there is unsatisfied demand, Presby estimates the lost goodwill cost at $.10. Complete the table below, and answer the questions that follow.

DEMAND	PROBABILITY
21	.25
22	.15
23	.10
24	.20
25	.30

DAY	PAPERS ORDERED	RANDOM NUMBER	DEMAND	REVENUE	COST	GOODWILL COST	NET PROFIT
1	22	37					
2		19					
3		52					
4		8					
5		22					
6		61					

a)   What is the demand on day 3?
b)   What is the total net profit at the end of the 6 days?

c) What is the lost goodwill on day 6?

d) What is the net profit on day 2?

e) How many papers has Presby ordered for day 5?

F.12 Simkin's Hardware simulated an inventory-ordering policy for Ace electric drills that involved an order quantity of 10 drills, with a reorder point of 5. This first attempt to develop a cost-effective ordering strategy was illustrated in Table F.10 of Example F3 in your text. The brief simulation resulted in a total daily inventory cost of $6.65 in Example F4.

Simkin would now like to compare this strategy to one in which he orders 12 drills, with a reorder point of 6. Conduct a 10-day simulation and discuss the cost implications.

F.13 Every home football game for the last 8 years at Eastern State University has been sold out. The revenues from ticket sales are significant, but the sale of food, beverages, and souvenirs has contributed greatly to the overall profitability of the football program. One particular souvenir is the football program for each game. The number of programs sold at each game is described by the probability distribution given below:

NUMBER OF PROGRAMS SOLD	PROBABILITY
2,300	0.15
2,400	0.22
2,500	0.24
2,600	0.21
2,700	0.18

Each program costs $.80 to produce and sells for $2.00. Any programs that are not sold are donated to a recycling center and do not produce any revenue.

a) Simulate the sales of programs at 10 football games. Use the last column in the random-number table (Table F.4 in your text and on page F-5 of this Lecture Guide) and begin at the top of the column.

b) If the university decided to print 2,500 programs for each game, what would the average profits be for the 10 games that were simulated?

c) If the university decided to print 2,600 programs for each game, what would the average profits be for the 10 games that were simulated?

F.14 Refer to the data in Solved Problem F.1, in your text, which deals with Higgins Plumbing and Heating. Higgins has now collected 100 weeks of data and finds the following distribution for sales:

HOT-WATER HEATER SALES PER WEEK	NUMBER OF WEEKS THIS NUMBER WAS SOLD	HOT-WATER HEATER SALES PER WEEK	NUMBER OF WEEKS THIS NUMBER WAS SOLD
3	2	8	12
4	9	9	12
5	10	10	10
6	15	11	5
7	25		100

a) Assuming Higgins maintains a constant supply of 8 heaters, resimulate the number of stockouts incurred over a 20-week period.

b) Conduct this 20-week simulation two more times and compare your answers with those in part (a). Did they change significantly? Why or why not?

c) What is the new expected number of sales per week?

F.15 Taboo Tattoo and tanning has two tanning beds. One bed serves the company's regular members exclusively. The second bed serves strictly walk-in customers (those without appointments) on a first-come, first-served basis. Gary Clendenen, the store manager, has noticed on several occasions during the busy 5 hours of the day (2:00 P.M. until 7:00 P.M.) that potential walk-in customers will most often walk away from the store if they see one person already waiting for the second bed. He wonders if capturing this lost demand would justify adding a third bed. Leasing and maintaining a tanning bed costs Taboo $600 per month. The price paid per customer varies according to the time in the bed, but Gary has calculated the average net income for every 10 minutes of tanning time to be $2.00. A study of the pattern of arrivals during the busy hours and the time spent tanning has revealed the following:

TIME BETWEEN ARRIVALS (MINUTES)	PROBABILITY	TIME IN TANNING BED (MINUTES)	PROBABILITY
5	0.30	10	0.20
10	0.25	15	0.30
15	0.20	20	0.40
20	0.15	25	0.10
25	0.10		

a) Simulate 4 hours of operation (arrivals over 4 hours). Use the 14th column of Table F.4 (in your text and on page F-5 of this Lecture Guide) for arrival times and the 8th column for tanning times. Assume there is one person who has just entered the bed at 2:00 P.M. for a 20-minute tan. Indicate which customers balk at waiting for the bed to become available. How many customers were lost over the 5 hours?

b) If the store is open an average of 24 days a month, will capturing all lost sales justify adding a new tanning bed?

F.16   Jody Coffey owns and operates one of the largest Mercedes-Benz auto dealerships in Nebraska. In the past 36 months, her sales have ranged from a low of 6 new cars to a high of 12 new cars, as reflected in the following table:

SALES OF NEW CARS/MONTH	FREQUENCY
6	3
7	4
8	6
9	12
10	9
11	1
12	1
	36 months

Coffey believes that sales will continue during the next 24 months at about the same historical rates, and that delivery times will also continue to follow the following pace (stated in probability form):

DELIVERY TIME (MONTHS)	PROBABILITY
1	.44
2	.33
3	.16
4	.07
	1.00

Coffey's current policy is to order 14 cars at a time (two full truckloads, with 7 autos on each truck), and to place a new order whenever the stock on hand reaches 12 autos. What are the results of this policy when simulated over the next 2 years?

F.17   Refer to Problem F.16. Coffey establishes the following relevant costs: (1) carrying cost per Mercedes per month is $600; (2) cost of a lost sale averages $4,350; and (3) cost of placing an order is $570. What is the total inventory cost of the policy simulated in Problem F.16?

F.18   Refer to Problems F.16 and F.17. Coffey wishes to try a new simulated policy: ordering 21 cars per order, with a reorder point of 10 autos. Which policy is better, this one or the one formulated in Problems F.16 and F.17?

F.19   Johnny's Dynamo Dogs has a drive-through line. Customers arriving at this line during the busy hours (11:00 A.M. to 1:00 P.M.) either order items a la carte or on a value-meal basis. Currently 25% of meals are sold as value meals at an average contribution margin of $2.25. The a la carte meals earn $3.00 per meal but take longer to prepare and this slows the line. The following are the interarrival times that were recorded over the last 3 weeks of operation.

INTERARRIVAL TIMES FOR 500 OBSERVATIONS	
TIME BETWEEN ARRIVALS (MINUTES)	NUMBER OF OCCURRENCES
1	100
2	150
3	125
4	100
5	25

In addition, the following service times for a la carte and value meals were recorded:

CUSTOMER SERVICE TIMES FOR 500 ORDERS OF EACH TYPE			
SERVICE TIME (MINUTES)	A LA CARTE	SERVICE TIME (MINUTES)	VALUE MEALS
1	50	1	100
2	125	2	175
3	175	3	125
4	150	4	100

John Fishback ("Johnny") has always observed that because of street traffic the store loses all of the potential customers who arrive when 4 cars are in the drive-through line (ie, the line never exceeds four customers).

a) Simulate a 1-hour time period for the current mix of a la carte and value meal orders. To start, assume two cars are in the line, each with 2-minute service times. Determine the number of meals served, the income from those meals, and the number of missed sales due to customers going elsewhere.

b) Johnny is contemplating a reduction of $.25 in the prices of value meals. He believes that this will increase the percentage of meals that are value meals from 25% to 40%. This will result in faster service times and fewer lost sales. Using simulation, determine if this change will be financially beneficial. Assume that the benefits will be available for 2 hours a day over a 20-day month.

F.20 General Hospital in Richmond, Virginia, has an emergency room that is divided into six departments: (1) an initial exam station to treat minor problems or make a diagnosis; (2) an X-ray department; (3) an operating room; (4) a cast-fitting room; (5) an observation room (for recovery and general observation before final diagnosis or release); and (6) an outprocessing department (where clerks check out patients and arrange for payment or insurance forms).

The probabilities that a patient will go from one department to another are presented in the following table:

FROM	TO	PROBABILITY
Initial exam at emergency room entrance	X-ray department	.45
	Operating room	.15
	Observation room	.10
	Outprocessing clerk	.30
X-ray department	Operating room	.10
	Cast-fitting room	.25
	Observation room	.35
	Outprocessing clerk	.30
Operating room	Cast-fitting room	.25
	Observation room	.70
	Outprocessing clerk	.05
Cast-fitting room	Observation room	.55
	X-ray department	.05
	Outprocessing clerk	.40
Observation room	Operating room	.15
	X-ray department	.15
	Outprocessing clerk	.70

a) Simulate the trail followed by 10 emergency room patients. Proceed, one patient at a time, from each one's entry at the initial exam station until he or she leaves through outprocessing. You should be aware that a patient can enter the same department more than once.

b) Using your simulation data, determine the chances that a patient enters the X-ray department twice.

F.21 Management of First Syracuse Bank is concerned over a loss of customers at its main office. One proposed solution calls for adding one or more drive-through teller stations so that customers can get quick service without parking. President David Pentico thinks the bank should risk only the cost of installing one drive-through. He is informed by his staff that the cost (amortized over a 20-year period) of building a drive-through is $12,000 per year. It also costs $16,000 per year in wages and benefits to staff each new teller window.

The director of management analysis, Marilyn Hart, believes that the following two factors encourage the immediate construction of two drive-through stations. According to a recent article in *Banking Research* magazine, customers who wait in long lines for drive-through teller service will cost banks an average of $1 per minute in lost goodwill. Also, although adding a second drive-through will cost an additional $16,000 in staffing, amortized construction costs can be cut to a total of $20,000 per year if two drive-throughs are installed simultaneously, instead of one at a time. To complete her analysis, Hart collected 1 month's worth of arrival and service rates at a competing bank. These data follow:

INTERARRIVAL TIMES FOR 1,000 OBSERVATIONS	
TIME BETWEEN ARRIVALS (MINUTES)	NUMBER OF OCCURRENCES
1	200
2	250
3	300
4	150
5	100

CUSTOMER SERVICE TIME FOR 1,000 CUSTOMERS	
SERVICE TIME (MINUTES)	NUMBER OF OCCURRENCES
1	100
2	150
3	350
4	150
5	150
6	100

a) Simulate a 1-hour time period, from 1:00 P.M. to 2:00 P.M., for a single-teller drive-through.
b) Simulate a 1-hour time period, from 1:00 P.M. to 2:00 P.M., for a two-teller system.
c) Conduct a cost analysis of the two options. Assume that the bank is open 7 hours per day and 200 days per year.

  : F.22   Kansas's M. J. Riley Corp. is the nation's largest manufacturer of industrial-size washing machines. A main ingredient in the production process is 8-by-10 foot sheets of stainless steel. The steel is used for both interior washer drums and outer casings.

Steel is purchased weekly on a contractual basis from the RTT Foundry, which, because of limited availability and lot sizing, can ship either 8,000 or 11,000 square feet of stainless steel each week. When Riley's weekly order is placed, there is a 45% chance that 8,000 square feet will arrive and a 55% chance of receiving the larger-size order.

Riley uses the stainless steel on a stochastic (nonconstant) basis. The probabilities of demand each week are as follows:

STEEL NEEDED PER WEEK (SQ. FT)	PROBABILITY
6,000	.05
7,000	.15
8,000	.20
9,000	.30
10,000	.20
11,000	.10

Riley has a capacity to store no more than 25,000 square feet of steel at any time. Because of the contract, orders *must* be placed each week regardless of on-hand supply.

a) Simulate stainless steel order arrivals and use for 20 weeks. (Begin the first week with a starting inventory of 0.) If an end-of-week inventory is ever negative, assume that "back orders" are permitted and fill the demand from the next arriving order.
b) Should Riley add more storage area? If so, how much? If not, comment on its present system.

INTERNET HOMEWORK PROBLEMS

See our Internet homepage at **www.prenhall.com/heizer** for these additional homework problems: F.23 through F.29.

CASE STUDY

Alabama Airlines' Call Center

Alabama Airlines opened its doors in December 2001 as a commuter service with its headquarters and hub located in Birmingham. The airline was started and managed by two former pilots, David Douglas and Andrew Pollard. It acquired a fleet of 12 used prop-jet planes and the airport gates vacated by Delta Airlines' 2001 downsizing due to terrorist attacks.

With business growing quickly, Douglas turned his attention to Alabama Air's "800" reservations system. Between midnight and 6:00 A.M., only one telephone reservations agent had been on duty. The time between incoming calls during this period is distributed as shown in Table 1. Carefully observing and timing the agent, Douglas estimated that the time required to process passenger inquiries is distributed as shown in Table 2.

TABLE 1 ■ Incoming Call Distribution

TIME BETWEEN CALLS (MINUTES)	PROBABILITY
1	.11
2	.21
3	.22
4	.20
5	.16
6	.10

All customers calling Alabama Air go "on hold" and are served in the order of the calls unless the reservations agent is available for immediate service. Douglas is deciding whether a second agent should be on duty to cope with customer demand. To maintain customer satisfaction, Alabama Air wants a customer to be "on hold" for no more than 3 to 4 minutes; it also wants to maintain a "high" operator utilization.

Furthermore, the airline is planning a new TV advertising campaign. As a result, it expects an increase in "800" line phone inquiries. Based on similar campaigns in the past, the incoming call distribution from midnight to 6:00 A.M. is expected to be as shown in Table 3. (The same service time distribution will apply.)

TABLE 2 ■ Service-Time Distribution

TIME TO PROCESS CUSTOMER INQUIRIES (MINUTES)	PROBABILITY
1	.20
2	.19
3	.18
4	.17
5	.13
6	.10
7	.03

TABLE 3 ■ Incoming Call Distribution

TIME BETWEEN CALLS (MINUTES)	PROBABILITY
1	.22
2	.25
3	.19
4	.15
5	.12
6	.07

Discussion Questions

1. Given the original call distribution, what would you advise Alabama Air to do for the current reservation system? Create a simulation model to investigate the scenario. Describe the model carefully and justify the duration of the simulation, assumptions, and measures of performance.

2. What are your recommendations regarding operator utilization and customer satisfaction if the airline proceeds with the advertising campaign?

Source: Professor Zbigniew H. Przasnyski, Loyola Marymount University. Reprinted by permission.

APPENDIX I   NORMAL CURVE AREAS

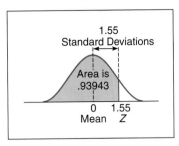

To find the area under the normal curve, you can apply either Table I.1 or Table I.2. In Table I.1, you must know how many standard deviations that point is to the right of the mean. Then, the area under the normal curve can be read directly from the normal table. For example, the total area under the normal curve for a point that is 1.55 standard deviations to the right of the mean is .93943.

TABLE I.1

	.00	.01	.02	.03	.04	.05	.06	.07	.08	.09
.0	.50000	.50399	.50798	.51197	.51595	.51994	.52392	.52790	.53188	.53586
.1	.53983	.54380	.54776	.55172	.55567	.55962	.56356	.56749	.57142	.57535
.2	.57926	.58317	.58706	.59095	.59483	.59871	.60257	.60642	.61026	.61409
.3	.61791	.62172	.62552	.62930	.63307	.63683	.64058	.64431	.64803	.65173
.4	.65542	.65910	.66276	.66640	.67003	.67364	.67724	.68082	.68439	.68793
.5	.69146	.69497	.69847	.70194	.70540	.70884	.71226	.71566	.71904	.72240
.6	.72575	.72907	.73237	.73536	.73891	.74215	.74537	.74857	.75175	.75490
.7	.75804	.76115	.76424	.76730	.77035	.77337	.77637	.77935	.78230	.78524
.8	.78814	.79103	.79389	.79673	.79955	.80234	.80511	.80785	.81057	.81327
.9	.81594	.81859	.82121	.82381	.82639	.82894	.83147	.83398	.83646	.83891
1.0	.84134	.84375	.84614	.84849	.85083	.85314	.85543	.85769	.85993	.86214
1.1	.86433	.86650	.86864	.87076	.87286	.87493	.87698	.87900	.88100	.88298
1.2	.88493	.88686	.88877	.89065	.89251	.89435	.89617	.89796	.89973	.90147
1.3	.90320	.90490	.90658	.90824	.90988	.91149	.91309	.91466	.91621	.91774
1.4	.91924	.92073	.92220	.92364	.92507	.92647	.92785	.92922	.93056	.93189
1.5	.93319	.93448	.93574	.93699	.93822	.93943	.94062	.94179	.94295	.94408
1.6	.94520	.94630	.94738	.94845	.94950	.95053	.95154	.95254	.95352	.95449
1.7	.95543	.95637	.95728	.95818	.95907	.95994	.96080	.96164	.96246	.96327
1.8	.96407	.96485	.96562	.96638	.96712	.96784	.96856	.96926	.96995	.97062
1.9	.97128	.97193	.97257	.97320	.97381	.97441	.97500	.97558	.97615	.97670
2.0	.97725	.97784	.97831	.97882	.97932	.97982	.98030	.98077	.98124	.98169
2.1	.98214	.98257	.98300	.98341	.98382	.98422	.98461	.98500	.98537	.98574
2.2	.98610	.98645	.98679	.98713	.98745	.98778	.98809	.98840	.98870	.98899
2.3	.98928	.98956	.98983	.99010	.99036	.99061	.99086	.99111	.99134	.99158
2.4	.99180	.99202	.99224	.99245	.99266	.99286	.99305	.99324	.99343	.99361
2.5	.99379	.99396	.99413	.99430	.99446	.99461	.99477	.99492	.99506	.99520
2.6	.99534	.99547	.99560	.99573	.99585	.99598	.99609	.99621	.99632	.99643
2.7	.99653	.99664	.99674	.99683	.99693	.99702	.99711	.99720	.99728	.99736
2.8	.99744	.99752	.99760	.99767	.99774	.99781	.99788	.99795	.99801	.99807
2.9	.99813	.99819	.99825	.99831	.99836	.99841	.99846	.99851	.99856	.99861
3.0	.99865	.99869	.99874	.99878	.99882	.99886	.99899	.99893	.99896	.99900
3.1	.99903	.99906	.99910	.99913	.99916	.99918	.99921	.99924	.99926	.99929
3.2	.99931	.99934	.99936	.99938	.99940	.99942	.99944	.99946	.99948	.99950
3.3	.99952	.99953	.99955	.99957	.99958	.99960	.99961	.99962	.99964	.99965
3.4	.99966	.99968	.99969	.99970	.99971	.99972	.99973	.99974	.99975	.99976
3.5	.99977	.99978	.99978	.99979	.99980	.99981	.99981	.99982	.99983	.99983
3.6	.99984	.99985	.99985	.99986	.99986	.99987	.99987	.99988	.99988	.99989
3.7	.99989	.99990	.99990	.99990	.99991	.99991	.99992	.99992	.99992	.99992
3.8	.99993	.99993	.99993	.99994	.99994	.99994	.99994	.99995	.99995	.99995
3.9	.99995	.99995	.99996	.99996	.99996	.99996	.99996	.99996	.99997	.99997

Source: From Richard I. Levin and Charles A. Kirkpatrick, *Quantitative Approaches to Management*, 4th ed. Copyright © 1978, 1975, 1971, 1965 by McGraw-Hill, Inc. Used with permission of McGraw-Hill Book Company.

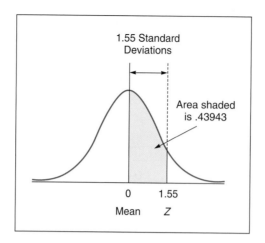

As an alternative to Table I.1, the numbers in Table I.2 represent the proportion of the total area away from the mean, μ, to one side. For example, the area between the mean and a point that is 1.55 standard deviations to its right is .43943.

z	.00	.01	.02	.03	.04	.05	.06	.07	.08	.09
0.0	.00000	.00399	.00798	.01197	.01595	.01994	.02392	.02790	.03188	.03586
0.1	.03983	.04380	.04776	.05172	.05567	.05962	.06356	.06749	.07142	.07535
0.2	.07926	.08317	.08706	.09095	.09483	.09871	.10257	.10642	.11026	.11409
0.3	.11791	.12172	.12552	.12930	.13307	.13683	.14058	.14431	.14803	.15173
0.4	.15542	.15910	.16276	.16640	.17003	.17364	.17724	.18082	.18439	.18793
0.5	.19146	.19497	.19847	.20194	.20540	.20884	.21226	.21566	.21904	.22240
0.6	.22575	.22907	.23237	.23565	.23891	.24215	.24537	.24857	.25175	.25490
0.7	.25804	.26115	.26424	.26730	.27035	.27337	.27637	.27935	.28230	.28524
0.8	.28814	.29103	.29389	.29673	.29955	.30234	.30511	.30785	.31057	.31327
0.9	.31594	.31859	.32121	.32381	.32639	.32894	.33147	.33398	.33646	.33891
1.0	.34134	.34375	.34614	.34850	.35083	.35314	.35543	.35769	.35993	.36214
1.1	.36433	.36650	.36864	.37076	.37286	.37493	.37698	.37900	.38100	.38298
1.2	.38493	.38686	.38877	.39065	.39251	.39435	.39617	.39796	.39973	.40147
1.3	.40320	.40490	.40658	.40824	.40988	.41149	.41309	.41466	.41621	.41174
1.4	.41924	.42073	.42220	.42364	.42507	.42647	.42786	.42922	.43056	.43189
1.5	.43319	.43448	.43574	.43699	.43822	.43943	.44062	.44179	.44295	.44408
1.6	.44520	.44630	.44738	.44845	.44950	.45053	.45154	.45254	.45352	.45449
1.7	.45543	.45637	.45728	.45818	.45907	.45994	.46080	.46164	.46246	.46327
1.8	.46407	.46485	.46562	.46638	.46712	.46784	.46856	.46926	.46995	.47062
1.9	.47128	.47193	.47257	.47320	.47381	.47441	.47500	.47558	.47615	.47670
2.0	.47725	.47778	.47831	.47882	.47932	.47982	.48030	.48077	.48124	.48169
2.1	.48214	.48257	.48300	.48341	.48382	.48422	.48461	.48500	.48537	.48574
2.2	.48610	.48645	.48679	.48713	.48745	.48778	.48809	.48840	.48870	.48899
2.3	.48928	.48956	.48983	.49010	.49036	.49061	.49086	.49111	.49134	.49158
2.4	.49180	.49202	.49224	.49245	.49266	.49286	.49305	.49324	.49343	.49361
2.5	.49379	.49396	.49413	.49430	.49446	.49461	.49477	.49492	.49506	.49520
2.6	.49534	.49547	.49560	.49573	.49585	.49598	.49609	.49621	.49632	.49643
2.7	.49653	.49664	.49674	.49683	.49693	.49702	.49711	.49720	.49728	.49736
2.8	.49744	.49752	.49760	.49767	.49774	.49781	.49788	.49795	.49801	.49807
2.9	.49813	.49819	.49825	.49831	.49836	.49841	.49846	.49851	.49856	.49861
3.0	.49865	.49869	.49874	.49878	.49882	.49886	.49889	.49893	.49897	.49900
3.1	.49903	.49906	.49910	.49913	.49916	.49918	.49921	.49924	.49926	.49929

TABLE I.2

APPENDIX II SOLUTIONS TO EVEN-NUMBERED PROBLEMS

Chapter 1

1.2 2 valves/hr.

1.4 Varies by site and source.

1.6 Productivity of labor: 9.3%
Productivity of resin: 11.1%
Productivity of capital: −10.0%
Productivity of energy: 6.1%

1.8 **(a)** .0096 rugs/labor-dollar
(b) .00787 rugs/dollar

1.10 Productivity of capital dropped, labor and energy productivity increased.

1.12 Before: 25 boxes/hr.
After: 27.08 boxes/hr.
Increase: 8.3%

1.14 Labor change: 0.0%
Investment change: 22.5%

Chapter 2

2.2 Cost leadership: Sodhexo–Mariott
Response: a catering firm
Differentiation: a fine-dining restaurant

2.4 The first few:
Arrow; Bidermann International, France
Braun; Gillette, U.S.
Lotus Autos; Proton, Malaysia
Firestone; Bridgestone, Japan
Godiva; Campbell Soup, U.S.

2.6 Some general thoughts to get you going:
(a) Energy costs change the cost structure of airlines.
(b) Environmental constraints may force changes in process technology (paint manufacturing and application) and product design (autos).

2.8 Look at current ranking at **www.weforum.org/pfd/gcr**.

Chapter 3

3.2 Here are some detailed activities for the first two activities for Jacob's WBS:
1.11 Set initial goals for fund-raising.
1.12 Set strategy, including identifying sources and solicitation place.
1.13 Raise the funds.
1.21 Identify voters' concerns.
1.22 Analyze competitor's voting record.
1.23 Establish position on issues.

3.4

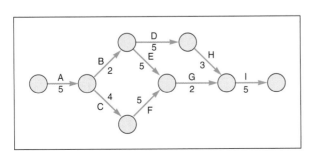

A-C-F-G-I is critical path; 21 days.
This is an AOA network.

3.6 **(a)**

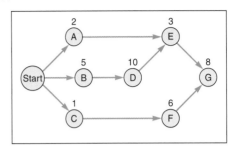

(b) B-D-E-G
(c) 26 days
(d)

Activity	Slack
A	13
B	0
C	11
D	0
E	0
F	11
G	0

3.8 **(a)**

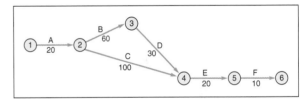

(b) Project completion time = 150 hr.

3.10

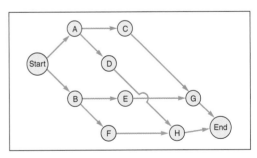

3.12 **(a)**

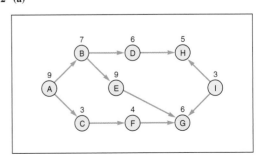

(b) A, B, E, G, I, is critical path.
(c) 34 wk.

3.14 A, 5.83, 0.69   G, 2.17, 0.25
      B, 3.67, 0.11   H, 6.00, 1.00
      C, 2.00, 0.11   I, 11.00, 0.11
      D, 7.00, 0.11   J, 16.33, 1.00
      E, 4.00, 0.44   K, 7.33, 1.78
      F, 10.00, 1.78

3.16 .946

3.18 Critical path currently is C-E for 12 days. $1,100 to crash by 4 days. Watch for parallel critical paths as you crash.

3.20 (a) 16 (A, D, G)
     (b) $12,300
     (c) D; 1 wk. for $75
     (d) 7 wk.; $1,600

3.22 (a) A, C, E, H, I, K, M, N; 50 wk.
     (b) 82.1%

3.24 (a) .0228
     (b) .3085
     (c) .8413
     (d) .9772

3.26 (a)

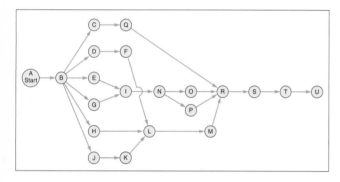

     (b) Critical path is A, B, J, K, L, M, R, S, T, U for 18 days.
     (c) i   No, transmissions and drivetrains are not on the critical path.
        ii   No, halving engine-building time will only reduce the critical path by 1 day.
        iii No, it is not on the critical path.
     (d) Reallocating workers not involved with critical-path activities to activities along the critical path will reduce the critical path length.

Chapter 4

4.2 (a) None obvious.
    (b) 7, 7.67, 9, 10, 11, 11, 11.33, 11, 9
    (c) 6.4, 7.8, 11, 9.6, 10.9, 12.2, 10.5, 10.6, 8.4
    (d) The 3-yr. moving average.

4.4 (a) 41.6
    (b) 42.3
    (c) Banking industry's seasonality.

4.6 (b) Naive = 23; 3-mo. moving = 21.33; 6-mo. weighted = 20.6; trend = 20.67
    (c) Trend projection.

4.8 (a) 91.3
    (b) 89
    (c) MAD = 2.7
    (d) MSE = 13.35
    (e) MAPE = 2.99%

4.10 (a) 4.67, 5.00, 6.33, 7.67, 8.33, 8.00, 9.33, 11.67, 13.7
     (b) 4.50, 5.00, 7.25, 7.75, 8.00, 8.25, 10.00, 12.25, 14.0

4.12 3-yr. Moving Average MAD = 2.54
     3-yr. Weighted Moving Average MAD = 2.31* (Best)
     Exponential Smoothing MAD = 2.4

4.14 α = .6 Exponential Smoothing MAD = 5.06
     α = .9 Exponential Smoothing MAD = 3.7
     3-yr. Moving Average MAD = 6.2
     Trend Projection MAD = 0.64* (Best)

4.16 $y = 421 + 33.6x$. When $x = 6$, $y = 622.8$.

4.18 MAD (α = .3) = 74.6
     MAD (3-yr. moving average) = 67.0
     MAD (Trend) = 5.6* (Best)

4.20 α = .1, β = .8 August forecast = $71,303; MSE = 12.7 for β = .8 vs. MSE = 18.87 for β = .2 in Problem 4.19.

4.22 Confirm that you match the numbers in Table 4.1.

4.24 (a) Observations do not form a straight line but do cluster about one.
     (b) $y = 1 + 1x$
     (c) 10 drums

4.26 270, 390, 189, 351 for fall, winter, spring, and summer, respectively.

4.28 Index is 0.709, winter; 1.037, spring; 1.553, summer; 0.700, fall.

4.30 (a) 337
     (b) 380
     (c) 423

4.32 (a) $y = 50 + 18x$
     (b) $410

4.34 (a) 28
     (b) 43
     (c) 58

4.36 (a) $452.50
     (b) Request is higher than predicted, so seek additional documentation.
     (c) Include other variables (such as a destination cost index) to try to increase r and r^2.

4.38 (a) $y = -.158 + .1308x$
     (b) 2.719
     (c) $r = .966$; $r^2 = .934$

4.40 131.2 → 72.7 patients; 90.6 → 50.6 patients

4.42 (a) They need more data and must be able to address seasonal *and* trend factors.
     (b) Try to create your own naïve model because seasonality is strong.
     (c) Compute and graph your forecast.

4.44 Trend adjustment does not appear to give any significant improvement.

4.46 (a) $y = 1.03 + .0034x$, $r^2 = .479$
     (b) For $x = 350$; $Y = 2.22$
     (c) For $x = 800$; $Y = 3.75$
     (Some rounding may occur, depending on software.)

4.48 (a) $\text{Sales}_{(x)} = -9.349 + .1121$ (contracts)
     (b) $r = .8963$; $S_{xy} = 1.3408$

Chapter 5

5.2 House-of-quality for a lunch:

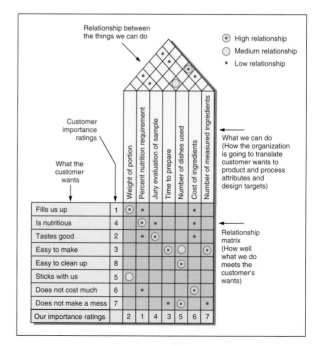

5.4 Individual answer. Build a house-of-quality similar to the one shown in Problem 5.2, entering the *wants* on the left and entering the *hows* at the top.

5.6 Assembly chart for a ballpoint pen:

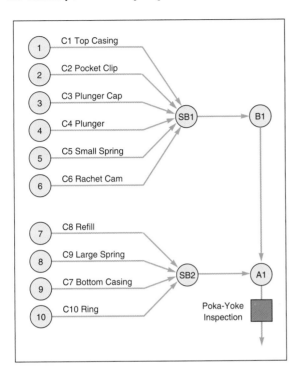

5.8 Assembly chart for a table lamp:

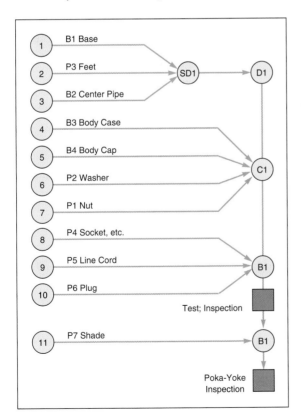

5.10 *Possible strategies*:

Notebook computers (growth phase):
Increase capacity and improve balance of production system.
Attempt to make production facilities more efficient.

Palm-held computer (introductory phase):
Increase R & D to better define required product characteristics.
Modify and improve production process.
Develop supplier and distribution systems.

Hand calculator (decline phase):
Concentrate on production and distribution cost reduction.

5.12 EMV of Proceed = $49,500,000
EMV of Do Value Analysis = $55,025,000
Therefore, Do Value Analysis.

5.14

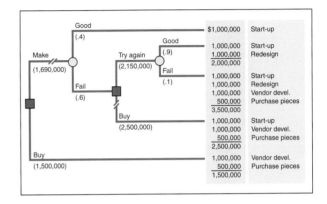

(a) The best decision would be to buy the semiconductors. This decision has an expected payoff of $1,500,000.
(b) Expected monetary value, minimum cost.
(c) The worst that can happen is that Ritz ends up buying the semiconductors and spending $3,500,000.
The best that can happen is that they make the semiconductors and spend only $1,000,000.

5.16 EMV (Design A) = $875,000
EMV (Design B) = $700,000

Chapter 6

6.2 Individual answer, in the style of Figure 6.5(b).
6.4 Individual answer, in the style of Figure 6.5(f).
6.6 Partial flowchart for planning a party:

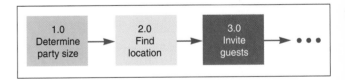

6.8

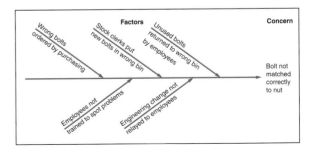

6.10 Individual answer, in the style of Figure 6.6 in the chapter.

6.12 Pareto chart, in the style of Example 1 with parking/drives most frequent, pool second, etc.

6.14 Materials: e and f; Methods: a, c, h; Manpower: b, g; Machinery: l; Ambiguous: d, i, j, k, m

6.16 **(a)** A scatter diagram in the style of Figure 6.5(b) that shows a strong positive relationship between shipments and defects.

(b) A scatter diagram in the style of Figure 6.5(b) showing a mild relationship between shipments and turnover.

(c) A Pareto chart in the style of Figure 6.5(d) showing frequency of each type of defect.

(d) A fish-bone chart in the style of Figure 6.5(c) with the 4 Ms showing possible causes of increasing defects in shipments.

Chapter 6 Supplement

S6.2 $UCL_{\bar{x}} = 52.31$

$LCL_{\bar{x}} = 47.69$

S6.4 $UCL_{\bar{x}} = 46.966$

$LCL_{\bar{x}} = 45.034$

$UCL_R = 4.008$

$LCL_R = 0$

S6.6 $UCL_{\bar{x}} = 3.728$

$LCL_{\bar{x}} = 2.236$

$UCL_R = 2.336$

$LCL_R = 0.0$

The process is in control.

S6.8 **(a)** $UCL_{\bar{x}} = 10.42$

$LCL_{\bar{x}} = 9.66$

$UCL_R = 1.187$

$LCL_R = 0$

(b) Yes.

(c) Increase sample size.

S6.10 **(a)** 1.36, 0.61

(b) Using $\sigma_{\bar{x}}$, $UCL_{\bar{x}} = 11.83$ and $LCL_{\bar{x}} = 8.17$.

Using A_2, $UCL_{\bar{x}} = 11.90$ and $LCL_{\bar{x}} = 8.10$.

(c) $UCL_R = 6.98$; $LCL_R = 0$

(d) Yes.

S6.12 $UCL_{\bar{x}} = 47.308$; $LCL_{\bar{x}} = 46.692$

$UCL_R = 1.777$; $LCL_R = .223$

Averages are increasing.

S6.14

UCL	LCL
.062	0
.099	0
.132	0
.161	0
.190	.01

S6.16 $UCL_p = .0313$; $LCL_p = 0$

S6.18 $UCL_p = .0901$; $LCL_p = 0$

Increased control limits by more than 50%. No.

S6.20 $UCL_p = .0581$

$LCL_p = 0$

S6.22 $UCL_c = 33.4$

$LCL_c = 7$ (or 6.6)

S6.24 $UCL_c = 26.063$

$LCL_c = 3.137$

S6.26 $C_p = 1.0$. The process is barely capable.

S6.28 $C_{pk} = 1.125$. Process *is* centered and will produce within tolerance.

S6.30 $C_{pk} = .166$

S6.32 AOQ = 2.2%

S6.34 **(a)** Yes, the process is in control for both $\bar{x}$- and R-charts.

(b) They support West's claim. But variance from the mean needs to be reduced and controlled.

Chapter 7

7.2

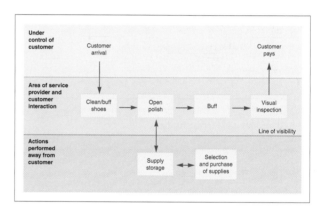

7.4

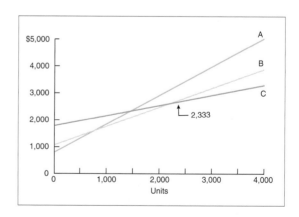

7.6 GPE is best below 100,000.

FMS is best between 100,000 and 300,000.

DM is best over 300,000.

7.8 Optimal process will change at 100,000 and 300,000.

7.10 **(a)**

(b) Plan c

(c) Plan b

7.12 Rent HP software, since projected volume of 80 is above the crossover point of 75.

Chapter 7 Supplement

S7.2 69.2%

S7.4 88.9%

S7.6 81 chairs

S7.8 Design = 88,920
Fabrication = 160,680
Finishing = 65,520

S7.10 (a) 4,590 in excess capacity
(b) 2,090 in excess capacity

S7.12 (a) 6,250 units
(b) 7,000 units

S7.14 $x = 10,000$

S7.16 (a) 12,500 units
(b) $100,000
(c) $350,000

S7.18 $BEP_x = 25,000$

S7.20 Present equipment = $1,000 profit
New equipment = 0 profit

S7.22 (a) 50,000 bags
(b) $125,000
(c) 60,000 bags
(d) $150,000
(e) $7,500
(f) 0.0
(g) Indifferent at 75,000.
(h) Manual process below 75,000.
Mechanized process above 75,000.

S7.24 $BEP_\$ = \$7,584.83$ per mo.
Daily meals = 9

S7.26 (a) $986.19
(b) 140.9 servings

S7.28 Large line payoff = $100,000
Small line payoff = $66,000

S7.30 NPV = $20,280

S7.32 NPV = $1,765

S7.34 (a) Purchase two large ovens.
(b) Equal quality, equal capacity.
(c) Payments are made at end of each time period. And future interest rates are known.

Chapter 8

8.2 China, $1.44

8.4 India is $.05 less than elsewhere.

8.6 Atlanta = 53; Charlotte = 60; select Charlotte.

8.8 Hyde Park with 54.5 points.

8.10 Location C, with a total *weighted* score of 1,530.

8.12 Great Britain at 36.

8.14 Italy is highest.

8.16 (a) Site 1 up to 125, site 2 from 125 to 233, site 3 above 233
(b) Site 2

8.18 Local supplier, 0–4,800; A, 4,800–8,000; B, 8,000–13,333; C, above 13,333

8.20 (5.15, 7.31)

8.22 (a) (6.23, 6.08)

8.24 5.6 East, 4.8 North is the weighted location.

Chapter 9

9.2 Benders to room (area) 1; Materials to 2; Welders to 3; Drills to 4; Grinder to 5; and Lathes to 6; Trips × Distance = 13,000 ft.

9.4 Layout #1, distance = 600 with rooms fixed
Layout #2, distance = 602 with rooms fixed

9.6 Layout #4, distance = 609
Layout #5, distance = 478

9.8 Cycle time = 9.6 min.; 8 workstations with 63.8% efficiency is possible.

9.10 Cycle time = 6.67 min./unit. Multiple solutions with 5 stations. Here is a sample: A, F, G to station 1; B, C to station 2; D, E to station 3; H to station 4; and I, J to station 5.

9.12 (a) Minimum no. of workstations = 2.6 (or 3).
(b) Efficiency = 86.7%.
(c) Cycle time = 6.67 min./unit with 400 min./day; minimum no. of workstations = 1.95 (or 2).

9.14 Cycle time = .5 min./bottle. Possible assignments with 4 workstations yields efficiency = 90%.

9.16 Minimum (theoretical) = 4 stations. Efficiency = 80% with 5 stations. Several assignments with 5 are possible.

9.18 There are three alternatives each with an efficiency = 86.67%; 160 units can be produced.

9.20 (a) "Longest operating time," "most following tasks," and "ranked positional weight" each require 12 workstations and give efficiencies of 84.61%.
(b) "Ranked positional weight," with 11 workstations, and efficiency = 90.1%.

Chapter 10

10.2

Time	Operator	Time	Machine	Time
	Prepare Mill			
1	Load Mill	1	Idle	1
2		2		2
3	Idle	3	Mill Operating (Cutting Material)	3
4		4		4
5	Unload Mill	5	Idle	5
6		6		6

10.4 The first 10 steps of 10.4(a) are shown below. The remaining 10 steps are similar.

OPERATIONS CHART			SUMMARY						
PROCESS: CHANGE ERASER			SYMBOL		PRESENT		DIFF.		
ANALYST: _____					LH	RH	LH	RH	LH	RH
DATE: _____			○ OPERATIONS		1	8				
SHEET: 1 of 2			⇨ TRANSPORTS		3	8				
METHOD: PRESENT PROPOSED			□ INSPECTIONS		1					
REMARKS:			D DELAYS		15	4				
			▽ STORAGE							
			TOTALS		20	20				
LEFT HAND	DIST.	SYMBOL	SYMBOL	DIST.	RIGHT HAND				
1 Reach for pencil		⇨	D		Idle				
2 Grasp pencil		○	D		Idle				
3 Move to work area		⇨	⇨		Move to pencil top				
4 Hold pencil		D	○		Grasp pencil top				
5 Hold pencil		D	○		Remove pencil top				
6 Hold pencil		D	⇨		Set top aside				
7 Hold pencil		D	⇨		Reach for old eraser				
8 Hold pencil		D	○		Grasp old eraser				
9 Hold pencil		D	○		Remove old eraser				
10 Hold pencil		D	⇨		Set aside old eraser				

10.6 Individual solution.

10.8 The answer is similar to Solved Problem 10.1, but crew activities C and D become the limiting activities.

10.10 The first portion of the activity chart is shown below.

10.12 The first portion of the process chart is shown below.

Chapter 10 Supplement

S10.2 9.35 sec.

S10.4 11 sec.

S10.6 55 sec.

S10.8 2.8 min.

S10.10 6.183 min.

S10.12 (a) Element 1 = .437 min.
  Element 2 = 1.79 min.
  Element 3 = 3.83 min.
  (b) Element 1 = .37 min.
  Element 2 = 1.58 min.
  Element 3 = 3.45 min.
  (c) Standard time = 6.75 min.

S10.14 Standard time = 6.67 min.; without the nonconforming observations of sealing and sorting, standard time = 5.40 min.

S10.16 (a) Normal time = 3.083
  (b) Standard time = 3.85 min.

S10.18 $n = 426$

S10.20 (a) 45.36, 13.75, 3.6, 15.09
  (b) 91.53 min.
  (c) 96 samples

S10.22 (a) 47.55 min.
  (b) 75 samples

S10.24 $n = 347$

S10.26 73.7%

S10.28 6.55 sec.

S10.30 (a) Standard time = 3.69 min.
  (b) Normal time = 3.026 min.

Chapter 11

11.2 Donna Inc, 8.2; Kay Inc., 9.8

11.4 Individual responses. Issues might include: academics, location, financial support, size, facilities, etc.

11.6 (a) $3.13
  (b) $7.69

11.8 (a) Option a is most economical.
  (b) The customer requirements may demand a faster schedule.

11.10 (a) Go with faster subcontractor.
  (b) Internal production or testing may require a faster schedule.

Chapter 11 Supplement

S11.2 General electric at **www.geis.com** provides GE Global Exchange Services, which enable small and medium sized companies to take advantage of e-commerce.

S11.4 **www.freemarkets.com** provides online auctions for industrial parts, raw materials, commodities, and services.

S11.6 Any move toward "perfect markets" should put downward pressure on prices.

Chapter 12

12.2 A items are G2 and F3; B items are A2, C7, and D1; all others are C.

12.4 108 items

12.6 600 units

12.8 (a) 80 units
  (b) 73 units

12.10 2,100 units

12.12 (a) 149 valves
  (b) 74.5 valves
  (c) 27 orders
  (d) $9 \frac{1}{4}$ days
  (e) $1,341.64
  (f) 80 valves

12.14 (a) Order quantity variations have limited impact on total cost.
  (b) EOQ = 50

12.16 2,309 units

12.18 (a) 1,217 units
  (b) 1,095 = max. inventory
  (c) 8.22 production runs
  (d) $657.30

12.20 $51,000 without discount
  $49,912.50 with discount

12.22 Order in quantities of 100. Total cost = $752.63.

12.24 (a) EOQ = 410
  (b) Vendor Allen has slightly lower cost.
  (c) Optimal order quantity = 1,000 @ total cost of $128,920

12.26 (a) EOQ (A) = 336; EOQ (B) = 335
  (b) Order 1,200 from Vendor B.
  (c) At 1,200 lb., total cost = $161,275.
  (d) Storage space and perishability.

12.28 (a) Z = 1.88
  (b) Safety stock = $Z\sigma = 1.88(5) = 9.4$ drives
  (c) ROP = 59.4 drives

12.30 150 sets

12.32 EOQ = 442

12.34 17 poles

Chapter 13

13.2 Cost = $53,320
  No, plan 2 is better.

13.4 Cost = $214,000 for plan B
13.6 Plan D; $122,000; plan E is $129,000
13.8 Each answer you develop will differ.
13.10 Plan C, $92,000; plan D, $82,300 assuming initial inventory = 0
13.12 (a) Cost is $314,000.
    (b) Cost is $329,000 (but an alternative approach yields $259,000).
    (c) Cost is $222,000.
    (d) Plan C.
    (e) Plan C with lowest cost and steady employment.
13.14 $1,186,810
13.16 $100,750
13.18 $90,850
13.20 (a, b) Cost using O.T. and Abernathy = $198,125.
    (c) A case could be made for either position.
13.22 Current model = $9,200 in sales; proposed model yields $9,350, which is only slightly better.

Chapter 14

14.2 The time-phased plan for the gift bags is:

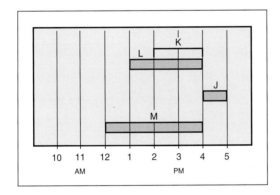

Someone should start on item "M" by noon.

14.4 Gross material requirements plan:

Item		Week								Lead Time (wk.)
			1	2	3	4	5	6	7	8	
S	Gross req								100		
	Order release						100				2
T	Gross req						100				
	Order release					100					1
U	Gross req						200				
	Order release				200						2
V	Gross req						100				
	Order release			100							2
W	Gross req						200				
	Order release	200									3
X	Gross req						100				
	Order release				100						1
Y	Gross req						400				
	Order release	400									2
Z	Gross req						600				
	Order release			600							1

14.6 Gross material requirements plan, modified to include the 20 units of U required for maintenance purposes:

Item		Week								Lead Time (wk.)
		1	2	3	4	5	6	7	8	
S	Gross req							100		
	Order release					100				2
T	Gross req						100			
	Order release				100					1
U	Gross req					200	20			
	Order release			200	20					2
V	Gross req					100				
	Order release		100							2
W	Gross req					200				
	Order release	200								3
X	Gross req					100				
	Order release		100							1
Y	Gross req				400	40				
	Order release	400	40							2
Z	Gross req				600	60				
	Order release		600	60						1

14.8 (a)

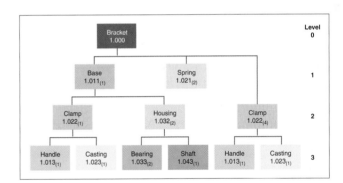

  (b) For 50 brackets, the gross requirements are for 50 bases, 100 springs, 250 clamps, 250 handles, 250 castings, 100 housings, 200 bearings, and 100 shafts.
  (c) For 50 brackets, net requirements are 25 bases, 100 springs, 125 clamps, 125 handles, 125 castings, 50 housings, 100 bearings, and 50 shafts.

14.10 (a) Gross material requirements plan for the first three items:

Item		Week											
		1	2	3	4	5	6	7	8	9	10	11	12
X1	Gross req								50		20		100
	Order release							50		20	100		
B1	Gross req								50		20		100
	Order release						50		20	100			
B2	Gross req								100		40		200
	Order release						100		40	200			

14.10 **(b)** The net materials requirement plan for the first two items:

Level: 0 Item:X1	Parent: Lead Time:					Quantity: Lot Size: L4L					
Week No.	1	2	3	4	5	6	7	8	9	10	11	12
Gross Requirement							50		20		100	
Scheduled Receipt												
On-Hand Inventory							50		0		0	
Net Requirement							0		20		100	
Planned Order Receipt									20		100	
Planned Order Release							20		100			

Level: 1 Item: B1	Parent: X1 Lead Time: 2					Quantity: 1X Lot Size: L4L					
Week No.	1	2	3	4	5	6	7	8	9	10	11	12
Gross Requirement									20		100	
Scheduled Receipt												
On-Hand Inventory									20		0	
Net Requirement									0		100	
Planned Order Receipt											100	
Planned Order Release									100			

14.12 Net material requirements schedule (only items A and H are shown):

	Week											
	1	2	3	4	5	6	7	8	9	10	11	12
A Gross required								100		50		150
On hand								0		0		0
Net required								100		50		150
Order receipt								100		50		150
Order release						100		50		150		
H Gross required								100		50		
On hand								0		0		
Net required								100		50		
Order receipt								100		50		
Order release							100		50			

14.14 **(a)**

Level	Description	Qty
0	A	1
1	B	1
2	C	1
2	D	1
3	E	1
1	F	1
2	G	1
2	H	1
3	E	1
3	C	1

(b) Solution for Items A, B, F:

Lot Size	Lead Time	On Hand	Safety Stock	Allo- cated	Low- Level Code	Item ID		Period (wk.)							
								1	2	3	4	5	6	7	8
Lot	1	0	—	—	0	A	Gross Requirements								10
for							Scheduled Receipts								
Lot							Projected On Hand								0
							Net Requirements								10
							Planned Receipts								10
							Planned Releases							10	
Lot	1	2	—	—	1	B	Gross Requirements							10^A	
for							Scheduled Receipts								
Lot							Projected On Hand	2	2	2	2	2	2	2	0
							Net Requirements							8	
							Planned Receipts							8	
							Planned Releases						8		
Lot	1	5	—	—	1	F	Gross Requirements							10^A	
for							Scheduled Receipts								
Lot							Projected On Hand	5	5	5	5	5	5	5	0
							Net Requirements							5	
							Planned Receipts							5	
							Planned Releases						5		

14.16 **(a)** Only item G changes.
  (b) Component F and 4 units of A will be delayed from week 6 to week 7.
  (c) Options include: delaying 4 units of A for 1 week; asking supplier of G to expedite production.

14.24 Selection for first 5 weeks:

Week	Units	Capacity Required (time)	Capacity Available (time)	Over/ (Under)	Production Scheduler's Action
1	60	3,900	2,250	1650	Lot split. Move 300 minutes (4.3 units) to week 2 and 1,350 minutes to week 3.
2	30	1,950	2,250	(300)	
3	10	650	2,250	(1,600)	
4	40	2,600	2,250	350	Lot split. Move 250 minutes to week 3. Operations split. Move 100 minutes to another machine, overtime, or subcontract.
5	70	4,550	2,250	2,300	Lot split. Move 1,600 minutes to week 6. Overlap operations to get product out door. Operations split. Move 700 minutes to another machine, overtime, or subcontract.

14.26 Individual answers: Use the Web page of the major vendors such as SAP, Oracle, and People Soft.

Chapter 15

15.2

15.4 **(a)** 1-D, 2-A, 3-C, 4-B
  (b) 40
15.6 A-61 to 4; A-60 to 1; A-53 to 3; A-56 to 5; A-52 to 2; A-59 to 6; 150 hr.
15.8 1–2 P.M. on A; 2–3 P.M. on C; 3–4 P.M. on B; 4–5 P.M. on Independent; 75.5 rating
15.10 **(a)** A, B, C, D, E
  (b) B, A, D, E, C
  (c) E, D, A, B, C
  (d) C, B, A, D, E
  SPT is best.
15.12 **(a)** A, B, C, D
  (b) B, C, A, D
  (c) D, A, C, B
  (d) C, B, D, A
  (e) D, C, A, B
  SPT is best on all measures.
15.14 **(a)** A, B, C, D, E
  (b) C, A, B, E, D
  (c) C, D, E, A, B
  (d) B, A, E, D, C
  EDD, then FCFS are best on lateness; SPT on other two measures.
15.16 1, 3, 4, 2, 5
15.18 E, D, C, A, B, F

14.18 EOQ = 57; Total cost = $1,630
14.20 $650
14.22 $455

Chapter 16

16.2 3.75, or 4 kanbans
16.4 Size of kanban = 66; number of kanbans = 5.9, or 6
16.6 **(a)** EOQ = 10 lamps
  (b) 200 orders/yr.
  (c) $200
16.8 7.26 min.
16.10 **(a)** Setup cost = $5.74
  (b) Setup time = 8.61 min.

Chapter 17

17.2 From Figure 17.2, about 13% overall reliability.
17.4 Expected daily breakdowns = 2.0
  Expected cost = $100 daily
17.6 **(a)** 5.0%
  (b) .00001026 failures/unit-hr.
  (c) .08985
  (d) 98.83
17.8 $R_s = .8145$
17.10 $R_p = .99925$
17.12 **(a)** $R_p = .984$
  (b) Increase by 11.1%.
17.14 $R = .7918$
17.16 **(a)** .972
  (b) .981
17.18 System B is slightly higher at .9397.

Quantitative Module A

A.2 **(a)**

Size of First Station	Good Market ($)	Fair Market ($)	Poor Market ($)	EV Under Equally Likely
Small	50,000	20,000	−10,000	20,000
Medium	80,000	30,000	−20,000	30,000
Large	100,000	30,000	−40,000	30,000
Very large	300,000	25,000	−160,000	55,000

(b) Maximax: Build a very large station.

(c) Maximin: Build a small station.

(d) Equally likely: Build a very large station.

A.4 EVPI = $13,800 − 12,200 = $1,600

where $13,800 = .3(22,000) + .5(12,000) + .2(6,000)

A.6 EVPI = $364,000 − $320,00 = $44,000

A.8 E(cost full-time) = $520

E(cost part-timers) = $475

A.10 Major expansion; EMV = $150,000

A.12 8 cases; EMV = $352.50

A.14 **(a)**

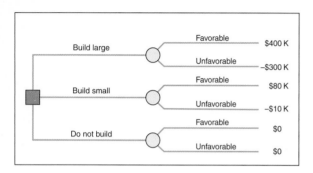

(b) Small plant with EMV = $26,000

(c) EVPI = $134,000

A.16 **(a)** Max EMV = $11,700

(b) EVPI = $13,200 − $11,700 = $1,500

A.18

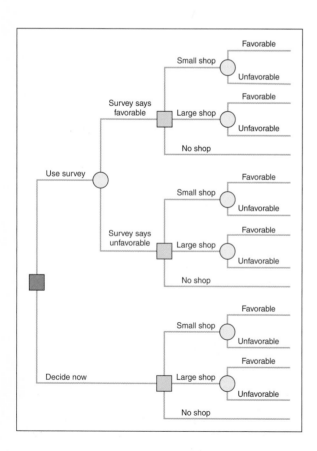

A.20 No information and build large; $4,500.

A.22

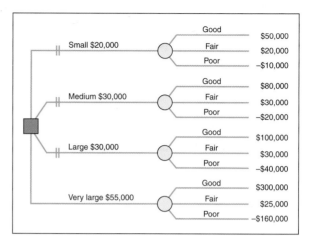

Quantitative Module B

B.2 Profit = $100 at $X = 0$, $Y = 10$

B.4 **(b)** Yes; $P = $3,000 at (75, 75) and (50, 150)

B.6 **(a)** Min $X_1 + 2X_2$

$X_1 + X_2 \geq 40$

$2X_1 + 4X_2 \geq 60$

$x_1 \leq 15$

(b) Cost = $.65 at (15, 25)

(c) 65¢

B.8 $x_1 = 200$, $x_2 = 0$, profit = $18,000

B.10 10 Alpha 4s, 24 Beta 5s, profit = $55,200

B.12 **(a)** $x_1 = 25.71$, $x_2 = 21.43$

(b) Cost = $68.57

B.14 **(a)** $x_1 = 7.95$, $x_2 = 5.95$, $x_3 = 12.6$, $P = $143.76

(b) No unused time.

(c) 26¢

(d) $7.86

B.16 Let X_{ij} = number of students bused from sector i to school j.

Objective: minimize total travel miles =

$$5X_{AB} + 8X_{AC} + 6X_{AE}$$
$$+ 0X_{BB} + 4X_{BC} + 12X_{BE}$$
$$+ 4X_{CB} + 0X_{CC} + 7X_{CE}$$
$$+ 7X_{DB} + 2X_{DC} + 5X_{DE}$$
$$+12X_{EB} + 7X_{EC} + 0X_{EE}$$

Subject to:

$X_{AB} + X_{AC} + X_{AE} = 700$ (number of students in sector A)

$X_{BB} + X_{BC} + X_{BE} = 500$ (number students in sector B)

$X_{CB} + X_{CC} + X_{CE} = 100$ (number students in sector C)

$X_{DB} + X_{DC} + X_{DE} = 800$ (number students in sector D)

$X_{EB} + X_{EC} + X_{EE} = 400$ (number students in sector E)

$X_{AB} + X_{BB} + X_{CB} + X_{DB} + X_{EB} \leq 900$ (school B capacity)

$X_{AC} + X_{BC} + X_{CC} + X_{DC} + X_{EC} \leq 900$ (school C capacity)

$X_{AE} + X_{BE} + X_{CE} + X_{DE} + X_{EE} \leq 900$ (school E capacity)

Solution: $X_{AB} = 400$

$X_{AE} = 300$

$X_{BB} = 500$

$X_{CC} = 100$

$X_{DC} = 800$

$X_{EE} = 400$

Distance = 5,400 "student miles"

B.18 Hire 30 workers; three solutions are feasible; two of these are:

16 begin at 7 A.M.

9 begin at 3 P.M.

2 begin at 7 P.M.

3 begin at 11 P.M.

An alternate optimum is:

3 begin at 3 A.M.

9 begin at 7 A.M.

7 begin at 11 A.M.

2 begin at 3 P.M.

9 begin at 7 P.M.

0 begin at 11 P.M.

B.20 Max $P = 9x_1 + 12x_2$

Subject to:

$x_1 + x_2 \leq 10$

$x_1 + 2x_2 \leq 12$

$x_1 = 8, x_2 = 2$; profit = $96

B.22 $x_1 = 14, x_2 = 33$, cost = 221

B.24 **(a)** $22.50–$30.00

(b) Shadow price for wiring = $5.00 between 210–280 hr.

B.26 **(a)** Minimize = $6X_{1A} + 5X_{1B} + 3X_{1C} + 8X_{2A} + 10X_{2B} + 8X_{2C}$
$+ 11X_{3A} + 14X_{3B} + 18X_{3C}$

Subject to:

$X_{1A} + X_{2A} + X_{3A} = 7$

$X_{1B} + X_{2B} + X_{3B} = 12$

$X_{1C} + X_{2C} + X_{3C} = 5$

$X_{1A} + X_{1B} + X_{1C} \leq 6$

$X_{2A} + X_{2B} + X_{2C} \leq 8$

$X_{3A} + X_{3B} + X_{3C} \leq 10$

(b) Minimum cost = $219,000

B.28 One approach results in 2,791 medical patients and 2,105 surgical patients, with a revenue of $9,551,659 per year (which can change slightly with rounding). This yields 61 medical beds and 29 surgical beds.

B.30 **(a)** Minimize total cost = $0.60X_1 + 2.35X_2 + 1.15X_3 + 2.25X_4$
$+ 0.58X_5 + 1.17X_6 + 0.33X_7$ subject to:

$295X_1 + 1,216X_2 + 394X_3 + 358X_4 + 128X_5 + 118X_6 + 279X_7 \leq 1,500$

$295X_1 + 1,216X_2 + 394X_3 + 358X_4 + 128X_5 + 118X_6 + 279X_7 \geq 900$

$.2X_1 + .2X_2 + 4.3X_3 + 3.2X_4 + 3.2X_5 + 14.1X_6 + 2.2X_7 \geq 4$

$16X_1 + 96X_2 + 9X_3 + 0.5X_4 + 0.8X_5 + 1.4X_6 + 0.5X_7 \leq 50$

$16X_1 + 81X_2 + 74X_3 + 83X_4 + 7X_5 + 14X_6 + 8X_7 \geq 26$

$22X_1 + 28X_5 + 19X_6 + 63X_7 \leq 50$

All $X_1 \geq 0$

(b) Each meal has a cost of $1.75.

(c) The meal is fairly well balanced (two meats, a green vegetable, and a potato). The weight of each item is realistic.

(d) This problem is very sensitive to changing food prices.

Quantitative Module C

C.2 Total cost = $2,000. Multiple optimal solutions exist. Cost after second iteration = $2,640; after third iteration = $2,160.

C.4 Optimal cost = $2,570

X-A = 50; X-C = 50; Y-B = 50; Z-B = 30; Z-C = 20; Z-Dummy = 25

C.6 **(a)** A-1, 10; B-1, 30; C-2, 60; A-3, 40; C-3, 15

(b) $1,775

C.8 Houston, $19,500

C.10 Total cost = $505

C.12 Initial cost = $260

Improved solution = $255

Final solution = $230

C.14 F1-W1, 1,000; F1-W4, 500; F2-W2, 2,000; F2-W3, 500; F3-W3, 1,500; F3-W4, 700; cost = $39,300

C.16 $60,900 with East St. Louis; $62,250 with St. Louis

Quantitative Module D

D.2 **(a)** 44%   **(d)** .53 min.

(b) .36 people   **(e)** 1.2 min.

(c) .8 people

D.4 **(a)** .5   **(d)** .5

(b) .5   **(e)** .05 hr.

(c) 1   **(f)** .1 hr.

D.6 **(a)** .667

(b) .667 min.

(c) 1.33

D.8 **(a)** .375

(b) 1.6 hr. (or .2 days)

(c) .225

(d) 0.141, 0.053, 0.020, 0.007

D.10 **(a)** 2.25

(b) .75

(c) .857 min. (.014 hr.)

(d) .64 min. (.011 hr.)

(e) 42%, 32%, 24%

D.12 **(a)** 6 trucks

(b) 12 min.

(c) .857

(d) .54

(e) $1,728/day

(f) Yes, save $3,096 in the first year.

D.14 **(a)** .666

(b) 1.33

(c) 10 sec.

D.16 **(a)** .113 hr. = 6.8 min.

(b) 1.13 cars

D.18 **(a)** .05

(b) .743

(c) .795

D.20 3, 2, 4 MDs, respectively

D.22 Individual responses.

Quantitative Module E

E.2 **(a)** 507 min.

(b) 456 min.

(c) 410 min.

(d) 369 min.

E.4 **(a)** 1,546 min.

(b) 2,872 min.

(c) 3,701 min.

(d) 6,779 min.

E.6 **(a)** 14.31 hr.

(b) $71,550

(c) $947,250

E.8 **(a)** 80%

(b) 3.51

(c) 3.2, 2.98, 2.81

(d) 21.5

E.10 **(a)** 72.2 hr.

(b) 60.55 hr.

(c) 41.47 hr.

E.12 Torri will take 3.67 hours and Kate 2.4 hours. Neither trainee will reach 1 hr. by the 10th unit.

E.14 $748,240 for fourth, $709,960 for fifth, $679,960 for sixth

E.16 **(a)** 70 millicents/bit

(b) 8.2 millicents/bit

E.18 26,755 hr.

E.20 **(a)** 32.98 hr., 49.61 hr.

(b) Initial quote is high.

E.22 **(a)** Four boats can be completed.

(b) Five boats can be completed.

E.24 $908 million is the total cost.

Quantitative Module F

F.2 0, 0, 0, 0, 0, 0, 0, 2, 0, 2

F.4 Profits = 20, −15, 20, 17.50, 20; average equals 12.50

F.6 At the end of 5 minutes, two checkouts are still busy and one is available.

F.8

Arrivals	Arrival Time	Service Time	Departure Time
1	11:01	3	11:04
2	11:04	2	11:06
3	11:06	2	11:08
4	11:07	1	11:09

F.10 (a, b)

No. Cars	Prob.	Cum. Prob.	R.N. Interval
3 or fewer	0	0	—
4	.10	.10	01 through 10
5	.15	.25	11 through 25
6	.25	.50	26 through 50
7	.30	.80	51 through 80
8	.20	1.00	81 through 00
9 or more	0	—	—

    (c) Average no. arrivals/hr. = 105/15 = 7 cars

F.12 Each simulation will differ. Using random numbers from right-hand column of the random number table, reading top to bottom, in the order used, results in a $9.20 cost. This is greater than the $6.65 in Example F3.

F.14 (a) 5 times (b) 6.95 times; yes (c) 7.16 heaters

F.16 Average demand is about 8.75, average lead time is 1.86, average end inventory = 6.50, average lost sales = 4.04. Values will vary with different sets of random numbers.

F.18 Average end inventory = 8.92; average lost sales = 3.5; total cost = $497,268 or $20,719/month. This new policy seems preferable.

F.20 Here are the random-number intervals for the first two departments. Random number intervals correspond to probability of occurrence.

From	To	R.N. Interval
Initial exam	X ray	01 through 45
	OR	46 through 60
	Observ.	61 through 70
	Out	71 through 00

From	To	R.N. Interval
X ray	OR	01 through 10
	Cast	11 through 35
	Observ.	36 through 70
	Out	71 through 00

Each simulation will produce different results. Some will indeed show a person entering X ray twice.

F.22 Expected supply exceeds expected demand.

CD Tutorial 1

T1.2 5.45; 4.06
T1.4 .2743; .5
T1.6 .1587; .2347; .1587
T1.8 (a) .0548;
    (b) .6554;
    (c) .6554;
    (d) .2119

CD Tutorial 2

T2.2

Fraction Defective	Mean of Poisson	$P(x \le 1)$
.01	.05	.999
.05	.25	.974
.10	.50	.910
.30	1.50	.558
.60	3.00	.199
1.00	5.00	.040

T2.4 The plan meets neither the producer's nor the consumer's requirement.

CD Tutorial 3

T3.2 (a) $x_1 + 4x_2 + s_1 = 24$
       $x_1 + 2x_2 + s_2 = 16$
    (b) See the steps in the tutorial.
    (c) Second tableau:

c_j	Mix	x_1	x_2	s_1	s_2	Qty.
9	x_2	.25	1	.25	0	6
0	s_2	.50	0	−.50	1	4
	z_j	2.25	9	2.25	0	54
	$c_j - z_j$	.75	0	−2.25	0	

    (d) $x_1 = 8$, $x_2 = 4$, Profit = $60

T3.4 Basis for 1st tableau:
    $A_1 = 80$
    $A_2 = 75$
Basis for 2nd tableau:
    $A_1 = 55$
    $x_1 = 25$
Basis for 3rd tableau:
    $x_1 = 14$
    $x_2 = 33$
Cost = 221 at optimal solution

T3.6 (a) x_1
    (b) A_1

CD Tutorial 4

T4.2 Cost = $980; 1-A = 20; 1-B = 50; 2-C = 20; 2-Dummy = 30; 3-A = 20; 3-C = 40

T4.4 Total = 3,100 mi.; Morgantown–Coaltown = 35; Youngstown–Coal Valley = 30; Youngstown–Coaltown = 5; Youngstown–Coal Junction = 25; Pittsburgh–Coaltown = 5; Pittsburgh–Coalsburg = 20

T4.6 (a) Using VAM, cost = 635; A–Y = 35; A–Z = 20; B–W = 10; B–X = 20; B–Y = 15; C–W = 30.
    (b) Using MODI, cost is also 635 (i.e., initial solution was optimal). An *alternative* optimal solution is A–X = 20; A–Y = 15; A–Z = 20; B–W = 10; B–Y 35; C–W = 30.

CD Tutorial 5

T5.2 (a) $I_{13} = 12$
    (b) $I_{35} = 7$
    (c) $I_{51} = 4$
T5.4 (a) Tour: 1-2-4-5-7-6-8-3-1; 37.9 mi.
    (b) Tour: 4-5-7-1-2-3-6-8-4; 39.1 mi.
T5.6 Vehicle 1: Tour 1-2-4-3-5-1 = $134
    Vehicle 2: Tour 1-6-10-9-8-7-1 = $188
T5.8 The cost matrix is:

	1	2	3	4	5	6	7	8
1	—	107.26	118.11	113.20	116.50	123.50	111.88	111.88
2		—	113.53	111.88	118.10	125.30	116.50	118.10
3			—	110.56	118.70	120.50	119.90	124.90
4				—	109.90	119.10	111.88	117.90
5					—	111.88	106.60	118.50
6						—	111.88	123.50
7							—	113.20
8								—